The Adam Smith Review

Volume 4

Adam Smith's contribution to economics is well-recognized but in recent years scholars have been exploring anew the multidisciplinary nature of his works. *The Adam Smith Review* is a refereed annual review that provides a unique forum for interdisciplinary debate on all aspects of Adam Smith's works, his place in history, and the significance of his writings for the modern world. It is aimed at facilitating debate between scholars working across the humanities and social sciences, thus emulating the transdisciplinary reach of the Enlightenment world which Smith helped to shape.

The fourth volume of the series contains contributions from a multi-disciplinary range of specialists, including, Henry C. Clark, Douglas J. Den Uyl, Ryan Patrick Hanley, Neven B. Leddy, David M. Levy and Sandra J. Peart, Robert Mankin, Leonidas Montes, James R. Otteson, Andrew S. Skinner, and Gloria Vivenza, who discuss:

- the sources and influences of Smith's work in the classics, the Scottish Enlightenment and eighteenth-century France
- the Glasgow Edition of Smith's Works and the *Wealth of Nations*.

Vivienne Brown is Professor of Intellectual History at The Open University, UK. She is the author of *Adam Smith's Discourse: Canonicity, Commerce and Conscience* (1994, Routledge) and numerous articles in a range of disciplinary and interdisciplinary journals. She is the founder/editor of *The Adam Smith Review* on behalf of the International Adam Smith Society.

The Adam Smith Review

Published in association with the International Adam Smith Society

Edited by Vivienne Brown

Faculty of Social Sciences, The Open University, UK

Book Reviews
Edited by Fonna Forman-Barzilai

Department of Political Science, University of California, San Diego, USA

Editorial Board

Books available in this series:

The Adam Smith Review Volume 1
Edited By Vivienne Brown
(Published in 2004)

The Adam Smith Review Volume 3
Edited By Vivienne Brown
(Published in 2007)

The Adam Smith Review Volume 2
Edited By Vivienne Brown
(Published in 2006)

The Adam Smith Review Volume 4
Edited By Vivienne Brown
(Published in 2008)

The Adam Smith Review
Volume 4

Edited by
Vivienne Brown

Routledge
Taylor & Francis Group

LONDON AND NEW YORK

IASS

First published 2008
by Routledge
2 Park Square, Milton Park, Abingdon, Oxon OX14 4RN

Simultaneously published in the USA and Canada
by Routledge
270 Madison Ave, New York, NY 10016

*Routledge is an imprint of the Taylor & Francis Group,
an informa business*

© 2008 The International Adam Smith Society
(www.adamsmithsociety.net)

Typeset in Times New Roman by
Florence Production Ltd, Stoodleigh, Devon
Printed and bound in Great Britain by
Biddles Digital, King's Lynn

British Library Cataloguing in Publication Data
A catalogue record for this book is available from the British Library

Library of Congress Cataloging in Publication Data
A catalog record has been requested for this book

ISSN 1743–5285
ISBN10: 0–415–45438–7 (hbk)
ISBN10: 0–203–88838–3 (ebk)

ISBN13: 978–0–415–45438–4 (hbk)
ISBN13: 978–0–203–88838–4 (ebk)

Editorial

The Adam Smith Review is a multidisciplinary refereed annual review sponsored by the International Adam Smith Society. It provides a unique forum for vigorous debate and the highest standards of scholarship on all aspects of Adam Smith's works, his place in history, and the significance of his writings for the modern world. *The Adam Smith Review* aims to facilitate interchange between scholars working within different disciplinary and theoretical perspectives, and to this end is open to all areas of research relating to Adam Smith. The *Review* also hopes to broaden the field of English-language debate on Smith by occasionally including translations of scholarly works at present available only in languages other than English.

The Adam Smith Review is intended as a resource for Adam Smith scholarship in the widest sense. The Editor welcomes comments and suggestions, including proposals for symposia or themed sections in the *Review*. The *Review* is also open to comments and debate relating to papers previously published in it.

For details of membership of the International Adam Smith Society and purchase of the *Review* on preferential terms for personal members of the Society, please contact the Membership Secretary, Remy A. Debes (rdebes@ memphis.edu) or visit the *Review*'s website (www.adamsmithreview.org).

Contents

Notes on contributors

S.M. Amadae is a political theorist in the Department of Political Science at Ohio State University and has written *Rationalizing Capitalist Democracy: The Cold War Origins of Rational Choice Liberalism* (2003).

Henry C. Clark is Professor of History at Canisius College. He is the author of several articles on Adam Smith, as well as *La Rochefoucauld and the Language of Unmasking in Seventeeth-Century France* and *Compass of Society: Commerce and Absolutism in Old-Regime France*, and is the editor of *Commerce, Culture and Liberty: Readings on Capitalism Before Adam Smith*.

Douglas J. Den Uyl is the Vice President of Educational Programs, Liberty Fund. He has published widely on Adam Smith and the Enlightenment.

Laurence W. Dickey is emeritus Professor of Modern Intellectual History at the University of Wisconsin, Madison. He is author of *Hegel: Religion, Economics and the Politics of Spirit* (1987) and many articles on modern German and British intellectual history. He is also editor of Adam Smith, *The Wealth of Nations* (1993), which contained substantial editorial commentary.

Fonna Forman-Barzilai is Assistant Professor of Political Theory at the University of California, San Diego. Her first book, *Adam Smith and the Circles of Sympathy: Cosmopolitanism and Moral Theory*, is forthcoming (2009). She is currently serving as Book Reviews Editor of *The Adam Smith Review*.

Christel Fricke, Professor of Philosophy at the University of Oslo, Norway, Director of the 'Centre for the Study of Mind in Nature' (CSMN – www. csmn.uio.no), has a PhD and Habilitation from Heidelberg University, Germany. She specializes in meta-ethics and moral psychology, including philosophy of the emotions, in aesthetics and semiotics, as well as in the history of modern philosophy. Her recent publications include *Adam Smith als Moralphilosoph* (2005), co-edited with **Hans-Peter**

Schütt who is professor of Philosophy at the University of Karlsruhe, Germany, has a PhD and Habilitation from Heidelberg University in Germany, and specializes in metaphysics, the philosophy of mind, moral psychology, meta-ethics and history of philosophy.

Caroline Gerschlager is an invited researcher at the Université Libre de Bruxelles (DULBEA) where she is preparing her Habilitation in economics at the Vienna University of Economics and Business Administration. She has a thematic interest in deception and self-deception in markets which she approaches with a variety of methods. She specializes in the history and philosophy of economics as well as in recent developments in micro-economics. Her books have come out with Metropolis (Germany), Kluwer and Palgrave Macmillan. Her recent research on Adam Smith includes 'Adam Smith's Account of Self-deceit and Informal Institutions' and 'Foolishness and Identity: Adam Smith and Amartya Sen' (at http://dev.ulb.ac.be/dulbea/fr/workingpaper.php).

Ryan Patrick Hanley is Assistant Professor of Political Science at Marquette University. His recent work on Smith has appeared in *American Journal of Political Science, European Journal of Political Theory*, and *Studies in Eighteenth-Century Culture*. His first book, *Adam Smith and the Character of Virtue*, is forthcoming 2009.

Charles Larmore is the W. Duncan MacMillan Family Professor in the Humanities and Professor of Philosophy at Brown University. His new book, *The Autonomy of Morality*, will appear in the Fall of 2008.

Neven Brady Leddy is completing his doctoral dissertation on the intellectual and cultural contexts of Smith's moral philosophy in the History Department at Oxford University. He is co-editor (with Avi Lifschitz) of a forthcoming volume of essays on the role of ancient paradigms in the eighteenth century, entitled *Epicurus in the Enlightenment*. Neven's next research project is an investigation of the reception of the Scottish Enlightenment in Geneva.

David M. Levy is Professor of Economics at George Mason University and Co-director of the Summer Institute for the Preservation of the History of Economic Thought. His first article on Adam Smith appeared in *Journal of History of Ideas* in 1978. The Peart and Levy symposium on econometric ethics first presented at the Summer Institute and the Joint Statistical Meetings was published in *Eastern Economic Journal* in 2008.

Iain McLean is Professor of Politics and Director, Public Policy Unit, Oxford University. Recent work includes *Adam Smith: Radical and Egalitarian* 2006), *Applying the Dismal Science: When Economists Give Advice to Governments*, ed. with Colin Jenings (2006), and *State of the Union: Unionism and the Alternatives in the United Kingdom since 1707*, with Alistair McMillan (2005).

Robert Mankin is Professor in the English Department of the University of Paris-Diderot and specializes in eighteenth- and seventeenth-century intellectual history. He is the editor of a forthcoming edition of early writing by the English historian Edward Gibbon.

Leonidas Montes obtained his PhD at the Faculty of Economics and Politics, King's College, University of Cambridge. He is the author of *Adam Smith in Context* (2004), co-editor with Eric Schliesser of *New Voices on Adam Smith* (2006) and has published some articles on Adam Smith and the Scottish Enlightenment. Leonidas is currently Dean of the School of Government at Universidad Adolfo Ibañez, Santiago, Chile.

James R. Otteson is Director of the Schottenstein Honors Program at Yeshiva University in New York. He is author of *Adam Smith's Marketplace of Life* (2002) and of *Actual Ethics* (2006), which won the 2007 Templeton Enterprise Award.

Maria Pia Paganelli is an Assistant Professor of Economics at Yeshiva University and an Associate Adjunct Professor at New York University. She specializes in history of economic thought, in particular in eighteenth century money theories and Adam Smith. She has published, among others, in *History of Political Economy*, *Journal of the History of Economic Thought*, *The Adam Smith Review* and *Eastern Economic Journal*.

Sandra J. Peart is Dean of the Jepson School of Leadership Studies at the University of Richmond and Co-director of the Summer Institute for the Preservation of the History of Economic Thought. She is past-president of the History of Economics Society. S.J. Peart and D.M. Levy, *'Vanity of the Philosopher': From Equality to Hierarchy in Post-Classical Economics* (2005), won a Choice award for Outstanding Academic Title. The collection of papers and conversations from the first five years of the Summer Institute, *The Street Porter and the Philosopher: Conversations on Analytical Egalitarianism*, edited by S.J. Peart and D.M. Levy, has just been published.

Tiziano Raffaelli is Professor of the History of Economic Thought at the Department of Philosophy of the University of Pisa. He has edited Alfred Marshall's philosophical papers and written extensively on him and the Cambridge School of Economics. He is managing editor of *Marshall Studies Bulletin* and co-editor of the *Elgar Companion to Alfred Marshall*. His other main interests include Adam Smith and classical economics, American institutionalism, Italian economic thought and the methodology of economics.

D.D. Raphael is emeritus Professor of Philosophy at Imperial College, London. He was much involved in the Glasgow Edition of the Works and Correspondence of Adam Smith and is joint editor of *The Theory* *of Moral Sentiments* (1976). His latest book, *The Impartial Spectator* (2007), is a study of Adam Smith's moral philosophy.

Dennis C. Rasmussen is Assistant Professor of Political Science at the University of Houston. He is the author of *The Problems and Promise of Commercial Society: Adam Smith's Response to Rousseau* (2008) and is currently working on a manuscript on the Enlightenment and its contemporary critics.

Eric Schliesser is an Assistant Professor of Philosophy at Leiden University and a research associate in History and Methodology of Economics, University of Amsterdam. He is co-editor (with Leon Montes) of *New Voices on Adam Smith* (2006) and has published in *Hume Studies*, *Journal for the History of Philosophy*, *British Journal for the History of Philosophy*, *Philosophy of the Social Sciences* and *Journal for Scottish Philosophy*.

Andrew S. Skinner is emeritus Professor of Political Economy at Glasgow University. He is editor of James Steuart, *Principles of Political Oeconomy* (1966); joint editor of the *Wealth of Nations* (1976) Clarendon Press; editor of the *Wealth of Nations* (1999, 1970) Penguin; author of *A System of Social Science: Papers Relating to Adam Smith* (1979, 1996); and numerous articles in the history of economics.

Craig Smith is a Lecturer in Philosophy at the University of St Andrews. He is the author of *Adam Smith's Political Philosophy: The Invisible Hand and Spontaneous Order* (2006).

Jan Toporowski is Senior Lecturer and Research Associate in the Department of Economics at the School of Oriental and African Studies, University of London; Research Associate in the Centre for the History and Methodology of Economics, University of Amsterdam; and a Senior Member of Wolfson College Cambridge. He has worked in fund management, international banking and central banking. He is currently working on an intellectual biography of Michal Kalecki.

Keith Tribe is Visiting Senior Research Fellow in History, University of Sussex, and Rowing Coach at The King's School, Worcester. He now works primarily as a professional translator and is presently engaged on a new translation of Max Weber's *Wirtschaft und Gesellschaft* Part I. His new book, *Making Economics*, a study of the creation of economics as a university discipline, will be published in 2009.

Gloria Vivenza is Professor of History of Economic Thought at the University of Verona, Italy. Her main interest is the influence of Greek and Latin classics on modern economic thought. She has written many articles and a book on the classical heritage in Adam Smith's thought, and she is also studying the influence of classical authors, especially Aristotle and Cicero, on modern thought. She wrote recently some articles about aspects of Cicero's 'economic' ideas in the Renaissance.

Symposium: Adam Smith and his sources

Guest editor: Douglas J. Den Uyl

Introduction

Adam Smith's sources

Guest editor: Douglas J. Den Uyl

When one thinks of the sources which were instrumental in developing Adam Smith's own ideas, the name of David Hume probably comes to mind first. Then, perhaps, other contemporary thinkers of the era, such as Francis Hutcheson or Henry Home, would follow closely behind. These thinkers were important contributors to a milieu in which Smith was intellectually nurtured and in which he reflected upon the central issues of his day. At the same time, one would likely recall that Smith spent two years in France and begin thinking of Turgot or the French Physiocrats as sources of his economic thought. In this connection too, one might remember some laudatory comments on Smith's part about Voltaire. In general, a list such as this seems to be the standard accounting of the sources of Adam Smith's thought.

It is interesting that in an open call for papers on the sources of Smith's thought, none of these traditional sources were submitted. Instead of Hume we get Shaftesbury and Swift. Instead of Turgot and Voltaire, we get Montesquieu and other somewhat lesser-known French writers and intellectuals. Instead of other Scottish Enlightenment figures, we have the Stoics. In addition, the vast majority of the submissions were in areas outside economics. I mention all this not as a roundabout way of suggesting that the traditional list of sources is in any way defective or unimportant. Rather I mention it as a way of indicating that the traditional list is far too narrow. Of course, it could be that our contributors were simply looking for the roads less-taken in submitting their papers. But even so, the fact remains that there are these roads less-taken to explore.

Perhaps because Smith's economics has been historically so much the focus, we have tended to look for the sources of his thought that may have had an impact there. The scholarly rejection of 'das Adam Smith problem', however, has opened the door to seeing Smith's writings as an integrated whole. If nothing else, that rejection puts *The Theory of Moral Sentiments* (TMS) on at least equal footing with the *Wealth of Nations* (WN). Since TMS has numerous allusions to thinkers and topics in fields outside economics as diverse as philosophy and the arts, a whole range of possible avenues of influence opens up to us. Add to that the fact that other works of Smith's, of widely differing subject areas (for example, jurisprudence,

The Adam Smith Review, 4: 1–205 © 2008 The International Adam Smith Society, ISSN 1743–5285, ISBN 13: 978–0–415–45438–4.

science and music), are readily available, the list of potential sources multiplies exponentially. The chance to explore whether these other subject areas further confirm the notion that Smith is an integrated thinker with a general systematic philosophy, rather than simply a social theorist, is thereby irresistible.

But even if Smith is not completely systematic, these other areas of his intellectual life are bound to shed light upon those facets of his thought ordinarily considered. Consequently, the question inevitably arises whether, and the degree to which, sources from other areas of interest to Smith may also have impacted his thought in the traditionally more influential and well-studied areas. Saying all that is not yet to say anything about the possible influences upon Smith's thought from alternative periods of history, such as the classical world. Smith, like other well-educated men of his generation, was certainly steeped in the classical sources, especially the Stoics, and at least three of our contributors to this volume have been inspired to look there for sources of influence.

The contributions to this volume clearly reflect the widening consideration of sources for Smith's thought. One cannot help feeling after reading them all, however, that we are only beginning to scratch the surface of what sources might be considered when thinking of potential influences upon Adam Smith. No doubt this feeling in large part stems from the fact that the face of Adam Smith has been changing significantly over the last few decades. Within living memory of many of us, Smith was thought to be little more than an advocate for free-market economics. Now a significant number of scholars are so-called 'left Smithians' who see Smith as the forerunner of egalitarian and social justice perspectives that tend to characterize those on the left side of the political spectrum. Even without any divisions in political perspectives, the increasing prominence of TMS in Smith scholarship, as we just noted, has also altered how we must think of Adam Smith. We can no longer say that WN is somehow the 'essential' Smith. Indeed, TMS is increasingly filling that role. In this connection too we cannot forget that scholars are beginning to pay attention to what Smith has to say in science, the arts, psychology and jurisprudence. In short, as the scholarly range of interest in Smith's thought expands and differing interpretations emerge, the range of sources expands as well. In a way, then, the contributors to this volume are pioneers in a field of scholarship that can only burgeon.

In themselves, the contributions to this volume certainly reflect the trend towards ever widening sources. Four of the contributions go back to antiquity in their quest to better understand Smith's thought. Gloria Vivenza has two of these contributions – one, 'A note on Adam Smith's first invisible hand', is a short note on the possible connection between Jupiter's hand and the more familiar 'invisible hand' imagery so much associated with Smith's thought. In her other longer contribution, 'Justice for the criminal: classical themes at the origin of Smithian ideas', Vivenza discusses both classical and seventeenth- and eighteenth-century discussions of the concept of justice and their impact on Smith, specifically with respect to Smith's manuscript on justice reprinted in 'The passage on atonement, and a manuscript fragment on justice' (TMS Appendix II). Though the manuscript was a youthful work, the sources from which it draws may be relevant to his more mature reflections. In the classical vein also is the contribution by Leonidas Montes, 'Adam Smith as an *eclectic* Stoic', considering Smith's connection to the Stoics. On this topic there is already considerable scholarship, including contributions by Montes himself. Montes reviews the connection with the purpose of arguing that the Stoic concept of *oikeiosis* as the basis for Smithian sympathy has been underestimated, and the influence of the Stoics on Smith's concept of self-command has been overestimated. As Montes' paper suggests, Smith selects from Stoic doctrines views that accord best with his own framework of analysis. Finally, David M. Levy and Sandra J. Peart, in 'Adam Smith and his sources: the evil of independence', also turn to the Stoics to help explain Smith's egalitarianism as well as his theory of socialization. It turns out that Stoic cosmopolitanism is a force towards impartiality and other-orientedness, both of which are critical to socialization as Smith understands it. In this connection too, Levy and Peart explore in the classical roots of sympathy the extent to which the place of sympathy in socialization compromises the assumption of independence in some modern social science approaches.

If we turn our attention to times closer to Smith's own and look to Anglophone authors, we have contributions by both Ryan Patrick Hanley and James R. Otteson. Hanley looks at the connection between Swift and Smith in 'Style and sentiment: Smith and Swift', while Otteson looks to that of Shaftesbury and Smith in 'Shaftesbury's evolutionary morality and its influence on Adam Smith'. Smith's love, not to mention extensive knowledge, of literature coupled with some rather positive statements about Swift would be sufficient reason to explore the connection between them. Hanley, however, has deeper issues in mind, arguing that Smith admired Swift's notions of moral sentiments especially with respect to pride, vanity, indignation and justice – critical terms in Smith's substantive moral theorizing. Smith's own balanced moral temperament is found to a large extent in Swift. Otteson looks at another important figure in the eighteenth century, though one perhaps less well-known today than Swift. Still, Otteson's purpose is similar to Hanley's in seeking to uncover an important source of Smith's moral theory. Shaftesbury was a highly influential thinker in the eighteenth century, and it is typical to see the connection to Smith through Hutcheson. Otteson, however, is interested in exploring more directly the influences of Shaftesbury upon Smith in their rejection of Hobbesian models of human nature and sociality. Moreover, Otteson holds that central elements of the evolving character of Smith's moral philosophy are to be found in Shaftesbury.

If we turn our attention now to French sources, we find three rather diverse contributions presented here. The first source, and the most obvious one outside the realm of economics, is Montesquieu. Like Shaftesbury, Montesquieu had a large influence on thinkers in the eighteenth century, including members of the Scottish Enlightenment. Unlike Shaftesbury, Montesquieu also has associated with him a large body of contemporary scholarship, including reflections on the connection between Smith and Montesquieu. Henry C. Clark, in 'Montesquieu in Smith's method of "theory and history"', surveys the relevant literature on the connection and then offers his own reflections on the similarities and differences exhibited in these two thinkers, especially with respect to the connection between theory and history.

Our other two contributors who focus upon the French connection work with sources less well-known than Montesquieu's *Spirit of the Laws*. Neven B. Leddy, for example, in 'Adam Smith's moral philosophy in the context of eighteenth-century French fiction', considers the fictional writings of Pierre Marivaux, Crébillon and Marie-Jeanne Riccoboni. Leddy seeks to examine how French fictional writers like these may have been a source for Smith's reflections upon moral philosophy and moral psychology. Smith speaks favourably of these authors in precisely this context, so Leddy's purpose is to examine how certain components of their fiction, namely sympathetic love as opposed to *amour-propre*, are similar to what we find in Smith. Part of Leddy's purpose also includes opening our horizons on just what kinds of sources we should be considering when thinking about Smith in these matters. In a way, Robert Mankin wishes to do something very similar. The approach to ideas in the eighteenth century was often, to say the least, encyclopaedic. In 'Pins and needles: Adam Smith and the sources of the *Encyclopédie*', Mankin wishes to explore this milieu by looking directly at the connections between Smith and some of the contributors to the French *Encyclopédie*. Not only will such an examination help establish Smith's interest and intentions towards a synthetic intellectual vision, but also some direct connections between the *Encyclopédie* and some early pieces by Smith will help give us insights into the nature of that synthesis. That in turn could have important implications for how we see some of the relationships between Smith's extant writings.

The richness of these contributions to the sources of Smith's thought should be evident even from these extremely brief remarks about what one will find herein. But as I suggested at the outset, it is equally true that one has no trouble now imagining many other sources one might consider when thinking of Adam Smith. That is why I suggested that the contributors to this volume are, in a way, pioneers in opening some doors through which many of us should want to follow. *The Adam Smith Review* is certainly doing this branch of Smith scholarship a significant service by devoting an issue to Smith's sources.

Of course, no issue can be put together without help and encouragement. In this regard, the general editor, Vivienne Brown, is to be thanked especially. Besides the general call for papers and the selection of the most promising submissions, the papers to follow were all read critically by me and commentary provided to the authors. Each was also submitted to a blind review by at least one other author. In some cases, one author now in this volume was blindly reviewed by another, because I believed that person to be the best available for that task. Among those outside this volume who deserve special thanks for their part in the review process are Lauren Brubaker, Jack Weinstein and Michael Zuckert. In addition, Elizabeth Hiestand helped me immensely in proofreading these papers. Such is the basic process that brought these papers forward. It is certainly a great pleasure to have had a part in bringing this collection to you.

Justice for the criminal
Classical themes at the origin of Smithian ideas

Gloria Vivenza

I have deliberately avoided the word 'sources' in the title of this article, because what I will discuss are not sources in a technical sense, so much as ideas of classical origin, elaborated on considerably by seventeenth- and eighteenth-century scholarship. I have already devoted a great deal of work to the classical sources of Adam Smith: up to now this has consisted of researching, as reliably as possible, what Smith could have derived from his outstanding knowledge of the classical authors. In this article it is my intention to postulate a possible, but unverified, influence of classical origin on Adam Smith. Perhaps it would be more accurate to call it modern, since it goes back to the seventeeth-century treatment of classical subjects. I will offer an account – hypothetical but, I hope, well grounded – of the origin of an expression used by Adam Smith, found not in his principal works but in what we might call a 'minor' text: an original manuscript fragment on justice, unearthed in 1831 and published by Raphael and Macfie in 'The passage on atonement, and a manuscript fragment on justice' (TMS Appendix II: 383–401). The editors date the manuscript fragment to the period when Smith was teaching in Glasgow, between 1751–2 and 1764.

On this particular aspect of justice Smith was never to dwell again; and, as he never fulfilled his project of writing a treatise on natural jurisprudence, where perhaps he could have dealt with a theory of punishment, we may conclude that this juvenile note is the witness of a lifelong reflexion on problems of justice.

I will begin by briefly summarizing a part of the treatment of justice found in *The Theory of Moral Sentiments*. At TMS VII.ii.1.10, Smith affirms that the term 'justice' has different meanings, both in Greek and the other languages. In fact, Smith sets about distinguishing between at least two types of justice: simply abstaining from doing harm, and correct behaviours or actions in relations with others. Justice which compels us not to harm, and punishes anyone who does, has already been treated by Smith at TMS II.ii.1.5, within the context of legal justice, which can be imposed by force and the violation of which is an injury, that is, *iniuria*. Similarly, we read at TMS VII.ii.1.10 that: 'In one sense we are said to do justice to our neighbour when we abstain from doing him any positive harm, and do not directly hurt him, either in his person, or in his estate, or in his reputation'.

But there is a second aspect of justice which Smith describes immediately after: 'In another sense we are said *not* to do justice to our neighbour' (TMS VII.ii.1.10; my italics) when we do not treat him with the respect and consideration warranted by his position. It is no longer sufficient 'to abstain from hurting him'; we must 'exert ourselves to serve him and to place him in that situation in which the impartial spectator would be pleased to see him' (TMS VII.ii.1.10).

Smith has thus discerned two different meanings for the concept which in both cases goes by the name of justice: 'in one sense' it is sufficient to abstain from *iniuria*; 'in another sense' it is necessary to render honours and services: the fact that we abstain from *iniuria* is somehow taken for granted, and, above all, is insufficient. The justice to which Smith alludes here consists of honouring and serving certain people when their status so obliges us, in a society which has recently been defined as 'strategically unequal' (Levi 2003: 195) due to a question of institutional differences. In the medieval and modern worlds, the feudal system recognized rights to individuals according to their status: what was right for a commoner differed from what was right for a gentleman. The ancient world may seem less complex in this respect; it is true that there were two categories with different rights, free men and slaves. But there was slavery even in the modern world in Smith's day; what is more, there also was the feudal hierarchy of the *ancien régime*, unknown to the ancient world.

Smith's passage goes on to clarify how the first form of justice is what Aristotle and the Schoolmen called commutative justice, and Grotius *justitia expletrix*; it consists of refraining from the property of others, and of spontaneously complying with what the law commands. The second form of justice, described as distributive justice by some, is what Grotius calls *justitia attributrix*, and consists of 'proper beneficence, in the becoming use of what is our own, and in the applying it to those purposes either of charity or generosity, to which it is most suitable, in our situation, that it should be applied' (TMS VII.ii.1.10). At this point, a note added by Smith to 'distributive justice' explains that 'the distributive justice of Aristotle is somewhat different. It consists in the proper distribution of rewards from the public stock of a community. See Aristotle Ethic. Nic. 1.5.c.2'.

In the manuscript fragment on justice, we find a slightly different version, which the editors analyse by careful comparison with TMS and *Lectures on Jurisprudence* (LJ). They highlight the most substantial difference: in the fragment, a parallel is drawn between 'improper punishment' and 'improper benevolence', the conclusion of which is not cited in full in TMS, just the part which treats 'improper benevolence'. In the manuscript, and only in the manuscript, we find the phrase 'Improper punishment, punishment which is either not due at all or which exceeds the demerit of the Crime, is an injury to the Criminal' (TMS Appendix II: 394). The editors very rightly ask themselves why Smith did not include this passage in his criticism of the utilitarian account of justice; they conclude that, if it is just, for reasons of general utility, to inflict a punishment which may seem excessively severe (the well-known example of the sentinel falling asleep and endangering the whole army, TMS II.ii.3.11), it is impossible to define excessive punishment as 'an injury to the Criminal' because injury is a breach of justice (TMS Appendix II: 394; Norrie 1989: 228). The editors conclude their analysis by comparing the passage from TMS with the two passages from LJ in which Smith once again gives the example of the sentinel (LJA ii.92; LJB 182), underlining how the punishment should be considered 'just', but not in the same way as the punishment of a thief or assassin.

Within this context, the editors comment on Adam Smith's note on Aristotle and conjecture that 'In preparing his earlier thought for publication, Smith would have checked many of his statements, and in this instance he would have found, by reference to Aristotle, that some qualification was needed to the bare statement in the lecture that 'in the Schools' the name of distributive justice was used for the proper allocation of beneficence' (TMS Appendix II: 396–7).

In reality, Smith did specify something in the manuscript on justice, but it was not enough. In TMS, he bases his ideas constantly on Grotius for both types of justice; for commutative justice he quotes Aristotle and the Schoolmen, while for distributive justice he merely refers to 'some' (TMS VII.ii.1.10).[1] The manuscript is equally vague: Smith speaks of 'most writers' or 'those writers' (TMS Appendix II: 390), without mentioning names. However, he writes that: 'The Rules of punishment have been by most Writers referred to distributive Justice as well as the Rules of Beneficence, and they seem to have imagined that improper vengeance was an impropriety of the same kind with improper Benevolence'. Later he explains that the 'rules' of punishment and beneficence have something in common and something which distinguishes them. They are similar in that both are difficult to establish, and vary with circumstances; they differ on one essential point, which 'those Writers have not, perhaps, sufficiently attended to' (TMS Appendix II: 390), namely that excessive punishment is an 'injury to the Criminal' and as such should in turn be punished, while 'improper Beneficence' requires no punishment. Thus Smith distinguishes between Aristotle's distributive justice and that of the unknown writers, which, if anything, corresponds to Grotius's *justitia attributrix* more than to Aristotle.

The fundamentals of the Aristotelian passage cited, which refers to 'sharing of honours, riches and anything else that can be divided among the members of the political community' (Aristotle 1994, NE 1130 b: 31–32), are substantially respected in Smith's reference, although summarized to the extreme. What Smith does not detect, perhaps because not essential to his argument, is that this distribution may be performed by several individuals or by a *super partes* judge. This is by no means irrelevant to the subsequent evolution of the concept; many years ago I happened to notice that in the Middle Ages there came to be only one distributor: St. Thomas's *gubernator* or *dispensator*. However, Aristotle very probably considered that the distribution of all that can be divided among the members of a community depended on the political regime of the community: a sole distributor will be typical of a monarchy, and will be suited only to a monarchy. Aristocracies, oligarchies and democracies will behave differently (Vivenza 1996: 31; Theocarakis 2006: 13–14). Such pluralism would have been hard to maintain in an age of absolute monarchies like the Modern Age, in which the power of the monarchy had, since the Middle Ages, come to be likened to the power of God, which was, by definition, unique (Lambertini 1985).

Adam Smith was thus aware that although the core meaning of commutative justice had to some extent been maintained from Aristotle to the Schoolmen and as far as Grotius, distributive justice had taken on a meaning somewhere between Aristotle's concept and that of the 'some' who were closer to Grotius than to Aristotle.

In effect, the passage from Aristotle in which he distinguishes between the two types of justice (NE 1130 b 30–1132 b 20) provided plenty of work for the Schoolmen and even their successors. The following is a brief summary of their principal arguments. The most significant argument is that both types of justice are grounded on the principle of equality, except that in the case of distributive justice, it is an equality of proportions (De Molina 1615: 10). In my opinion, this was a way to ensure that an unequal distribution was accepted as 'just': nearly all scholars refer to a division of the goods of the community on the basis of how much single members have contributed, or deserved, or according to their status. It is important to emphasize that this distribution is performed by authority: distributive justice is the prerogative of power, and cannot be exercised privately by individuals (De Molina 1615: 10).

Now from the times of Buridan to the German jurist Cocceius (who was well-known to Smith),[2] many people maintained that there was no reason to distinguish between the two types of justice: they were the same. Why? Because if an amount of something is 'distributed' to someone in an 'unjust' quantity for that person, a wrong is done, an *iniuria* – very like a theft. To right this wrong, it is necessary to resort to commutative justice: it is like incurring a debt with that person (De Molina 1615: 11).[3] Here, the two types of justice are connected at least: *distributiva in sua functione includit commutativam* (Lessius 1612: 18).

Conversely, Cocceius, an authoritative commentator of Grotius, argued that there was absolutely no reason for the division into corrective and distributive justice, and that effectively it did not exist in any part of the law (Cocceius 1751, vol. I: 35, *ad* § VIII, and *Additio*). Cocceius also declared, in disagreement with Grotius, that if it really was necessary to apply this distinction to the punishment, it should be considered a part of corrective justice, and not distributive justice.[4]

Distributive justice, according to Cocceius, was an invention of Aristotle, for which we get the impression that there was no need: it belonged to the field of ethics and not to justice. Aristotle reasoned in terms of proportions, and his justice was a proportion based on the golden mean between more and less (NE 1131 a 11–12). However, since Aristotle was familiar with two types of proportion – arithmetic and geometric – he seems to have created for this reason two types of justice: commutative *sive absoluta, ut in contractibus* ('absolute as in contracts') for its mathematical proportion, and distributive *sive comparata; ut in distributione praemiorum [. . .] omnibusque virtutibus quae aliis hominibus utilitatem afferunt* ('or relative, as in the distribution of rewards and in all the virtues which bring benefits to men', Cocceius 1751: 35 *ad* § VIII) for its geometrical proportion. Is it a coincidence that Smith considered justice to be the virtue distinguished by certain and 'grammatical' rules? He mentioned neither arithmetic nor geometry, the two subjects that Aristotle (and after him legions of interpreters, among them Grotius) always brought up when discussing the two types of justice. Yet Smith said the same thing: justice, unlike other virtues, must be grounded on fixed rules. Perhaps the fact that he renounces arithmetic/geometrical proportion and its implied dualism indicates agreement with Cocceius, according to whom justice was in reality unique, an 'exact' form. Distributive justice had already shifted, prior to Adam Smith, towards a meaning connected with 'dispensing' virtues (beneficence, magnanimity, liberality, charity), rather than with strict justice.

As regards terminology, it is important to emphasize that when Grotius alludes to the two Aristotelian forms of justice – distributive and commutative – he uses the correct term for the former (*dianemetike*) but not for the latter, which he calls *sunallaktike*, while Aristotle defines it *diorthotike*. Aristotle describes the latter as the justice assigned to voluntary/involuntary transactions, in Greek *sunallagmata*; however, the verb he uses for this type of justice is *diorthoo*, which means to straighten, to correct.[5] So it seems that Grotius focused his attention on the principle of the transaction itself (*sunallagma*: covenant, contract, dealings, transactions), rather than on the principle of straightening or correcting, which was what Aristotle meant. It has been observed that Aristotle's text, especially in *Nicomachean Ethics*, seems to point to a third type of justice, which concerns only economic transactions and hence differs from both distributive and corrective justice (NE 1132 b 21–1133 b 28).[6] However, this is a much-discussed passage: a part of the scholarship includes it in the category of 'commercial' justice, and another part in that of 'reciprocity', which has a special economic meaning relating mainly to anthropological studies. I will not dwell on these problems here, but only recall that medieval philosophy unified corrective and commutative justice, assigning even 'economic' justice to the field of the rectificatory version. Grotius and Pufendorf followed suit; indeed Grotius 'dropped the name "commutative" precisely because the major part of rectifying justice has nothing to do with the rights acquired from contractual exchange'(Raphael 2001: 58).

Gronovius paid great attention to Grotius's text, and although he based his discussion on the latter scholar's scheme, he did not hesitate to observe

– albeit in brackets – that the *vir doctissimus* could have added that in Aristotle's text *sunallagma* represented the object of justice in question, rather than its foundation;[7] Gronovius limited himself to concluding that he was not interested in bringing out exactly what the Stagirite meant, since Grotius did not follow the text closely – and here we cannot fail to agree. What follows is also significant: Aristotle's text 'is by now ignored by many'.[8]

In conclusion, Grotius believed that Aristotle had identified two types of justice; however, he translated them into Latin using words that differed from those used up to that time. R. Grosseteste's medieval Latin translation rendered the two Aristotelian forms of justice as *distributivum iustum*, and *aequale* (or *directivum*) *iustum* (Gauthier 1972, XXVI.3: 236).[9] Grotius, on the other hand, opted for *attributrix* (or sometimes *assignatrix*) and *expletrix*, respectively. The difference is evident: from the Aristotelian 'rectifying' or 'correcting' we arrive at a word (*ex-pleo*) whose meaning is closer to 'fulfilling, satisfying, or performing'.[10]

The second translation (*attributrix*) reveals another important departure from the Aristotelian meaning, as well as from the Latin translation. Both the Greek and the Latin terms are preceded by a prefix (*dia-*, *dis-*) which means 'in different directions', which in this case means precisely a distribution among different recipients. Grotius maintains the verb *tribuo*, but uses the opposite prefix: *dis-* becomes *ad-*: rather than spreading here and there, the movement is focused in one direction.[11]

What is the difference between distribute and attribute or assign? In the first case, the accent is on the plurality of recipients; in the second we are more concerned with the act of assigning in itself. It is obvious in the second case that there is nothing against numerous assignations, and hence numerous recipients, but the emphasis is more on the act of giving the goods in question than on their ultimate destination: an emphasis on the donor rather than on the receiver.

I realize that these arguments may seem excessively painstaking; however, if – as I have argued elsewhere[12] – the relationship between justice and benevolence (which evolved into charity), of Ciceronian origin but expanded greatly in the Modern Age, has acquired such considerable importance and above all has prompted so much discussion and so many technical formulations from the Middle Ages onwards (Raphael 2001: 60–1), it is precisely because it represented a kind of dialectics between rights and benefits, within a social structure based on inequality. So even something as trifling as a shift from *distributrix* to *attributrix* demonstrates a rather shrewd use of language, which reveals a progression from a community-type idea of distribution – based on consensus – to an idea of distribution based on authority, which is not open to discussion.

In the fragment, Smith returns to Grotius's phrase to the effect that true justice is only commutative/corrective (*quae proprie aut stricte iustitiae nomen obtinet*, ['which strictly speaking is given the name of justice']

De iure I.1.viii: 1; cf. TMS, Appendix II: 390); perhaps he also derives from here the concept that the rules of justice are precise, unlike the 'loose, vague and indeterminate' (TMS III.6.11) rules of the other virtues: Grotius affirms that such rules are *laxius*. According to Cocceius's criticism (Cocceius 1751, I: 34 *ad* § VII) Grotius confused natural right with whatever concerns virtue or perfection. Distributive justice concerns things that are 'measured' by merit, so it is a problem of ethics.

Thus distributive justice changed in the Modern Age, into *comes earum virtutum, quae aliis hominibus utilitatem adferunt, ut liberalitatis, misericordiae, providentiae rectricis* ('a companion of those virtues which bring some advantage to others: like liberality, compassion, prudence in government' Grotius 1751 *De iure* I.1.viii.1), the last becoming what Smith defined as 'superior prudence' (TMS VI.i.15): in short, the discretionary virtues, namely those an individual is free to exercise or not. From here medieval and modern thought established a connection between distributive justice and liberality that is absent in Aristotle. In fact, modern distributive justice has a double character: on the one hand, it is connected with institutional hierarchies (it is 'just' that society be divided in different parts with different functions, different rights and different forms of justice); on the other hand, there is a connection with ethical issues relating to virtue and merit (you will receive more or less according to your merit or worth).

Coming back to our argument, Grotius's positions were criticized not only by Cocceius but also by other jurists (Tuck 1995: 75) who observed the discrepancies with Aristotle. In any case, it is impossible to treat the fierce discussions on this argument in this brief contribution.

Let us take the subject of punishment (Lat. *poena*). Smith claims that most writers have treated both punishment and beneficence as aspects of distributive justice. He goes on to observe that these authors seem to think that even improper vengeance is the same kind of impropriety. This brings the question of merit into play: one of the cornerstones of the various treatments of beneficence is that it must not be given to the undeserving – a typical example of improper beneficence. *Ex regulis iustitiae distributivae homo liberalis esse debet non nisi in merentes* ('according to the rules of distributive justice, man must not be liberal except with those who deserve it'), which means that giving to the undeserving should constitute a violation of distributive justice, which in reality is not the case: *An igitur, si in immerentes liberalis est, pecat [sic] contra regulas iustitiae? Omnino: quia imitari perfectiones divinas [. . .] pars cultus divini est* ('and therefore, if one is liberal towards him who does not deserve it, he sins against the rules of justice? Not at all: because a part of worship is to imitate divine perfection – and God gives his benefits even to undeserving men' [Cocceius 1751, 1: 37 *ad* § VIII]).[13] Besides, improper beneficence cannot be punished because it does not violate any *right*.

However, justice is exercised through sanctions (the problem of the *poena* was perceived strongly), which at times may be disproportionate to their cause. According to Smith's more mature theory, resentment should arise at this point; but as the editors have noted, he had not yet fully elaborated his theory. The figure of the impartial spectator does not appear in the fragment on justice, while resentment is mentioned twice (TMS Appendix II: 389 and 390), seemingly to offer Smith an opportunity to explain that this sentiment tends to induce men to seek retribution, and that precisely to avoid this they resort to magistrates and justice. Smith affirms (p. 390) that while it is easy to establish exactly which right has been violated by the illegal act, it is more difficult to establish what degree of resentment is appropriate: it varies according to the circumstances. He raises a very singular issue: an excessive punishment appears to be an *iniuria*, an illicit act which in turn deserves punishment. However, Smith was mistaken in believing that an excess of punishment could be considered in juridical theory as a wrong inflicted to the criminal, because, in that case, the wrongdoer would have been the punisher. This could not be accepted because law and justice were represented by the punisher himself. So, in order to maintain that right and justice were always on the side of the punisher, it was necessary to claim that the punished had no right: and this is what Grotius and others said.

Perhaps this is why Smith removed the phrase 'improper punishment [. . .] is an injury to the Criminal' from published texts, because, according to the sharply focused commentary of the editors, 'injury is a breach of justice', namely the violation of a right.[14]

Once again, it is appropriate to start from a phrase of Grotius: *nocentibus iniuria non fieri si puniantur* ('to him who harms, no *iniuria* is done if punishment is inflicted', *De iure* II.20.iv.1). The problem had effectively been debated at length, in the sense that the punishment, although *due* to the criminal, was not his *right*. For example, Grotius speaks out against the customary expression (*vulgaris locutio qua dicitur poenam deberi ei, qui deliquit*) according to which punishment was *due* to the criminal. This 'due' should not be interpreted as a right of the criminal, as we might be led to believe, since '*cui proprie debetur aliquid, is in alterum ius habet*' ('the person to whom something is due, has a right over another' – namely, the person indebted to him [Grotius 1751, *De iure*, II.20.ii.2]).[15] Therefore the punishment was due for reasons of equity, because it was right for a wrongdoing to be punished, but it was not intended to confer rights to any criminal, not even the 'negative' right of receiving punishment – and hence not even the right to demand that the punishment be just. Pufendorf, who also maintained that 'punishment is properly owed, not to the wrongdoer, as something which cannot rightly be denied him [. . .] but to society', a little further states that 'wrong is not done to the delinquent, if he undergo the degree of punishment which he knew had been set for the degree of his misdeed [. . .] even if, perchance, the punishment, absolutely considered, may seem more severe than the wrong done' (Pufendorf 1931 [1712]: 178).[16]

This probably explains Smith's afterthought. If the criminal, in the legal theories of the time, effectively had no rights, not even to receive a just punishment, it was evident that he could not receive *iniuria* either, so the problem of excessive punishment had no reason to exist. Grotius and other scholars maintained that the punishment of a crime did NOT come under the category of *iniuriae*; on this point Smith should have agreed that precisely for this reason, it should not cause resentment. Grotius in reality did not offer any depth of analysis of the problem of unjust punishment: he simply affirmed that the punishment was to be proportionate to the crime committed. Many authors spoke out against excessive punishment, but none said that it was an injustice to the criminal (Grotius 1751, *De iure*, II.20.ii.1).[17] Smith, on the other hand, had raised the question of an 'inappropriate' punishment (disproportionate in relation to the crime or not due), and in such instances must have considered resentment inevitable.

The problem is that at this point rights and sentiments enter a (difficult) relationship. In the case of sentiments (which include resentment) we know that there is always a question of 'degree' involved; this is not the case for rights, which in general are defined precisely. This is one of the traditional points of friction between justice and the other virtues, often highlighted in the recent upsurge of 'virtue ethics'. It was Grotius who observed that Aristotle was in difficulty with his theory of the golden mean when he came to treat justice (Schneewind 1990: 46), a virtue whose extremes are not easy to establish: one cannot give too much or too little justice.

Smith reasoned in terms of 'perfect propriety of conduct', describing behaviour which is neither excessive nor defective; and, like Aristotle, entrusted the definition of the 'point of propriety' to sensibility rather than reason.[18] It is not, however, a question of more or less perfect 'propriety' when we are dealing with civil or criminal justice: quite simply, there are rules. Hence, even punishment should be subject to these rules, and be 'automatically' determined by the degree of the crime, without the need to appeal to individual sensitivity.

Some commentators on Grotius – for example, Gronovius, but also Lessius – elucidated Grotius's claim that punishment should be proportionate to the crime, affirming that the two types of justice differed only in so far as one concerned people, the other things. Even contracts, argued Gronovius rather speciously, belonged to distributive justice: in this case we can reasonably suppose that Aristotle would have been rather surprised by such a claim. Gronovius asserted that both types of justice are concerned with unequal parts, with more or less: only that distributive justice assigns the more or less *aestimatis personis*, that is, by evaluating the persons, while corrective justice assigns *aestimatis inter se rebus, nullo personarum discrimine*: by having evaluated the things, without having made any difference between the persons.

Commutative justice effectively presupposed, as Aristotle clearly asserted in NE 1132 a 4–5, that people were considered equal. Gronovius therefore appeared to believe that, if people are not unequal, then things must be. This justifies his explanation that since precious goods yield more than other

17

goods, contracts belong to distributive justice because it is distributive justice which is concerned with more or less. Gronovius's position appears to be the mirror image of Cocceius's, which said that all justice was ultimately commutative. Here, on the other hand, it is all distributive, in so far as it originates from inequalities. The fact that numerous modern authors attempted in various ways to unify the two types of justice is probably due to the fact that modern society was structurally unequal: the medieval and modern world were more unequal than the ancient, which did not know aristocracy[19] and did not have different classes. Aristotle's justice based on equality (*to ison*, cf. NE 1131 a 13; *Pol.* 1282 b 18–20) was problematic to the moderns. Numerous solutions were put forward, and I do not claim to have examined them all; however, we have seen that it was possible to suggest that distributive justice was also egalitarian, thus becoming commutative; or that distributive justice, part of ethics, was not justice; or that one of the two concerned persons and the other things; or even that commutative justice (in a contractual sense) was part of distributive justice.

Cocceius in fact held that commutative justice did not contain all the *capita iuris* since it referred only to relations of a contractual nature, or which originate from a condition of equality, which, if altered, it was necessary to restore (Cocceius 1751, I: 36–37). So we are inclined to conclude that commutative justice concerns rights deriving from juridical consensus, while it excludes all rights deriving from *status*, which refers to distributive justice. Are we revolving around the great dichotomy of modern political thought: consensus or authority? Social contract or theory of divine rights? This is the difference between a society based on common consent and one based on authority. Obviously the Church sided with authority, and was suspicious of the autonomy that 'virtue ethics' presupposed: even in their personal behaviour, men could not be left to decide by themselves; they were to follow the Church's guidance. Justice is distinct from other virtues because it cannot be reduced to the golden mean, nor to the correlated notion of an individual urge to behave virtuously, motivated by the person's character and sensibility rather than 'external' rules to be obeyed: it is the person himself, the wise man (*phronimos*) who finds the right balance, corresponding to the golden mean. But for the Church, a virtuous man who wishes to be so independently of his faith in God is not a good Christian, to such a point that in Catholic orthodoxy his virtue is not even recognized as such.[20]

It has been recently claimed that Adam Smith was 'the last virtue ethicist'.[21] In fact, Smith considered morals based on a spontaneous choice of conduct more appropriate than the slavish respect of rules (which, however, he did allow, in the name of an acceptable morality: TMS III.5.1–2). Spontaneous choice of conduct implies autonomous command of one's own behaviour, independent of authority.

To conclude, we may recall that this subject cannot receive adequate treatment in a short article. We have evidence of a deep reflection on widely debated topics, the subject of numerous treatises, many with similar or even identical titles: Lessius, De Molina, Suarez and De Soto wrote treatises with the title *de iustitia et iure*. This distinction, and at the same time, connection, between *iustitia*, of which God is the author, and *ius*, of which man is the author, dating back to the glossator Azo, the jurist from Bologna (twelfth–thirteenth century),[22] explains how attempts have been made to clarify the relationship between virtue in an abstract sense and the concrete practice of its application, which in the case of legal relationships is very complex.

As regards Smith, we can detect an attempt at personal reasoning which was perhaps ahead of the juridical thought of his time. Today nobody would dream of denying that an excessive punishment constitutes an 'injury to the criminal', but in Smith's day it was, to say the least, an unusual position, considering that the criminal could not suffer *iniuria*.

The most significant aspect of the entire discussion, echoes of which can be perceived in Smith's manuscript on justice, is the attempt to give distributive justice an acceptable 'statute'. I have already referred to the fact that Smith, like Grotius and others, considered true justice to be the commutative type. Now we are perhaps in a better position to understand why distributive justice was not adequate. Starting from equality, and from the fact that for Aristotle *iustum = aequale* – as nearly all the moderns repeat – it is clear that commutative justice, which puts all persons on the same level, appeared more neutral, impersonal and 'equal' than the other form.

Distributive justice had been elaborated in medieval and modern times so as to justify a power structure that had not existed in Aristotle's day,[23] but which nevertheless had found in the works of Aristotle (and Plato) very strong support. It was Plato, in effect, who had maintained that there were two kinds of *equality*: one 'determined by measure, weight and number' (Plato 1984, *Laws* 757B); and another, variously defined by the moderns as 'proportionate equality' or 'symmetrical inequality', consisting of an equality of ratios by which 'there should be unequal valuations, in order that offices and contributions may be assigned in accordance with the assessed valuation in each case, being framed not in proportion only to the moral excellence of a man's ancestors or of himself, nor to his bodily strength and comeliness, but in proportion also to his wealth or poverty' (*Laws* 744C). It was on this double concept of equality that Aristotle based his double justice, grounded on the one hand on 'the "arithmetical" equality, which merely counts heads and treats all alike', and, on the other, on 'that truer "proportional" equality which takes account of human inequality, and on which "distributive justice" (as Aristotle terms it) is based'.[24] But it would be unfair to Plato if his observation that the two kinds of equality 'though identical in name' are frequently 'almost opposite in their practical results' (*Laws* 757B) were to pass unnoticed. The same may be said of the two forms of Aristotle's justice, as I observed some time ago.[25] But Aristotle did not stress this contradiction, and the philosophers and political writers who followed him found various ways, as I have tried to show in this paper, to represent the two justices as the sides of the same coin.

In fact Adam Smith realized that Aristotle's distributive justice was something different from the medieval and modern concept. In Smith's day, distribution decided by authority had long been presented as fair: the authorities ratified – and indeed themselves represented – the stratification of society, which, as we have said, resulted in different forms of justice for different social strata. Why there was so much insistence on justifying this is clear: attempts have always been made to cover up harsh realities, above all to ensure their acceptance by those who are sacrificed for the benefit of the privileged few; there is also a tendency to make the necessity and expediency of those disagreeable realities evident, for reasons of social (and political) order and stability.

Smith himself does the same, and this has been noted several times ('Nature has wisely judged that the distinction of ranks, the peace and order of society, would rest more securely upon the plain and palpable difference of birth and fortune, than upon the invisible and often uncertain difference of wisdom and virtue'; slightly above he also wrote 'The peace and order of society, is of more importance than even the relief of the miserable', TMS VI.ii.1.20).

We should also observe, and indeed underline, that Smith treats Aristotle's two kinds of justice within a Platonic framework. Just above the passage in TMS with which I opened this paper, Smith briefly summarized Plato's philosophy, describing it as that 'perfect propriety of conduct' we have when each of the three mental faculties performs their respective function, and reason governs passions (TMS VII.ii.1.9). After commenting on the way Grotius describes Aristotle's two justices, at TMS VII.ii.1.10, Smith alludes to a third type of justice, namely the ability to attribute the right value to things, including 'any particular object of self-interest'. Perhaps even this is reminiscent of Aristotle: at NE 1136 b 18–19 Aristotle says: 'if a man knowingly and voluntarily gives too much to another and too little to himself, he does injustice to himself'. Directly after, however, Smith returns to the Platonic scheme by asserting that men who possess 'this' justice also possess all the other virtues, and concludes by reaffirming that Plato considered the nature of the virtue to be the 'state of mind in which every faculty confines itself within its proper sphere without encroaching upon that of any other' (TMS VII.ii.1.11).

As usual, Smith's definition is precise. From his original absolute equality, Plato proceeds with a categorization into classes, or functions of the state, according to the different 'material' of which human beings are made. An individual could only very exceptionally leave the category in which he found himself.[26] Smith may have felt that the Platonic 'framework' could to some extent be adapted to feudal society: class differences were presented as the inevitable product of distributive *justice*, which had helped to resolve the issue of inequality. As a result, Smith inserted Aristotle's two justices into the Platonic framework, although strictly speaking they were out of place here – unless he had perhaps connected them with the Platonic discussion of the two kinds of equality mentioned above, but this we shall never know. Smith speaks of Aristotle henceforth at TMS VII.ii.1.12–14, but limits himself to the golden mean ('habit of moderation').

According to some recent scholarship, Smith is to be considered 'egalitarian', in the sense that sympathy and in general the mechanism of evaluation imply that every man is capable of mentally putting himself in the position of others, and considering the interests of others 'equal in value to our own' (Fleischacker 2004: 73, cf. also Darwall 1999; and Griswold 1999). For Smith every human being should have 'equal dignity' (Darwall 1999: 145), and we can undoubtedly agree with this.

I should clarify that I am speaking of another type of equality, or rather inequality: institutional inequality, by which society is stratified into layers, each with different rights according to the various categories of people. Smith accepted this situation, as did almost everyone in his day: after all, the French Revolution was imminent but had not yet exploded. So we should acknowledge that although Smith recognized equal dignity to every individual, he was not ready to treat everyone in the same way: to render justice to someone with whom we have a given type of relationship, we must *serve* him (TMS VII.ii.1.10). Distributive justice justified precisely this type of inequality. Many of the classical doctrines (Ulpian's *suum cuique tribuere*, for instance) were interpreted by the moderns in the sense of making every man 'stay in his own place'. Who decided that place was not open to question; but men could find ways to understand, and justify, the unequal distribution of rank and wealth that characterized distributive 'justice'. Both reasons of authority and of merit were offered: from the medieval 'it is just because it is the will of God' to the modern 'if you have less this means that you are less worthy – yourself or your forefathers'.

It is well-known that Adam Smith justified the ownership of great property by the labour of the owner or his ancestors in acquiring it, which is a kind of merit. But he did not ascribe status to the worth of the person, or of his/her ancestors. Men were born equal: only environment and education gave rise to differences (of wealth and welfare deriving from status). However, Smith did consider this kind of difference a useful stimulus to human activity (TMS IV.1.10–11), although the same passage begins with a famous description of the deceitful efforts of the ambitious poor man's son who tries to reach wealth and greatness (TMS IV.1.8).

We know that Smith would have liked to have written a tract on the principles of jurisprudence, but did not succeed in his intent. Justice is obviously one of these principles – indeed, the most important. It has always been acknowledged as one of the virtues, although different from others. In the various elaborations, there is clear evidence of a widespread effort to include under the name 'justice' both punishment, compensation for damage; and the distribution of privileges, which are two totally different things. This resulted in two different levels of reasoning; various attempts were made to make them tally, by emphasizing equality (of numbers or proportions) or differences (between people and things). What was left formed the 'strange pair' of justice and benevolence.[27]

Smith therefore seems to have thought that if distributive justice concerned both the rules of punishment and of beneficence (after all, both were 'distributed' from above, putting the receiver at the mercy of the giver), the similarity should end here. An excess of benefits cannot cause harm, unlike an excess of punishment. Smith was convinced that the authors who had treated this point had not reflected adequately. On the contrary, they had, concluding that for a criminal no rights are violated and no *iniuria* takes place. Exactly like beneficence, punishment was a discretional event, and one did not ask the person who assigned it for explanations – or at least the receiver of the punishment was not entitled to ask. The circle closed with a grim symmetry, and Smith removed the phrase 'injury to the criminal', although this did, in my opinion, reflect his thought.

Generally speaking, when we read the *Early Draft*, or some of the *Lectures* – works which represent Smith's early thought and which were not destined to be published, or at least not immediately – we notice that his positions are slightly more radical than in the versions published subsequently, and are expressed with less caution (Alvey 2003: 241).

The phrase on 'injury to the criminal' belongs to this category. Personally I remain convinced that Smith continued to consider an excessive or undue punishment an injury, but he certainly did not write this 'officially'. And if his non-utilitarian position on justice (Raphael 2001: chap. II) allows an exception here, in so far as punishment for reasons of common utility is accepted even if the level of resentment is modest due to the triviality of the violation, the impression remains that Smith does not entirely agree with the principle whereby a criminal cannot be a victim of injustice because he has no rights: a point, perhaps, in favour of supporters of the egalitarian Smith.

Notes

1 'Some' emphasized by the editors in Appendix II, p. 396.
2 Cf. LJA i.87, LJB 3–4 and *passim*. Smith owned two editions of Cocceius's commentary on Grotius's *de iure belli ac pacis*. I could not use them in writing the present article, but I used a 1751 Swiss edition where the commentaries of Cocceius the father, and some observations of his son Samuel, are added at the end of each chapter of the *de iure*, whereas Gronovius's and Grotius's observations are collected in the footnotes.
3 Cf. also Lessius (1612: 18): *si distributor aliquem fraudaverit minus dando quam postulabat eius conditio, faciet ei iniuriam* ('if the distributor cheats someone by giving him less than his status requires, he will have wronged him').
4 *Si quaedam proportio attendenda esset, poenae ad expletricem iustitiam potius pertinent, quia tendunt ad reparationem iniuriae, adeoque ad expletionem iustitiae* ('if we are to attend to proportion, punishments should rather belong to commutative justice, because they aim to rectify offences, and therefore to fulfill

justice', Cocceius 1751, III: 333, *ad* § II). Commutative justice is here called *expletrix*, following Grotius.

5 The evolution of the rendering of Aristotle's terminology by the Church's Fathers, the Scholastics, and modern thinkers is explained in Raphael (2001: 57–8). Cf. also Theocarakis (2006: 29 with n.1). The 'rectifying' justice was called 'commutative' by Scholastic philosophers, and, as we have seen, this term still prevailed in Adam Smith's day; now the best translations and comments use 'corrective' or 'rectificatory'.

6 Cf Spengler (1980: 96 with note 103), referring to that part of the scholarship which distinguished between commutative justice (justice in exchanges) and the other two forms, corrective and distributive. In fact, commutative and corrective are frequently used as synonymous, probably because both rely on 'arithmetical' equality (Spengler 1980: 88.) See note 5 above. I treated this subject in Vivenza (1999).

7 *Potuisset addere Vir Doctissimus, to sunallagma, apud Aristotelem, non significare fundamentum obligationis ex hac Iustitia oriundae, sed tantum rem ipsam, circa quam versatur Iustitia* ('that very wise man could have added that *sunallagma* in Aristotle does not mean the foundation of the obligation originating from this justice, but only the object with which this justice deals' (Cocceius 1751, I: 5, Gronovii n. 46).

8 *Sed parum refert, quid senserit Stagyrita, cuius divisio non accurate respondet divisioni Auctoris nostri, & a plerisque jam negligitur* ('it matters little what the Stagirite meant; his subdivision does not correspond exactly to our author's division, and has come to be disregarded by many', Cocceius 1751, I: 5).

9 I shall not deal with the third type of justice, *antipeponthos* in Greek and *contrapassum* in Latin (NE, ch. VIII of book V), since its particular character is not relevant to the present argument.

10 Grotius does mention the Greek *epanorthotike*, which includes the root of the verb to straighten, as a better word than *sunallaktike* for Aristotle's commutative justice (Grotius, *De iure*, I.1.viii.1). The problem is that it was *sunallaktike*, which did not suit Aristotle's text, as I have said above. About *expletrix*, cf also Gronovius (1702), p. 6.

11 A thorough discussion of Grotius's use of terms in relation to perfect/imperfect rights is in Pufendorf (1712), I.vii.11 (pp. 123–24).

12 Cf. Vivenza (1996).

13 Here we enter the dialectics of beneficence–gratitude, cf. Vivenza (1996).

14 While I share Haakonssen's opinion that Smith could not define as punishable an improper punishment because this 'would conflict with his theory of sovereignty' (Haakonssen 1981: 115), here I prefer to enlighten another aspect upon which Smith did not dwell, but which he may have deduced from his natural-law sources: that punishment cannot be seen as an injury to the guilty.

15 Grotius is at pains to exclude that punishment be due to the delinquent as in a sort of contract: *quasi nocenti aliquid reddatur, sicut in contractibus fieri solet* ('as if something were due to a wrongdoer as it happens in contracts'). Also Cocceius (1751), III: 334 *ad* § II. Cf. Norrie (1989: 231); and Salter (1999: 210).

16 Not all were of this opinion; see for instance De Vattel: he spoke against those who maintained that 'all punishment is just when the criminal knows in advance the penalties to which he exposes himself' (De Vattel 1916: 71).

17 (*Aequalitas inter culpam et poenam*), with Grotius's own note quoting Seneca, Tacitus, Ammianus, Horace's scholiast and the Lex Wisigothorum, in Cocceius 1751, III: 260.

18 Vivenza (forthcoming).

19 In the case of the Romans, equality was reached after the plebeians obtained the same rights of the patricians, at a very early stage of Roman history.
20 I should add that I cannot deal succinctly with these kinds of subjects; nevertheless, they are very relevant. For instance, this concept of man's independence from God, so to speak, marks an important point of difference between Enlightenment and religion. Cocceius even denies the very existence of a natural human society, and consequently of a 'social' natural law. We read sentences like: *demonstrabimus, doctrinam de societate humana ex impiis theologiae gentilis principiis ortam esse* ('we'll demonstrate that the theory of human society derived from impious principles of pagan theology'); or *supponi enim deberet, socialitatem esse ens a se, quod a nulla alia causa pendet* ('one should even suppose that sociality existed by itself, as it derives from no other cause', Cocceius 1751, I.§46). See Haakonssen (1996: 141–142). The subject of natural human society was a cornerstone of Enlightenment thought, which was, from this point of view, closer to the 'pagan' (Aristotle's) principle of a natural society among men.
21 McCloskey (forthcoming).
22 *Nam author iuris homo, iustitiae vel Deus* ('man is the author of right, God of justice'), *Azonis Summa Institutionum* I.1.
23 What is different in Smith's time and Aristotle's is that in eighteenth-century Europe there were three classes with different rights: aristocracy, clergy and commoners. In the ancient political community, every citizen had the same rights as any other. I think that they were rather similar to *our* world: there were differences of wealth, so at the end the poor were not treated in the same way as the rich, but this was not due to laws or institutions.
24 Comment of R.G. Bury to Plato, *Laws* 757B, also referring to Plato's *Gorgias* and Aristotle's *Politics* and *Nicomachean Ethics*. Cf also Spengler (1980: 88).
25 Vivenza (2001: 199): 'By the eighteenth century it perhaps began to seem slightly incongruous that both forms were called "justice", when in fact they represented opposing concepts'.
26 Incidentally, if anything, he changed category for intrinsic motives: Plato admits that sometimes a member of the guardian's class (the 'golden' men, best endowed with the qualities for command) may be transferred to the auxiliaries' class (the 'silver' men) if they have traces of silver in their gold: out of the metaphor, if their essential qualities are not first-class as they should be for the functions they have to perform. It is obvious that the 'material' of which these men are made (*Republic* 415 a–e; 420b–421c), represents precisely those 'invisible and often uncertain difference(s) of wisdom and virtue' which in Smith's view could not constitute a solid basis for the division of men into classes.
27 I have dealt with this topic in Vivenza (1996; 2001: 198–202).

Bibliography

Alvey, J.E. (2003) *Adam Smith: Optimist or Pessimist? A New Problem Concerning the Teleological Basis of Commercial Society*, London: Ashgate.
Aristotle (1994) *The Nicomachean Ethics*, Cambridge, MA/London: Loeb.
Azonis Summa Institutionum (1966), Papiae 1506, reprint ex officina Erasmiana, Augusta Taurinorum.
Cocceius (1751) *Hugonis Grotii De jure belli ac pacis libri tres, cum Annotationes Auctoris, nec non J.F.Gronovii Notis, & J.Barbeyracii Animadversionibus; Commentariis insuper locupletissimis Henr.L.B. De Cocceii [. . .] insertis quoque observationibus Samuelis L.B.De Cocceii,* [. . .] Lausannae, Sumptibus Marci-Michaelis Bousquet & Sociorum, MDCCLI.

Darwall, S. (1999) 'Sympathetic liberalism: recent work on Adam Smith', *Philosophy and Public Affairs*, 28:139–64.

De Molina, L. (1615) *De iustitia et iure*, Antwerpiae.

De Vattel, E. (1916) [1758] *Le droit des gens, ou principes de la loi naturelle, appliqués à la conduite et aux affaires des nations et des souverains*, The Carnegie Institute of Washington.

Fleischacker, S. (2004) *On Adam Smith's* Wealth of Nations: *A Philosophical Companion*, Princeton: Princeton University Press.

Gauthier, R.A. (ed.) (1972) *Aristoteles Latinus*, Leiden/Bruxelles, vol. XXVI, 3 (*Nicomachean Ethics*).

Griswold, C.L. Jr (1999) *Adam Smith and the Virtues of Enlightenment*, Cambridge: Cambridge University Press.

Gronovius (1702): *Hugonis Grotii De jure belli ac pacis libri tres, in quibus Jus Naturae & Gentium, item Juris Publici praecipua explicantur. Cum annotates auctoris [. . .] nec non Joann. Frid. Gronovii V.C. Notae in totum opus de Jure Belli ac Pacis editio novissima [. . .]*, Amstelaedami, Apud Henricum Wetstenios, H.FF.

Grotius (1751): cf Cocceius (1751).

Haakonssen, K. (1981) *The Science of a Legislator: The Natural Jurisprudence of David Hume and Adam Smith,* Cambridge: Cambridge University Press.

Haakonssen, K. (1996) *Natural Law and Moral Philosophy: From Grotius to the Scottish Enlightenment*, Cambridge: Cambridge University Press.

Lambertini, R. (1985) 'Per una storia dell'*oeconomica* tra alto e basso Medioevo', *Cheiron* II:4, 45–74.

Lessius, L. (1612) *De iustitia et iure caeterisque virtutibus cardinalibus libri quatuor*, Antwerpiae, ex officina Platiniana.

Levi, G. (2003) 'Aequitas *vs* fairness. Reciprocità ed equità fra età moderna e contemporanea', *Rivista di storia economica* XIX, 2.

McCloskey, D. (forthcoming), 'The last great virtue ethicist', in *The Elgar Companion to Adam Smith*, J.T. Young (ed.), Cheltenham: Edward Elgar.

Norrie, A. (1989) 'Punishment and justice in Adam Smith', *Ratio Juris*, 2: 227–39.

Plato (1984) *The Laws*, with an English translation by R.G. Bury, Cambridge, MA/London: Loeb, 2 vols.

Polybius (1992) *The Histories*, Cambridge, MA/London: Loeb.

Pufendorf, S. (1931) [1712] *Droit de la nature et des gens*, Amsterdam: De Coup.

Raphael, D.D. (2001) *Concepts of Justice*, Oxford: Oxford University Press.

Salter, J. (1999) 'Sympathy with the poor: theories of punishment in Hugo Grotius and Adam Smith', *History of Political Economy*, XX: 205–24.

Schneewind, J.B. (1990) 'The misfortunes of virtue', *Ethics*, 101: 42–63.

Smith, A. (1976a) *The Theory of Moral Sentiments,* D.D. Raphael and A.L. Macfie (eds), Oxford: Clarendon Press.

—— (1976b) *An Inquiry into the Nature and Causes of the Wealth of Nations*, R.H. Campbell & A.S. Skinner (eds), Oxford: Clarendon Press.

—— (1980) *Essays on Philosophical Subjects*, W.P.D. Wightman, J.C. Bryce and I.S. Ross (eds), Oxford, Clarendon Press.

Spengler, J.J. (1980) *Origins of Economic Thought and Justice*, London/Amsterdam: Southern Illinois University Press.

Strabo (1917–1932), *Geography*, with an English translation by H.L. Jones, Cambridge, MA/London: Loeb, 8 vols.

Theocarakis, N.J. (2006) '*Nicomachean Ethics* in political economy: the trajectory of the problem of value', *History of Economic Ideas*, XIV: 9–53.

Tuck, R. (1995) *Natural Right Theories*, Cambridge: Cambridge University Press.

Vivenza, G. (1996) 'Benevolenza pubblica, benevolenza privata e benevolenza reciproca: la virtù del dono e dello scambio dall'antichità al Settecento', *Studi storici Luigi Simeoni*, XLVI: 15–37.

—— (1999) 'Translating Aristotle: at the origin of terminology and content of economic value', in *Incommensurability and Translation: Kuhnian Perspectives on Scientific Communication and Theory Change*, R. Rossini Favretti, G. Sandri and R. Scazzieri (eds), Cheltenham/Northampton: Edward Elgar, 331–350.

—— (2001) *Adam Smith and the Classics*, Oxford: Oxford University Press.

—— (forthcoming) 'Aristotle and Adam Smith', in *The Elgar Companion to Adam Smith*, J.T. Young (ed.), Cheltenham: Edward Elgar.

A note on Adam Smith's first invisible hand

Gloria Vivenza

At WN V.ii.h.3, in reference to *vicesima hereditatum*, the famous inheritance tax imposed by the Emperor Augustus, Adam Smith cites a classical historian, Dio Cassius, and adds a note containing a reference to a modern tract on the Roman system of taxation: P. Burman, *De vectigalibus populi romani*.[1]

The book Smith cites was published for the first time in 1714; he possessed a 1734 edition, also in Latin, to which Burman added another early work previously published separately, four years after the *Vectigalia*: a brief tract of a philological–numismatic character, a totally different subject area. The full title of the 1734 edition was thus: *Petri Burmanni De vectigalibus populi romani, et Zeus kataibates sive Jupiter Fulgurator in Cyrrhestarum nummis* (Leidae, Wishoff).

Here we will deal with the second essay, since Smith is very likely to have read it, and may perhaps have derived some ideas about its protagonist, Jupiter. On the coins of the ancient Asian town of Cyrrhus,[2] Jupiter appeared seated, a thunderbolt in his hand, encircled by the words *Dios kataibatou* (or *katebatou*) *Kyrreston*. The coins are reproduced in an illustration at the end of the book, inserted between pages 344 and 345 on an unnumbered page. The God appears, seated, on both sides of the coin: on a cliff on one side, and on a throne inside a temple on the reverse. In both cases a thunderbolt is in his hand. An attempt to interpret the writing had already been made by Eduard Holtenus in 1699, in a letter to the eminent philologist Johann Georg Graevius. Burman reproduces the letter (pp. 216–22) in order to discuss it further.

Holtenus asserts that scholars connected the adjective *kataibatou*[3] with thunder, thus translating *Jovis Fulminantis* or, by analogy with a coin of Diocletian, *Fulguratoris*. The brief survey (p. 218), which also mentions a Latin epithet with a similar meaning, taken from Roman augural language (*Elicius*, that descends in the thunderbolt, *Fulgurator*) as a counterpart of the Greek *kataibates*, concludes with a fundamental objection raised by Holtenus: how can we consider the god to be in the act of hurling a thunderbolt if he is comfortably seated? It is necessary to seek an alternative translation.

I will briefly summarize this question, because it is not the philologist–antiquarian aspect that interests us here. Holtenus proposed *descensoris*, from the verb *descendere*, which effectively corresponds to the Greek *katabaino*; however, not in the sense of a true descent of the god – it could readily have been objected that the god was always seated, and the new translation seemed no more fitting. However, Holtenus reminds us that in the ancient pagan religion, in certain places images of divinities believed to have fallen from the sky were worshipped; he suggests that the inscription on the coins can be interpreted as *Jovis coelo delapsi* (221–22).

Burman resumes the argument with some very close reasoning, which here I shall summarize briefly. First and foremost, Jupiter has often been considered synonymous with the sky or heaven, that part of the universe associated with winds, rain, snow, thunder and lightning. The verb *katabaino* was apparently used because all these phenomena *in illius quasi* manu *& potestate, & totidem tela & arma essent, quae summus Deorum in mortales jacularetur* (p. 224: 'in his *hand* and in his power were virtually weapons or munitions which the God of Gods hurled against mortals'; my italics). By launching them from the sky to the earth, he made them 'descend'.

Burman continues his argument, explaining how at times the gods came down from Mount Olympus, and includes numerous literary examples to demonstrate how their descent could be beneficial; only with thunder and lightning was there the intent to punish (227). Taking his cue from the fact that during their frequent descents to earth the gods were able to take on different forms – Jupiter in particular was well-known for the numerous disguises which allowed him to copulate with mortal women[4] – Burman explains with a note from the Holy Scriptures: *Deus nulli mortalium conspici poterat vera & divina specie* ('God could not be seen by any mortal in his true and divine form'), a characteristic at least partially shared by the pagan gods, as numerous literary sources confirm (230–32). The gods in general are a sight that men cannot tolerate. Finally, one last consideration (pp. 233 and ff.): if all gods could come down to earth in their relations with human beings, why is it that the epithet *kataibates*, or 'he who descends' is reserved only for Jupiter? How did he differ from the other gods, who were referred to in a variety of ways (*custodes, tutelares, praesides*), but never with that word?

Well, the only thing that distinguished Jupiter from the other gods was his command of bad weather (p. 234). Even the polytheists, continues Burman, had a divinity they considered superior to the others, who administered things divine and human. The Greeks and Romans entrusted this role to Jupiter, who from Mount Olympus watched over the actions of men in order to praise or punish;[5] *hujus* manum *ventis, imbribus, procellis, tonitribus, & quidquid id genus est, armabant* (*sc.* Greeks and Romans: 'armed his *hand* with winds, rains, storms, thunder and whatever else belongs to this kind of things', p. 234; my italics). Essentially Jupiter hurling lightning is reconsidered in this version, criticized by Holtenus: *katabaino* is a descent, made to carry out the god's vengeance, in the sense that the above *prodigia* (thunder, lightning etc.) hurled from the sky are signs of his majesty and his wrath.

This is the gist of the part of Burman's text that interests us here. Let us now turn to Smith's invisible hand of Jupiter. At 'The History of Astronomy' (HA) III.2 the invisible hand is invoked to alter things, not in the normal course of events: this function, which is somehow opposed to the function attributed to it in economic thought, has been noted several times: in HA it interrupts and obstructs the normal course of events, rather than facilitating it (cf. A.L. Macfie 1971).[6] But here Smith is precisely considering traumatic, unforeseen events, which terrorize primitive men since they understand neither their reason nor their origin: '. . . they proceed from some intelligent, though *invisible* causes, of whose vengeance and displeasure they are either the signs or the effects' (HA III.1; my italics). The appearance of the 'hand' may remind us of Burman's two phrases cited above, in which it is clearly stated that all weather phenomena are in the *hand* of Zeus; I would add that in Holtenus's letter to Graevius we find a quote from Ovid: *Dextra libratum fulmen ab aure* (*Metam*.II, 311[7]), which is pertinent, despite the use of '*dextra*' rather than 'hand'. And it is a threatening hand, as we have already seen: the epithet refers to the god only when he intends to punish, and therefore he himself is an object of fear.

Smith appears to have somehow extrapolated the weather phenomena, presenting them as sources of terror given the ignorance of primitive peoples, who tended to attribute them to the wrath of an angry god. Up to this point, a certain parallelism exists, apart from the fact that Burman does not indulge in any 'anthropological' considerations on the ignorance of primitive peoples. Jupiter reappears in Smith's argument when he specifies that divine intervention, just like human intervention, served to alter the natural course of events, to prevent them from carrying on as usual: 'Fire burns, and water refreshes; heavy bodies descend, and lighter substances fly upwards, by the necessity of their own nature; nor was the invisible hand of Jupiter ever apprehended to be employed in those matters. But thunder and lightning, storms and sunshine, those more irregular events, were ascribed to his favour, or his anger' (HA III.2). As we have observed, even in Burman's essay a difference is made between normal, beneficial relations between men and the gods, including Zeus, and the latter's intervention with lightning which indicates a sudden, brusque change.

Perhaps even the invisibility of the god, mentioned by Burman as I said above, may have given Smith the idea of a hand that acts without being seen, just as the presence of the gods was not always visible even in the pagan religion, although it was perceived all the same. I realize that it would hardly be appropriate to claim that I have discovered from where Smith derived the well-known image. But it is a fact that points of contact do exist, and several at that; in addition it may be useful to bear in mind that Smith wrote the 'History of Astronomy' when he was very young: during his Oxford or Edinburgh years (Vivenza 2001: 10, n. 8), namely in the forties (1740–6 or 1748–50). Burman's publication of the *Zeus kataibates* together with his *Vectigalia* (1734) was quite recent. Although young, however, Smith already demonstrated the capacity to assimilate and make his own the various ideas offered by his extensive classical culture; the end result is, as always, quite different and, above all, exclusively his own.

Notes

1 In fact, there are two references: there is also Bouchard's work, *De l'impot du vingtième*; however, in this note we will deal only with the first.
2 Or of the region called Cyrrhestica: there is scanty information about it, going back to Strabo 16,2 and Polybius 50,7 and 57,4, who speak of it as a Syrian region or people, respectively. Stephen of Byzantium also speaks of a city, Cyrrhus.
3 From the verb *katabaino*, to descend.
4 The adventures of Jupiter are summarized by Burman with an almost facetious *peccaturum in terris* (p. 229: 'preparing himself to sin on earth') in which the use of the verb 'to sin' gives a singular Christian taint to these mythological amorous exploits.
5 I will not digress on the fact that this is a characteristic of the Christian God more than of a pagan god.
6 Most scholars have concerned themselves, as we know, with Smith's other two 'invisible hands': those at TMS IV.i.10 and WN IV.ii.9. For a survey and discussion, see Rothschild (2001, pp. 116 and ff.).
7 '(Jupiter), balancing in his right hand a bolt (struck Phaeton from the chariot and from life)'.

Bibliography

Macfie, A.L. (1971) 'The invisible hand of Jupiter', *Journal of the History of Ideas*, 32: 595–99.
Rothschild, E. (2001) *Economic Sentiments: Adam Smith, Condorcet and the Enlightenment*, Cambridge, MA/London, Harvard University Press.
Smith, A. (1980) 'The History of Astronomy', in *Essays on Philosophical Subjects*, W.P.D. Wightman (ed.), Oxford: Clarendon Press.
Vivenza, G. (2001) *Adam Smith and the Classic: The Classical Heritage in Adam Smith's Thought*, Oxford: Oxford University Press.

Adam Smith as an *eclectic* Stoic

Leonidas Montes

I Introduction

With different nuances, the Stoics' influence on Adam Smith and the Scottish Enlightenment is generally taken for granted.[1] The many references to the Stoics, mainly in Smith's *Theory of Moral Sentiments* (TMS),[2] and the importance of this classical tradition within the Scottish Enlightenment, have led scholars to acknowledge this apparently obvious influence. However, this influence is at times more elusive than obvious. If there are clear traces of this 'famous sect' (TMS Advertisement 1) in Smith's legacy, first of all it is difficult to refer to Stoicism as one unified philosophical system, and secondly, some well-known features of Stoicism bluntly contradict Smith's ethical conceptions.

Stoicism as a source of Adam Smith's legacy is a complex matter. Moreover, Adam Smith, '*the* great eclectic' (Viner 1927: 199; emphasis in the original), to borrow Jacob Viner's appropriate description, does not make things easier for modern interpreters. For the purpose of this essay, Emma Rothschild is quite right when she declares 'he [Smith] was eclectic in his use of Stoic ideas' (2001: 132). I would add that if we take the original Greek meaning of *eklektikos*, her judgment makes more sense in Smith as the verb *eklegein* means selecting or choosing from what is best. Smith clearly knew what to take and what not to take from the Stoics, as the title and purpose of this essay suggest.

As it would be the subject of an ambitious project to fully investigate the overall influence and implications of Smith's *eclectic* position on Stoicism, in this essay I will only concentrate on Smith's sympathy and self-command and their Stoic sources. On the one hand, the influence of the Stoics concept of *oikeiosis* in sympathy – the cornerstone of Smith's moral thought – has been underestimated. On the other hand, the influence of the Stoics in self-command – Smith's chief virtue – has been overestimated. If Smith's sympathy is underpinned by the idea of *oikeiosis*, self-command does not necessarily derive from the Stoics. This chief virtue reflects an important Socratic source quite different from that of the Stoics. Sympathy has generally been taken simply as a 'modern' idea, and self-command has been routinely considered as a Stoic virtue. I will challenge these widely held views, uncovering what Smith selected and did not select from the Stoics for sympathy and self-command, respectively.

We know that Smith devoted the last years of his life to work on TMS.[3] The last edition (sixth) was published posthumously and it contains substantial revisions and extensive additions that amount to nearly one third of the definitive sixth edition of TMS. Some of those changes, specifically related to the Stoics, will provide important indications of Smith's mature thinking on Stoicism. They will be analyzed in the course of this essay.

The next section will explore the context of Stoicism and Smith's account of the Stoics. It will also be argued that Smith might have known many different sources of the Stoics. Section 3 begins with an account of Smith's sympathetic process in order to analyze the importance of the concept of *oikeiosis* as a distinctively Stoic source. In section 4 it will be argued that the common view of Smith's self-command as a Stoic virtue is disputable. Finally some brief conclusions about the Stoics as a principal source for Smith's thought will be drawn.

II Adam Smith and Stoicism in context

The importance of Stoicism

Charles Taylor, in his *Sources of the Self* (1989), shows, among other things, the crucial importance of Stoicism in the formation of modern identity during the seventeenth and eighteenth centuries. Smith's reliance on the Stoics, and their influence upon the Scottish Enlightenment, has been widely acknowledged. In their authoritative introduction to TMS, the editors Raphael and Macfie declare that 'Stoic philosophy is the primary influence on Smith's ethical thought' (TMS Intro. 5). Soon after they refer to 'the pervasive character of Stoic influence' (ibid.), arguing that regardless of some changes in the successive editions of TMS 'Stoicism never lost its hold over Smith's mind' (TMS Intro. 5–6). Any serious scholar who reads Smith would rapidly recognize the Stoics' explicit and implicit importance in the shaping of Smith's moral philosophy.

It has been traditionally argued that this phenomenon was pervasive within the Scottish Enlightenment tradition as a whole. Relying on the Stoics, Shaftesbury, Grotius and Pufendorf, to name a few, transmitted this classical tradition to foundational figures of the Scottish Enlightenment such as the 'never to be forgotten' Hutcheson (*Corr.* Letter 274) and the influential Carmichael. Stoicism was certainly extremely relevant to the shaping of the Scottish Enlightenment. But as Macfie has argued '[t]he Scots gave it their own typical turn but their thought is in the broad Stoic stream' (1967: 20). For this, and many other reasons that I will attempt to explain, it is an extremely complex influence.[4] The Scottish literati adopted Stoicism, but they also adapted it in many different ways.

Roughly speaking, Early Stoicism is foremost represented by Zeno of Citium (334–262 BC), who initiated this tradition at the *Stoa Poikile*. He is followed by Cleanthes (331–232 BC) and then by Chrysippus (c.280–c.206 BC). Smith refers to all of them, but mainly by assigning Chrysippus the famous paradoxes, he is to be blamed for the corruption of Early Stoicism:

> At any rate, I cannot allow myself to believe that such men as Zeno or Cleanthes, men, it is said, of the most simple as well as of the most sublime eloquence, could be the authors, either of these, or of the greater part of the other Stoical paradoxes, which are in general mere impertinent quibbles, and do so little honour to their system that I shall give no further account of them. I am disposed to impute them rather to Chrysippus, the disciple and follower, indeed, of Zeno and Cleanthes, but who, from all that has been delivered down to us concerning him, seems to have been a mere dialectical pedant, without taste or elegance of any kind.
>
> (TMS VII.ii.1.41)

Middle Stoicism is mainly represented by Panaetius (c.180–110 BC) and Posidonius of Apamea (c.135–c.51 BC). Roman or Late Stoicism is principally represented by Seneca (4 BC–65 AD), Epictetus (50–138 AD), Marcus Aurelius (121–180 AD) and Hierocles (second century AD). What we know today about Stoicism is basically from doxography and some fragments, and mainly through the legacy of Cicero, Diogenes Laertius, Marcus Aurelius, Hierocles, the fifth century Greek anthologist Stobaeus, Sextus Empiricus, Epictetus and Galen. From antiquity we have just inherited a great amount of fragmentary and diverse material bearing on Stoic philosophy. With all these different sources in different periods, Stoicism as a source is rather elusive. Therefore there is not only a problem of reconstruction, but also a problem of internal coherence as we find differences within Stoicism.

Another important point to keep in mind on Smith and his classical sources is that during the Enlightenment Latin was the language of the literati. Yet Adam Smith possessed also a serious command of Greek. The writer Henry Mackenzie, to whom Walter Scott referred as the 'Scottish Addison', is reported to have compared Smith with Dr. Johnson. The former was 'an exception' in terms of character and knowledge, and the latter 'only knew one language well, the Latin' (Clayden 1887: 166–7). A simple look into Smith's impressive collection of classical works in his library (Mizuta 1967), his repeated emphasis on the study of the Greek language in his letters regarding the education of Viscount Fitzmaurice (cf. *Corr.* Letters 28, 29 and 31), and his command of Greek explicit in LRBL, are sufficient proof to confirm this testimony as evidence.

If we look at Smith's library, it is quite possible that he had access to a diversity of Stoic sources.[5] In fact, he refers to 'the few fragments of their [Stoics'] philosophy which have come down to us' (TMS VII.ii.26). In addition, as any serious classic scholar would do, when Smith refers with his occasional, but delightful sense of humour to the possible suicide of Zeno, he enumerates the '[t]hree different accounts [which] have been given of the death of Zeno the Stoic' (TMS VII.ii.31).

During the seventeenth and eighteenth centuries Cicero was undoubtedly the main source for Stoicism. Cicero was widely read, but so were Marcus Aurelius and Epictetus, although to a lesser extent.[6] Smith continuously cites Cicero, and in his LRBL he is even reported to have said that '[t]here is no character in antiquity with which we are better acquainted than with that of Cicero' (LRBL ii.235).[7] Indeed, in LRBL and also in LJ, Smith shows an intimate knowledge of Cicero's works. Smith's best friend, David Hume, in his first *Inquiry*, reflects the favourable intellectual atmosphere towards Cicero when he says that the 'fame of CICERO flourishes at present' (Hume 1993 [1748]: 3; emphasis in the original). In his *My Own Life*, Hume recalls that during his youth 'Cicero and Virgil were the authors which I was secretly devouring' (Hume 1987 [1777]: xxxiii). But among Cicero's works, his masterpiece *De Officiis* was, in particular, widely read and extremely popular during the eighteenth century.[8]

The assumption of Cicero as the spokesman of the Stoic tradition might be misleading. Some modern interpretations of the Stoics' influence on Smith take for granted that Cicero is the main, if not the only source of Stoicism. Yet, while Cicero follows 'the Stoics above all, not as an expositor, but, as is my custom, drawing from their fountains when and as it seems best, using my own judgment and discretion' (Cicero 1991, I.6: 4), and while he is undoubtedly a very important source for Stoical thought, his writings are hardly an uncomplicated summary of Stoic ideas, to say nothing of the neo-Stoicism that deeply influenced the Scottish context. Cicero adopted but also criticized different aspects of Stoicism. But the intellectual and cultural value of the 'romanization', of what had been said by his Greek predecessors, is indeed very relevant.

In sum, the intellectual landscape is much more complicated than simply accepting the influence of the Stoics on Adam Smith. If there are explicit references and clear traces of the 'famous sect' in Smith's writings, the first problem we face is that it is difficult to refer to Stoicism as one unified philosophical system.

Smith's evolution on Stoicism

In the Advertisement for the sixth edition of TMS, Smith claims that in Part VII he has 'brought together the greater part of the different passages concerning the Stoical Philosophy, which, in the former Editions, had been scattered about in different parts of the work'. The editors of TMS believe he is exaggerating (TMS Adv., note 1), and they are correct if we take this statement only literally. But Smith immediately adds that 'I have likewise endeavoured to explain more fully, and examine more distinctly, some of

the doctrines of that famous sect' (TMS Adv. 1). His intention is clear; so
is his concern with the Stoics. Perhaps Smith was not only exaggerating, but
also consciously acknowledging the importance of the evolution of his
own thought about the Stoics. If that is so, we should not only worry about
what he 'brought together', but also about what he actually changed. To
complement and underpin the latter, we need to assess how and why his
position regarding the Stoics evolved.

Another example one might use to understand the evolution of Smith's
thought about classical sources concerns the Epicureans. Since the early
editions of TMS, Smith attempts to distance himself from any Epicurean
connection. He declares: '[t]his system is, no doubt, altogether inconsistent
with that which I have been endeavouring to establish' (TMS VII.ii.2.13).
However, his account of the virtue or prudence, friendship and even some
characteristics of Smith's sympathy and his concept of tranquillity of mind,
especially in the last edition of TMS, are pervaded by an Epicurean tenet.
Referring to the Epicureans, Smith's change in the last edition of TMS from
'the worst' to simply the 'most imperfect system' (TMS VII.ii.4.5) is not
casual as it might signal a late acknowledgment of Epicurean sources.

Although some changes in the last edition of TMS have been attributed
to his old age,[9] I tend to view the sixth edition of TMS as a product of mature
thought, rather than senility. In this sense his completely new added Part VI
'Of the Character of Virtue' reflects a shift towards a virtue ethics in its
title and its content. In addition, many of the changes that come up in his
last lifetime edition of TMS deviate from Smith's original and more decided
endorsement of some aspects of Stoicism.

For example, the Stoics' influence in Smith's account of his four chief
virtues (prudence, beneficence, self-command and justice) in the newly
added Part VI of TMS, which was written only a few years before Smith's
death, shows some important differences. These changes reflect the actual
evolution of Smith's virtues from TMS first edition (1759) to the sixth edition
(1790).[10] Norbert Waszek, referring to these four Smithian virtues, states that
'it can be argued that the particular manner in which Smith defined those
traditional virtues distinctly echoes Stoic ideas and terminology' (1984: 603).
In addition, Athol Fitzgibbons considers that 'Smith's four virtues . . .
prudence, justice, self-command, and benevolence, were his eighteenth-
century namesakes for the traditional Stoical virtues' (1995: 104). Recent
scholarship, by delving into this and other issues, has questioned the tendency
of too readily accepting the view of Smith's Stoicism. Moreover, some
scholars have recently begun to argue against this commonly held view
(Forman-Barzilai 2002; Montes 2004; Brubaker 2006), and new connections
have emerged linking, for example, Smith to Aristotle and virtue ethics
(Fleischacker 1999; Vivenza 2001; Carrasco 2004; Hanley 2006).

At this stage it is appropriate to discuss some of the main and most common
themes of the Stoic doctrines, analyzing Smith's responses. Following
Eckstein's (1926) pioneering work pinpointing differences among editions,

and Dickey's (1986) ablest effort, I will try to underline some of those changes related to Stoicism. This will be done through Smith's own account of some relevant aspects of Stoicism.

For the Stoics reason (*logos*) and nature (*physis*) are a unity in a living *kosmos* of which we form part. Therefore their maxim: living in accordance with nature.

> The ancient stoics were of opinion, that as the world was governed by the all-ruling providence of a wise, powerful, and good God, every single event ought to be regarded, as making a necessary part of the plan of the universe, and as tending to promote the general order and happiness of the whole: that the vices and follies of mankind, therefore, made as necessary a part of this plan as their wisdom or their virtue; and by that eternal art which educes good from ill, were made to tend equally to the prosperity and perfection of the great system of nature.
>
> (TMS I.ii.3.4)

Literally the word *physis* means growth. This word also refers to the way a thing grows and by extension it relates to an action or behaviour of something growing, like a human being. Thus the notion of a human being whose 'natural life' is in accord with nature makes more sense as a cosmic process. However, the Stoics' maxim of living in accordance with nature assumes a *summum bonum*, which is beyond this world. This also requires that things in this life (including life itself)[11] are indifferent to us. Related to the latter, the Stoics developed the famous concept of *apatheia*. This concept demands not only complete indifference to events in this world, but also a rational acceptance of whatever destiny may hold:

> If I am going to sail, says Epictetus, I chuse the best ship and the best pilot, and I wait for the fairest weather that my circumstances and duty will allow. Prudence and propriety, the principles which the Gods have given me for the direction of my conduct, require this of me; but they require no more: and if, notwithstanding, a storm arises, which neither the strength of the vessel nor the skill of the pilot are likely to withstand, I give myself no trouble about the consequence. All that I had to do is done already. The directors of my conduct never command me to be miserable, to be anxious, desponding, or afraid. Whether we are to be drowned, or to come to a harbour, is the business of Jupiter, not mine. I leave it entirely to his determination, nor ever break my rest with considering which way he is likely to decide it, but receive whatever comes with equal indifference and security.
>
> (TMS VII.ii.1.20)

The content of this classical example of Epictetus is repeated through other examples by Smith in other passages (see, for example, TMS VII.ii.1.26;

III.3.11), but in the last edition of TMS Smith's conclusion about this attitude is that:

> From this perfect confidence in that benevolent wisdom which governs the universe, and from this entire resignation to whatever order that wisdom might think proper to establish, it necessarily followed, that, to the Stoical wise man, all the events of human life must be in a great measure indifferent.
>
> (TMS VII.ii.1.21)

Complete indifference in the form of apathy for Smith is against the 'plan and system' of nature:

> By the perfect apathy which it prescribes to us, by endeavouring, not merely to moderate, but to eradicate all our private, partial, and selfish affections, by suffering us to feel for whatever can befall ourselves, our friends, our country, not even the sympathetic and reduced passions of the impartial spectator, it endeavours to render us altogether indifferent and unconcerned in the success or miscarriage of every thing which Nature has prescribed to us as the proper business and occupation of our lives.
>
> (TMS VII.ii.1.46)

The Stoics' neglect of sentiments and their consequences is contrary to Smith's common sense, and even to nature, as Smith suggests in the last passage, also added to the last edition of TMS. Perfect apathy understood literally as no sentiments, no passions or no emotions,[12] is just contrary to the essence of *The Theory of Moral Sentiments*. Smith's ethics is founded on sentiments, on the passions and emotions that constitute, through sympathy, the cement of society. Simply following what happens with sheer and cold resignation, the Stoic would lose his human nature. Smith's *zoon politikon* demands, ethically and politically, an active social being. Human beings feel, and feelings influence human behaviour. The Stoic sage would lack Smith's understanding of the close relationship between morality and sentiments.

It is important to underline that Smith's self-command is not apathy as it requires feelings. As it will be shown in the next section, Smith's account of self-command is more complicated than a simple understanding of this virtue as self-control. If apathy demands not only the control of emotions, but the eradication of passions, Smith's self-command represents an inward movement that derives in an outward enabling action.

For Smith feelings are interrelated to virtuous behaviour. Following Aristotle's concept of *mesotes* and his understanding of the cardinal virtue of courage, Smith borrows the idea that to have courage in excess (acting with temerity) is not virtuous (does not deserve merit) as courage demands the sentiment of fear. The apathetic courageous man would be simply insensible. He who has the virtue of courage feels fear but also has the virtue of self-command. This Aristotelian passage explaining this idea was also added to the sixth edition of TMS:

> Concerning the subject of self-command, I shall only observe further, that our admiration for the man who, under the heaviest and most unexpected misfortunes, continues to behave with fortitude and firmness, always supposes that his sensibility to those misfortunes is very great, and such as it requires a very great effort to conquer or command. The man who was altogether insensible to bodily pain, could deserve no applause from enduring the torture with the most perfect patience and equanimity. The man who had been created without the natural fear of death, could claim no merit from preserving his coolness and presence of mind in the midst of the most dreadful dangers.
>
> (TMS III.3.44)

Another important point for the Stoics is that in political terms there is the recurrent idea of the citizen of the world. Using again Epictetus, Smith also gives some examples of cosmopolitanism:

> Man, according to the Stoics, ought to regard himself, not as something separated and detached, but as a citizen of the world, a member of the vast commonwealth of nature. To the interest of this great community, he ought at all times to be willing that his own little interest should be sacrificed. Whatever concerns himself, ought to affect him no more than whatever concerns any other equally important part of this immense system. We should view ourselves, not in the light in which our own selfish passions are apt to place us, but in the light in which any other citizen of the world would view us. What befalls ourselves we should regard as what befalls our neighbour, or, what comes to the same thing, as our neighbour regards what befalls us. 'When our neighbour', says Epictetus, 'loses his wife, or his son, there is nobody who is not sensible that this is a human calamity, a natural event altogether according to the ordinary course of things; but, when the same thing happens to ourselves, then we cry out, as if we had suffered the most dreadful misfortune. We ought, however, to remember how we were affected when this accident happened to another, and such as we were in his case, such ought we to be in our own'.
>
> (TMS III.3.11)

According to the Stoics only the sage will attain virtue, but they also consider life as a journey of moral development. Remember that living in accordance with nature also involves a process of growth. In a beautiful metaphor Smith explains that for the Stoics the important thing was to play well, regardless of the result:

Human life the Stoics appear to have considered as a game of great skill; in which, however, there was a mixture of chance, or of what is vulgarly understood to be chance. In such games the stake is commonly a trifle, and the whole pleasure of the game arises from playing well, from playing fairly, and playing skilfully.

(TMS VII.ii.1.24)

The popular interpretation that Stoicism emerged in a political context that somehow forced a detachment from public life is worth exploring.[13] Stoicism and also Epicureanism, as intellectual phenomena, can also be seen as a political reaction towards the end of Athenian democracy, or a political longing for it. The Stoics left the agora and secluded themselves in a painted colonnade (*Stoa Poikile*); the Epicureans in the Garden.[14] In this context, Vivienne Brown's interpretation of Smith's discourse relying on the private virtues epitomized by the Stoics, leaving aside the public virtues that they had to abandon (Brown 1994, chapter 4), is quite suggestive. Yet our pragmatic Adam Smith was also well aware of these circumstances and their social, psychological and intellectual consequences. I will quote this long passage, also added to the last edition of TMS, in full, as it is an interesting proof of Smith's political sensibility to the importance of context:

The propriety, upon some occasions, of voluntary death, though it was, perhaps, more insisted upon by the Stoics, than by any other sect of ancient philosophers, was, however, a doctrine common to them all, even to the peaceable and indolent Epicureans. During the age in which flourished the founders of all the principal sects of ancient philosophy; during the Peloponnesian war and for many years after its conclusion, all the different republics of Greece were, at home, almost always distracted by the most furious factions; and abroad, involved in the most sanguinary wars, in which each sought, not merely superiority or dominion, but either completely to extirpate all its enemies, or, what was not less cruel, to reduce them into the vilest of all states, that of domestic slavery, and to sell them, man, woman, and child, like so many herds of cattle, to the highest bidder in the market. The smallness of the greater part of those states, too, rendered it, to each of them, no very improbable event, that it might itself fall into that very calamity which it had so frequently, either, perhaps, actually inflicted, or at least attempted to inflict upon some of its neighbours. In this disorderly state of things, the most perfect innocence, joined to both the highest rank and the greatest public services, could give no security to any man that, even at home and among his own relations and fellow-citizens, he was not, at some time or another, from the prevalence of some hostile and furious faction, to be condemned to the most cruel and ignominious punishment. If he was taken prisoner in war, or if the city of which he was a member was conquered, he was exposed, if possible, to still greater injuries and insults. But every man naturally, or rather necessarily, familiarizes his imagination with the distresses to which he foresees that his situation may frequently expose him. It is impossible that a sailor should not frequently think of storms and shipwrecks, and foundering at sea, and of how he himself is likely both to feel and to act upon such occasions. It was impossible, in the same manner, that a Grecian patriot or hero should not familiarize his imagination with all the different calamities to which he was sensible his situation must frequently, or rather constantly expose him. As an American savage prepares his death-song, and considers how he should act when he has fallen into the hands of his enemies, and is by them put to death in the most lingering tortures, and amidst the insults and derision of all the spectators; so a Grecian patriot or hero could not avoid frequently employing his thoughts in considering what he ought both to suffer and to do in banishment, in captivity, when reduced to slavery, when put to the torture, when brought to the scaffold. But the philosophers of all the different sects very justly represented virtue; that is, wise, just, firm, and temperate conduct; not only as the most probable, but as the certain and infallible road to happiness even in this life. This conduct, however, could not always exempt, and might even sometimes expose the person who followed it to all the calamities which were incident to that unsettled situation of public affairs. They endeavoured, therefore, to show that happiness was either altogether, or at least in a great measure, independent of fortune; the Stoics, that it was so altogether; the Academic and Peripatetic philosophers, that it was so in a great measure. Wise, prudent, and good conduct was, in the first place, the conduct most likely to ensure success in every species of undertaking; and secondly, though it should fail of success, yet the mind was not left without consolation. The virtuous man might still enjoy the complete approbation of his own breast; and might still feel that, how untoward soever things might be without, all was calm and peace and concord within. He might generally comfort himself, too, with the assurance that he possessed the love and esteem of every intelligent and impartial spectator, who could not fail both to admire his conduct, and to regret his misfortune.

(TMS VII.ii.1.28)

Another obvious candidate to suggest that Smith might have changed his early position regarding the Stoics is the significant alteration in the atonement passage (TMS II.ii.3.12; see also Appendix II: 383–401). This famous passage discussing the Deity, charged with Stoics overtones, determinism and religious discourse, is substituted in the sixth and last edition by a short and quite Humean sentence: 'In every religion and in every superstition that the world has ever beheld, accordingly, there has been a Tartarus as well as an Elysium; a place provided for the punishment of the wicked, as well as one for the reward of the just' (TMS II.ii.3.12). Walter

Eckstein, in his introduction to his 1926 German translation of Smith's TMS, compares some of the changes in the sixth edition, suggesting that 'from certain additions and above all from a few omissions one could perhaps conclude the presence of a transformation in Smith's religious views' (Eckstein 2000 [1926]: 29), referring immediately to the controversial atonement passage as evidence for this change.

After Eckstein described this new passage as 'the somewhat sceptical-sounding sentence' (Eckstein 2000 [1926]: 30), this change has generated much speculation among scholars. This change might suggest a turn in his religious beliefs, or simply a blunt affirmation of his undisclosed private position on this issue.[15]

Nearly at the end of Smith's account of the Stoics, he bluntly concludes that '[t]he plan and system which Nature has sketched out for our conduct, seems to be altogether different from that of the Stoical philosophy' (TMS VII.ii.43). Is there anything left after this rather conclusive closing? I believe there is. If Smith does not adopt the main doctrines of the Stoics, he borrows some aspects of Stoicism that fit within his system. In particular the Stoic concept of *oikeiosis* is fundamental to understand Smith's sympathetic process and his notion of self-interest. It is very likely that Smith would have used this distinctively Stoic concept as an important source.

III Smith's concept of sympathy and *oikeiosis*

Smith's sympathy

Before investigating directly *oikeiosis* as a Stoic source for Smith's sympathy, it is necessary to explain briefly Smith's own understanding of the sympathetic process. The first sentence in the TMS, 'How selfish soever man may be supposed, there are evidently some principles in his nature, which interest him in the fortune of others, and render their happiness necessary to him, though he derives nothing from it except the pleasure of seeing it' (TMS I.i.1.1), defines sympathy as a principle in human nature. But Smith is aware that common language might mislead readers to what he actually means by sympathy. In fact:

> Pity and compassion are words appropriated to signify our fellow-feeling with the sorrows of others. Sympathy, though its meaning was, perhaps, originally the same, may now, however, without much impropriety, be made use of to denote our fellow-feeling with any passion whatever.
>
> (TMS I.i.1.5)

This passage is important for at least three reasons. First, it clarifies what Smith does not mean by sympathy. Second, it opens up the way for defining

Smith's complex sympathetic process. And finally, what concerns us in this essay, it will lead us to an important Stoic influence.

The Greek prefix *sun* (later *syn*), which means together or simply with (as Plato's *Sym-posium* means drinking with), is joined to *pathos*. Therefore *sun-pathos* is etymologically equivalent to com-passion (the Latin prefix *cum* is the equivalent of the Greek *sun*, and *pathos* and passion are also the same). Smith is clearly aware of this etymological analogy, therefore he clarifies that 'though its meaning was . . . originally the same', sympathy is different from merely com-passion. Then by making clear that sympathy should 'be made use of to denote our fellow-feeling with any passion whatever', he also clarifies that sympathy is not simply fellow-feeling related to pity, but also with joy.

But two additional concepts are needed to give full meaning to Smith's sympathetic process: imagination and the cause that triggers any passion. It is by the 'very illusion of the imagination' and 'the idea of those circumstances' that this broad concept of sympathy takes place. The nature of the sympathetic process is determined by 'the imaginary change of situations from which it arises' (TMS I.i.4.1). Also imagination affects the importance of the causes that trigger our passions, as '[s]ympathy, therefore, does not arise so much from the view of the passion, as from that of the situation which excites it' (TMS I.i.1.10). I can have fellow-feeling with any passion, but I cannot sympathize '. . . till informed of its cause' (TMS I.i.1.8). We can even feel 'the dread of death' (TMS I.i.1.13), and I may even sympathize with a pregnant woman (TMS VII.iii.1.4), even though I cannot ever have a baby. In sum, the role of imagination combines with a circumstantial deliberative process that finally allows the agent to sympathize. Strictly speaking, Smith's sympathy would be etymologically and conceptually a special kind of *empatheia*, as the Greek prefix *en* means in, into or within.

Smith's sympathy naturally requires an impartial spectator consistent with human beings' inherently social nature. But sympathy is not only about fellow-feeling as a natural social phenomenon, as it also requires understanding the reasons behind that feeling. Sympathy involves deliberation. Sympathy is not only standing in your shoes, but also knowing where those shoes are standing. Moreover, responding to Thomas Reid's accusation that his sympathy was a selfish concept,[16] Smith stresses that it 'cannot, in any sense, be regarded as a selfish principle' (TMS VII.iii.1.4).

The Greek word *sumpatheia* was very important for the Stoics. Actually, the editors of TMS argue that 'The Stoics themselves applied the notion of society no less than to the physical universe, and used the Greek *sympatheia* (in the sense of organic connection) of both' (TMS, Intro. p. 7).[17] For the Stoics *sumpatheia* also had a cosmic significance that entailed social overtones, and though it was an important word for the Stoic tradition, it had already been used by Plato, Aristotle and Epicurus. For example, Cicero refers to the Greek *sumpatheia*, especially in his *De Divinatione*, and translates the Greek word as *consensus* (Cicero 1971, II.xiv), and then as a *natural connexion.* According to the Stoics, who were chief apologists of divination, there is a sympathy or connexion that permits communication between the divine soul and the human soul.[18] This is related to the Stoic idea of Nature with a capital 'N'. We live in accordance with Nature. There is a connexion and a consensus, to follow both of Cicero's translations, with nature. Not surprisingly during the seventeenth and early eighteenth centuries, sympathy was also closely linked to physiology (see Forget 2003) and even to alchemical studies as Levy and Peart suggest in this volume (2008).

Sympathy and oikeiosis

Of course there would be no sympathetic process without an impartial spectator. Sympathy, without attaining mutual sympathy, would be like exchange without a market for Smith. It is the process of the concordance of sentiments that finally uncovers the social nature of Smith's project.[19] In this sense sympathy also relates to Cicero's translation of the Stoic's word *sumpatheia* as a 'natural connexion'. Sympathy for Smith not only pre-supposes the social nature of human beings, very much like Hume's concept of sympathy, but it is the sympathetic process, through the attainment of mutual sympathy, that finally determines Smith's ethics of social interaction. For Smith a human being without society would simply not be a human being, and society without sympathy, would simply not be society:

> Were it possible that a human creature could grow up to manhood in some solitary place, without any communication with his own species, he could no more think of his own character, of the propriety or demerit of his own sentiments and conduct, of the beauty or deformity of his own mind, than of the beauty or deformity of his own face. All these are objects which he cannot easily see, which naturally he does not look at, and with regard to which he is provided with no mirror which can present them to his view. Bring him into society, and he is immediately provided with the mirror which he wanted before.
>
> (TMS III.i.3)

Now according to Smith we tend naturally to sympathize more easily with those that are close to us, and it is more difficult to sympathize with strangers. There is a sort of sympathetic gradient,[20] whereby sympathy decreases with emotional distance. Nieli's (1986) article about the spheres of intimacy treats this issue, and recently Otteson (2002) has suggestively expanded this intuition to defend a marketplace of morals. According to James Otteson's suggestive thesis there is no *Das Adam Smith Problem*, as we should understand that Smith intends a combination of morality and markets. Therefore both of his books (TMS and WN) are consistent as far as they represent a single conception of human institutions.

This propensity to sympathize is naturally self-centred. In TMS last edition this social phenomenon is wonderfully described by Smith:

> After himself, the members of his own family, those who usually live in the same house with him, his parents, his children, his brothers and sisters, are naturally the objects of his warmest affections. They are naturally and usually the persons upon whose happiness or misery his conduct must have the greatest influence. He is more habituated to sympathize with them. He knows better how every thing is likely to affect them, and his sympathy with them is more precise and determinate, than it can be with the greater part of other people. It approaches nearer, in short, to what he feels for himself.
>
> (TMS VI.ii.1.2)

There is a clear Stoic source in relation to this idea that Smith develops for his last TMS edition. Hierocles, according to Stobaeus, stated:

> Each one of us is as it were entirely encompassed by many circles . . . the first and closest circle is the one which a person has drawn as though around the center, his own mind . . . Next . . . contains parents, siblings, wife, and children. The third one has in it uncles and aunts, grandparents, nephews, nieces, and cousins . . . The next circle includes other relatives, and this is followed by the circle of local residents, then the circle of fellow-tribesmen, next that of fellow-citizens, and the in the same way the circle of people from neighbouring towns, and the circle of fellow-country men. The outermost and largest circle, which encompasses all the rest, is that of the whole human race . . . it is the task of a well tempered man . . . to draw the circles together somehow towards the centre.
>
> (Long and Sedley 1987, vol. 1: 349)

This relates to the Stoic's fundamental concept of *oikeiosis*, which after Pohlenz (1987 [1940]) became firmly linked as a crucial idea of Stoic ethics. It is very well treated in Brown (1994: chapters 4 and 5).[21] This concept is a primary impulse of human beings to what is familiar, to what belongs to oneself. *Oiken* is the opposite of *allotrion*, what is alien. Therefore it relates to what is familiar and also to the process of making a thing belong to you. It is self-love in a morally good sense, not related to selfishness. It relates, one might say, to Smith's enlightened self-interest, or, recalling Rousseau's famous distinction in his second *Discourse, amour de soi-meme* (with *amour de soi-meme* different from *amour propre*).[22]

Vivenza (2001: 204–5) has questioned the Stoic origins of *oikeiosis*, emphasizing the Aristotelian pedigree of the concept. I side with Vivienne Brown who takes *oikeiosis* as a Stoic concept. Moreover, Vivenza claims that it is unlikely that Smith could have interpreted *oikeiosis* (2001: 204).

I tend to believe that Smith was aware of the concept of *oikeiosis* through his readings of Diogenes Laertius, Plutarch and Stobaeus, for example, not only through Marcus Aurelius.[23] In addition it is possible that Smith might probably have known the piece of doxography just quoted on *oikeiosis* quite well, as Stobaeus's works were part of his library (Mizuta 1967: 143).

But there is more to be dealt with in terms of *oikeiosis* and sympathy. One problem is whether we consider Smith's sympathy as a 'change of places' or whether the sympathetic process takes place within oneself. This can be labelled as the identity problem.[24] If we assume, and follow his assertion that sympathy 'cannot, in any sense, be regarded as a selfish principle' (TMS VII.iii.I.4), we might find a contradiction if we read the following passage:

> By the imagination we place ourselves in his situation, we conceive ourselves enduring all the same torments, we enter as it were into his body, and become in some measure the same person with him, and thence form some idea of his sensations, and even feel something which, though weaker in degree, is not altogether unlike them.
>
> (TMS I.i.1.2)

If we endure 'all the same torments' and feel what she or he feels, it seems that the sympathetic process is selfish, as it depends on our imagination, on our thinking about what another person is feeling. What a person actually feels is only part of the process; we must check what we should feel if we were in his situation. Given this apparent paradox, that is whether the sympathetic process is selfish or not, resorting to the Stoics concept of *oikeiosis* we should explain this dilemma, and suggest that Smith might have been using this tradition as an important source for developing his concept of sympathy.

The sympathetic process is naturally self-centered. So is the Stoics concept of *oikeiosis*. In the process we assess the situation and imagine what we would feel. This does not necessarily imply that it is selfish. Neither is the Stoics concept of *oikeiosis*. Smith's self-interest is inherently social and moral, as it is the Stoics concept of *oikeiosis* that informs Smith's sympathy and his notion of self-interest. Therefore 'the doctrine of *oikeiosis* is seen as having two aspects, an inward-looking aspect and an outward-looking aspect' (Brown 1994: 96). It is certainly this *ad intra* and *ad extra* characteristic of *oikeiosis* that makes it such a fundamental influence on Smith's system. Within a continuous interaction of agents and society, it is from the agent outwards, and then from the outside inwards. Perhaps it could be argued that when the German Historical School created *Das Adam Smith Problem*, they did not only consider a proper understanding of Smith's benevolence, but neither did they understand sympathy and self-interest with their clear Stoic influence. If they had done so, probably much intellectual energy would have been saved.[25]

The capacity to sympathize with strangers decreases as the emotional ties diminish. For the Stoics this is simply natural. For Smith's concept of sympathy and self-interest, it is natural too. Smith distinguishes between self-interested behaviour and selfish behaviour. The latter is especially criticized in his TMS when he refers to the Licentious Systems (TMS VII.ii.4). The former is defended:

> Regard to our own private happiness and interest, too, appear upon many occasions very laudable principles of action. The habits of oeconomy, industry, discretion, attention, and application of thought, are generally supposed to be cultivated from self-interested motives, and at the same time are apprehended to be very praise-worthy qualities, which deserve the esteem and approbation of every body.
>
> (TMS VII.ii.3.16)

As the Stoic concept of *oikeiosis* involves self-love, I agree with Vivienne Brown (1994) who argues that 'the Stoic concept of self-love is not egoistical in a material sense, but describes nature's mechanism for motivating the development or moral awareness in the individual agent' (95). But neither is it egoistical in a moral nor in a philosophical way. To love oneself, to love our family, to love a friend more than any stranger, is simply to live in accordance with nature. If Cropsey (1957) would claim this natural tendency to self-preservation as a Hobbesian influence, in my view this is based on the Stoic sources:

> Every man, as the Stoics used to say, is first and principally recommended to his own care; and every man is certainly, in every respect, fitter and abler to take care of himself than of any other person. Every man feels his own pleasures and his own pains more sensibly than those of other people. The former are the original sensations; the latter the reflected or sympathetic images of those sensations. The former may be said to be the substance; the latter the shadow.
>
> (TMS VI.ii.1.1)

Furthermore, he attributes this crucial notion to the founder of Stoicism:

> According to Zeno, the founder of the Stoical doctrine, every animal was by nature recommended to its own care, and was endowed with the principle of self-love, that it might endeavour to preserve, not only its existence, but all the different parts of its nature, in the best and most perfect state of which they were capable.
>
> (TMS VII.ii.1.15)

Relying on the Stoics, Smith is also continuing the classical liberal tradition initiated by Locke that considers property in its more general and broad sense as a 'sacred rule':

> One individual must never prefer himself so much even to any other individual, as to hurt or injure that other, in order to benefit himself . . . and who does not inwardly feel the truth of that great stoical maxim, that for one man to deprive another unjustly of any thing, or unjustly to promote his own advantage by the loss or disadvantage of another, is more contrary to nature, than death, than poverty, than pain, than all the misfortunes which can affect him, either in his body, or in his external circumstances.
>
> (TMS III.3.6)

This idea that connects justice and property, that begins with life, liberty and property rights, is reminiscent of Locke's famous definition of 'Lives, Liberties and Estates, which I call by the general name, Property' (Locke 2000 II.123: 350).

Smith's concept of sympathy might be influenced by the Stoic concept of *oikeiosis* to a large extent. So does his hotly debated concept of self-interest, which resembles what the Stoics were aiming at with *oikeiosis*. Brown (1994) is quite clear about the significance of *oikeiosis* for Smith's discourse, as she argues that the 'Stoic concept of self-love falls under the doctrine of *oikeiosis*' (95).[26] Moreover, I would suggest that Smith's concept of propriety, which literally relates to *proprius*, to something belonging to one, might also have an important connection with this all-encompassing classical source of *oikeiosis*. Propriety has a moral meaning related to one's own, in particular to property in its liberal Lockean sense of 'Lives, Liberties and Estates'.[27] Furthermore propriety is possibly linked to Cicero's *officium*, which corresponds to the Stoics term *kathekon*, that is, appropriate action, a term that involves duties in society. With these additional classic sources in mind, the Stoics influence on Adam Smith acquires a new and more important dimension.[28] In this important passage, also added for the last edition of TMS, we can find this connection:

> The Stoics in general seem to have admitted that there might be a degree of proficiency in those who had not advanced to perfect virtue and happiness. They distributed those proficients into different classes, according to the degree of their advancement; and they called the imperfect virtues which they supposed them capable of exercising, not rectitudes, but proprieties, fitnesses, decent and becoming actions, for which a plausible or probable reason could be assigned, what Cicero expresses by the Latin word *officia,* and Seneca, I think more exactly, by that of *convenientia.* The doctrine of those imperfect, but attainable virtues, seems to have constituted what we may call the practical morality of the Stoics. It is the subject of Cicero's Offices; and is said to have been that of another book written by Marcus Brutus, but which is now lost.
>
> (TMS VII.ii.1.42)[29]

But Smith's sense of propriety has clearly nothing to do with *apatheia*, as he clarifies in this powerful passage added to TMS last edition:

> The sense of propriety, so far from requiring us to eradicate altogether that extraordinary sensibility, which we naturally feel for the misfortunes of our nearest connections, is always much more offended by the defect, than it ever is by the excess of that sensibility. The stoical apathy is, in such cases, never agreeable, and all the metaphysical sophisms by which it is supported can seldom serve any other purpose than to blow up the hard insensibility of a coxcomb to ten times its native impertinence. The poets and romance writers, who best paint the refinements and delicacies of love and friendship, and of all other private and domestic affections, Racine and Voltaire; Richardson, Maurivaux, and Riccoboni; are, in such cases, much better instructors than Zeno, Chrysippus, or Epictetus.
>
> (TMS III.3.14)

Soon after Smith lowers his tone, conceding that '[t]he sense of propriety is much more apt to be offended by the excess, than by the defect of our sensibility, and there are but very few cases in which we can approach too near to the stoical apathy and indifference' (TMS III.3.16).

In a passage that begins talking about self-love as self-preservation, Smith again refers to the Stoics:

> By choosing and rejecting with this just and accurate discernment, by thus bestowing upon every object the precise degree of attention it deserved, according to the place which it held in this natural scale of things, we maintained, according to the Stoics, that perfect rectitude of conduct which constituted the essence of virtue. This was what they called to live consistently, to live according to nature, and to obey those laws and directions which nature, or the Author of nature, had prescribed for our conduct.
>
> (TMS VII.ii.1.16)

In the next paragraph, Smith claims: 'So far the Stoical idea of propriety and virtue is not very different from that of Aristotle and the ancient Peripatetics' (TMS VII.ii.1.17). He is referring to the Middle Stoics, who developed a notion closer to his concept of propriety.

Even though there are signs that Smith changed his attitude towards the Stoics in the last edition of TMS (especially distancing himself further from *apatheia*), he remains influenced by the Stoics (especially in terms of sympathy and *oikeiosis*).

Emma Rothschild might be correct when she provocatively suggests that Stoicism could be seen in the eighteenth century as an acceptable substitute for religion. In her own words, 'to be demonstratively Stoic was to be a safe deist' (2001: 304, endnote 104). Certainly nobody wanted to be called a

Hobbist or an Epicurean during the eighteenth century. Smith witnessed what happened to his friend David Hume in trying to get a university position. Thus his narrative unfolds in an historical context favorable to Stoicism. If we follow the suggestive explanation offered by Emma Rothschild, that appealing to the Stoics was a safe haven for an agnostic like Smith, any account of the invisible hand that relies upon its Stoic origins must be dismissed.[30] If it were, Smith would be simply pulling our legs, which is similar to Rothschild's own explanation of the invisible hand.

Samuel Fleischacker, in his recent *On Adam Smith's* Wealth of Nations: *A Philosophical Companion* (2004), holds that Smith was a believer (Fleischacker 2004: 44–5 and 70–2), and recently Evensky (2005) is firmly convinced that Smith was pious and that his invisible hand is simply the hand of God.[31] Although there is a lot of debate on this issue – whether Smith merely drew on the widely used deistic language, or whether his use of this language was deeply felt – it will most probably remain a subject of controversy. The references to God and its many metaphors in TMS might obey to the fact that this book was based on his moral philosophy lectures. In contrast, in WN there is no mention of God at all. If we consider that Smith's lectures were aimed mainly at young men destined to follow an ecclesiastical career, and remember that his TMS was based on his actual lectures on ethics, this might be a good explanation for his reliance on religious discourse. We must also recall, as Rothschild suggests, that Smith was too cautious and mindful of public opinion to ignore the use of deistic rhetoric.

IV Smith's self-command

I will attempt to show, *pace* the editors of the TMS and the prevailing view on the nature of self-command, that the underlying assumption for considering self-command as 'distinctively Stoic' (TMS Intro. p. 6), is disputable.[32] Vivienne Brown (1994, chapters 3 and 4), in what is probably one of the best available analyses of Smith and Stoicism, simply refers to 'Stoic virtue of self-command' (Brown 1994: 215), or more cautiously to 'self-command, a pre-eminently Stoic virtue' (Brown 1994: 98). There is general agreement in the literature on the Stoic nature of Smith's virtue of self-command. Even Gloria Vivenza, in the most thorough and developed analysis of Smith and the classics, argues that self-command 'is indeed a virtue with undeniably Stoic characteristics' (2001: 57). I will briefly argue that self-command is originally a Socratic virtue, with some important nuances in its meaning.[33]

As I have already developed this idea in Montes (2004: 76–86), there are only two points that I want to underline in relation to Smith's self-command. First, Smith added for the last edition of TMS that self-command 'is not only a great virtue, but from it all the other virtues seem to derive their principal lustre' (TMS VI.iii.11). Self-command is not only an important virtue, but for Smith has a foundational character. But also we must consider that Smith asserts that '[t]he most perfect knowledge, if it is not supported by the most perfect self-command, will not always *enable* him to do his duty' (TMS VI.iii.1, emphasis added). Both characteristics of self-command determine its unique distinctiveness.

In sum we have this virtue of self-command that initially (especially before the last edition of TMS) looks like control of passions, but acquires a special character: it is a fundamental and enabling virtue. Smith is purposefully not using self-control, nor self-restraint as it was common to refer to the negative reading of this virtue (negative in terms of 'absence of'). If Smith would have been talking simply of control of passions, he might have used self-control, or even self-restraint. Moreover, self-command was a term not widely used during the eighteenth century. It was more common to see self-restraint or self-control. In my view Smith knew he was using self-command, which includes the idea of command, a sense of direction. Contrary to mere control of passions, self-command has a positive (in terms of command 'for') and enabling characteristic. Its source is not Stoic, but much resembles the Socratic virtue of *enkrateia*.

The Greek word *en-krateia* literally means 'inner power' or 'power within oneself', making 'self-command' a fairly good translation of the term. Its opposite is *akrasia*. In his *Memorabilia* Xenophon portrays Socrates as referring to *enkrateia* as the 'foundation of all virtues' (Xenophon 1997, I.v.4: 67), and later in a dialogue with Euthydemus discussing the importance of *enkrateia*, Socrates suggests that '*enkrateia* is a very great blessing [*ariston*] to a man' (Xenophon 1997, IV.v.9: 329). *Memorabilia* was a widely read and a very important classical text during the eighteenth century. It was also in Smith's library (Mizuta 1967: 153), and surely he did know it well.

It is very likely that Smith was thinking in terms of a Socratic self-command as *enkrateia* when he developed his corrections of TMS last edition. There are also interesting connections of this philosophical concept, considered by Werner Jaeger as a 'central conception in our moral code' (Jaeger 1965 [1939], vol. 2: 53), in Aristotle's cardinal virtue of *sophrosune* (see North 1966). In fact, for Aristotle the cardinal virtue of temperance (*sophrosune*) also has a positive turn that allows us to attain the golden mean. Similarly, Smith's self-command can be seen as a process of inward looking and then outward acting.

My second point is that at the end of Part VI, completely added to TMS last edition, we find that of all Smith's four main virtues only self-command is morally assessed by its propriety, regardless of its effects or consequences. It is noteworthy that Smith finishes with a 'Conclusion' to his newly added part VI of TMS comparing all his chief virtues, underlining the particular character of self-command. I will only reproduce the last paragraph:

> But in our approbation of the virtues of self-command, complacency with their effects sometimes constitutes no part, and frequently but a small

part, of that approbation. Those effects may sometimes be agreeable, and sometimes disagreeable; and though our approbation is no doubt stronger in the former case, it is by no means altogether destroyed in the latter. The most heroic valour may be employed indifferently in the cause either of justice or of injustice; and though it is no doubt much more loved and admired in the former case, it still appears a great and respectable quality even in the latter. In that, and in all the other virtues of self-command, the splendid and dazzling quality seems always to be the greatness and steadiness of the exertion, and the strong sense of propriety which is necessary in order to make and to maintain that exertion. The effects are too often but too little regarded.

(TMS VI Concl. 7)

If we judge prudence, justice and benevolence by their effects, the story with self-command is different.[34] It finally relates to what Smith considers praise-worthy, as 'we' (the supposed impartial spectator) assess the moral value of those *proper* actions related to self-command. If we can find a connection between Smith's self-command and the Stoics, it is not in terms of control of passions, but may be in relation to our individual responsibility to behave properly (the *propriety* of our conduct). Smith and the Stoics were concerned 'not about the event, but about the propriety of his own endeavours' (TMS VII.ii.1.21). In this sense sympathy, propriety and the chief virtue of self-command constitute a philosophical trilogy that sheds new light in our understanding of Smith's ethics.

V Conclusions

In this essay it has been my aim to show that using the Stoics as a source of Smith is a complex issue. In fact, Stoicism is by itself complicated, and the way Smith benefited from the Stoics, and the classics, does not help to clarify this connection. Yet I argued that Smith heavily relies upon the Stoic concept of *oikeiosis* for developing his conception of sympathy. Finally I briefly reconsidered an argument that views the other face of Smith's self-command, not simply as control of passions, but as an enabling virtue that has a sense of direction to do what one has to do.

The discussion of Smith and the Stoics is relevant in many aspects. If we assume a theological determinism in Smith it would be easy to conclude that 'the invisible hand is only one of the many names given in the *Moral Sentiments* to the Deity. . . There is little doubt that Adam Smith did believe (as a matter of faith) in this final reconciler' (Macfie 1967: 111). With this assumption that relies on Smith as a believer, we could solve many problems. In his *On Adam Smith's Moral Philosophical Vision*, Jerry Evensky gives a great and plausible example of Smith's belief in the deity to explain his 'liberal plan of equality, liberty and justice' (WN IV.ix.3).[35] After all he is not alone in believing in Smith's faith. From Jacob Viner up to Samuel

Fleischacker we have an important tradition of scholars assuming Smith's faith. A similar and quite interrelated conclusion can be reached regarding the Stoics as a source on Adam Smith. When Emma Rothschild persuasively claims that 'Smith's descriptions of Stoic doctrine should be read, it seems to me, with much the same discrimination as his descriptions of Christian religion' (2001: 133), she is persuasively suggesting the interrelation of Smith's beliefs and his Stoicism. The influence of the Stoics in Adam Smith has been generally taken for granted. But it is complex, even elusive.

Acknowledgement

I am much indebted to Doug Den Uyl and one anonymous referee for their very helpful comments. And to the editor of this *Review* for her thorough work and some sharp remarks.

Notes

1 Since the early reception of Adam Smith, up to classic works such as Bryson (1945) and Macfie (1967), the Stoics' influence has been widely treated by scholars as a general phenomenon within the Scottish Enlightenment, and as a particularly relevant influence on Adam Smith. On the latter, Brown (1994) did some pioneering work uncovering some aspects of Smith's Stoicism. Vivenza (2001) also presents a compulsory and original reading for anyone interested in Smith and the classics in general, particularly analyzing some relevant aspects of Smith and the Stoics.

2 In this essay I shall refer to five of the six standard books of *The Glasgow Edition of the Works and Correspondence of Adam Smith* by their abbreviations for references and quotations: *The Theory of Moral Sentiments* (TMS), *An Inquiry into the Nature and Causes of the Wealth of Nations* (WN), *Lectures on Jurisprudence* (LJ), *Lectures on Rhetoric and Belles Lettres* (LRBL), and *Correspondence of Adam Smith* (*Corr.*).

3 TMS went through six editions (1759, 1761, 1767, 1774, 1781 and 1790). Early in 1785 Smith agreed to publish a sixth edition thinking that 'I have a few alterations to make of no great consequence' (*Corr.* Letter 244). His position at the Board of Customs at Edinburgh did not allow him to pursue this task, but during the last two years of his life he was 'labouring very hard' in preparing the sixth edition. In March 1789 Smith acknowledged that 'the subject has grown upon me' (*Corr.* Letter 287).

4 To give only one example, Francis Hutcheson, the founding father of the Scottish Enlightenment, translated Marcus Aurelius into English. Hutcheson represents a neo-Stoicism that is different from the Ciceronian heritage. It has Platonic connotations that might be informed by Shaftesbury's influence on Hutcheson. All these great intellectuals interpreted a particular reading of the Stoics informed by complex and even scattered references to the Stoics in the classical tradition. Certainly Smith was no exception.

5 In Smith's library we find Stobaeus's *Eclogarum* and *Loci Communes* (Mizuta 1967: 143), three different editions of Sextus Empiricus's works (Mizuta 1967: 55, 139), two complete works of Diogenes Laertius (p. 88), four editions of Plutarch (p. 130), three works by Marcus Aurelius (p. 117), four works by Hierocles (p. 102), five editions of Epictetus (pp. 20, 91), three works of Seneca (pp. 55, 138–9) and of course different editions of Cicero (pp. 14, 81).

6 Although Seneca is also an important figure in the Stoic tradition, he was out of favour during the Scottish Enlightenment. The cause might be the historical reasons surrounding his life. For example, the influential Lord Kames, in his *Sketches of the History of Man* (Home 1778 [1773]), refers to Seneca as 'a great corrupter of the Roman taste' (Home 1778: 284). In TMS Smith harshly refers to Seneca as 'that great preacher of insensibility' (TMS I.iii.1.13). He also judges 'one of the extravagancies of Seneca, that the Stoical wise man was, in this respect, superior even to a God' (TMS III.3.44). The change of Seneca from 'a stoical philosopher' (first five editions) to 'a cynical philosopher' (last edition, TMS VII.ii.1.20) might also be significant in understanding Smith's view of Seneca.

7 In Smith's library there are actually four different editions of Cicero's complete works, plus a single edition of *De Officiis* and his *Lettres* (Mizuta 1967: 14 and 81).

8 It is not negligible that Frederick the Great called *De Officiis* 'the best work on morals that has been or can be written', and that the influential Grotius followed Cicero by writing his *De Iure Belli ac Pacis* (1625) also in three books, quoting extensively from Cicero's *De Officiis*.

9 As Walter Eckstein nicely put it: 'the sober circumspection of old age' (2000 [1926]: 29) which might have hampered his initial idealism.

10 The most provocative and thorough analysis of Smith's four main virtues and its classical sources comes from Gloria Vivenza, who argues that the four Smithian virtues 'do not correspond to the cardinal virtues of Christianity, or even those of the classical world' (2001: 202). In my view, Smith's account of virtues relies upon the 'never to be forgotten' Francis Hutcheson, who was also deeply influenced by Shaftesbury. Their account of those chief virtues, *pace* Vivenza, would also follow a Platonic scheme, with Christian and Stoic overtones (see Montes 2004).

11 Smith admired the Stoics as they prepared for death. Among all those who thought there 'could be any evil in death', the Stoics 'I think it must be acknowledged, had prepared by far the most animated and spirited song' (TMS VII.ii.1.29). According to Smith 'The Stoics . . . sometimes talk of leaving life with gaiety' (TMS VII.ii.1.26). Note that all of these passages were included for TMS last edition.

12 Let me say that there is a debate on how we should understand the Stoics' *apathy*. For example Frede claims: 'it must be a caricature of the wise man to think that he has become insensitive to human concerns . . . Things do move him, but not in such a way as to disturb his balanced judgment' (1986: 100). In fact some scholars persuasively argue that the Stoics did not aim at eradicating emotions, but simply the 'mental disturbance' produced by passions.

13 If Zeno, Cleanthes and Chryssipus preached that men should participate in the political life of the city, they did not (or could not) do it in Athens. An anecdote shows Chryssipus answering, when asked why he took no part in political life, 'that bad politics would displease the gods and good politics the citizens' (Sandbach 1975: 141).

14 For a visual image of the location of the philosophical schools of Hellenistic Athens see (Long and Sedley 1987, vol. 1: 4). Schofield (1991) suggests that Zeno's *Republic* would follow Plato in a political ideal communism.

15 I tend to believe that Adam Smith was an agnostic (see Montes 2004: 37–8), but Smith's religious beliefs, if any, will remain a subject of speculation.

16 In a 1778 letter to Lord Kames, Thomas Reid states that 'I have always thought Dr. Smith's System of Sympathy wrong. It is indeed a Refinement of the selfish System' (in Reeder 1997: 66).

17 However, Gloria Vivenza claims that '[a]n immediate point to make is that despite the similarity of terminology Smith's "sympatheia" has little in common with classical *sumpatheia* apart from the basic sense of taking the part of, or "suffering together with", another person' (2001: 41).

18 Chrysippus had also talked of *sympatheia*, and later Posidonius developed a kind of 'cosmic sympathy' (Sandbach 1975: 130–8).

19 The fact that mutual sympathy is agreeable to Smith triggered Hume's famous letter to Smith arguing, 'I wish you had more particularly and fully prov'd, that all kinds of Sympathy are necessarily Agreeable. This is the Hinge of your System . . . Now it would appear that there is a disagreeable Sympathy, as well as an agreeable . . . An Hospital woud be a more entertaining Place than a Ball' (*Corr.* p. 43).

20 I am indebted to David Levy who coined this complex philosophical idea into simple neoclassical economic language. From an economist's point of view it would be even feasible to go all the way down thinking in terms of a sympathetic marginal rate of substitution.

21 On the Stoic concept of *oikeiosis* see Schofield (1995, 1999: 760–8), Inwood and Donini (1999: 677–82), Long (1996: 250–64), Sandbach (1975: 34–5), Engberg-Pedersen (1990, 1995), and Edelstein (1966: 35). On Smith and the Stoics see also Vivenza (2001). Heise (1995) also analyses the importance of *oikeiosis* for Smith.

22 Related to this connection see Brown (1994: 94). She persuasively argues that by simply conflating self-love and self-interest in Adam Smith we 'overlook the Stoic context for the sympathetic account of self-love'. Moreover, in footnote 30 (Brown 1994: 94), she makes a sharp observation warning about an important difference between Rousseau's *amour de soi*, as an a-social concept, against the social and moral nature of Smith's Stoic self-love. The latter is crucial, as will be soon argued.

23 Marcus Aurelius refers only once to *oikeiosis*, and compared to the other classical authors just mentioned, he does not develop the conception of *oikeiosis*.

24 Fontaine (1997) has treated this issue.

25 On *Das Adam Smith Problem*, the context around it, its debate, and some possible consequences for our understanding of sympathy, see Montes (2003).

26 Heise (1995: 19) also states that 'the self-interest or self-betterment of Smith is the *oikeiosis* of the Stoics', but he too readily concludes that '[i]n the sixth edition of TMS, Smith became even more Stoic' (Heise 1995: 23).

27 Propriety and property were both used interchangeably during the seventeenth and eighteenth century. The connection between property's particular meaning of material possession and propriety's more general classical liberal meaning, that also includes a moral connotation, is quite interesting. Property finally acquired a material meaning, but retained a moral connotation with, for example, 'acting with propriety'. In my view this might be a reflection of the corruption debate – commercial progress versus moral decay or wealth versus virtue – that began to take place in seventeenth-century England up to the eighteenth century. I have argued that in a way Adam Smith represents the twilight of a republican tradition, and that some important vestiges of this tradition can be found in his works (see Montes 2004, chapters 3 and 4). The context of Smith's initial support of a militia, a republican cause, and then his endorsement of a standing army in his WN, is a wonderful example for understanding the corruption debate (see Montes forthcoming).

28 Brown (1994: 76–86) makes the link between Cicero's *officia* (Cicero's translation for *kathekonta*) as appropriate acts, resembling Smith's crucial moral concept of propriety. I develop a similar idea in Montes (2004, chapter 4), but if Brown states that propriety (as Cicero's *officia*) relies 'upon rules/precepts to guide external behaviour' (Brown 1994: 86), I argue that there is also an important component of moral autonomy in this concept.

29 In Montes (2004: 127, footnote 56) I argue that the link with Seneca's *convenientia* is not inimical to the argument of assuming *officia* as a classical source for Smith's propriety. On the contrary, it reinforces this argument.

30 However, I believe this suggestive thesis does not necessarily lead to Rothschild's provocative interpretation of the invisible hand as an ironic metaphor, neither to

a theological interpretation or any reading of the invisible hand as a matter of religious faith.
31   Similar arguments are earlier found in Jacob Viner (1927, 1972), Veblen (1933 [1899–1900]) and Macfie (1967).
32   The only exception I am aware of that challenges this widely held view is Athol Fitzgibbons, who, correctly but without further arguments states that '[s]elf-command was a synonym for Platonic temperance' (1995: 105).
33   The fact that *enkrateia* is a Socratic virtue of course does not necessarily imply that it did not influence the Stoics. Moreover, it must be stressed that the language of *vir virtutis* is often overlapped with the ethical discourse of the Stoics. Not in vain does Smith refer to the 'spirit and manhood of their [the Stoics'] doctrines' (TMS VII.ii.29).
34   Let me clarify that Smith was clear since the first edition between the dichotomy of cause and effect in terms of moral assessment (see TMS I.i.3.5 and TMS II.i.2).
35   According to Evensky, the invisible hand 'is for Smith the hand of the deity that designed the "oeconomy of nature"' (2005: 163).

Bibliography

Brown, V. (1994) *Adam Smith's Discourse: Canonicity, Commerce and Conscience*, London: Routledge.
Brubaker, L. (2006) 'Does the "wisdom of nature" need help?', in *New Voices on Adam Smith*, L. Montes and E. Schliesser (eds), London: Routledge.
Bryson, G. (1945) *Man and Society: The Scottish Inquiry of the Eighteenth Century*, Princeton: Princeton University Press.
Carrasco, M.A. (2004) 'Adam Smith, Aristotle, and the virtues of commerce', *Review of Metaphysics*, 58: 81–116.
Cicero (1991) *On Duties*, M.T. Griffin and E.M. Atkins (eds), Cambridge: Cambridge University Press.
—— (1971) *De Divinatione*, W.A. Falconer (ed.), Cambridge, MA: Harvard University Press.
—— (1997) *De Officiis*, G.P. Goold (ed.), Cambridge, MA: Harvard University Press.
Clayden, P.W. (1887) *The Early Life of Samuel Rogers*, London: Smith, Elder & Co.
Cropsey, J. (1957) *Polity and Economy: An Interpretation of the Principles of Adam Smith*, The Hague: Martinus Nijhoff.
Dickey, L. (1986) 'Historicizing the "Adam Smith Problem": conceptual, historiographical, and textual issues', *Journal of Modern History*, 58: 579–609.
Eckstein, W. (2000) [1926] 'Introduction to *The Theory of Moral Sentiments*', reprinted in *Adam Smith: Critical Responses*, H. Mizuta (ed.), vol. 5, pp. 12–49, London: Routledge.
Edelstein, L. (1966) *The Meaning of Stoicism*, Cambridge, MA: Harvard University Press.
Engberg-Pederson, T. (1990) *The Stoic Theory of Oikeiosis: Moral Development and Social Interaction in Early Stoic Philosophy*, Denmark: Aarhus University Press.
—— (1995) 'Discovering the good: *oikeiosis* and *kathekonta* in Stoic ethics' in *Hellenistic Social and Political Philosophy: Proceedings of the Sixth Symposium Hellenisticum*, M. Schofield (ed.), Cambridge: Cambridge University Press.
Evensky, J. (2005) *Adam Smith's Moral Philosophy. A Historical and Contemporary Perspective on Markets, Law, Ethics, and Culture*, Cambridge: Cambridge University Press.

Fitzgibbons, A. (1995) *Adam Smith's System of Liberty, Wealth, and Virtue: The Moral and Political Foundations of The Wealth of Nations*, Oxford: Clarendon Press.

Fleischacker, S. (1999) *A Third Concept of Liberty: Judgment and Freedom in Kant and Adam Smith*, Princeton: Princeton University Press.

—— (2004) *On Adam Smith's* Wealth of Nations: *A Philosophical Companion*, Princeton: Princeton University Press.

Fontaine, P. (1997) 'Identification and economic behaviour: sympathy and empathy in historical perspective', *Economics and Philosophy*, 13: 261–80.

Forget, E.L. (2003) 'Evocations of sympathy: sympathetic imagery in eighteenth-century social theory and physiology', *History of Political Economy*, vol. 35, Annual Supplement, pp. 282–308.

Forman-Barzilai, F. (2002) 'Adam Smith as globalization theorist', *Critical Review*, 14: 391–419.

Frede, M. (1986) 'The Stoic doctrine of the affections of the soul', in *The Norms of Nature: Studies in Hellenistic Ethics*, M. Schofield and G. Striker (eds), Cambridge: Cambridge University Press.

Hanley, R. (2006) 'Adam Smith, Aristotle and virtue ethics', in *New Voices on Adam Smith*, L. Montes and E. Schliesser (eds), London: Routledge.

Heise, P.A. (1995) 'Stoicism in the EPS: the foundation of Adam Smith's moral philosophy', in *The Classical Tradition in Economic Thought: Perspectives on the History of Economic Thought*, vol. XI, I.H. Rima (ed.), Aldershot: Edward Elgar.

Home, H., Lord Kames (1778 [1773]) *Sketches of the History of Man: Considerably enlarged by the last additions and corrections of the author*, London: A. Strahan and T. Cadell.

Hume, D. (1993) [1748] *An Enquiry Concerning Human Understanding*, E. Steinberg (ed.), Indianapolis: Hackett Publishing Company.

—— (1987) [1777] 'My Own Life', in *Essays Moral, Political and Literary*, E.F. Miller (ed.), Indianapolis: Liberty Fund.

Inwood, B. and Donini, P. (1999) 'Stoic Ethics', in *The Cambridge History of Hellenistic Philosophy*, Cambridge: Cambridge University Press.

Jaeger, W. (1965) [1939] *Paideia: The Ideas of Greek Culture*. Oxford: Oxford University Press.

Levy, D.M. and Peart, S.J. (2008) 'Adam Smith and his sources: the evil of independence', *The Adam Smith Review*, 4: 57–87, V. Brown (ed.), London and New York: Routledge.

Locke, J. (2000) *Two Treatises of Government*, P. Laslett (ed.), Cambridge: Cambridge University Press.

Long, A.A. (1996) *Stoic Studies*, Cambridge: Cambridge University Press.

Long, A.A. and Sedley, D.N. (1987) *The Hellenistic Philosophers*, 2 vols., Cambridge: Cambridge University Press.

Macfie, A.L. (1967) 'Adam Smith's Moral Sentiments as foundation for his Wealth of Nations', reprinted in *The Individual in Society: Papers on Adam Smith*, A.L. Macfie (ed.), pp. 59–81, London: George Allen & Unwin.

Mizuta, H. (1967) *Adam Smith's Library: A Supplement to Bonar's Catalogue with a Checklist of the whole Library*, Cambridge: Cambridge University Press.

Montes, L. (2003) 'Das Adam Smith Problem: its origins, the stages of the current debate, and one implication for our understanding of sympathy', *Journal of the History of Economic Thought*, 25: 64–90.

—— (2004) *Adam Smith in Context: A Critical Reassessment of some Central Components of His Thought*, London: Palgrave-Macmillan.

—— (forthcoming) 'Adam Smith and the militia issue: wealth over virtue?', in *The Elgar Companion to Adam Smith Companion*, J.T. Young (ed.), Aldershot: Edward Elgar.

—— Montes, L. and Schliesser, E. (eds) (2006) *New Voices on Adam Smith*, London: Routledge.

Nieli, R. (1986) 'Spheres of intimacy and the Adam Smith Problem', *Journal of the History of Ideas*, 47: 611–24.

North, H. (1966) *Sophrosyne: Self-knowledge and Self-Restraint in Greek Literature*, Ithaca: Cornell University Press.

Otteson, J.R. (2002) *Adam Smith's Marketplace of Life*, Cambridge: Cambridge University Press.

Pohlenz, M. (1987) [1940] *Grundfragen der Stoichen Philosophie*, Gottingen: Vandenhoeck & Ruprecht, reprinted Garland Publishing Inc.

Reeder, J. (1997) *On Moral Sentiments: Contemporary Responses to Adam Smith*, Bristol: Thoemmes Press.

Rothschild, E. (2001) *Economic Sentiments: Adam Smith, Condorcet, and the Enlightenment*, Cambridge, MA: Harvard University Press.

Sandbach, F.H. (1975) *The Stoics*, London: Chatto & Windus.

Schofield, R.E. (1991) *The Stoic Idea of the City*, Cambridge: Cambridge University Press.

—— (1995) 'Two Stoic approaches to justice', in *Justice and Generosity: Studies in Hellenistic Social and Political Philosophy*, Proceedings of the Sixth Symposium Hellenisticum, Cambridge: Cambridge University Press.

—— (1999) 'Social and political thought', in *The Cambridge History of Hellenistic Philosophy*, Cambridge: Cambridge University Press.

Smith, A. (1976a) *The Theory of Moral Sentiments*, D.D. Raphael and A.L. Macfie (eds), Oxford: Clarendon Press, reprinted, Indianapolis: Liberty Fund (1984).

—— (1976b) *An Inquiry into the Nature and Causes of the Wealth of Nations*, R.H. Campbell and A.S. Skinner (eds), Oxford: Clarendon Press; reprinted, Indianapolis: Liberty Fund (1981).

—— (1978) *Lectures on Jurisprudence*, R.L. Meek, D.D. Raphael, and P.G. Stein (eds), Oxford: Clarendon Press, reprinted, Indianapolis: Liberty Fund (1982).

—— (1983) *Lectures on Rhetoric and Belles Lettres*, J.C. Bryce (ed.), Oxford: Clarendon Press, reprinted, Indianapolis: Liberty Fund (1985).

—— (1987) *Correspondence of Adam Smith*, E.C. Mossner and I.S. Ross (eds), Oxford: Clarendon Press; reprinted, Indianapolis: Liberty Fund.

Taylor, C. (1989) *Sources of the Self: The Making of Modern Identity*, Cambridge: Cambridge University Press.

Veblen, T. (1933) [1899–1900] 'The preconceptions of economics', in *The Place of Science in Civilization and other Essays*, New York: Viking Press.

Viner, J. (1927) 'Adam Smith and laissez faire', *Journal of Political Economy*, 35: 198–232.

—— (1972) *The Role of Providence in the Social Order, An Essay in Intellectual History*, Philadelphia: American Philosophical Society.

Vivenza, G. (2001) *Adam Smith and the Classics: The Classical Heritage in Adam Smith's Thought*, Oxford: Oxford University Press.

Waszek, N. (1984) 'Two concepts of morality: a distinction of Adam Smith's ethics and its Stoic origin', *Journal of the History of Ideas*, 45: 591–606.

Xenophon (1997) *Memorabilia*, G.P. Goold (ed.), Cambridge, MA: Harvard University Press.

Adam Smith and his sources

The evil of independence

David M. Levy and Sandra J. Peart

The following statements constitute a *non sequitur*:

'I am richer than you are, therefore I am superior to you'; or,
'I am more eloquent than you are, therefore I am superior to you.'

But the following conclusions are better:

'I am richer than you are, therefore my property is superior to yours'; or,
'I am more eloquent than you are, therefore, my elocution is superior to yours.'

But *you* are neither property nor elocution.

Epictetus, *Encheiridion*, para. 44

... the Stoics ... have the glory of being the earliest thinkers who grounded the obligation of morals on the brotherhood, the *sungeneia*, of the whole human race.

John Stuart Mill, *On Grote* (1866: 419)

Introduction

This paper explores the foundations of Adam Smith's view that the philosopher is the same as the street porter. Despite their innate similarity, Smith recognized that the *role* of the philosopher, someone who provides useful instruction to fellow humans, is not that of the street porter (Peart and Levy 2005; Schliesser 2005, 2006). He also saw that this potentially useful employment may entail a biased perspective on human conduct. Motivated by matters too distant for ordinary people to notice, the philosopher may come to believe that he is better than those he studies and to regard himself as independent from their concerns. Viner expressed Smith's position:

Under normal circumstances, the sentiments make no mistake. It is reason which is fallible. Greatest of all in degree in fallibility is the speculative reason of the moral philosopher, unless the legislator is on a still lower level.

(Viner 1972: 78–9)[1]

In Smith's account, ordinary people overcome a bias in perspective by relying upon proverbs that summarize common experience (Peart and Levy 2005). The philosopher, steeped in the study of ancient texts, does not avail himself of proverbial wisdom. Instead, Smith locates the means to correct the bias of philosophers in Stoicism. He singles out Stoicism as a philosophy which, in spite of the failings of Stoic philosophers, directed its adherents toward the greatest good. It reached 'the judgments of the man within the breast' and motivated selfish and partial beings toward unselfishness and impartiality.[2]

This paper locates the foundations of Smith's egalitarianism in Stoic cosmopolitanism. Cosmopolitanism implies that our place in the world ought to be immaterial; every one should be valued impartially. Smith offered a solution to the deep problem in Stoicism: how the Stoic maxim of life according to natural inclinations also served cosmopolitanism.[3] For Smith 'right' and 'wrong' are natural and motivating and so they constrain us to act reciprocally even though, by nature, we value those closest to us more than we do those further away. Like the Stoics, Smith developed a coherent theory of the human, characterized by innate sociability and for whom beliefs articulated in language have motivational force. Finally, we show how Smith's proposed cure for the intolerance of religious factions appeals to innate sociability. Rather than risk being alone, religious teachers will exchange beliefs and intolerance becomes attenuated.

We recognize that the relationship between Smith's doctrine and Stoic teaching is contested in recent secondary literature (Raphael and Macfie 1976; Waszek 1984; Griswold 1999; Vivenza 2001; Montes 2004, 2008; Fleischacker 2004; Brubaker 2006). While the common identification of liberalism with cosmopolitanism (Mill 1866: 419; Furniss 1920: 6; Heckscher 1935: 35–6; Montes 2008) suggests Stoic roots to Smith's teaching, the Stoics were providentialists and the consensus among scholars is that Smith 'never requires belief in God as a condition for his empirical explanations to work' (Fleischacker 2004: 45). In what follows, we shall attempt to reconcile these seemingly contradictory assessments. To suggest how the argument will unfold, consider whether beliefs motivate. Supposing they do, then even if the consensus view that God or providence does not provide motivational force in Smith's system, as long as we believe in God or providence, these beliefs might motivate. Smith is clear that people are, in fact, motivated by religious beliefs, although he allows that whether for good or for ill must be discovered. He is also clear that, in spite of Stoicism's seeming conflict with human nature, it was a force for good.

Philosophy in Smith

We divide this section into three parts. First, we consider a Stoic discussion in which the pride of the teacher is corrected by appeal to the teaching. Second, we sketch Smith's account of Stoic doctrine and the temptation of the Stoics. Third, we discuss Smith's account of the context in which the attitude commonly called 'stoicism' was both natural and necessary. The modality of necessary and possible do not often enter into the history of economics, so we need to be aware that Smith appeals to necessity in a Stoic context. In what is necessary for humans we find what is true for all.

Stoic teaching and the teacher. As a clue to what Smith might find attractive in Stoicism, consider the following passage from Epictetus, who came to the occupation of philosopher from slavery. When he discussed the importance of reason and logic, Epictetus countered the unjustified pride of the philosopher with his own philosophy. The passage starts with the student who seeks to understand nature by first understanding the greatest logician in the Stoic tradition:[4]

> What, then, is your admirable achievement? To understand the will of nature. Very well; do you understand it all by yourself? And if that is the case, what more do you need? For if it is true that 'all men err involuntarily', and you have learned the truth, it must needs be that you are doing right already. But, so help me Zeus, I do not comprehend the will of nature. Who, then, interprets it? Men say, Chrysippus. I go and try to find out what this interpreter of nature says. I begin not to understand what he says, and look for the man who can interpret him. 'Look and consider what this passage means', says the interpreter, 'just as if it were in Latin!' What place is there here, then, for pride on the part of the interpreter?
>
> (Epictetus *Discourses* I.xvii.13–15)

Stoicism levels. One can always replace the teacher with the teaching common to all:

> Why, there is no just place for pride even on the part of Chrysippus, if he merely interprets the will of nature, but himself does not follow it; how much less place for pride, then, in the case of his interpreter! For we have no need of Chrysippus on his own account, but only to enable us to follow nature. No more have we need of him who divines through sacrifice, considered on his own account, but simply because we think that through his instrumentality we shall understand the future and the signs given by the gods . . . nor do we admire the crow or the raven, but God, who gives His signs through them.
>
> (Epictetus *Discourses* I.xvii.18–19)

We shall explore how Stoicism might be employed to correct the biases of its adherents.

Stoic teachings and temptation. Smith taught us how to understand the teachings of 'antient philosophy':

In the antient philosophy, whatever was taught concerning the nature
either of the human mind or of the Deity, made a part of the system of
physicks. Those beings, in whatever their essence might be supposed to
consist, were parts of the great system of the universe, and parts too
productive of the most important effects. Whatever human reason could
either conclude, or conjecture, concerning them, made, as it were, two
chapters, though no doubt two very important ones, of the science which
pretended to give an account of the origin and revolutions of the great
system of the universe.

(WN V.i.f.28)

As an example of the sources from which Smith drew, consider the report
in Diogenes Laertius:

The doctrine that the world is a living being, rational, animate and
intelligent, is laid down by Chrysippus in the first book of his treatise
On Providence, by Apollodorus in his *Physics*, and by Posidonius. It is
a living thing in the sense of an animate substance endowed with
sensation; for animal is better than non-animal, and nothing is better than
the world, *ergo* the world is a living being.

(Laertius 1925, vii.143)

Providentialism follows from the claim that nothing is 'better than the
world'. The link between God and the world will be important:

The substance of God is declared by Zeno to be the whole world and
the heaven, as well as by Chrysippus in the first book *Of the Gods*, and
by Posidonius in his first book with the same title.

(Laertius 1925, vii.148)

Humans are given pride of place in the providential order: 'Also they hold
that there are dæmons who are in sympathy with mankind and watch over
human affairs' (Laertius 1925, vii.151).

Sympathy will be discussed at length below.

From ancient philosophy Smith draws the lesson that there is no outside
vantage from which to the judge the universe. There is no external vantage
to which a philosopher might escape and obtain a god's view of the universe.
Instead, all places in the Stoic world provide God's eye views (TMS
VII.ii.i.39), but, from our place in the world, social connections emerge
naturally.[5] When the Stoic philosopher distances himself from his fellow
creatures, he contradicts his teaching of innate sociability.

Smith's characterization of Stoic teaching supposes that we must view
ourselves as a 'citizen of the world', a cosmopolitan:

Among the moralists who endeavour to correct the natural inequality of
our passive feelings by diminishing our sensibility to what peculiarly

concerns ourselves, we may count all the ancient sects of philosophers, but particularly the ancient Stoics. Man, according to the Stoics, ought to regard himself, not as something separated and detached, but as a citizen of the world, a member of the vast commonwealth of nature. To the interest of this great community, he ought at all times to be willing that his own little interest should be sacrificed. Whatever concerns himself, ought to affect him no more than whatever concerns any other equally important part of this immense system. We should view ourselves, not in the light in which our own selfish passions are apt to place us, but in the light in which any other citizen of the world would view us. What befalls ourselves we should regard as what befalls our neighbour, or, what comes to the same thing, as our neighbour regards what befalls us. 'When our neighbour', says Epictetus, 'loses his wife, or his son, there is nobody who is not sensible that this is a human calamity, a natural event altogether according to the ordinary course of things; but, when the same thing happens to ourselves, then we cry out, as if we had suffered the most dreadful misfortune. We ought, however, to remember how we were affected when this accident happened to another, and such as we were in his case, such ought we to be in our own'.

(TMS III.3.11)

In Smith's view, the Stoics have their moral facts in order. There is no 'commonly honest man' who does not 'inwardly feel the truth of that great stoical maxim' that unjust acts are 'contrary to nature'. Maxims are motives in Smith's account. This is so even when simple 'utilitarian' considerations argue against justice:[6]

One individual must never prefer himself so much even to any other individual, as to hurt or injure that other, in order to benefit himself, though the benefit to the one should be much greater than the hurt or injury to the other. . . . There is no commonly honest man . . . who does not inwardly feel the truth of that great stoical maxim, that for one man to deprive another unjustly of any thing, or unjustly to promote his own advantage by the loss or disadvantage of another, is more contrary to nature, than death, than poverty, than pain, than all the misfortunes which can affect him, either in his body, or in his external circumstances.

(TMS III.3.6)[7]

A central passage in Smith's *Moral Sentiments* establishes the link between providential order and individual responsibility. Rational creatures within the creation, such as ourselves, who act to enhance the happiness of mankind, 'co-operate with the Deity'. God's will depends upon our actions on His behalf:[8]

The happiness of mankind, as well as of all other rational creatures, seems to have been the original purpose intended by the Author of nature, when he brought them into existence. . . . But by acting according to the dictates of our moral faculties, we necessarily pursue the most effectual means for promoting the happiness of mankind, and may therefore be said, in some sense, to co-operate with the Deity, and to advance as far as in our power the plan of Providence. By acting otherways, on the contrary, we seem to obstruct, in some measure, the scheme which the Author of nature has established for the happiness and perfection of the world, and to declare ourselves, if I may say so, in some measure the enemies of God. Hence we are naturally encouraged to hope for his extraordinary favour and reward in the one case, and to dread his vengeance and punishment in the other.

(TMS III.5.7)

This is an important line of argument because it implies that the providential order depends upon people following the 'dictates of our moral faculties'. Smith believes religious teaching is the method by which that moral instruction is diffused.[9] We shall encounter the question below of what it is that insures that religious teaching will have a beneficial impact.

Teachers fail. In Smith's telling, the Stoic philosophers were tempted by their providentialism towards apathy. Apathetic providentialism denies the importance of our place in the world. That place forms the centre of all the connections we make in life. We naturally judge on the basis of our place in the world and we are better judges of near than remote events:

The ancient stoics were of opinion, that as the world was governed by the all-ruling providence of a wise, powerful, and good God, every single event ought to be regarded, as making a necessary part of the plan of the universe, and as tending to promote the general order and happiness of the whole: that the vices and follies of mankind, therefore, made as necessary a part of this plan as their wisdom or their virtue; and by that eternal art which educes good from ill, were made to tend equally to the prosperity and perfection of the great system of nature. *No speculation of this kind, however, how deeply soever it might be rooted in the mind, could diminish our natural abhorrence for vice, whose immediate effects are so destructive, and whose remote ones are too distant to be traced by the imagination.*

(TMS I.ii.3.4; emphasis added)

Stoical disdain for this central fact of place denied the innate sociability of humans with those close to them. Smith is contemptuous of the stoic doctrine of the irrelevance of experience (Vivenza 2001: 58; Montes 2004) in which the murder of one's father is said to be no more important than the death of a chicken.

The stoical apathy is, in such cases, never agreeable, and all the meta-physical sophisms by which it is supported can seldom serve any other purpose than to blow up the hard insensibility of a coxcomb to ten times its native impertinence. The poets and romance writers, who best paint the refinements and delicacies of love and friendship, and of all other private and domestic affections, Racine and Voltaire; Richardson, Maurivaux, and Riccoboni; are, in such cases, much better instructors than Zeno, Chrysippus, or Epictetus.

(TMS III.3.14)

In everyday experience, connections with others are the centre of life. Those who deny the importance of ordinary morality, deny human experience and human nature.

The necessity of Stoicism. The question then arises, why is Stoic teaching so important to Smith? Smith explains the origin of Stoic doctrine by appeal to the facts of life in the ancient world. In that world of factional violence, people were treated like cattle, butchered or brutalized by enslavement. All were at risk and no social distinction mattered:

During the age in which flourished the founders of all the principal sects of ancient philosophy; during the Peloponnesian war and for many years after its conclusion, all the different republics of Greece were, at home, almost always distracted by the most furious factions; and abroad, involved in the most sanguinary wars, in which each sought, not merely superiority or dominion, but either completely to extirpate all its enemies, or, what was not less cruel, to reduce them into the vilest of all states, that of domestic slavery, and to sell them, man, woman, and child, like so many herds of cattle, to the highest bidder in the market. The smallness of the greater part of those states, too, rendered it, to each of them, no very improbable event, that it might itself fall into that very calamity which it had so frequently, either, perhaps, actually inflicted, or at least attempted to inflict upon some of its neighbours. In this disorderly state of things, the most perfect innocence, joined to both the highest rank and the greatest public services, could give no security to any man that, even at home and among his own relations and fellow-citizens, he was not, at some time or another, from the prevalence of some hostile and furious faction, to be condemned to the most cruel and ignominious punishment. If he was taken prisoner in war, or if the city of which he was a member was conquered, he was exposed, if possible, to still greater injuries and insults.

(TMS VII.ii.1.28)

Smith proposes that the attitude we call stoicism is the *natural*, the *necessary*, response to this situation. What is true in the ancient world holds true in the American world of Smith's time:

But every man *naturally*, or rather *necessarily*, familiarizes his imagination with the distresses to which he foresees that his situation may frequently expose him. It is *impossible* that a sailor should not frequently think of storms and shipwrecks, and foundering at sea, and of how he himself is likely both to feel and to act upon such occasions. It was *impossible,* in the same manner, that a Grecian patriot or hero should not familiarize his imagination with all the different calamities to which he was sensible his situation must frequently, or rather constantly expose him. As an American savage prepares his death-song, and considers how he should act when he has fallen into the hands of his enemies, and is by them put to death in the most lingering tortures, and amidst the insults and derision of all the spectators; so a Grecian patriot or hero could not avoid frequently employing his thoughts in considering what he ought both to suffer and to do in banishment, in captivity, when reduced to slavery, when put to the torture, when brought to the scaffold. But the philosophers of all the different sects very justly represented virtue; that is, wise, just, firm, and temperate conduct; not only as the most probable, but as the certain and infallible road to happiness even in this life. This conduct, however, could not always exempt, and might even sometimes expose the person who followed it to all the calamities which were incident to that unsettled situation of public affairs.

(TMS VII.ii.1.28; emphasis added)

All the great schools of ancient philosophy separated happiness from fortune.

> They endeavoured, therefore, to show that happiness was either altogether, or at least in a great measure, independent of fortune; the Stoics, that it was so altogether; the Academic and Peripatetic philosophers, that it was so in a great measure. . . . though it should fail of success, yet the mind was not left without consolation. The virtuous man might still enjoy the complete approbation of his own breast; and might still feel that, how untoward soever things might be without, all was calm and peace and concord within. He might generally comfort himself, too, with the assurance that he possessed the love and esteem of every intelligent and impartial spectator, who could not fail both to admire his conduct, and to regret his misfortune.

(TMS VII.ii.1.28)

Our situation encourages us to embrace permanent things. We are encouraged to abstract from the applause of those we see to concern ourselves with approbation from those we imagine. In this imaginative act, we begin to generalize. For Smith, the Stoics were simply the most systematic of all the schools because they separated happiness entirely from the randomness of fortune and so they removed the importance of the particular from their teaching. Stoic cosmopolitanism is a systematic version of the natural response to a common fate.

Perhaps the Stoics are more Smithian than Smith found them to be. Epictetus, the former slave who was, for Smith, the 'greatest apostle' of the Stoic 'contempt of life and death' (TMS, VII.ii.1.35), asked about the worst case, the 'forlorn' state. He wondered why it would be natural to believe that God Himself could be forlorn and he concluded that we cannot even 'conceive of the mode of life of one who is all alone'.

> Why, if being alone is enough to make one forlorn, you will have to say that even Zeus himself is forlorn at the World-Conflagration, and bewails himself: 'Wretched me! I have neither Hera, nor Athena, nor Apollo, nor, in a word, brother, or son, or grandson, or kinsman'. There are even those who said that this is what he does when left alone at the World-Conflagration; for they cannot conceive of the mode of life of one who is all alone, starting as they do from a natural principle, namely, the facts of natural community of interest amongst men, and mutual affection, and joy in intercourse. But one ought none the less to prepare oneself for this also, that is, to be able to be self-sufficient, to be able to commune with oneself; even as Zeus communes with himself. . . .
>
> (Epictetus *Discourses* III.xiii.4–7)

In Epictetus's Stoicism, happiness entails mutuality. That fear of loneliness appears in a critical aspect of Smith's argument when he explains how to combat the biases of religious teachers.

Motivation and necessity

Natural and necessary, as well as the motivational force of language, comprise the logical centre of Stoicism. The topics covered in Stoic logic were wider than in modern logic. Epictetus pointed out the fallacy of the inference from unequal possession or skill to inequality of persons.[10] Many of the broader aspects of Stoic logic link to Smith's enterprise. The motivational force of language is part of a central puzzle of Stoic teaching that serves to distinguish between 'true' and 'truth'.[11] As we have seen, Smith talks about the development of attitudes that the Stoics referred to as 'natural' and 'necessary'. These, too, are concepts in Stoic logic. To this background we now turn.

Motivation by truth. Stoic logical doctrine holds that truth is corporal (soma) and popular, democratic even (demos). From corporality and popularity, we can infer that the words of ordinary people serve to motivate. As these texts are not widely discussed in the context of Smith's teaching on the motivational impact of language, we quote at length. The Stoic consensus is that only body can move body. So, for language to have motivational impact, it needs to be embodied. We quote from Sextus Empiricus's *Against the Logicians*:

As for the truth, some people, and especially the Stoics, think that it differs from what is true in three ways, in being, in composition, and in power. In being, in so far as the truth is a body (soma) while what is true is incorporeal. And reasonably so, they say: for the latter is a proposition and the proposition is a sayable, and the sayable is incorporeal. The truth, by contrast, is a body in so far as it is thought to be knowledge that is capable of asserting everything that is true and all knowledge is the leading part in a certain state (just as the hand in a certain state is thought of as a fist). But the leading part, according to these people, is a body; therefore the truth too is bodily in kind.

(Sextus Empiricus 2005 and 1935, i:38–9)

Modern logicians note the Stoic distinction between 'true' and 'truth' with care, but have emphasized the 'true' and, perhaps, neglected 'truth'.[12] Sextus continues, making a distinction in composition between 'true' and 'truth'. 'Truth' as knowledge, is 'an aggregation of many things':

In composition, in so far as what is true is thought of as something uniform and simple in nature, such as (at present) 'It is day' and 'I am having a discussion', while the truth, on the contrary, is supposed (on the assumption that it consists of knowledge) to be composite and an aggregation of many things. Thus, just as the populace is one thing and the citizen another, and the populace is the aggregation of many citizens while the citizen is the single one, by the same reasoning truth differs from what is true, and the truth resembles the populace (dêmos) and what is true resembles the citizen, because the former is composite, and the latter simple.

(Sextus Empiricus 2005 and 1935, i.40–1)

What Bett translates as 'populace' and Mates (1996: 52) transliterates as *deme*, Liddell-Scott-Jones's *Lexicon* defines as ordinary country people.

If truth is corporal and only body affects body, then we need a corporal explanation of the adoption of opinions that come to be accepted as the truth. The Stoics explained the criterion of truth by sense impressions.[13] Smith takes a Stoic path when he explains the adoption of opinions by a desire for approbation, not in terms of whether the opinion is true or not. The desire for approbation provides the motivational link to the language community and allows Smith to pass from mind to mind:

Every faculty in one man is the measure by which he judges of the like faculty in another. I judge of your sight by my sight, of your ear by my ear, of your reason by my reason, of your resentment by my resentment, of your love by my love. I neither have, nor can have, any other way of judging about them.

(TMS I.i.3.10)

Acceptance of opinions is driven by a desire for approbation:[14]

> To approve of another man's opinions is to adopt those opinions, and to adopt them is to approve of them. If the same arguments which convince you convince me likewise, I necessarily approve of your conviction; and if they do not, I necessarily disapprove of it: neither can I possibly conceive that I should do the one without the other. To approve or disapprove, therefore, of the opinions of others is acknowledged, by every body, to mean no more than to observe their agreement or disagreement with our own. But this is equally the case with regard to our approbation or disapprobation of the sentiments or passions of others.
>
> (TMS I.i.3.2)

Necessity. In a logic of necessity, one can make statements about the nature of things. Stoic logic begins when Zeno studied with Diodorus (Laertius 1925, vii.25). We quote a report of an argument between Diodorus and another one of his students, Philo, about the logic of conditionals:

> Philo says that a true conditional is one which does not have a true antecedent and a false consequent, e.g., when it is day and I am conversing, 'if it is day, then I am conversing'; but Diodorus defines it as one which neither is nor ever was capable of having a true antecedent and a false consequent. According to him, the conditional just mentioned seems to be false, since when it is day and I have become silent, it will have a true antecedent and a false consequent; but the following conditional seems true: 'if atomic elements of things do not exist, then atomic elements of things do exist', since it will always have the false antecedent . . . and the true consequent.
>
> (Mates 1949: 235)

Philo's conditional is the 'material implication' of modern fame. The question is what to make of Diodorus's conditional? As reconstructed by Mates (1949, 1953) and Prior (1955), the Diodorean implication holds for all time. In the example given, it is the nature of things to be atomic and nature, unlike the fact of talking, this does not change.[15]

We can thus define human nature by appeal to what is true for all members of the species. Some goal is natural for a species if and only if all members of the species have that goal.[16] All animals have at least one goal in common, to continue to exist:

> An animal's first impulse, say the Stoics, is to self-preservation, because nature from the outset endears it to itself, as Chrysippus affirms in the first book of his work *On Ends:* his words are, 'The dearest thing to every animal is its own constitution and its consciousness thereof'; for it was

not likely that nature should estrange the living thing from itself or that she should leave the creature she has made without either estrangement from or affection for its own constitution.

(Laertius 1925, vii.85)

While humans have the ability to reason logically in pursuit of our goals, we know from Chrysippus that this does not make us unique. Dogs too can solve logical problems in pursuit of desire.[17] The distinction between action for pleasure and action by nature depends upon the time structure. All species are directed by impulses which precede pleasure:

As for the assertion made by some people that pleasure is the object to which the first impulse of animals is directed, it is shown by the Stoics to be false. For pleasure, if it is really felt, they declare to be a by-product, which never comes until nature by itself has sought and found the means suitable to the animal's existence or constitution; it is an aftermath comparable to the condition of animals thriving and plants in full bloom.

(Laertius 1925, vii.85–6)

Then follows the argument for human exceptionality. Like other species, we start impulsively but then we come to understand the consequences. Here is the organization of later Stoic ethical teaching:

The ethical branch of philosophy they divide as follows: (1) the topic of impulse; (2) the topic of things good and evil; (3) that of the passions; (4) that of virtue; (5) that of the end; (6) that of primary value and of actions; (7) that of duties or the befitting; and (8) of inducements to act or refrain from acting. . . .

And nature, they say, made no difference originally between plants and animals, for she regulates the life of plants too, in their case without impulse and sensation, just as also certain processes go on of a vegetative kind in us. But when in the case of animals impulse has been superadded, whereby they are enabled to go in quest of their proper aliment, for them, say the Stoics, Nature's rule is to follow the direction of impulse. But when reason by way of a more perfect leadership has been bestowed on the beings we call rational, for them life according to reason rightly becomes the natural life. For reason supervenes to shape impulse scientifically.

(Laertius 1925, vii.84–6)

If we think of the Stoic doctrine that action precedes foresight of advantage, then Smith's explanation of trade, so disconnected from modern economics (Levy 1992; Rubinstein 2000), comes into clearer focus:

This division of labour, from which so many advantages are derived, is not originally the effect of any human wisdom, which foresees and intends that general opulence to which it gives occasion. It is the necessary, though very slow and gradual, consequence of a certain propensity in human nature which has in view no such extensive utility; the propensity to truck, barter, and exchange one thing for another.

(WN I.ii.1)

We trade because it is in our nature to trade. It is a defining characteristic of our species:

Whether this propensity be one of those original principles in human nature, of which no further account can be given; or whether, as seems more probable, it be the necessary consequence of the faculties of reason and speech, it belongs not to our present subject to enquire. It is common to all men, and to be found in no other race of animals, which seem to know neither this nor any other species of contracts. Two greyhounds, in running down the same hare, have sometimes the appearance of acting in some sort of concert. Each turns her towards his companion, or endeavours to intercept her when his companion turns her towards himself. This, however, is not the effect of any contract, but of the accidental concurrence of their passions in the same object at that particular time. Nobody ever saw a dog make a fair and deliberate exchange of one bone for another with another dog. Nobody ever saw one animal by its gestures and natural cries signify to another, this is mine, that yours; I am willing to give this for that.

(WN I.ii.2)

'Indifference' is a Stoic concept which can refer to a goal that is not universal but only specific to a time and a place. While thought experiments can rationalize otherwise odd choices,[18] sexual practices provide a real world example of Stoic indifference. If we believe an account of Smith's view of sodomy as a 'thing indifferent'[19] then again we find a Stoic source in Smith's views.[20] Less dramatically, Smith is clear in WN that moral codes appealing to poor people carry different imperatives about sexuality than moral codes attractive to the rich.[21]

Providence and sympathy

Smith told us that Stoic doctrine comes in fragments that need to be read with care.[22] It is often recited only to be opposed in part or in whole. The teaching of the Stoics on providence and sympathy provides a case in point. If the truth is carried by what people in fact believe, what do we make of their views on the gods? From the universal consensus that the gods exist, the Stoics and others inferred that the gods exist.[23] From the existence of gods and their beneficence, the Stoics inferred the efficacy of divination. This is the context in which the Stoic teaching on cosmic sympathy encounters great controversy even among their students.

Fragments carrying Posidonius's work on divination come to us in the account *On Divination* of his friend and student, Cicero:[24]

> 2.41. The Stoics actually argue when they are particularly eager: 'If there are gods, there is divination; the gods are; therefore, there is divination'. It would make much more sense to say, 'There is no divination; therefore, there are no gods'.
> 2.81. But all kings, peoples, nations, make use of auspices. As if anything were as universal as the fact that people are stupid!
>
> (Luck 1985: 273)

Concluding that 'people are stupid' is precisely what we do not wish to do. Instead, we attempt to follow the Stoics' reasoning on this matter. So, we step into their universe, containing as it does a place for magic.

'Sympathy' enters the discussion. In this famous text Epictetus is questioned about persuading a man that he is under the eye of God 'Do you not think, he answered, that all things are united in one? – I do, said the other. – Very well, do you not think that what is on earth feels the influence [*sumpatheia*] of that which is in heaven?' (Epictetus I.xiv.2–3).

'*Sumpatheia*' is translated by modern specialists as 'co-affection' or 'interaction'.[25] Epictetus's translator adds the following note:

> This is the famous principle of *sumpatheia* . . . the physical unity of the cosmos in such a form that the experience of one part necessarily affects every other. This doctrine, especially popular with the Stoics, is essentially but a philosophic formulation of the vague ideas that underlie the practices of sympathetic magic.
>
> (Oldfather 1925 at Epictetus I.xiv.2)[26]

An extraordinarily interesting passage from Cicero denies the divination but not that sympathy is a principle in interconnections; indeed, it is principle of unanimity. We quote from Kidd's translation which points to the fact that Cicero does not offer a Latin equivalent of *sumpatheia* but simply gives the Greek:

> You can put forward hundreds of examples like that to illustrate a natural relationship between remote separate things. Well, let's grant this natural relationship. In no way does it overturn this argument of mine: in what way can any kind of split in the liver forecast financial gain? What natural coupling, what concord (to put it so) or unanimity, which the Greeks call 'sympathy' [the Stoic technical term, *sumpatheia*] can be the cause of a harmonisation between a split in a liver and my

petty cash, or between my little windfall and heaven, earth and the laws of nature?

(Posidonius 1999, F106)

'Sympathy' is a word of magic. As such, it was attacked by mechanical philosophers. Francis Bacon was particularly sharp, but there were others.[27] A belief in what seems to us to be magic has been hard to accept in those who made great contributions to natural science.[28] Knowing the relationship between Bacon and Thomas Hobbes, Bacon's attack on sympathetic explanations helps us appreciate why both Shaftesbury and Smith provide sympathetic accounts in opposition to Hobbes and the Hobbesianism in Hume (Pack and Schliesser 2006).

Shaftesbury's distinction between ancient and modern philosophy is central in this response to Hobbes.[29] Shaftesbury explains the difference between ancient philosophical accounts and the modern philosophy taught by Hobbes when dealing with the messy aspects of human motivation – '*Passion, Humour, Caprice, Zeal, Faction*' (2000 [1711] i.72):

> Modern Projectors, I know, wou'd willingly rid their hands of these *natural* Materials; and wou'd fain build after a more uniform way. They wou'd new-frame the human Heart; and have a mighty fancy to reduce all its Motions, Balances and Weights, to that one Principle and Foundation of a cool and deliberate *Selfishness*. Men, it seems, are unwilling to think they can be so outwitted, and impos'd on by Nature, as to be made to serve her Purposes, rather than their own. They are asham'd to be drawn thus out of *themselves*, and forc'd from what they esteem their *true Interest*.
>
> (Shaftesbury 2000 [1711] i.73)

The question of 'interest' and 'selfishness' will be important in what follows. Shaftesbury's target, Hobbes, made his contribution to later 'rational choice' considerations by formulating self-interest accounts in terms of the independence of acting agents. For Hobbes, words which connect people are of no consequence:

> For the Lawes of Nature (as *Justice, Equity, Modesty, Mercy*, and (in summe) *doing to others as wee would be done to*,) of themselves, without the terrour of some Power, to cause them to be observed, are contrary to our naturall Passions, that carry us to Partiality, Pride, Revenge, and the like. And Covenants, without the Sword, are but Words and of no strength to secure a man at all.
>
> (Hobbes 1985 [1651] ii.17.2)

In terms of twentieth-century game theory, the independence assumption implies that all cells in a game matrix are feasible. What is best for me, given that I do not expect you to reciprocate, is often very different from what is best for me given that I expect you to reciprocate.

To challenge Hobbes's account of the independence of acting agents, Shaftesbury appealed to the hidden property of sympathetic vibration among agents which establishes harmony.[30] Harmony is both a musical and an ethical concept.[31] In Shaftesbury's account, the awareness of our sympathetic inter-relationship with others is a key to our happiness:

> And in the next place, as PARTIAL AFFECTION is fitted only to a short and slender Enjoyment of those Pleasures of *Sympathy* or *Participation with others*; so neither is it able to derive any considerable Enjoyment from that other principal Branch of human Happiness, *viz. Consciousness of the actual or merited Esteem of others.*
>
> (Shaftesbury 2000 [1711] ii.64–5)

As Smith explained Stoic teaching, the esteem we merit may substitute for happiness when fortune fails and we get less than we deserve.

From truth claims to belief claims

Viner never averted his attention from the role Smith assigned to providence in the social order. As Viner found the role of providence more pronounced in *Theory of Moral Sentiments* than in *Wealth of Nations*, he took his position on the 'Adam Smith Problem'.[32] His explanation for the disconnect between Smith's two great books was that Smith analyzed one human in two spheres. Here is Irwin's summary, quoting Viner's final position on the problem:

> Smith dealt with only one man 'who operates in two worlds, which impinge on him psychologically in different manners: first, in the non-market world, the world of his family, his neighbors, his community and country, and second, the world of market transactions, of impersonality and anonymity, where the sense of justice is the only moral sentiment which has an important psychological role to play'.
>
> (Irwin 1991: 19)[33]

Viner's 'two world' reading of Smith is in line with how students of Viner have read Smith.[34]

In our view, by contrast, TMS offers an explanation of what people believe, while people act on the basis of such beliefs in both TMS and WN. We give two examples of this below. The first is taken from WN and is developed without any explicit discussion of whether Smith thinks the belief is 'true' or 'false'. It is simply there. The deleterious consequences will be noted in the last edition of TMS. In the second example, from TMS, the difference between 'true' and 'false' belief becomes important. Smith judges factional beliefs that violate universality to be 'false'.

In our reading, Smith moved Stoic thinking about magic from claims about the world to claims about how people interpret the world. Consequently, the providentialism with which Smith disagrees in Stoic doctrine will appear in the troubling beliefs of ordinary people. Contrary to Viner's argument that there are no flaws in the beneficent order in *Theory of Moral Sentiments*, we point to Smith's worry about 'false' religious belief driving the problem of faction. But Smith does not, as a consequence, endorse Cicero's conclusion that people are stupid. Instead, he addressed the problem in *Wealth of Nations* with the argument that harmful religious beliefs would be exorcised in a competitive equilibrium by what is most natural to humans, the desire to avoid loneliness.

Gambling for approbation. Consider one widely deplored aspect of Smith's economics, his explanation of why individuals systematically engage in gambles that fail plausible expected value calculations. One aspect of his explanation is worthy of some attention. A class of gambles interests spectators who reward the winners with approbation and this changes the calculations of the gamblers (Levy 1999). We need to ask why the spectators reward the winners with approbation. For Smith, spectators impute from 'win', the judgment 'deserve to win' (Peart and Levy 2005). Smith explains Stoic teaching in terms of a gamble with life itself:

> Human life the Stoics appear to have considered as a game of great skill; in which, however, there was a mixture of chance, *or of what is vulgarly understood to be chance*. In such games the stake is commonly a trifle, and the whole pleasure of the game arises from playing well, from playing fairly, and playing skillfully. If notwithstanding all his skill, however, the good player should, by the influence of chance, happen to lose, the loss ought to be a matter, rather of merriment, than of serious sorrow. He has made no false stroke; he has done nothing which he ought be ashamed of . . . Human life, with all the advantages which can possibly attend it, ought, according to the Stoics, to be regarded but as a mere two-penny stake; a matter by far too insignificant to merit any anxious concern.
>
> (TMS VII.ii.1.24; emphasis added)

For the Stoics, chance is the doctrine of the uninstructed. Chance does not really exist in the *kosmos*:

> If I am going to sail, says Epictetus, I chuse the best ship and the best pilot, and I wait for the fairest weather that my circumstances and duty will allow. Prudence and propriety, the principles which the Gods have given me for the direction of my conduct, require this of me; but they require no more: and if, notwithstanding, a storm arises, which neither the strength of the vessel not the skill of the pilot are likely to withstand, I give myself no trouble about the consequences. . . . Whether

we are to be drowned, or come to a harbour, is the business of Jupiter, not mine.

(TMS VII.ii.1.20)

The spectator who believes as the Stoics do would of course impute from the successful arrival of the ship that the passengers travelled with the will of God. But we must remember that, for Smith, the doctrines of moral philosophy are a systematical ordering of the commonplace.[35]

Now consider what Smith tells us in the chapter on market wages in competitive equilibrium. Here is how spectators interpret the outcome of a high stakes gamble:

> To excel in any profession, in which but few arrive at mediocrity, is the most decisive mark of what is called *genius* or superior talents. The public admiration which attends upon such distinguished abilities, makes always a part of their reward; a greater or smaller in proportion as it is higher or lower in degree. It makes a considerable part of that reward in the profession of physick; a still greater perhaps in that of law; in poetry and philosophy it makes almost the whole.
>
> (WN I.x.b.24; emphasis added)

'Genius' is from a Latin word which is sometimes used to translate *daimon* a Greek spirit. The spectator interprets outcomes by imputing providential design, so those who are successful are seen as having deserved success. What for the Stoics is a claim about the *kosmos* is for Smith a commonplace belief.

What if merited approbation is supposed to be payment for virtue, but public applause, actual approbation, is a payment for wealth obtained by any sort successful gamble? Smith flags this for attention in the modifications of TMS made post-WN:

> This disposition to admire, and almost to worship, the rich and the powerful, and to despise, or, at least, to neglect persons of poor and mean condition, though necessary both to establish and to maintain the distinction of ranks and the order of society, is, at the same time, the great and most universal cause of the corruption of our moral sentiments.
>
> (TMS I.iii.3.1)

Thus, a failure of approbation occurs as a result of a belief in the beneficence of the *kosmos*, the providentialism of the people Smith studies. From a win people impute that the win was deserved. Smith appeals to proverbial wisdom as a way to disregard the extremes:

> In the middling and inferior stations of life, the road to virtue and that to fortune, to such fortune, at least, as men in such stations can reasonably

expect to acquire, are, happily in most cases, very nearly the same. In all the middling and inferior professions, real and solid professional abilities, joined to prudent, just, firm, and temperate conduct, can very seldom fail of success. Abilities will even sometimes prevail where the conduct is by no means correct. . . . The success of such people, too, almost always depends upon the favour and good opinion of their neighbours and equals; and without a tolerably regular conduct these can very seldom be obtained. The good old proverb, therefore, That honesty is the best policy, holds, in such situations, almost always perfectly true. In such situations, therefore, we may generally expect a considerable degree of virtue; and, fortunately for the good morals of society, these are the situations of by far the greater part of mankind.

(TMS I.iii.3.5)

The universalism in proverbial wisdom that honesty is the best policy, can help counteract the common providentialism of imputing desert from winning an unjust gamble.

When belief is 'false'. Smith does not move directly from sympathetic judgments to behaviour. Rules, religion and education are all intermediate steps between sympathy and behaviour. We come to believe in the gods and we enter into their situation in our imagination. Just as we project our mind into the situation of the dead, we impute our sentiments into the situation of the gods. Sympathetic projection, as Smith describes, equalizes. We suppose the gods are just like us:

This opinion or apprehension, I say, seems first to be impressed by nature. Men are naturally led to ascribe to those mysterious beings, whatever they are, which happen, in any country, to be the objects of religious fear, all their own sentiments and passions. They have no other; they can conceive no other to ascribe to them. Those unknown intelligences which they imagine but see not, must necessarily be formed with some sort of resemblance to those intelligences of which they have experience. During the ignorance and darkness of pagan superstition, mankind seem to have formed the ideas of their divinities with so little delicacy, that they ascribed to them, indiscriminately, all the passions of human nature, those not excepted which do the least honour to our species, such as lust, hunger, avarice, envy, revenge.

(TMS III.5.4)

Reflection and discussion make a difference as we move from gods who are just like us to gods who are what we would become:

They could not fail, therefore, to ascribe to those beings, for the excellence of whose nature they still conceived the highest admiration, those sentiments and qualities which are the great ornaments of humanity, and which seem to raise it to a resemblance of divine perfection, the love of virtue and beneficence, and the abhorrence of vice and injustice.

(TMS III.5.4)

Our sympathy is embodied in our beliefs about the gods. This argument is consistent with Viner's reading.

What is not consistent, is Smith's next step. Smith asks, do things always work out well? A problem arises when religious beliefs are factional:

> *False notions of religion* are almost the only causes which can occasion any very gross perversion of our natural sentiments in this way; and that principle which gives the greatest authority to the rules of duty, is alone capable of distorting our ideas of them in any considerable degree.
>
> (TMS III.6.12; emphasis added)

Has Smith abandoned Stoicism to appeal to the stupidity of people? Smith's answer is found in WN. A natural characteristic of humans will purge religion of evil if we do not hinder it:[36]

> The teachers of each sect, seeing themselves surrounded on all sides with more adversaries than friends, would be obliged to learn that candour and moderation which is so seldom to be found among the teachers of those great sects, whose tenets being supported by the civil magistrate, are held in veneration by almost all the inhabitants of extensive kingdoms and empires, and who therefore see nothing round them but followers, disciples, and humble admirers. The teachers of each little sect, finding themselves almost alone, would be obliged to respect those of almost every other sect, and the concessions which they would mutually find it both convenient and agreeable to make to one another, might in time probably reduce the doctrine of the greater part of them to that pure and rational religion, free from every mixture of absurdity, imposture, or fanaticism, such as wise men have in all ages of the world wished to see established; but such as positive law has perhaps never yet established, and probably never will establish in any country: because, with regard to religion, positive law always has been, and probably always will be, more or less influenced by popular superstition and enthusiasm.
>
> (WN V.i.g.8)

There is a trade in the passage.

The Stoic context of the 'invisible hand'

Smith insists that our natural inclinations are to seek our own happiness and, because our place in the world has motivational weight, the approval of our friends and neighbours (TMS III.2.15). Smith's critical worry is that religions might create factions. With factions, the connection between the actual approval of our neighbours and the merited approval of the wider universe is attenuated. Smith's answer, quoted above, emphasizes the importance of connections. It is not natural for a person to be alone. That is the fundamental axiom of the doctrine of human sociability. To cure loneliness people talk. In a system of natural liberty in religion, they find that they disagree. What happens? 'The teachers of each little sect, finding themselves almost alone, would be obliged to respect those of almost every other sect . . .'. By trade in the space of belief, they keep the conversation going. They compromise and agree to disagree because without the trade, they risk being alone. As Epictetus argued, it is natural to believe that even God fears loneliness.

Smith's 'invisible hand' is offered to encapsulate the argument that individuals, pursuing their natural inclinations, will be led to promote a larger good, the interests of 'the great society of mankind'.[37] Smith presupposes the doctrine of human sociability. The Stoic philosophers put forward the imperative of universal happiness and connection.[38] A life according to nature is the Stoic maxim.[39] The question that arises is to what degree these Stoic teachings are consistent. The barrier for Smith between a life by natural inclination and instruction and the goal of universal happiness is faction. Since for Smith there is no difference between trade and discussion, we cure faction by making it necessary to trade as we discuss.

Situation matters. The Stoics lived in a world in which it was natural to ask whether God cries. But Smith also lived in a world in which people were still treated as if they were cattle and from that vantage point, perhaps, he could read more deeply into Stoic texts than those of us who inherited a happier world. We who do not see the social world that way but who are still troubled by the problem of factions might consider that Adam Smith and his Stoic masters have something still to teach us. The faction which most concerns us, to speak to our research, is the faction of experts. The problem which Smith encountered, to remove the bias of the teacher from the teaching, is precisely what we have encountered there (Peart and Levy 2005, Levy and Peart 2008).

Acknowledgements

An earlier version of this paper was presented in the History of Economics Society meeting June 2006, Grinnell, Iowa. We benefited from discussion with Joe Persky, Leon Montes and Eric Schliesser. We would also like to thank an anonymous reader for suggesting improvements. Special thanks to Doug Den Uyl for his encouragement.

Notes

1 Smith's celebrated 'man of system' passage gives a context in which philosopher and legislator come together (TMS VI.ii.2.17).

2   'The reasonings of philosophy, it may be said, though they may confound and perplex the understanding, can never break down the necessary connection which Nature has established between causes and their effects. The causes which naturally excite our desires and aversions, our hopes and fears, our joys and sorrows, would no doubt, notwithstanding all the reasonings of Stoicism, produce upon each individual, according to the degree of his actual sensibility, their proper and necessary effects. The judgments of the man within the breast, however, might be a good deal affected by those reasonings, and that great inmate might be taught by them to attempt to overawe all our private, partial, and selfish affections into a more or less perfect tranquility. To direct the judgments of this inmate is the great purpose of all systems of morality. That the Stoical philosophy had very great influence upon the character and conduct of its followers, cannot be doubted; and that though it might sometimes incite them to unnecessary violence, its general tendency was to animate them to actions of the most heroic magnanimity and most extensive benevolence' (TMS VII.ii.1.47).

3   'The plan and system which Nature has sketched out for our conduct, seems to be altogether different from that of the Stoical philosophy' (TMS VII.ii.1.43).

4   '. . . most people thought, if the gods took to dialectic, they would adopt no other system than that of Chrysippus' (Diogenes Laertius, 1925, vii.180). '[O]ften said to have been the greatest logician of ancient times. Chrysippus was regarded as the second founder of Stoicism; according to an old saying, "If there had been no Chrysippus, there would have been no Stoa". . . . It seems likely that Chrysippus was responsible for the final organization of Stoic logic into a calculus' (Mates 1953: 7).

5   In terms of the Stoic technicalities Smith has given 'place' motivational weight. We are born at a particular place. Appealing to an axiom of innate sociability which Smith and the Stoics share, we know that the connections which we develop in that place will naturally matter to us. Therefore, place is corporeal in Smith's system. In the classical Stoic systems place along with sayables, void and time are the incorporeals (Long and Sedley 1987: 162–65). 'True' is defined in terms of sayables and is distinguished from 'truth' as we see below.

6   We argue that utilitarianism in the classical period (before F.Y. Edgeworth) needs to be read with the supposition of sympathetic agents, Peart and Levy (2005).

7   Vivenza (2001: 2) uses this passage as the first classical text in her book.

8   'Zeno formulated the concept and ideal of cosmopolitanism. Since there is only one world, we must believe that all human beings are citizens of this world. This ideal is contrary to all the ancient and modern particularisms and nationalisms, but it has had wide appeal in many ages, and also in our own century. It has often been forgotten that the merit of this concept is due to Zeno . . .' (Kristeller 1991: 34–5). Thus, the identification of liberalism with 'cosmopolitan' – (Mill (1978) [1866]: 419; Furniss 1920: 6; and Heckscher 1935: 35–6) – pays homage to the Stoic roots of the liberal tradition. Our obligations to 'all other rational creatures' may speak to Hume's 'other rational species' problem (Levy and Peart 2004).

9   'These natural hopes and fears, and suspicions, were propagated by sympathy, and confirmed by education; and the gods were universally represented and believed to be the rewarders of humanity and mercy, and the avengers of perfidy and injustice. And thus religion, even in its rudest form, gave a sanction to the rules of morality, long before the age of artificial reasoning and philosophy. That the terrors of religion should thus enforce the natural sense of duty, was of too much importance to the happiness of mankind, for nature to leave it dependent upon the slowness and uncertainty of philosophical researches' (TMS III.5.4).

10 Epictetus (44) is quoted as the first epigraph.

11 'Now it might be thought that "truth" meant merely the characteristic of being true and that consequently when the senses of "true" were determined, the senses of "truth" would *ipso facto* be determined. In Stoic usage, this was not the case' (Mates 1953: 35).

12 'The criterion for determining the truth of presentations, much discussed by the Stoics, is an epistemological problem and not within the scope of this work' (Mates 1953: 35–6). 'By the "leading part" Sextus here means the intellect, which is part of the soul and therefore, for the Stoics, material. They held, then, that the "truth" refers to a complete body of knowledge as it may be possessed by a person or persons, while "true" is an adjective applied to an *axioma*. The linguistic distinction appears to be a little eccentric, but it perfectly intelligible. We shall not be further concerned with the truth in the Stoic sense' (Kneale and Kneale 1962: 150).

13 'A presentation (or mental impression) is an imprint on the soul: the name having been appropriately borrowed from the imprint made by the seal upon the wax' (Laertius 1925, vii.46). 'The Stoics agree to put in the forefront the doctrine of presentation and sensation, inasmuch as the standard by which the truth of things is tested is generically a presentation. . . .' (Laertius 1925, vii.49).

14 In the years immediately preceding his work on Stoic logic, Prior questioned the motivational claims which Smith makes. 'It would probably be acknowledged that we would in fact approve of all opinions coinciding with our own, and of no others; but *why* would we? Plainly, many would say, because to make an opinion "our own" is to regard it as true, i.e., as a perception or representation of a fact beyond the opinion itself; and it is because of the supposed accordance of another man's opinion with this fact, rather than because of its known accordance with our own opinion, that we approve of it, i.e., we consider it true' (Prior 1949: 66–7). Schliesser (2005) gives evidence that Smith's practice in the 'History of Astronomy' is as much in accord with Prior's principles as his own!

15 'Diodorus managed to define a plausible sense of "implication" that is stronger than Material implication and weaker than Strict Implication – a feat requiring no little skill' (Mates 1949: 235). The technical context of debates over necessity – the 'master argument' – is reported in Epictetus *Discourses* II.xix.1–6 (Mates 1953: 38). Prior (1955) offers a solution to the master argument which shows how classical discussions of modal logic fit into the modern systems.

16 From the logic of natural as universal, the sceptic denies that there are natural goods. 'Fire, which heats by nature, appears to everyone to be productive of heat, and snow, which cools by nature, appears to everyone to be productive of coolness, and all the things which are affective by nature affect in the same way those who are, as the Dogmatists put it, "in a natural condition". But, as we shall show, none of the so-called "goods" affects everyone as being good; therefore, there does not exist anything that is good by nature' (Mates 1996 = Sextus Empiricus *Outlines*, 3.23.179).

17 'And according to Chrysippus, who was certainly no friend to non-rational animals, the dog even shares in the celebrated Dialectic. In fact, this author says that the dog uses repeated applications of the fifth undetermined argument-schema when, arriving at a juncture of three paths, after sniffing at the two down which the quarry did not go, he rushes off on the third without stopping to sniff. For, says, this ancient authority, the dog in effect reasons as follows: the animal either went this way or that way or the other; he did not go this way and he did not go that; therefore, he went the other' (Mates 1996 = Sextus Empiricus *Outlines*, I.14.69).

18 'But some say that none of the things indifferent by nature are simply preferred or rejected; for every indifferent thing appears, in different circumstances, sometimes preferred and sometimes rejected. For surely, they say, if the wealthy are being plotted against by a tyrant while the poor are left in peace, everyone would

choose to be poor rather than wealthy, so that wealth becomes a thing rejected. Consequently, since every so-called "indifferent" thing is called "good" by some people and "bad" by others, whereas all alike would consider it were indifferent by nature, nothing is indifferent by nature' (Mates 1996 = Sextus Empiricus *Outlines* 2.24.192–3).

19   'Adam Smith, whom I knew well, was a man of much investigation, knowledge, and sagacity; with a heart overflowing with benevolence and sociability; but he was strong tinctured with *French Philosophy* and *systime!* To mention two circumstances, in which I cannot be *mistaken,* because spoken to myself, and although contradictory to the sentiments I had expressed, not spoken in publick, where men often sport opinions for argument, but in the familiarity of individual conversation, where the unreserved sentiments are spoke. These were "That the Christian Religion *debased* the *human mind*;" and that "Sodomy was a thing in itself *indifferent*"' (Dalrymple 1800: 4). Salim Rashid first pointed out this text to us.

20   '... among us sodomy is regarded as shameful ... whereas by the Germani, they say, it is not considered shameful but just a customary thing. ... But is there anything surprising about this, when not only the followers of the Cynic philosophy but also those of Zeno of Citium, namely Cleanthes and Chrysippus, say that this practice is indifferent?' (Mates 1996 = Sextus Empiricus *Outlines*, 3.24.199–200).

21   In TMS Smith responds to Mandeville on temperance and chastity, suggesting that approbation follows consequences: 'Those virtues, however, do not require an entire insensibility to the objects of the passions which they mean to govern. They only aim at restraining the violence of those passions so far as not to hurt the individual, and neither disturb nor offend the society' (TMS VII.ii.4.11). WN makes it clear that consequences depend upon where in society one is. 'In the liberal or loose system, luxury, wanton and even disorderly mirth, the pursuit of pleasure to some degree of intemperance, the breach of chastity, at least in one of the two sexes, &c. provided they are not accompanied with gross indecency, and do not lead to falsehood or injustice, are generally treated with a good deal of indulgence, and are easily either excused or pardoned altogether. In the austere system, on the contrary, those excesses are regarded with the utmost abhorrence and detestation. The vices of levity are always ruinous to the common people' (WN V.i.g.10).

22   In his published work, 'fragment' is used only in a Stoic context. 'The Stoics, in the few fragments of their philosophy which have come down to us, sometimes talk of leaving life with a gaiety, and even with a levity, which, were we to consider those passages by themselves, might induce us to believe that they imagined we could with propriety leave it whenever we had a mind, wantonly and capriciously, upon the slightest disgust or uneasiness' (TMS VII.ii.1.26). 'The few fragments which have come down to us of what the ancient philosophers had written upon these subjects, form, perhaps, one of the most instructive, as well as one of the most interesting remains of antiquity. The spirit and manhood of their doctrines make a wonderful contrast with the desponding, plaintive, and whining tone of some modern systems' (TMS VII.ii.1.29).

'Fragment' also appears when Smith wrote to David Hume to make arrangement for his papers in the event of his death, 'I must tell you that except those which I carry along with me there are none worth the publishing, but a fragment of a great work which contains a history of the Astronomical Systems that were successively in fashion down to the time of Des Cartes. Whether that might not be published as a fragment of an intended juvenile work, I leave entirely to your judgment' (*Corr.* Letter 137, 16 April 1773).

23   Sextus Empiricius *Against Physicists* I: 60–61 discusses proofs for the existence of gods and puts universal agreement about the existence of the gods in first place.

This seems to be a persuasive argument. The argument that myths about Hades are incoherent (Sextus Empiricus I: 70–72) does not apply to beliefs about the gods. Sextus credits the Stoics here.

24 Posidonius 1989/1999, F26: 'Our friend Posidonius published five books on divination'. Kidd comments: 'Posidonius was without doubt used by Cicero, but certainly exclusively'. Cicero's respect and affection is as clear as can be. Posidonius 1989/1999, T31: 'Posidonius by whom I was trained'. T33: '. . . the famous Posidonius, the greatest of all the Stoics'.

With the Edelstein-Kidd/Kidd *Posidonius* as guide, one might read what Smith read and hear Posidonius argue with Chrysippus. Posidonius's emphasis on the role of emotion in ethics, (F30–5) is important for Smith's stoicism. Edelstein-Kidd/Kidd could help determine what texts of the ancient world could have told Smith about Posidonius's contributions (Kristeller 1991: 123–39) and so saved Smith from his assertion that there was no Stoic who was a competent astronomer (Smith (1980) [1795] 'Astronomy', iv.14).

25 Long & Sedley (1987: 489). Liddell-Scott-Jones's *Lexicon* gives an older translation 'fellow feeling, sympathy'. 'Co-affection' suggests the denial of independent agency which we take as critical to Smith's argument and suggests his opposition well-documented in the literature to the apathetic idea, *apatheia*.

26 Luck 1985: 3–4. 'One important concept in all magic is the principle of cosmic sympathy, which has nothing to do with compassion but means something like "action and reaction in the universe". All creatures, all created things, are united by a common bond. If one is affected, another one, no matter how distant or seemingly unconnected, feels the impact. This is a great and noble idea, but in magic it was mainly applied in order to gain control. Scientists think in terms of cause and effect, while *magi* think in terms of "sympathies" or "correspondences" in the sense defined above. . . . not by some sort or direct mechanical influence but rather by a hidden "vibration". . . . This doctrine was held, with variations, by Pythagoreans, Platonists, and Stoicists. Among the Stoicists, Posidonius of Apamea (c. 135–50 BC) should be mentioned'.

Perhaps the most famous linkage between magic and sympathy via vibration occurs in Plotinus *Ennead* (1991) IV.4.40–1. The magician is inside the world of enchantment 'Supposing the mage to stand outside the All, his evocations and invocations would no longer avail to draw up or call down . . .'. 'The prayer is answered by the mere fact that part and other part are wrought to one tone like a musical string which, plucked at one end, vibrates at the other also'. The complicated issue of Stoic sources for Plotinus are discussed by Dodds *et al.* (1957).

There are hundreds of references to 'sympathy' and 'sympathetic magic' in Thorndike (1923–58). For instance in volume 8 the index entry 'sympathy' (1958, 8: 787) is approximately the same size as the entry for 'star' (1985, 8: 783). Two modern specialist accounts of ancient science link astrology of the Stoic doctrine of sympathy: Dijksterhuis (1950: 84) and Lloyd (1987: 44). The discussion in Walker (1958: 6–10) distinguishes between the impact of sound and other senses.

27 Bacon (1620, para. 85): 'Again the students of natural magic, who explain everything by sympathies and antipathies, have in their idle and most slothful conjectures ascribed to substances wonderful virtues and operations; and if ever they have produced works, they have been such as aim rather at admiration and novelty than at utility and fruit'. Eric Schliesser found this for us.

Leibniz's comment on Newton's principle of attraction catches the mysticism of sympathetic explanations: 'laquelle estant accordée, on passeroit bientost à d'autres suppositions semblables, comme à la pesanteur d'Aristote, à l'attraction de Mons. Newton, à des sympathies ou antipathies et à mille autres attributs semblables', Letter to Huygens of 20 March 1693, quoted by Dijksterhuis (1950: 480).

Keynes (1995: 34): 'The major innovation in Newton's scientific work, the concept of force, was derived from his beliefs in the occult powers of the natural magic tradition, of which, for him, the most important part was alchemy'. Cf. Henry (1986).

28 Keynes purchased a box of Newton's alchemical manuscripts and described the reaction of earlier scholars who looked inside. 'After his death Bishop Horsley was asked to inspect the box with a view to publication. He saw the contents with horror and slammed the lid. A hundred years later Sir David Brewster looked into the box. He covered up the traces with carefully selected extracts and some straight fibbing. His latest biographer, Mr. More, has been more candid', Keynes (1951: 317). A later specialist's judgment is even harsher than Keynes's (Dobbs 1975: 11–14).

29 'Our modern Philosopher' says '*Courage is constant anger*' (Shaftesbury 2000 [1711] i.75). The reference is *Leviathan's* definition of 'anger'.

30 'Upon the whole: It may be said properly to be the same with the Affections or Passions in an Animal-Constitution, as with the Cords or Strings of a Musical Instrument. If these, tho in ever so just proportion one to another, are strain'd beyond a certain degree, 'tis more than the Instrument will bear: The Lute or Lyre is abus'd, and its Effect lost. On the other hand, if while some of the Strings are duly strain'd, others are not wound up to their due proportion; then is the Instrument still in disorder, and its Part ill perform'd. The several Species of Creatures are like different sorts of Instruments: And even the same Species of Creatures (as in the same sort of Instruments) *one* is not entirely like the *other*, nor will the same Strings fit each. The same degree of Strength which winds up *one,* and fits the several Strings to a just Harmony and Concert, may in *another* burst both the Strings and Instrument it-self. Thus Men who have liveliest Sense, and are the easiest affected with Pain or Pleasure, have the need of the strongest Influence or Force of the Affections, such as Tenderness, Love, Sociability, Compassion, in order to preserve a *right* BALANCE *within,* and to maintain them in their Duty, and in the just performance of their Part: whilst others, who are of a cooler Blood, or lower Key, need not the same Allay or Counterpoint; nor are made by Nature to feel those tender and endearing [?] Affections in so exquisite a degree' (Shaftesbury 2000 [1711] ii.55).

31 Walker gives suggestions as to why the sense of hearing was considered more important than that of sight (1958: 10–11). Long (1996) also attends to the role of sound in the Stoic tradition. Using Aristotelian texts, he conjectures: 'May we take the Stoics to be drawing a comparable analogy between musical and ethical harmony?' (1996: 204). Levy and Peart (2004) find sympathy as vibration in Hume's *Treatise*. Accounts of sympathy as vibration did not end with Smith. One can be found in Erasmus Darwin's *Botanic Garden* (1791). Peart and Levy (2005) discuss nineteenth-century biological thinking about sympathy.

32 Irwin (1991: 18) summarizes Viner's settled position: '[In TMS] The beneficent order in nature shows no serious flaws and operates to promote the welfare of mankind. Viner maintains that although traces of this approach appear in the *Wealth of Nations*, "on the points at which they come into contract there is a substantial measure of irreconcilable divergence between the *Theory of Moral Sentiments* and the *Wealth of Nations,* with respect to the character of the natural order"'.

33 Justice is not the only moral sentiment in the *Wealth of Nations*. In TMS Smith explains carefully the distinction between justice and generosity (Levy and Peart 2004). There is generous behaviour in the *Wealth of Nations*, as witness beggars who live by the generosity of others (WN I.ii.2; I.x.c.38; III.iv.5). The mendicant orders receive considerable attention (WN IV.vii.b.20; V.i.g.2). There is also the more complicated issue to which we return below that of the desire for approbation

which is central to Smith's theory of the equalization of net advantages of employment in competitive equilibrium, rightly regarded by Stigler as one of Smith's triumphs (Stigler 1976: 1201).

34 Viner's description of the sympathetic machinery in terms of psychology speaks to whether there is any substantial difference between Viner's and Stigler's reading of Smith, as argued in Medema (forthcoming). Stigler (1960: 44) traces the independence between economics and psychology to Smith: 'In fact Smith's professional work on psychology (in the *Theory of Moral Sentiments*) bears scarcely any relationship to his economics, and this tradition of independence of economics from psychology has persisted . . .'. Stigler mentions Smith's asceticism in Stigler (1961: 5) and treats it more carefully in the context of Smith's psychological account of the stability of labour disutility (1976: 1207). He emphasizes that he is not sure whether Smith is in error here.

35 Thus, the doctrine that the lot reveals the will of God can be found most clearly in Jonah. This is cited as a point upon which adherents of all doctrines agree in Bodin's *Colloquium*. 'If a storm arose and could not be calmed with prayer, men of old used to cast lots and throw overboard the one on whom the lot had fallen. Thus when the prophet Jonah, on whom the lot had fallen, was thrown overboard, the storm suddenly subsided. . . . Would that custom were again put into practice. The lot used to fall rather often upon a very influential man, though never unless he deserved it. However, because of his powerful bodyguard he was able to elude the sacred lots. Therefore, the lots on ships fell into disuse' (Bodin 1975: 12–13).

36 Smith's argument is sketched in Levy (1978) bereft of Stoic context and concern for connections. Brubaker (2006: 184, 186) rightly stresses the importance of factions for the reading of *Theory of Moral Sentiments* but seems not to appreciate the importance of competition of religions in *Wealth of Nations* as a way out.

37 'The rich only select from the heap what is most precious and agreeable. They consume little more than the poor, and in spite of their natural selfishness and rapacity, though they mean only their own conveniency, though the sole end which they propose from the labours of all the thousands whom they employ, be the gratification of their own vain and insatiable desires, they divide with the poor the produce of all their improvements. They are led by an invisible hand to make nearly the same distribution of the necessaries of life, which would have been made, had the earth been divided into equal portions among all its inhabitants, and thus without intending it, without knowing it, advance the interest of the society, and afford means to the multiplication of the species. When Providence divided the earth among a few lordly masters, it neither forgot nor abandoned those who seemed to have been left out in the partition' (TMS IV.1.10). The more famous passage in WN is less unqualified. 'He generally, indeed, neither intends to promote the public interest, nor knows how much he is promoting it. By preferring the support of domestic to that of foreign industry, he intends only his own security; and by directing that industry in such a manner as its produce may be of the greatest value, he intends only his own gain, and he is in this, as in many other cases, led by an invisible hand to promote an end which was no part of his intention. Nor is it always the worse for the society that it was no part of it. By pursuing his own interest he frequently promotes that of the society more effectually than when he really intends to promote it' (WN IV.ii.9).

38 'Each one of us is as it were entirely encompassed by many circles, some smaller, others larger, the latter enclosing the former on the basis of their different and unequal dispositions relative to each other. The first and closest circle is the one which a person has drawn as though around a centre, his own mind. This circle encloses the body and anything taken for the sake of the body. For it is virtually the smallest circle, and almost touches the centre itself. Next, the second one further

removed from the centre . . . contains parents, siblings, wife, and children. The third one has in it uncles and aunts, grandparents, nephews, nieces, and cousins. The next circle includes the other relatives, and this is followed by the circle of local residents, then the circle of fellow-tribesman, next that of fellow-citizens, and then in the same way the circle of people from the neighbouring towns, and the circle of fellow-countryman. The outermost and largest circle, which encompasses all the rest, is that of the whole human race. Once these have been all surveyed, it is the task of a well tempered man, in his proper treatment of each group, to draw the circles together somehow towards the centre, and to keep zealously transferring those from the enclosing circles into the enclosed ones . . .', Hierocles (Long and Sedley 1987: 349).

39   'They [the Stoics] say that being happy is the end, for the sake of which everything is done, but which is not itself done for the sake of anything. This consists in living in accordance with virtue, in living in agreement, or, what is the same, in living in accordance with nature', Stobaeus (Long and Sedley 1987: 394).

Bibliography

Bacon, F. (1620) *The New Organon or True Directions Concerning the Interpretation of Nature*. Online. Available <http://ebooks.adelaide.edu.au/b/bacon/francis/organon/> (accessed 26 July 2008).

Bodin, J. (1975) *Colloquium of the Seven about Secrets of the Sublime = Colloquium Heptaplomeres de Rerum Sublimium Arcanis Abditis*, trans. M.L.D. Kuntz, Princeton: Princeton University Press.

Brubaker, L. (2006) 'Does the "wisdom of nature" need help?', in *New Voices on Adam Smith*, L. Montes and E. Schliesser (eds), New York: Routledge.

Dalrymple, A. (1800) *Thoughts of an Old Man, of Independent Mind, though Dependent Fortune, on the Present High Price of Corn*, London: T. Reynolds.

Darwin, E. (1791) *The Botanic Garden; a Poem, in Two Parts. Part I. Containing The Economy of Vegetation. Part II. The Loves of the Plants. With Philosophical Notes*, London, Printed for J. Johnson.

Dijksterhuis, E.J. (1986) [1950] *The Mechanization of the World Picture*, trans. C. Dikshoorn, Princeton: Princeton University Press.

Dobbs, B.J.T. (1975) *The Foundations of Newton's Alchemy: or, 'The Hunting of the Greene Lyon'*, Cambridge: Cambridge University Press.

Dodds, E.R., Theiler, W., Hadot, P., Puech, H.C., Dörrie, H., Cilento, V., Harder, R., Schwyzer, H.R., Armstrong, A.H., and Henry, P. (1957) *Les Sources de Plotin*, Geneva: Vandœuvres-Genève.

Epictetus (1925) *Discourses and The Encheiridion*, trans. W.A. Oldfather, Cambridge, MA: Loeb Classical Library.

Fleischacker, S. (2004) *On Adam Smith's* Wealth of Nations*: A Philosophical Companion*, Princeton: Princeton University Press.

Furniss, E.S. (1920) *The Position of the Laborer in a System of Nationalism: A Study in the Labor Theories of the Later English Mercantilists*, Boston and New York: Houghton Mifflin Company.

Griswold, C.L., Jr (1999) *Adam Smith and the Virtues of Enlightenment*, Cambridge: Cambridge University Press.

Heckscher, E.F. (1935) *Mercantilism*, trans. M. Shapiro, revised edn (1962), E.F. Söderlund (ed.), London: George Allen & Unwin.

Henry, J. (1986) 'A Cambridge Platonist's materialism: Henry More and the concept of soul', *Journal of the Warburg and Courtauld Institutes*, 49: 172–95.

Hobbes, T. (1985) [1651] *Leviathan*, C.B. Macpherson (ed.), London: Penguin Books.

Irwin, D.A. (1991) 'Introduction', in J. Viner, *Essays in the Intellectual History of Economics*, Princeton: Princeton University Press.

Keynes, J.M. (1951) 'Newton, the man', in *Essays in Biography*, G. Keynes (ed.), New York: Horizon Press, 2nd edn.

Keynes, M. (1995) 'The personality of Isaac Newton', *Notes and Records of the Royal Society of London*, 49: 1–56.

Kneale, W. and Kneale, M. (1962) *The Development of Logic*, Oxford: Clarendon Press.

Kristeller, P.O. (1991) *Greek Philosophers of the Hellenistic Age*, trans. G. Woods, New York: Columbia University Press.

Laertius, D. (1925) *Lives of Eminent Philosophers*, trans. R.D. Hicks, Cambridge: Loeb Classical Library.

Levy, D.M. (1978) 'Adam Smith, "The Law of Nature", and contractual society', *Journal of the History of Ideas*, 39: 665–74.

—— (1992) *Economic Ideas of Ordinary People: From Preferences to Trade*, London: Routledge.

—— (1999) 'Adam Smith's katallactic model of gambling: approbation from the spectator', *Journal of the History of Economic Thought*, 21: 81–91.

—— and Peart, S.J. (2004) 'Sympathy and approbation in Hume and Smith: a solution to the other rational species problem', *Economics and Philosophy*, 20: 331–49.

—— (2008) 'Inducing greater transparency: towards the establishment of ethical rules for econometrics', *Eastern Economic Journal* 34, 103–14.

Lloyd, G.E.R. (1987) *The Revolutions of Wisdom*, Berkeley: University of California Press.

Long, A.A. (1996) *Stoic Studies*, Cambridge: Cambridge University Press.

Long, A.A. and Sedley, D.N. (1987) *The Hellenistic Philosophers: Translations of the Principal Sources with Philosophical Commentary,* Cambridge: Cambridge University Press.

Luck, G. (1985) *Arcana Mundi: Magic and the Occult in the Greek and Roman Worlds*, Baltimore: Johns Hopkins University Press.

Mates, B. (1949) 'Diodorean implication', *Philosophical Review*, 58: 234–42.

—— (1953) *Stoic Logic*, Berkeley: University of California Press.

—— (1996) *The Skeptic Way: Sextus Empiricus's Outlines of Pyrrhonism*, Oxford: Oxford University Press.

Medema, S.G. (forthcoming) 'Adam Smith and the Chicago School', in *The Elgar Companion to Adam Smith*. J.T. Young (ed.), Cheltenham: Edward Elgar.

Mill, J.S. (1978) [1866] 'Grote's Plato', in *Essays on Philosophy and the Classics*, Vol. 11 of *The Collected Works of John Stuart Mill*, J.M. Robson (ed.), Toronto: University of Toronto Press.

Montes, L. (2004) *Adam Smith in Context: A Critical Reassessment of Some Central Components of His Thought*, New York: Palgrave Macmillan.

—— (2008) 'The origins of *Das Adam Smith Problem* and our understanding of sympathy', in *The Street Porter and the Philosopher: Conversations on Analytical Egalitarianism*, S.J. Peart and D.M. Levy (eds), Ann Arbor: University of Michigan Press.

Pack, S.J. and Schliesser, E. (2006) 'Smith's Humean criticism of Hume's account of the origin of justice', *Journal of the History of Philosophy*, 44: 47–63.

Peart, S.J. and Levy, D.M. (2005) *The 'Vanity of the Philosopher': From Hierarchy to Equality in Post-Classical Economics*, Ann Arbor, University of Michigan Press.

Plotinus (1991) *The Enneads*, trans. by S. MacKenna, John Dillon (ed.), London: Penguin Books.

Posidonius (1989) *I. The Fragments*, L. Edelstein and I.G. Kidd (eds), 2nd edn, Cambridge: Cambridge University Press.

—— (1999) *III. The Translation of the Fragments*, trans. I.G. Kidd, Cambridge: Cambridge University Press.

Prior, A.N. (1949) *Logic and the Basis of Ethics*, Oxford: Clarendon Press.

—— (1955) 'Diodoran modalities', *Philosophical Quarterly*, 5: 205–13.

Raphael, D.D. and Macfie, A.L. (1976) 'Introduction' in A. Smith, *Theory of Moral Sentiments*, Indianapolis: Liberty Fund, 1982.

Rubinstein, A. (2000) *Economics and Language*, Cambridge: Cambridge University Press.

Schliesser, E. (2005) 'Wonder in the face of scientific revolutions: Adam Smith on Newton's "proof" of Copernicanism', *British Journal for the History and Philosophy of Science*, 13: 697–732.

—— (2006) 'Adam Smith's benevolent and self-interested conception of philosophy', in *New Voices on Adam Smith*, L. Montes and E. Schliesser (eds), New York: Routledge.

Sextus Empiricus (2005) *Against the Logicians*, trans. R. Bett, Cambridge: Cambridge University Press.

—— (1935) *Against the Logicians*, trans. R.G. Bury, Cambridge: Loeb Classical Library.

—— (1935) *Against the Physicists. Against the Ethicists*, trans. R.G. Bury, Cambridge: Loeb Classical Library.

[Shaftesbury] A., Third Earl of Shaftsbury (2000) [1711] *Characteristicks of Men, Manners, Opinions, Times*, Indianapolis: Liberty Fund.

Smith, A. (1979) [1759] *The Theory of Moral Sentiments*, D.D. Raphael and A.L. Macfie (eds), Oxford: Clarendon Press; reprinted, Liberty Fund (1982).

—— (1979) [1776] *An Inquiry into the Nature and Causes of the Wealth of Nations*, R.H. Campbell, A.S. Skinner and W.B. Todd (eds), Oxford: Clarendon Press, reprinted, Liberty Fund (1982).

—— (1980) [1795] *Essays on Philosophical Subjects*, W.P.D. Wightman and J.C. Bryce (eds), Oxford: Clarendon Press; reprinted, Liberty Press (1982).

—— (1987) [1977] *The Correspondence of Adam Smith*, E.C. Mossner and I. Ross (eds), Oxford Clarendon Press; reprinted, Liberty Classics (1982).

Stigler, G.J. (1960) 'The influence of events and policies on economic theory', *American Economic Review*, 50: 36–45.

—— (1961) 'Private vice and public virtue', *Journal of Law and Economics*, 4: 1–11.

—— (1976) 'The successes and failures of Professor Smith', *Journal of Political Economy*, 84: 1199–1213.

Thorndike, L. (1923–58) *A History of Magic and Experimental Science*, New York: Columbia University Press.

Viner, J. (1927) 'Adam Smith and laissez faire', *Journal of Political Economy,* 35: 198–232.

—— (1972) *The Role of Providence in the Social Order: An Essay in Intellectual History*, Philadephia: American Philosophical Society.

Vivenza, G. (2001) *Adam Smith and the Classics: The Classical Heritage in Adam Smith's Thought*, Oxford: Oxford University Press.

Walker, D.P. (1958) *Spiritual and Demonic Magic: From Ficino to Campanella*, Notre Dame: University of Notre Dame Press.

Waszek, N. (1984) 'Two concepts of morality: a distinction of Adam Smith's ethics and its Stoic origin', *Journal of the History of Ideas*, 45: 591–606.

Style and sentiment

Smith and Swift

Ryan Patrick Hanley

Readers of Smith know that he was sometimes given to hyperbole. One of the most striking instances of such in his corpus is to be found in his ninth rhetoric lecture. Here he claims that when combined, the systems of Jonathan Swift and Lucian form 'a complete system of ridicule'. With Swift satirizing the gay and Lucian the grave, 'both together form a System of morality from whence more sound and just rules of life for all the various characters of men may be drawn than from most set systems of Morality' (Smith 1985, LRBL i.124–25). But this claim raises several questions. First, how did Smith come to shower such praises on a composite 'system of morality' neither of whose elements are mentioned in the review of 'Systems of Moral Philosophy' in Part VII of *The Theory of Moral Sentiments*? Second, even though Smith explains why it is necessary to couple Lucian and Swift (namely so that each might balance out the 'prejudices' characteristic of the other), it is hardly clear, on its face, why he should have recommended either in the first instance. It is this second question that will occupy us here, and specifically with reference to Swift.[1] What did Smith find so compelling in Swift to lead him to make such a pointed recommendation of the Dean?

Some hint might be found in another hyperbolic comment ostensibly made by Smith about Swift – a comment again recorded by an anonymous transcriber. This time the report is given by a 1791 contributor to an Edinburgh literary magazine writing under the pseudonym 'Amicus'. Reporting the details of a conversation said to have occurred eleven years prior, Amicus claims that 'Of Swift, Dr. Smith made frequent and honorable mention', and is said to have affirmed that Swift 'wanted nothing but inclination to have become one of the greatest of all poets'. Yet this extravagance aside, Amicus goes on to report the more substantive claim that Smith 'regarded Swift, both in stile and sentiment, as a pattern of correctness' (cited in LRBL, pp. 228–9).[2] Herein lies, I argue below, the seed of Smith's admiration for Swift. Smith's comments on Swift in LRBL suggest that his admiration is not limited to Swift's style in prose or verse, but extends to the substantive moral sentiments Swift sought to convey and direct by employing such a style. To demonstrate this claim, this essay first examines the comments in LRBL on Swift's style and its relationship to his practical moral project; and then turns to a demonstration of how these same elements manifest themselves in the style and substance of Smith's own practical moralizing, and especially in his treatments of two characteristically Swiftian subjects: the place of pride and vanity in the process of self-assessment, and the relationship of indignation and resentment to justice.

I

Smith's only extended treatment of Swift is to be found in lectures seven and eight of LRBL. The treatment is largely positive throughout. At the start of the lecture course Smith introduced Swift as the writer whose language 'is more English than any other writer we have' (LRBL i.4). Later he would note that 'there is perhaps no writer whose works are more generally read than his, and yet it has been very late, that very few in this country particularly understand his real worth' (LRBL i.100).[3] Smith's explanation for this neglect is itself of interest. Noting that his 'sentiments in Religious matters are not at all suitable to those which for some time past have prevail'd in this country', Smith explains that Swift's under-appreciation owes not to heterodoxy but to orthodoxy; hence his observation that Swift 'never has such warm exclamations for civill or religious liberty as are now generally in fashion' (LRBL i.101). But these conjectures on Swift's neglect aside, what does Smith believe constitutes Swift's 'real worth'?

Smith's assessment of Swift's achievement focuses on his mastery of the 'plain style'. This is the subject of TMS's only substantive reference to Swift, portrayed there as a poetic innovator who replaced the 'quaintness' of Butler with 'plainness' (Smith 1984, TMS V.1.7). But the significance of such plainness does not receive a full explanation until Smith's well-known account of the difference between the plain style and the simple style in LRBL. Both the substance and the methods of this account are of interest to the student of his debts to Swift. The first striking aspect of the account is its departure point: namely the claim that there exists no single archetype of the best or most beautiful style, and the accompanying claim that beauty of style – and the genius of an author – lies in the choice of a fitting style that conforms to the natures of the author, the audience, and the given circumstance (see LRBL i.76–79). The second striking aspect of the account lies in Smith's decision to introduce the distinction between the plain and the simple styles with a consideration of the difference between plain and simple characters – a decision which itself attests to the degree to which Smith shared Swift's conviction that styles and sentiments are inseparable.[4]

Smith begins his comparison of the plain and the simple with the observation that 'no two stiles have a greater connexion than a plain and a simple one, but they are far from being the same' (LRBL i.85). But what then marks the difference? The simple man, he explains, is distinguished not only by the goodness of his heart but by his indifference to 'all the outward marks of civility and breeding that he sees others of a more disingenuous temper generally put on' and his embrace of 'customs that do'nt look affected'. Indeed throughout this portrait of the simple man Smith continually returns to this conjunction of authenticity and humility, emphasizing not only the simple man's 'unaffected modesty' but also his 'diffidence of his own judgement' and 'the diffidence he entertains of his own capacity'. The consequence of such diffidence, we are then told, is that 'contempt never enters into his mind, he is more ready to think well than meanly both of the parts and the conduct of others', and hence is chiefly given to the sentiments of 'admiration and pity' and 'compassion' (LRBL i.88–90). The plain man, in contrast, evinces a subtle twist on the same themes. Like the simple man, he is largely indifferent to 'the common civilities and forms of good breeding', is 'far from affecting any graces or civilities' and 'despises the fashion in every point and neither conforms himself to it in dress, in language, nor manners, but sticks by his own downright ways'. He is, in a word, 'not at all sedulous to please'. Yet it soon becomes clear that the plain man's indifference to affected appearances stems from a much different provenance than the simple man's. The humility characteristic of the latter leads him to be indifferent to vain shows of superiority, but it is rather the pride of the plain man that leads him to despise such external affectation and to embrace in its stead a very different demeanor; 'his confidence in his own superior sense and judgement' and not humility constitutes the root of his indifference, with the result that 'compassion finds little room in his breast; admiration does not at all suit his wisdom; contempt is more agreeable to his selfsufficient imperious temper' (LRBL i.85–87).

The distinction between the plain and the simple, as drawn above, is of central import to an appreciation of Smith's interest in Swift as well as to his own project. First, the central line of demarcation between the simple and the plain man is their orientation towards the opinions of others, with the deference and humility of the simple contrasted with the haughty pride of the plain. This would in time prove to be a principal theme of Smith's own ethics, most obviously in his sketch of the differences between the vain man and the proud man in the sixth (1790) edition of TMS, for which the distinction between the plain and simple man in LRBL can be regarded largely as a preparative. In addition, Smith's contrast between the plain and the simple man would receive a second and even more explicit echo in Part VI of the sixth edition in the portrait there drawn of the archetype of human perfection, the wise and virtuous man. There Smith explains that the wise and virtuous man is characterized by his ability to balance the fact that he is 'sensible of his own superiority' when comparing himself to others with the fact that he is yet 'humbled' when he compares himself to perfection – a combination that produces what Smith calls 'the character of real modesty', and a capacity to resist the proud man's contempt of his inferiors and a corresponding embrace of a desire to 'promote their further advancement' (TMS VI.iii.25). Put differently, the wise and virtuous man, characterized by this dual sense of genuine superiority before the human standard and genuine inferiority before the divine standard, is the perfect amalgamation of the plain and the simple man, and in this respect also reflects one of Smith's most characteristic projects as a theorist of virtue, namely the reconciliation of the seemingly incommensurate virtues of the plain and the simple, the selfish and the other-directed, the awful and the amiable, and ultimately those of Lucian and Swift.

In LRBL, Smith uses the distinction between the simple and the plain to introduce his association of Swift with the literary style corresponding to the plain man, and William Temple with the style of the simple man. In making such an association, he picks up a hint given by Swift himself. In *Gulliver's Travels* we are repeatedly told that its 'Style is very plain and simple' (Swift 1939, PW XI, xxxvii, xxxi; X, 29). This claim is evidence of Swift's awareness of the need to harmonize prose style and intent. And indeed it is this same concept of fittingness that explains Smith's own interest in the use made by Swift of the plain style. Smith considers this style particularly fitting for two reasons. In the first place, Smith admires Swift's style not because it is perfect in itself, but because it is peculiarly appropriate to his character. Smith indeed continually reminds us of his basic rules of style: 'that the expression ought to be suited to the mind of the author' and that the best authors 'did not attempt what they thought was the greatest perfection of stile but that perfection which they thought most suitable to their genius and temper' (LRBL i.79; i.137; cf. i.99).[5] Swift was particularly successful on this front, Smith insists – even as he makes clear that Swift's temper was less than attractive. Thus he frequently calls attention to Swift's 'morose temper' and 'natural moroseness' which 'joined to the constant disappoint- ments and crosses he met with in life would make contempt naturall to his character'. Smith further suggests that Swift might have lacked the proud indifference to such disappointments so characteristic of the plain man; thus his claim that Swift's interest in exposing the follies of the frivolous stemmed precisely from his having repeatedly witnessed 'those that had little else to recommend them not only have some tollerable character and pass thro life with some sort of applause, but even be preferred before himself'. His, in short, was a contempt fueled by 'the reverence he had for his own good sense and judgement which he thought far above that of the common stamp'. Smith's psychobiographical diagnosis of Swift's envy is then the foundation of his claim that Swift's style harmonized with his character, as the characters he exposed 'were those which best suited his taste', namely 'grave men who had any thing of levity or folly in their character', and especially 'those who went about their follies with an air of importance' (LRBL i.118–22).

But Smith also insists that Swift's style is fitting for a second and indeed more important reason. Swift's plain style was not only appropriate to his character, but also to the nature of the project for which he employed it and the character of the audience for which this project was intended. Smith makes this clear in his most significant praise of Swift, which also constitutes one of his most important, if sweeping, indictments of modern moral philosophy:

> The thoughts of most men of genius in this country have of late inclined to abstract and Speculative reasonings which perhaps tend very little to the bettering of our practise. Even the Practicall Sciences of Policticks and Morality or Ethicks have of late been treated too much in a Speculative manner. These studies Swift seems to have been rather entirely ignorant of, or what I am rather inclined to believe, did not hold them to be of great value. His generall character as a plain man would lead him to be of this way of thinking; he would be more inclined to prosecute what was immediately beneficial. Accordingly we find that all his writings are adapted to the present time, either in ridiculing some prevailing vice or folly or exposing some particular character.
>
> (LRBL i.101–2)

Here Smith makes clear why he admires both Swift's style and sentiments: his sentiments are admirable because they are geared towards practical reform, and his style is admirable because, unlike the methods of the moderns, they are well suited to such a project. In this account Smith again picks up a hint from Swift himself. In his account of the quarrel of the ancients and the moderns in the *Battle of the Books*, Swift disparages the moderns, observing that 'being light-headed, they have in Speculation a wonderful Agility, and conceive nothing too high for them to mount; but in reducing them to Practice, discover a mighty Pressure about their Posteriors and their Heels' (PW I, 145). As moralists, both Smith and Swift thus reject the 'generall and abstract speculations' of the moderns and rather hark back to the type of moralizing characteristic of the classical tradition as partially revived by Hutcheson (LRBL i.102). In particular, Smith proved to be sympathetic to Hutcheson's attempt to recover the importance of practical judgment and common sense. And thus with regard to the charge that one of his teachings 'you'll say is no more than common sense', Smith is in wholehearted agreement: 'Indeed it is no more. But if you'll attend to it all the Rules of Criticism and morality when traced to their foundation, turn out to be some Principles of Common Sence which every one assents to; all the business of those arts is to apply these Rules to the different subjects and shew what their conclusion is when they are so applyed' (LRBL i.133).[6] Again, this itself is a Swiftian sentiment, evident from Swift's own observation that politics themselves 'were nothing but common sense' (PW VIII, 77).

Smith is also keen to note a paradoxical effect of Swift's commitment to practical common-sense moralism combined with his utilization of the plain style so that he might communicate to a wider audience. The fact that Swift rejected 'ornaments of language' and instead spoke plain truths in plain language caused him not only to be widely read, but also little admired – or at least not admired to a degree consistent with his genius, Smith thinks (LRBL i.91). Hence his claim that Swift, though 'the plainest as well as the most proper and precise of all the English writers, is despised as nothing out of the common road; each of us thinks he could have wrote as well; And our thoughts of the language give us the same idea of the substance of his writings' (LRBL i.104). This assessment is interesting first for its provenance; here again Smith's judgment seems to take up a hint supplied by Swift, who earlier had made precisely the same point: 'tis certain that all Men of Sense depart from the Opinions commonly received, and are consequently more or less Men of Sense, according as they depart more or less from the Opinions commonly received' (PW IV, 47). But Smith's explanation of the reasons for Swift's neglect also helps to explain one of the most perplexing and least attractive aspects of LRBL, namely the uncharacteristically savage attack that Smith launches on Shaftesbury on the heels of his Swift analysis. The critique of Shaftesbury is notorious for its shallow ad hominems, foremost among them its attack on Shaftesbury's 'very puny and weakly constitution' which ostensibly rendered him too weak for love, ambition, or serious philosophical researches (LRBL i.138). But this far-fetched assessment aside, a substantive point is also being made here. Smith's attempt to dethrone Shaftesbury and his corresponding attempt to reclaim a higher place for Swift are emblematic of his larger project to reorient modern moral discourse to the practical judgments and dispositions of classical morality and the practical methods of plain speech that accompany it. Indeed, even though Smith points out Shaftesbury's debts to Platonism (see LRBL i.145), his error, Smith insists, lies in his having been too modern rather than too ancient. Shaftesbury is thus condemned by Smith for his penchant for both abstract moral theorizing characteristic of the moderns, and then also for his embrace of the convoluted prose characteristic of such an approach; thus Shaftesbury, we are told, is of the sort of authors who are 'so obscure that their meaning is not to be discovered without great attention and being altogether awake' (LRBL i.v.10). Such wakefulness, Smith seems to imply, is unreasonable to expect from audiences of treatises on morality. Swift, however, wrote in a style 'so plain that one half asleep may carry the sense along with him' (LRBL i.10).[7] The methods and the audience of the metaphysician, Smith suggests, must not be confused with the methods and audience of the moralist.

II

Our focus thus far has been on Smith's assessment of Swift's style. But what matters of substance attracted Smith to Swift? That he was attracted to and familiar with Swift's corpus there can be no doubt. From the extant records of his library catalogue we know that Smith owned complete sets of both a ten volume edition of Swift's works of unknown date and publisher and a seventeen volume set published in London in 1784 (Mizuta 2000: 244–45).

Smith also makes a number of direct references to specific writings which suggest demonstrable firsthand knowledge, including to such major works as *Gulliver's Travels* (LRBL i.106), *A Tale of A Tub* (LRBL i.119 and ii.127), the *Treatise on Good Manners and Good Breeding* and *Directions to Servants* (LRBL i.104); to such political essays as *Some Free Thoughts on the Present State of Affairs* (LRBL i.91), *An Answer to a Paper Called a Memorial* (Smith 1981, WN V.ii.k.27), *Short View of the State of Ireland* (Smith 1982, LJA vi.167) and the *Drapier's Letters* (LRBL i.120); and to such poems as 'The Grand Question Debated' (TMS V.i.6), 'On Poetry: A Rhapsody' (LRBL i.v.52), the *Verses to Stella* and the 'Verses on the Death' (both at LRBL 229). On these grounds it seems safe to assume that Smith was reasonably familiar with a broad range of Swift's writings. But what in particular drew him to Swift? Two specific themes seem to have attracted his particular attention: first Swift's practical moralizing related to the theme of self-love; and second, Swift's account of the relationship between indignation and justice with regard to the treatment of others.

Smith presents the grounds of his admiration for Swift's practical moralizing in his account of the aim of comedy. Here he distinguishes legitimate comedy from mere buffoonery. The latter focuses not on characters but on circumstances, whereas 'the only species of Ridicule which is true and genuine wit is that where Real foibles and blemishes in the Characters or behaviour of men are exposed to our view in a ridiculous light. This is altogether consistent with the character of a Gentleman as it tends to the reformation of manners and the benefit of mankind' (LRBL i.v.116). Two aspects of this assessment are striking. The first is its emphasis on exposing hidden vices; true and genuine wit is distinguished from its false impostor on the grounds that it brings to light genuine but concealed faults. The second aspect is its emphasis on the 'gentlemanliness' of this approach on the grounds that it leads to reformation and hence 'the benefit of mankind'. As we shall see, these twin concepts of exposure and reformation constitute the principal elements both of Swiftian moralizing as seen by Smith and of Smith's own moralizing.

Smith's and Swift's shared commitment to exposing moral vices is most evident in their respective treatments of vanity. The fundamental aim of these treatments is to penetrate the false veneer of appearances by exposing the comparatively vulgar and petty sentiments that constitute the genuine motivations of the vain. In this, Smith claims, lies 'the foundation of Ridicule': 'either when what is in most respects Grand or pretends to be so or is expected to be so, has something mean or little in it or when we find something that is realy mean with some pretensions and marks of grandeur' (LRBL i.108). This explains, Smith insists, the effectiveness of Swift's use of the mock heroic. In TMS, Smith cites in this context Swift's poem 'The Grand Question Debated' as an example of how English burlesque verse satirizes French heroic verse (TMS V.1.6). In LRBL he cites *Gulliver's Travels* as a more substantive example, noting especially that the humour of its first two voyages depends on the juxtaposition of the great and the small (LRBL i.109). Indeed, throughout his discussion of ridicule, Smith repeatedly claims that its humour lies in such a 'combination of the Ideas of admiration and contempt' (LRBL i.121; cf. i.107, 110). But at the same time, Smith recognizes that the satirical aim of the motif is not to elicit physical but moral comparisons. Thus again his interest in Swift and Lucian, who both use the trope of comparative juxtaposition to make their point, with Swift employing the type of satire in which 'mean objects are exposed by considering them as Grand', and Lucian the type in which 'Grand ones or such as pretend to or are expected to be so, are ridiculed by exposing the meaness and the littleness which is found in them' (LRBL i.117).

Smith's subsequent analysis of how Swift exposes the mean is revealing for both its account of the substantive targets at which Swift aimed and the methods he employed. Swift's principal target is of course vanity. Swift's satirical writings, Smith thus notes, 'are wrote with a design to ridicule some one of the prevailing gay follies of his Time. They are chiefly levelled against Coxcombs, Beaus, Belles and other characters where gay follies rather than the graver ones prevail' – in a word, 'any that encouraged themselves in employments of no moment or importance of life' (LRBL i.119, 122). Yet such an assessment, while surely right, is more revealing of Smith than of Swift. Smith's own contempt for the coxcomb who squanders his life in frivolous pursuits is every bit as pronounced as Swift's:

> Politeness is so much the virtue of the great, that it will do little honour to any body but themselves. The coxcomb, who imitates their manner, and affects to be eminent by the superior propriety of his ordinary behaviour, is rewarded with a double share of contempt for his folly and presumption. Why should the man, whom nobody thinks it worth while to look at, be very anxious about the manner in which he holds up his head, or disposes of his arms while he walks through a room? He is occupied surely with a very superfluous attention, and with an attention too that marks a sense of his own importance, which no other mortal can go along with.
>
> (TMS I.iii.2.5)

His critique of the coxcomb culminates with a remarkable excoriation of the 'man of rank and distinction' who 'is unwilling to embarrass himself with what can be attended either with difficulty or distress', and consequently prefers an easier path: 'to figure at a ball is his great triumph, and to succeed in an intrigue of gallantry, his highest exploit' (TMS I.iii.2.5). Smith's rhetoric is, to be sure, more earnest than Swift's, yet they agree on the vulgarity of this species of vanity and the need to expose it in plain language in order to disabuse their audiences of a propensity to it.

In addition to vanity, a second species of corrupt self-love is also a favorite target of both Swift and Smith: ambition. Swift's is perhaps the more famous critique. His portraits of court corruptions are a striking aspect of the political satire of *Gulliver's Travels*; readers do not soon forget his sketches of the tightrope-walking and 'leaping and creeping' of the Lilliputian courtiers, the dust-licking of the lords of Luggnagg, and the report given by Gulliver to the Houyhnhnms of the methods used by British ministers to ascend (PW XI, 23, 188–89, 239). But Smith too seeks to impress on his audience the vulgarity of such pursuits:

> In the courts of princes, in the drawing-rooms of the great, where success and preferment depend, not upon the esteem of intelligent and well-informed equals, but upon the fanciful and foolish favour of ignorant, presumptuous, and proud superiors; flattery and falsehood too often prevail over merit and abilities. In such societies the abilities to please, are more regarded than the abilities to serve. . .The external graces, the frivolous accomplishments of that impertinent and foolish thing called a man of fashion, are commonly more admired than the solid and masculine virtues of a warrior, a statesman, a philosopher, or a legislator. All the great and awful virtues, all the virtues which can fit, either for the council, the senate, or the field, are, by the insolent and insignificant flatterers, who commonly figure the most in such corrupted societies, held in the utmost contempt and derision.
>
> (TMS I.iii.3.6)

Swift is the more famous for his ostensible misanthropy, but it is evident that Smith had within his generally sympathetic character some impatience and even contempt for this type. That he wanted to steer his students from its seductions is also clear; hence the most explicit moral admonishment in the whole of TMS. Do you wish to live 'free, fearless, and independent?' Only one path presents itself: 'Never enter the place from which so few have been able to return; never come within the circle of ambition; nor ever bring yourself into comparison with those masters of the earth who have already engrossed the attention of half mankind before you' (TMS I.iii.2.7).

With these substantive comments on vanity and ambition in place, we can begin to discern the thread that unites Smith's various interests in Swift's person, his style, and his sentiments. In sketching Swift's character, Smith calls particular attention to Swift's indifference to appearances and his contempt of fashion; so too in analyzing Swift's plain style, Smith emphasizes Swift's renunciation of the flowery and fashionable for the plain and blunt. But this same lesson lies at the heart of Swift's practical moralizing, according to Smith. The problem with the vain and the ambitious, both thinkers agree, is that they are more concerned with appearances than with the cultivation of authenticity. Indeed the dismantling of such affectation lies at the heart of both of their projects. Hence Smith's own definition of vanity: the foolish liar and the self-aggrandizing coxcomb are pleased with the applause that they expect to claim, but Smith is also quick to say that 'their vanity arises from so gross an illusion of the imagination, that it is difficult to conceive how any rational creature should be imposed upon by it'. The problem that Smith here isolates is that those caught in the grip of vanity are unable to step outside themselves and see themselves for what they are – that is, by seeing themselves as others see them. But this is the only possible remedy:

> They look upon themselves, not in that light in which, they know, they ought to appear to their companions, but in that in which they believe their companions actually look upon them. Their superficial weakness and trivial folly hinder them from ever turning their eyes inwards, or from seeing themselves in that despicable point of view in which their own consciences must tell them that they would appear to every body, if the real truth should ever come to be known.
>
> (TMS III.2.4)

The fundamental problem at issue – namely the self-deception of the vain – was also one of Swift's central concerns. Gulliver tells us it was only through his encounters with the Houyhnhnms that he came to be conscious of 'a thousand faults in my self, whereof I had not the least perception before' (PW XI, 242). In his previous blindness he manifests what Swift takes to be the classic human shortcoming: 'Of such mighty Importance every man is to himself, and ready to think he is so to others; without once making this easy and obvious Reflection; that his Affairs can have no more Weight with other Men, than theirs have with him, and how little that is, he is sensible enough' (PW IV, 89).[8] For both Swift and Smith then, the chief task of the moralist is to assist his audience in the removal of what Smith famously calls 'the mysterious veil of self-delusion' in an attempt to bring individuals to a more modest assessment of their merits via a cultivation of the capacity to see ourselves as others in fact see us. Central to this process is the disassociation of our self-consciousness of our worth from any dependence on the external recognition and verification afforded by the praises of others. Just as the sweating and striving for the praises of others makes the vain miserable, Smith insists, complacent indifference to such struggle constitutes the happiness of the wise man. 'What can be added to the happiness of the man who is in health, who is out of debt, and has a clear conscience? To one in this situation, all accessions of fortune may properly be said to be superfluous' (TMS I.iii.1.7). Indeed, the cultivation of such tranquillity is a chief end of both Swift and Smith; hence Swift's claim that the aim of writing is to increase 'my reader's Repose, both of Body and Mind' – which he immediately calls 'the true ultimate End of Ethics' (PW I, 87). This concern to promote the tranquillity that comes from self-approbation might be the strongest bond that unites Swift and Smith. It can be no accident that Smith chose as his favorite line of Swift's poetry, 'Say, Stella, feel you no content, reflecting on a life well-spent' – a line Smith surely admired as much for its substantive emphasis on self-approbation as for its style (LRBL 229).

III

The previous section emphasized Smith's and Swift's shared commitment to reorienting more dependent forms of self-regard towards a genuinely virtuous and self-sufficient disposition. Similar transformations of base passions into noble virtues are to be found in Smith's and Swift's respective treatments of the relationship of the sentiment of indignation to justice. With regard to justice understood as an individual virtue, both argue that the savage passion of indignation is capable of being transformed into an other-directed sentiment distinguished both by its commitment to justice and by its moderation. And with regard to justice understood as a political virtue, both suggest that just practical political action can be motivated by the feelings of indignation experienced by witnesses to injustice. Indeed the practical political activities of both Smith and Swift themselves – and especially their understandings of the proper ends of political economy – find a common root in their concern for justice, despite their seemingly opposed positions on protectionism and free markets.

Swift's treatment of the relationship of indignation to justice begins with the story of his character. As he famously proclaimed in his epitaph, his ruling passion was the 'savage indignation' that led him to 'serve human liberty'. Smith would have known of this aspect of Swift's character most explicitly from the poem that Amicus says he considered 'the Dean's poetical master-piece': the 'Verses on the Death' (LRBL, p. 229). Among the central aims of the 'Verses' is to show how such a savage passion might be redirected to practical political action.[9] And this would have been an achievement with which Smith likely would have been impressed. In his rhetoric lectures, Smith observes that 'indignation everyone knows is the most irregular of all Passions in its movements', lacking any sort of 'regularity in its cadence' (LRBL i.v.51). In what follows, he admits that Swift himself is 'harsh and unpleasant in many of his compositions', owing to his 'morose humour' (LRBL i.v.52). Yet at the same time, Smith also would have found much to admire in the way in which Swift himself was capable, in other compositions, of using a light touch that defied such moroseness; thus Samuel Fleischacker has noted that Smith often 'emulates this tight-lipped way of conveying moral outrage' so characteristic of Swift (Fleischacker 2004: 4). Indeed it is this moderation that might have particularly attracted Smith to Swift. In the *Tale of a Tub* Swift claims 'zeal' is 'perhaps, the most significant Word that hath been ever yet produced in any language' (PW I, 86). Zeal is particularly troubling insofar as it has largely displaced another 'very good Word, which hath of late suffered much by both Parties, I mean MODERATION' (PW II, 13). Both Smith and Swift recognized the import of moderating the fury of contending parties; Smith himself insists that identified faction is 'by far the greatest' source of corruption (TMS III.3.43; see also WN V.i.f.40). With this in mind, we can assume that Smith would have found much to admire in Swift's claim that 'the truest Service a private Man may hope to do to his Country is by unbiassing his Mind so much as possible, and then endeavouring to moderate between the Rival Powers' (PW II, 2). And it should also be noted that Swift's commitment to moderation extended to reform initiated by philosophers. Swift delighted in critiquing the irrational exuberance of the rational for their favorite projects and schemes (see, for example, PW I, 108), and he repeatedly calls attention to the danger that philosophical reform poses to common life. 'Some Men, under the Notions of weeding out Prejudices, eradicate Religion, Virtue and common Honesty', he observed (PW I, 243). This would in time lead to his ironic decrying of 'the noble effects of Free-thinking' (PW IV, 47). The same sentiment is expressed by Smith in admiring the man who 'respects with an almost religious scrupulosity, all the established decorums and ceremonials of society', and lamenting the baneful effects of those who 'in all ages, from that of Socrates and Aristippus, down to that of Dr. Swift and Voltaire, and from that of Philip and Alexander the Great, down to that of the great Czar Peter of Moscovy, who have too often distinguished themselves by the most improper and even insolent contempt of all the ordinary decorums of life and conversation, and have thereby set the most pernicious example to all those who wish to resemble them' (TMS VI.i.10).

As Smith thus recognized, one of the defining characteristics of Swift's political engagement was his ability to balance the passion of indignation with the trimmer's love of moderation; for Swift, the indignation witnessed upon seeing the suffering did not lead to an equal outpouring of righteous zeal, but to a different form of engagement altogether. This is echoed in Smith's own account of the ways in which indignation leads to justice. The origin of justice, he explains, lies in what he calls 'sympathetic indignation'.[10] His central claim is that lacking the more forceful motive afforded by indignation, sympathy is insufficient to prompt spectators to action. For both Swift and Smith, sympathy is important for establishing social bonds; indeed while Smith is the more famous theorist of sympathy, Swift much earlier observed that 'there is a peculiar String in the Harmony of Human Understanding, which in several individuals is of exactly the same Tuning. This, if you can dexterously screw up to its right Key, and then strike gently upon it; Whenever you have the Good Fortune to light among those of the same Pitch, they will by a secret necessary Sympathy' (PW I, 106; cf. TMS I.i.4.7). But sympathy alone can only elicit sentiments and not actions; thus Smith's claim that nature has implanted in man's breast the more forceful and immediate passion of 'sympathetic indignation':

When we think of the anguish of the sufferers, we take part with them more earnestly against their oppressors; we enter with more eagerness into all their schemes of vengeance, and feel ourselves every moment wreaking, in imagination, upon such violators of the laws of society, that punishment which our sympathetic indignation tells us is due to their crimes. Our sense of the horror and dreadful atrocity of such conduct, the delight which we take in hearing that it was properly punished, the indignation which we feel when it escapes this due retaliation, our whole sense and feeling, in short, of its ill desert, of the propriety and fitness of inflicting evil upon the person who is guilty of it, and of making him grieve in his turn, arises from the sympathetic indignation which naturally boils up in the breast of the spectator, whenever he thoroughly brings home to himself the case of the sufferer.

(TMS II.i.5.6; cf. II.ii.2.1–4)

Herein lies Smith's explanation of the origins of justice as well as his recognition of the limits of sympathy. Sympathy, Smith thinks, is too gentle to be efficacious; what it requires, nature knew, is to be supplemented with a more direct and immediate passion capable of stimulating more direct and immediate action.

The concept of sympathetic indignation also helps to explain the motives behind specific aspects of Smith's and Swift's own practical political interventions. The several treatments of poverty in Swift's political writings provide obvious examples of the ways in which indignation might lead to political action. Throughout his Irish writings, his explicit indignation is manifest; Swift himself introduces his *Short View of the State of Ireland* with the admission that though he has 'been using all Endeavours to subdue my Indignation', he is unable to continue to subdue such passions – and hence his foray into political commentary (PW XII, 5). This same indignation is also expressed elsewhere more subtly; for example we also find elements of this same resentment in Gulliver's report to the Houyhnhnms on the social conditions of Britain: 'The rich Man enjoyed the Fruit of the poor Man's labour, and the latter were a Thousand to One in the Proportion to the former', yet 'the Bulk of our People was forced to live miserably, by labouring every Day for small Wages to make a few live plentifully' (PW XI, 235). In many ways this sounds much like the concluding lines of another text well known to Smith, Rousseau's *Discours sur l'inégalité*, which ends with the famous lament that it is 'manifestly against the Law of Nature' that 'a handful of people abound in superfluities while the starving multitude lacks in necessities' (Rousseau 1997: 188). In any case, it is this observation that led Swift to dedicate a great deal of his practical political energies to the amelioration of the conditions of the Irish poor. Yet here too we might find another reason for Smith's attraction to Swift.

To suggest that Smith and Swift shared much common ground in their thinking on economics will initially come as a surprise. In several respects they seem to represent two opposing poles in the eighteenth-century commercialization debate with regard to the value of luxury, with Swift embracing the traditional doctrine of balance of trade and the republican insistence on autarchic economic self-sufficiency, and Smith clearly arguing against protectionism, famously in his critique of mercantilism in Book IV of the *Wealth of Nations*. Indeed, Swift's oft-repeated warnings against the dangers of corruption at the hands of luxury (see, for example, PW I, 45) seem to directly violate fundamental ideas of Smith, and indeed he directly criticizes Swift's shortsighted critique of free trade and his naïve belief that wealth consists in ready money (LJA vi.167–68; LJB 261–66). But this notwithstanding, there are yet similarities in their economic doctrines. Like Hume, Smith approvingly cites Swift's witticism about the mathematics of custom duties (WN V.ii.k.27; from PW XII, 21). Smith also embraces Swift's main assumption concerning the foundational interdependence of commercial society. Gulliver thus observes that in Britain 'the Bulk of our People supported themselves by furnishing the Necessities and Conveniences of Life to the Rich and to each other. For Instance, when I am at home and dressed as I ought to be, I carry on my Body the Workmanship of a Hundred Tradesmen; the Building and Furniture of my House employ as many more; and five Times the Number to adorn my Wife' (PW XI, 236–7). The concluding castigation of female vanity aside, it is not difficult to hear in Swift's description of economic interdependence Smith's accounts of the interdependence necessary to fabricate the shears of the shepherd and the woolen coat of the labourer (WN I.i.11).[11]

But the most important substantive similarity in their economic thought is to be found in their conceptions of how best to serve the weakest and most vulnerable. Swift made this a principal theme of his political writings, especially with regard to the unjust and oppressive restrictions placed by the British on Irish woollen exportation. These restrictions, Swift insists, owe only to 'the Superiority of meer Power' and directly violate a basic principle of natural justice: that men should be free to trade (PW XII, 8).[12] But Smith takes up this same theme (perhaps directly influenced by his reading of Swift's Irish writings) and indeed does not hesitate to use the language of justice and sympathetic indignation to launch his critique. Thus in his correspondence he insists, with reference to the restrictions governing Irish access to English ports, that 'a very slender interest of our own Manufacturers is the foundation of all of these unjust and oppressive restraints. The watchful jealousy of those Gentlemen is alarmed lest the Irish, who have never been able to supply compleatly even their own market with Glass or Woollen manufacturs, should be able to rival them in forraign Markets'. Smith calls the alternative of free trade a 'most just and reasonable freedom of exportation and importation; in restraining which we seem to me rather to have gratified the impertinence than to have promoted any solid interest of our Merchants and Manufacturers', and goes so far as to insist that he 'should think it madness not to grant' the Irish whatever freedom they desire in this respect (Smith 1987, *Corr.* pp. 243, 242; cf. WN V.iii.72).[13] But Smith's indignation is not limited to the oppression of the Irish by the English, but also focuses on the oppression within Ireland itself, which he describes as 'divided between two hostile nations, the oppressors and the oppressed, the protestants and the Papists' (*Corr.* p. 244). Indeed Smith even defends a union of Ireland with England along the same lines as Scotland's 1707 Act of Union on the grounds that, along with freedom of trade, it might serve to promote the delivery of the weak from the strong:

> By a union with Great Britain, Ireland would gain, besides the freedom of trade, other advantages much more important, and which would much more than compensate any increase of taxes that might accompany that union. By the union with England, the middling and inferior ranks of people in Scotland gained a compleat deliverance from the power of an aristocracy which had always before oppressed them. By an union with Great Britain the greater part of the people of all ranks in Ireland would gain an equally compleat deliverance from a much more oppressive aristocracy; an aristocracy not founded, like that of Scotland, in the natural and respectable distinctions of birth and fortune; but in the most odious of all distinctions, those of religious and political prejudices; distinctions which, more than any other, animate both the insolence of the oppressors and the hatred and indignation of the oppressed, and which commonly render the inhabitants of the same country more hostile to one another than those of different countries ever are. Without a union with Great Britain, the inhabitants of Ireland are not likely for many ages to consider themselves as one people.
>
> (WN V.iii.89)[14]

Even though Swift and Smith arrived at their discussions of free trade with different theoretical commitments, their shared commitment to the amelioration of the condition of the worst off led them to reach the same conclusion with regard to the practical effects of the liberalization of the Anglo-Irish woollen trade, namely an increase in the freedom of the disenfranchised through a 'complete deliverance' from their former dependence on an oppressive aristocracy.

IV

Above I have sought to demonstrate that Smith was chiefly attracted to Swift for his public moralism. Smith several times calls attention to the duty of philosophers to attend to the needs of their fellows (see WN I.ii.4–5; TMS VI.ii.3.6); and so too Swift's oft-repeated mantra that his writings are always intended solely for 'the noblest End, to inform and instruct Mankind' (PW XI, 276–77; cf. I, 23, 77, 117). Moreover, Smith particularly admired Swift's capacity to teach his lessons in a light-handed and satirical manner. Smith's aversion to 'whining and melancholy moralists' is well known, and hence he was likely to have been all the more admiring of Swift's claim that 'as Mankind is now disposed, he receives much greater Advantage by being

Diverted than Instructed' – and hence his efforts to teach by employing 'a Layer of Utile and a Layer of Dulce' (PW I, 77).

At the same time, there is reason to believe that Smith would have balked were Swift too much of a moralist. Some of Smith's strongest theoretical attachments – and specifically his preference for the 'system of natural liberty' and his aversion to 'men of system' – would seem to preclude both his admiration for and his willingness to join the ranks of those who would seek to impose a system of morality on others. But herein lies perhaps the most significant reason for why Smith was particularly attracted to Swift's (and Lucian's) moralism. Unlike most conventional moralists, Swift is able to balance two seemingly opposed ideals. On the one hand, he harboured within his moralism an optimistic vision: 'Whatever Philosopher or Projector can find out an Art to sodder and patch up the Flaws and Imperfections of nature', he observes, 'will deserve much better of Mankind and teach us a more useful Science, than that so much in present esteem, of widening and exposing them' (PW I, 110). Yet this same optimism is tempered by Gulliver's own reflection that it seems universal for moralists to take as their departure point 'the Quarrels we raise with Nature' – a set of quarrels, he insists, that will, 'upon a strict Enquiry', be shown to be 'ill-grounded' (PW XI, 121–2). Put differently, the main moral lesson that both moralists teach is that the disposition to reform nature may itself be unnatural; hence Swift, despite his optimism expressed elsewhere, speaks in his own name when he has Gulliver admit that his once-envisioned project 'to reform the Yahoo race' was itself a 'visionary scheme' that could only have arisen from 'some corruptions of my Yahoo Nature which had been revived in me by Conversing with a few of your species' (PW XI, xxxvi). Less charitable readers of Swift might think this points to an inconsistency. But more likely is the fact that this reflects the unique balance that Swift achieved and Smith admired: the combination of the beneficent man's sincere desire to promote the betterment of his fellows with the modest man's humble realization of the limits of the material with which he works. The result, in each case, is the moralism of a moderate.

Notes

1 Focusing on Swift hardly implies that Smith's interest in Lucian is unworthy of further study. On the contrary, it is striking that that the excellent and thus far most comprehensive study to date of Smith's debts to the classics (Vivenza 2001) does not mention Lucian, in spite of Smith's claim that 'in a word there is no author from whom more reall instruction and good sense can be found than Lucian' (LRBL i.126). The present study focuses on Swift in order to provide an initial remedy for what has been recently described as a conspicuous area of 'unexplored territory' within Smith research (Montes and Schliesser 2006: 5).

2 Amicus's contribution to *The Bee, Or Literary Weekly Intelligencer* of 11 May 1791 is reprinted in LRBL at pp. 228–31.

3 The editor of LRBL has suggested that Smith's homage constitutes 'perhaps the earliest appreciation of Swift as writer'; see Bryce (1985: 16).

4 Thus Smith somewhat defensively claims that 'the consideration of this variety of characters affords us often no small entertainment, it forms one of the chief pleasures of a sociall life, and few are so foolish as to blame it or consider it as any defect' (LRBL i.178–79). Smith's interests in character and characterization have been largely overlooked, but for a helpful remedy to this oversight see especially Bullard (forthcoming).
5 On this point, see Phillips (2006: 67–71), which helpfully illustrates how Smith's study of Swift led him to emphasize the effect on style of an 'author's choice of persona' (69), and how 'literacy structure and moral choice characteristically converge' (71).
6 For important treatments of Smith's commitment to an ethics respectful of common sense or ordinary morality, see especially Griswold (1999) and Fleischacker (2004).
7 Whether in fact Swift's irony is so easily followed as Smith would have it seem is of course a point of considerable debate; see, for instance, the reservations noted in Brown (1994: 15). Smith himself seems to be of two minds in this respect, noting at one point that one can easily miss a word in a Swift sentence and still follow its meaning (LRBL i.10) and at another point suggesting that every word is necessary for an appreciation of the whole (LRBL i.92).
8 Compare to Smith's observation: 'Of such mighty importance does it appear to be, in the imaginations of men, to stand in that situation which sets them most in the view of general sympathy and attention. And thus, place, that great object which divides the wives of aldermen, is the end of half the labours of human life, and is the cause of all the tumult and bustle, all the rapine and injustice, which avarice and ambition have introduced into this world' (TMS I.iii.2.8).
9 I offer an extended explication of the intentions of the 'Verses' in Hanley (2006).
10 For a helpful examination of this relationship, see especially Pack and Schliesser (2006: 60–3). I am also much indebted to Eric Schliesser and Eduardo Velasquez for suggesting to me the similarities between Smith's and Swift's conceptions of justice in this respect.
11 It is interesting to note that Smith's famous passage concerning 'the benevolence of the butcher, the brewer, or the baker' two paragraphs later at WN I.ii.2 is itself presaged by the Drapier's promise, in his first letter, that he will sooner 'truck with my Neighbors the Butchers, and Bakers, and Brewers' than accept Wood's halfpence (PW X, 7).
12 For Swift's claims that free trade is a natural right denied to the Irish, see PW IX, 200; X, 141; XII, 6–8. Also, in addition to his general indignation at the treatment of the Irish by the British, Swift often attests to the personal indignation that he feels on witnessing the miserable spectacle of the destitute native Irish; see for example PW IX, 209; XII, 10f, 136.
13 It is in fact these restrictions on the woollen trade that Smith calls the laws which 'the clamour of our merchants and manufactures has extorted from the legislature, for the support of their own absurd and oppressive monopolies', ending his critique with the claim, worthy of Swift, that 'Like the laws of Draco, these laws may be said to be all written in blood' (WN IV.viii.17).
14 Smith's defence of the advantages of union shares much with Swift's own case for union as presented in his 'Story of the Injured Lady' (see esp. PW IX, 6).

Bibliography

Brown, V. (1994) *Adam Smith's Discourse: Canonicity, Commerce and Conscience*, London: Routledge.

Bryce, J.C. (1985) 'Introduction', Adam Smith, *Lectures on Rhetoric and Belles Lettres*, Indianapolis: Liberty Fund.

Bullard, P. ' "Physiognomy of the mind": conceptions of character from the Augustans to Adam Smith', unpublished manuscript.

Fleischacker, S. (2004) *On Adam Smith's* Wealth of Nations*: A Philosophical Companion*, Princeton: Princeton University Press.

Griswold, C.L. (1999) *Adam Smith and the Virtues of Enlightenment*, Cambridge: Cambridge University Press.

Hanley, R.P. (2006) 'Swift sailing', in *Enlightening Revolutions: Essays in Honor of Ralph Lerner*, Svetozar Minkov (ed.), Lanham, Maryland: Lexington.

Montes, L. and Schliesser, E. (eds) (2006) *New Voices on Adam Smith*, London: Routledge.

Mizuta, H. (2000) *Adam Smith's Library: A Catalogue*, Oxford: Oxford University Press.

Pack, S. and Schliesser, E. (2006) 'Adam Smith's "Humean" criticism of Hume's account of the origin of justice', *Journal of the History of Philosophy*, 44: 47–63.

Phillips, M.S. (2006) 'Adam Smith, belletrist', in *The Cambridge Companion to Adam Smith*, K. Haakoussen (ed.), Cambridge: Cambridge University Press.

Rousseau, J.-J. (1997) [1755] *Discourse on the Origins of Inequality*, in *The* Discourses *and Other Early Political Writings*, Victor Gourevitch (ed.), Cambridge: Cambridge University Press.

Smith, A. (1981) *An Inquiry into the Nature and Causes of the Wealth of Nations*, R.H. Campbell and A.S. Skinner (eds), Indianapolis: Liberty Fund.

—— (1982) *Lectures on Jurisprudence*, R.L. Meek, D.D. Raphael and P.G. Stein (eds), Indianapolis: Liberty Fund.

—— (1984) *The Theory of Moral Sentiments*, D.D. Raphael and A.L. Macfie (eds), Indianapolis: Liberty Fund.

—— (1985) *Lectures on Rhetoric and Belles Lettres*, J.C. Bryce (ed.), Indianapolis: Liberty Fund.

—— (1987) *Correspondence of Adam Smith*, E.C. Mossner and I.S. Ross (ed.), Indianapolis: Liberty Fund.

Swift, J. (1939) *The Prose Works of Jonathan Swift*, Herbert Davis (ed.), 12 vols, Oxford: Basil Blackwell.

Vivenza, G. (2001) *Adam Smith and the Classics: The Classical Heritage in Adam Smith's Thought*, Oxford: Oxford University Press.

Shaftesbury's evolutionary morality and its influence on Adam Smith

James R. Otteson

During the Scottish Enlightenment, philosophers like David Hume, Adam Smith and Adam Ferguson developed spontaneous-order or 'market' models for understanding large-scale human social institutions like law, language and morality (Hamowy 1987). For these Scots, and for Adam Smith in particular, these models served two principal purposes: explanation and strategy. They explained, first, where such institutions came from, how they developed over time, and what their stages of development were. They also served as bases for policy recommendations: once knowledge of the nature of such institutions could be coupled with knowledge of relatively stable human nature, strategies for realizing human ends could be developed.

A large part of the sociological projects these Scots undertook was in some way or another a reaction to Hobbes. For it was Hobbes who so brilliantly articulated and choreographed all the false positions on human nature, on the nature of human society, and on proper politics. Hobbes, they thought, argued that human beings are always narrowly self-interested, when they are not; Hobbes argued that human social life is made of inescapable Prisoner's-Dilemma-type social action problems, when it is not; and Hobbes argued that what is required to rescue us from the natural state of war resulting from the Prisoner's Dilemmas was a tyrannical state, when it is not. The central challenge Hobbes, or Hobbesianism, posed was thus to human sociality: Are human beings naturally inclined to form peaceable social groups – or not? People like Smith and Hume thought Hobbes was wrong about human sociality, despite the evident violence in the world. Their task, then, was to show what human nature really was and how human social institutions really work to explain why most of human life is indeed made up of peaceable social interactions, occasional (and recurring) violent outbreaks to the contrary notwithstanding. If in the process some institutional policies could be discovered that would help encourage the peaceable and discourage the violent aspects of humanity, then strategies for improving human life could be developed.

Of the Scots working in these areas, Adam Smith's market model was the most sophisticated (Otteson 2002). Although Smith built on the work of contemporaries or near contemporaries like Gershom Carmichael, Francis

Hutcheson, Lord Kames, and David Hume, it is not widely appreciated how he, as well as other figures of the Scottish Enlightenment, drew on the earlier work of Anthony Ashley Cooper, Third Earl of Shaftesbury (1671–1713). In this paper I will narrow the focus. I propose to lay out and reconstruct some of the central elements of Shaftesbury's thought that found their way, usually without attribution, into the arguments Smith developed to answer the Hobbesian challenge and to develop his own alternative accounts of natural human social institutions. Let us begin, then, by looking at Shaftesbury.

Shaftesbury on the origins of 'politeness' and moral order

One of the central works that was widely read by the learned and lay audiences in the eighteenth century was Shaftesbury's *Characteristicks of Men, Manners, Opinions, Times*, first published in 1711. *Characteristicks* is a relatively long work made up of several joltingly different pieces, so it is hard to take in, let alone assess, as a whole. Yet its influence can be seen in the several ideas, and in some cases the actual words and phrasings, from the work that find their way into the works of the Scots, including Adam Smith. With the exception of one section of this work, namely the *Inquiry Concerning Virtue or Merit*, Shaftesbury's *Characteristicks* is not a systematic treatise and does not usually develop arguments in stepwise or straightforwardly 'philosophical' fashion. Shaftesbury himself recognizes this. Referring to himself in the third person, he says, for example, that 'he does not, in his own model and principal performance, attempt to unite his philosophy in one solid and uniform body nor carry on his argument in one continued chain or thread' (Shaftesbury 1999: 459).[1] That underscores the difficulties in interpretation, but it does not mean that there is no philosophy in Shaftesbury's work, or that his conclusions did not become part of the moral and political repertoire exploited by later philosophers.[2]

Let us look first at Shaftesbury's conception of the origins and nature of moral order. The central passage with which to begin comes from *Sensus Communis, an Essay on the Freedom of Wit and Humour*. In it Shaftesbury is concerned to defend a robust freedom of speech, defending in particular 'raillery' even regarding sensitive topics like religion. Shaftesbury argues that the vigorous clash of thoughts and opinions – including 'wit', which, according to Shaftesbury, is higher than 'burlesque' and 'buffoonery' – is the surest means of both discovering truth and polishing manners. He is quite aware of the potential dangers his opponents anticipate if we all are allowed to 'make as free with our own opinions as with those of other people' (29): in particular, the truth might get lost amidst a sea of falsehood, and our manners and civility might descend to mere 'scurrilous buffoonery' (31). Yet, Shaftesbury writes, 'Truth, it is supposed, may bear *all* lights, and one of those principal lights, or natural mediums, by which things are to be viewed, in order to a thorough recognition, is ridicule itself, or that manner of proof by which we discern whatever is liable to just raillery in any subject' (30).

Shaftesbury acknowledges, however, that 'It is real humanity and kindness to hide strong truths from tender eyes', and that indeed 'we can never do more injury to truth than by discovering too much of it on some occasions' (30). But Shaftesbury's claim is that on those occasions when 'strong truths' should be either hidden altogether or revealed only slowly or piecemeal, one should not effect this restraint either by 'harsh denial or remarkable reserve'; instead, doing so 'by a pleasant amusement is easier and civiller' (30). Whom does Shaftesbury have in mind when he speaks of the necessity of shielding them from 'strong truths'? He might have in mind the young, as suggested by the phrase 'tender eyes'. But his continuing argument suggests he also has some adults in mind, perhaps in particular those who have strong, even dogmatic, beliefs that an interlocutor like Shaftesbury might like to question and who also have a strong, and humourless, attachment to them. That would not make their eyes 'tender', but it might make them prickly and easily upset, which can have the same effect and thus require the same delicacy. It is indeed especially for such people that Shaftesbury recommends the use of humour in beginning a conversation: like few other things, a shared chuckle can ease a person's grip on his dogmatically held beliefs and uncover a jointly shared humanity.

Now of course one can take humour too far: if one makes light of *everything,* others will be left guessing as to what one's actual views are, and they may be put off by the complete lack of seriousness. Thus Shaftesbury distinguishes between, on the one hand, the humane and kind humour he recommends, and, on the other, 'that gross sort of raillery which is so offensive in good company' (31). He continues: 'And indeed there is as much difference between one sort and another as between fair dealing and hypocrisy, or between the genteelest wit and the most scurrilous buffoonery'. Here is Shaftesbury's recommendation:

> But by freedom of conversation, this illiberal kind of wit will lose its credit. For wit is its own remedy. Liberty and commerce bring it to its true standard. The only danger is laying an embargo. The same thing happens here as in the case of trade. Impositions and restrictions reduce it to a low ebb. Nothing is so advantageous to it as a free port.
>
> (Shaftesbury 1999: 31)

A number of questions arise at this point. How are we to know when to disclose 'strong truths' and when to hide them, and to whom to expose them and whom to protect? How exactly are we to distinguish the 'scurrilous buffoonery' from 'the genteelest wit'? Shaftesbury seems to presume that we have the judgment to answer these questions, and we probably do. But that immediately raises another, and perhaps more important, question: what is the mechanism that produces shared or common judgments respecting these matters? Moreover, how are we to encourage in others proper – and properly edifying – humour while discouraging humour of the improper sort? Here is Shaftesbury's answer, perhaps the central passage from *Sensus Communis* on this point:

> And thus, in other respects, wit will mend upon our hands and humour will refine itself, if we take care not to tamper with it and bring it under constraint by severe usage and rigorous prescriptions. All politeness is owing to liberty. We polish one another and rub off our corners and rough sides by a sort of amicable collision. To restrain this is inevitably to bring a rust upon men's understandings. It is a destroying of civility, good breeding and even charity itself, under pretence of maintaining it.
>
> (Shaftesbury 1999: 31)

The way to answer the questions raised above, according to Shaftesbury, is to employ good judgment in the particular situations in which people find themselves.[3] That is what he means by 'men's understandings', which, Shaftesbury believes, prior rules and restrictions weaken rather than strengthen. He is withering in his indictment of such prior restrictions in the form of official or unofficial speech codes:

> Nor is it a wonder that men are generally such faint reasoners and care so little to argue strictly on any trivial subject in company, when they dare so little exert their reason in greater matters and are forced to argue lamely where they have need of the greatest activity and strength. The same thing therefore happens here as in strong and healthy bodies which are debarred their natural exercise and confined in a narrow space. They are forced to use odd gestures and contortions. They have a sort of action and move still, though with the worst grace imaginable. For the animal spirits in such sound and active limbs cannot lie dead or without employment. And thus the natural free spirits of ingenious men, if imprisoned and controlled, will find out other ways of motion to relieve themselves in their constraint and, whether it be in burlesque, mimicry or buffoonery, they will be glad at any rate to vent themselves and be revenged on their constrainers.
>
> (Shaftesbury 1999: 34)

Such humour, however, does not engage the understanding of its auditors the way 'wit' does, because it tends either merely to offend them or 'confound' them because of its 'mysterious manner' (30). The solution, according to Shaftesbury, is not, however, to restrict conversation to only those topics that have been antecedently approved (by someone), but, rather, to remove all restrictions on what topics may be discussed, and let the clash of opinions and ideas that results give rise to the invigorated understandings, and then ultimately to the politeness and polished manners, that we seek.

'A free conference is a close fight' (34), writes Shaftesbury, but it is an intellectual fight that leaves people in a mutual state of 'pleasantry and humour' (35). On the contrary, previously vetted orations or declamations are:

> merely a brandishing or beating the air. To be obstructed therefore and manacled in conferences and to be confined to hear orations on certain subjects must needs give us a distaste and render the subject so managed and disagreeable as the managers. Men had rather reason upon trifles, so they may reason freely and without the imposition of authority, than on the usefullest and best subjects in the world, where they are held under a restraint and fear.
>
> (Shaftesbury 1999: 34)

The recommendation, therefore, is to allow complete freedom of discussion, on the grounds that that will invigorate our understandings, uncover truth, provide a beneficial exercise of our capacities of reasoning and proper raillery, and in the end polish our manners and encourage a high form of politeness. Thus this 'collision' and subsequent 'polishing' indicate Shaftesbury's conception of both the origin and nature of moral orders: they arise from the clashing of competing goals and purposes and are patterns of behaviour that help people to cooperate to satisfy their wants. But Shaftesbury has not yet given us a complete picture, for he has omitted the crucial element: *how* does freedom do all these things? Douglas J. Den Uyl tells us that 'Shaftesbury was clearly one of the first to see how a "marketplace of ideas" could function to promote truth and the reformation of character' (Klein 1994, ch. 10; Den Uyl 1998: 314), and it seems right to suggest that Shaftesbury had this belief: but stating that one thing leads to another does not, even if true, explain how or why it does so. What is the mechanism that the Shaftesburian 'marketplace of ideas' creates or allows or constitutes that can generate the desirable consequences? Whatever one's sympathies for the robust freedom of speech Shaftesbury endorses, the account is incomplete, and thus the recommendation unconvincing, without an explanation of the putative mechanism at work. What does Shaftesbury offer us in this regard?

The missing mechanism

Unfortunately, Shaftesbury does not address this question squarely. Another of Shaftesbury's central contentions in *Sensus Communis* allows us, however, to elaborate a Shaftesburian argument about clashes of opinions producing politeness. Shaftesbury believes that there is something objectively good, or 'intrinsically worthy' (56), about virtue, and that there is a union between individual virtue and the public good. Thus, Shaftesbury tells us, 'There is no real love of virtue without the knowledge of public good' (50). I shall return momentarily to the notion of 'intrinsic goodness', but here I would indicate a different conclusion Shaftesbury draws from these premises, namely that in the state of nature not only would the virtues themselves still have meaning and 'intrinsic worth' but individuals in that state would also recognize them as such. He writes, 'Thus faith, justice, honesty and virtue must have been as early in the state of nature or they could never have been at all' (51); and he concludes: 'The natural knave has the same reason to be a civil one and may dispense with his politic capacity as often as he sees occasion' (ibid.). These passages appear in one of the many places Shaftesbury disputes, explicitly or implicitly, part of the Hobbesian argument. His specific point here goes on to become a commonplace among anti-Hobbesians, namely the *reductio* argument that if every man had been an enemy to every man in the state of nature, then no society could have ever developed. That is a fair point against Hobbes, but what are Shaftesbury's reasons for thinking that indeed people would recognize and respond to the standard list of virtues even outside any formally imposed state? The answer requires some construction to see.

On the one hand, Shaftesbury suggests that all human beings recognize the virtues as virtues because of their (the virtues') intrinsic merit and natural beauty. 'And thus, after all', says Shaftesbury, 'the most natural beauty in the world is honesty and moral truth. For all beauty is truth' (65); 'Some moral and philosophical truths are, withal, so evident in themselves, that it would be easier to imagine half mankind to have run mad and joined precisely in one and the same species of folly, than to admit anything as truth which should be advanced against such natural knowledge, fundamental reason and common sense' (68). The repeated insistence on the 'naturalness' and obviousness of this moral knowledge reflects Shaftesbury's belief that *akrasia,* or weakness of will, is impossible: once one knows what morality requires or once one recognizes the (moral) beauty in virtue, one therefore strives to achieve it. No intermediary step is required. As he argues in the *Letter Concerning Enthusiasm*:

> It is not the same with goodness as with other qualities, which we may understand very well and yet not possess. We may have an excellent ear in music without being able to perform in any kind. We may judge well of poetry without being poets or possessing the least of a poetic vein. But we can have no tolerable notion of goodness without being tolerably good.
>
> (Shaftesbury 1999: 22)

Yet on the other hand, it seems Shaftesbury's argument *should* be that interaction with others triggers in people an attempt to discover and then follow rules of behaviour that lead to successful personal relationships and exchanges. He even suggests in places that the bundle of moral judgments that arise in this way are amoral – that is, neither good nor bad in themselves, only useful or not according to whether they do in fact conduce to mutually beneficial social interaction. He writes in the *Inquiry,* for example, 'Whatsoever therefore is done which happens to be advantageous to the species through an affection merely towards self-good, does not imply any more goodness in the creature than as the affection itself is good' (171). This passage and those surrounding it have distinct Scottish 'spontaneous-order' overtones, to which I shall return. If Shaftesbury's response to Hobbesianism here, however, is that the virtues are transcendently fixed and intrinsically good, and recognized or apprehended by people as such, then it is not clear why the freedom to 'polish' our morals that results from the negotiation that takes place in competitive market-like social interactions is necessary. Why should people have extensive individual freedom, for speech or indeed for anything else, since (an objector might claim) open-ended and totally free clashing might result in any number of false, unproductive, or even counter-productive behavioural patterns? On the other hand, once moral virtue – *true* moral virtue – has been discovered, why not encourage or enforce it, or at the very least limit the freewheeling 'collision' so that it has a higher probability of leading to what we already know is true virtue? In other words, why leave things to a market-like process and just hope it 'spontaneously' arrives at what we already know?

A separate but related question is whether there might not be some other, better way to encourage people to develop virtue and proper politeness. That is, even if we concede to Shaftesbury that freedom and the unfettered marketplace of ideas and behaviours can lead *both* to the discovery of truth and virtue *and* to the more widespread belief in true ideas and recognition and pursuit of virtue, Shaftesbury would still have to show us that the marketplace is the best means, or at least a better means, of effecting these desirable ends than other possible means. After all, perhaps a Hobbesian method of establishing an absolute leviathan (or, for that matter, the Rousseauvian recommendation to empower a censor to properly superintend citizens' morals [Rousseau 1988, 4.7]) would turn out in fact to be a more effective means of realizing society-wide virtue than letting each individual discover it – or not – as he goes about his daily business.

Virtue and goodness: historical and evolutionary, or intrinsic and transcendent?

The contention that virtue has some intrinsic goodness seems to conflict with the 'spontaneous-order' view that morality is an unintended result of individuals interacting with only local aims in view. I believe that Shaftesbury is in fact deeply divided on this issue, though it is not clear he fully appreciates the tension.

On one side of this divide, his conception of manners and politeness being the result of market-like, 'polishing' forces extends through a surprising number of details. First, he has clear suggestions of a marketplace of morals, the unintentional creation of moral habits as a result of free interchanges among people; here is one example: 'It is the habit alone of reasoning which can make a reasoner. And men can never be better invited to the habit than when they find pleasure in it. A freedom of raillery, a liberty in decent language to question everything, and an allowance of unravelling or refuting any argument without offence to the arguer, are the only terms which can render such speculative conversations any way agreeable' (33).[4] Shaftesbury also acknowledges the existence both of overall systems of orders and of smaller suborders: although one set of rules applies to 'the freedom of *public* assemblies' (my emphasis), nevertheless:

> as to *private* society and what passes in select companies, where friends meet knowingly and with that very design of exercising their wit and looking freely into all subjects, I see no pretence for anyone to be offended at the way of raillery and humour, which is the very life of such conversations, the only thing which makes good company and frees it from the formality of business and the tutorage and dogmaticalness of the Schools.
>
> (Shaftesbury 1999: 36–7; my emphasis)[5]

Shaftesbury furthermore acknowledges the distinction between public or general goods and individuals' own private goods: 'We know that every creature has a private good and interest of his own' (167).[6] And he repeatedly argues for a connection between liberty and civilization, and the dependence of the latter on the former:

> Nothing therefore could have been the cause of these public decrees, and of this gradual reform in the commonwealth of wit, beside the real reform of taste and humour in the commonwealth or government itself. Instead of any abridgement, it was in reality an increase of liberty, an enlargement of the security of property, and an advancement of private ease and personal safety, to provide against what was injurious to the good name and reputation of every citizen.
>
> (112)

Further on the same point:

> But where persuasion was the chief means of guiding the society, where the people were to be convinced before they acted, there elocution became considerable, there orators and bards were heard, and the chief geniuses and sages of the nation betook themselves to the study of those arts by which the people were rendered more treatable in a way of reason and understanding, and more subject to be led by men of science and erudition. [. . .] Hence it is that those arts have been delivered to us in such perfection by free nations, who, from the nature of their government as from a proper soil, produced the generous plants, while the mightiest

bodies and vastest empires, governed by force and a despotic power, could, after ages of peace and leisure, produce no other than what was deformed and barbarous of the kind.

(Shaftesbury 1999: 107)[7]

Perhaps most strikingly, Shaftesbury anticipates Smithian invisible-hand explanations of selected social phenomena, based on a conception of natural human motivation, which would go on to become typical of the Scots, that holds that human nature is comprised of a combination of self-interest and other motives. Consider, for example, his account in *Sensus Communis* of the gradual and unintentional origins of communities from 'that affection which is between the sexes':

[this affection] is certainly as natural towards the consequent offspring and so again between the offspring themselves, as kindred and companions, bred under the same discipline and economy. And thus a clan or tribe is gradually formed, a public is recognized, and, besides the pleasure found in social entertainment, language and discourse, there is so apparent a necessity for continuing this good correspondency and union that to have no sense or feeling of this kind, no love of country, community or anything in common, would be the same as to be insensible even of the plainest means of self-preservation and most necessary condition of self-enjoyment.

How the wit of man should so puzzle this cause as to make civil government and society appear a kind of invention and creature of art, I know not. For my own part, methinks, this herding principle and associating inclination is seen so natural and strong in most men, that one might readily affirm it was even from the violence of this passion that so much disorder arose in the general society of mankind.

(Shaftesbury 1999: 51–2)

Packed into this one extraordinary passage is an impressive proportion of the required elements of a spontaneous-order explanation. There is a natural affection among people who know one another and interact regularly; there is a 'pleasure' in the 'union' or 'correspondency' of social entertainment (one might almost call it the Smithian 'pleasure of mutual sympathy of sentiments');[8] there is the gradual and unintentional growth of macro-order – 'society' and 'civil government' – from these micro-motives;[9] and there is even the characteristically Smithian consternation about the mistake of assuming human social institutions could only have been formed by rational deliberation.[10] Immediately after this passage, Shaftesbury writes, 'Universal good, or the interest of the world in general, is a kind of remote philosophical object. That greater community falls not easily under the eye. Nor is a national interest or that of a whole people or body politic so readily apprehended. In less parties, men may be intimately conversant and acquainted with one another' (52). In other words, individuals know their own peculiar, local situations better than they do either the situations of others or the situations of society as a whole; moreover, no one, regardless of his pretensions to the contrary, is able to stand outside the entire social order and survey it from afar – this 'greater community falls not easily under the eye'. Therefore (we can almost hear Shaftesbury concluding with Smith), they should be left free to regulate their own behaviours in their search to realize their private goods.

And Shaftesbury does indeed seem to believe in private goods, even if he does also seem to believe in a 'universal good' of all society. In the *Inquiry*, Shaftesbury writes:

> We know that every creature has a private good and interest of his own, which nature has compelled him to seek by all the advantages afforded him within the compass of his make. We know that there is in reality a right and wrong state of every creature, and that his right one is by nature forwarded and by himself affectionately sought.
>
> (Shaftesbury 1999: 167)[11]

The argument of this passage suggests that we should declass Shaftesbury's account, taking it even further from the transcendent and eternal to the terrestrial and local, which thereby brings it yet closer to Smith's account. The 'private good' of 'every creature', according to Shaftesbury here, is based on the individual creature's peculiar constitution: 'There being therefore in every creature a certain interest or good, there must also be a certain end to which everything in his constitution must naturally refer' (167). In what sense, then, can Shaftesbury here speak of there being 'in reality a right and wrong state of every creature', that is, an *objectively* right or wrong state? Precisely in the sense that individual creatures have actual natures – and, we might add, actual circumstances – that fix and determine their respective goods. So although one creature's good might well be distinct from another's – indeed, conceivably every single creature's good might be unique – nevertheless no given individual's good is arbitrary or changeable at the discretion or whim of the creature itself (or himself) or of any other creature. Thus we have an instance of what one might call *middle-way objectivity:* not transcendently or eternally fixed, but not arbitrary or subjectively relative either; rather, based on the facts of one's, and one's community's, actual material existence.[12]

Shaftesbury's insistence on individual freedom, in particular freedom of speech (consider again his repeated condemnations of speech codes[13]), also seems to be premised on an unstated argument like that indicated above about the market-like negotiation required to uncover and give rise to 'proper' moral attitudes, to politeness, to the discovery of truth, and indeed to civilization itself. This allows us to complete our construction of a Shaftesburian answer to the question raised earlier about the grounds on which Shaftesbury might claim that marketplaces of ideas, words, and behaviours are the best means for achieving virtue, or at least better means than Hobbesian centralized coercion. The argument would turn on the 'natural affection' Shaftesbury believes we have for one another, and what we can assume is the displeasure associated with being spurned or rejected in our affective overtures. We seek this affection in various aspects of our lives, and the search for it helps us to discover ideas, words, and behaviours that realize it. Built into this argument must be, perhaps contrary to other, rosier things Shaftesbury says about human nature, a claim about ineluctable human failings: either our ignorance of the true and the good, our inability to believe or follow them when discovered, or both. The latter of these possibilities would conflict with Shaftesbury's argument against the existence of *akrasia,* which means, perhaps, that Shaftesbury would argue the former. Regardless, both these claims would be addressed by the marketplace argument: it provides the medium through which both truths and good behaviours can be discovered, and it operates on the basis of natural incentives we would feel to seek them out.

Shaftesbury in at least one place seems to recognize, though obliquely, that he has not expressly specified the full explanatory mechanism. In *The Moralists, a Philosophical Rhapsody,* Shaftesbury has the following exchange take place between the interlocutors of this dialogue (the 'he' is the character Theocles; he is addressing the dialogue's other main character, Philocles):

> 'And when you', replied he, 'with your newly espoused system, have brought all things to be as uniform, plain, regular, and simple as you could wish, I suppose you will send your disciple to seek for deity in mechanism, that is to say, in some exquisite system of self-governed matter. For what else is it your naturalists make of the world than a mere machine'?
>
> (Shaftesbury 1999: II.5: 295)

Shaftesbury uses this obvious contempt for 'mechanical' explanations to introduce a conversation about evidence of intelligent design in the world and its connection to justified belief in God. The details of that conversation do not concern us here, but the philosophical point buried in Theocles' objection above does. For even if Shaftesbury does not identify with all of Theocles' position, I suspect this exchange nevertheless reveals Shaftesbury's awareness that it is in fact possible to give an account of perceived order by reference merely to an 'exquisite [mechanical] system of self-governed matter'. Yet the system does not in reality need to be 'exquisite' in its principles (though it may be in its ramifications): at bottom all that are required are principles motivating the actors in the system and a regular mechanism of selection, or relatively consistent selective rewards and punishments, of actions. Shaftesbury's claim about our disparate opinions clashing with one another and polishing our manners is a description of what the results of precisely such a self-organizing system can accomplish. If Shaftesbury has not investigated the requirements of such a system or does not quite see how such an explanation might proceed – indeed, if he in *Moralists* and perhaps elsewhere is sceptical about the prospects of such an explanation – he has still described some of the crucial elements and laid the groundwork for later investigation.

One final proto-Smithian detail: several passages suggest Shaftesbury's belief in or expectation that individual, private interests either do, or may well, unintentionally unite in a kind of harmony with the good of all. For example, in *Sensus Communis*, he writes that the 'affection which is between the sexes' leads naturally to community:

> And thus a clan or tribe is gradually formed, a public is recognized, and, besides the pleasure found in social entertainment, language and discourse, there is so apparent a necessity for continuing this *good correspondency and union* that to have no sense or feeling of this kind, no love of country, community or anything in common, would be the same as to be insensible even of the plainest means of self-preservation and most necessary condition of self-enjoyment.
>
> (Shaftesbury 1999: 51–2; italics supplied)

Shaftesbury's suggestion here is that because the larger community forms, gradually and unintentionally, out of the family and ultimately out of the union between men and women, their interests must at least partly harmonize. Later, in the *Inquiry Concerning Virtue or Merit,* Shaftesbury repeats a similar sentiment:

> Now if, by the natural constitution of any rational creature, the same irregularities of appetite which make him ill to others make him ill also to himself, and if the same regularity of affections which causes him to be good in one sense causes him to be good also in the other, then it is that goodness by which he is thus useful to others a real good and advantage to himself. And thus virtue and interest may be found at last to agree.
>
> (Shaftesbury 1999: 167)

In this case Shaftesbury discovers the unity in the reverse direction: what is good for the community will also be good for the individual, because of the former's dependence on the latter. One final passage reinforces the point. In *Moralists*, Shaftesbury writes: '*In short, if generation be natural, if natural affection and the care and nurture of the offspring be natural, things standing as they do with man and the creature being of that form and constitution he now is, it follows that society must be also natural to him and that out of society and community he never did, nor ever can, subsist*'

(287; Shaftesbury's italics). In this passage the connection is a bit more remote, since Shaftesbury's main point here is that human beings are inherently social. But Shaftesbury's repeated suggestion that there is an overlap or even union between individual interests and those of the larger community seems a precursor to the influential invisible-hand argument Smith will make some sixty years later, and a key part of an 'evolutionary' account of human social orders.

On the other side of the historical-and-evolutionary vs eternally-fixed-and-transcendent divide for Shaftesbury is his claim that the rules of morality, or at least the content of the moral virtues, enjoy an objectivity that transcends the 'middle-way' objectivity I have suggested Shaftesbury's position provides for. Shaftesbury introduces the idea in *Sensus Communis* rather gingerly:

> As for morals, the difference, if possible, was still wider. For without considering the opinions and customs of the many barbarous and illiterate nations, we saw that even the few who had attained to riper letters and to philosophy could never as yet agree on one and the same system or acknowledge the same moral principles. And some even of our most admired modern philosophers had fairly told us that virtue and vice had, after all, no other law or measure than mere fashion and vogue.
>
> (Shaftesbury 1999: 38)

This passage leaves open whether in fact there is some measure other than 'mere fashion and vogue', but Shaftesbury does not leave this an open question for long. In *Soliloquy*, he writes, 'Could we once convince ourselves of what is in itself so evident, that in the very nature of things there must of necessity be the foundation of a right and wrong taste, as well in the respect of inward characters and features as of outward person, behaviour and action, we should be far more ashamed of ignorance and wrong judgment in the former than in the latter of these subjects' (150). In *Miscellany III*, Shaftesbury writes: 'Let us therefore proceed in this view, addressing ourselves to the grown youth of our polite world. Let the appeal be to these whose relish is retrievable and whose taste may yet be formed in morals as it seems to be already in exterior manners and behaviour. That there is really *a standard* of this latter kind will immediately and on the first view be acknowledged' (414). In addition to reiterating Shaftesbury's belief in a moral standard that is apparently fixed because 'in the nature of things', this passage squares with his contention that morality is consistent with, or perhaps identical to, truth, and that there is little or no possibility of *akrasia*. In the *Inquiry* Shaftesbury makes this connection explicit:

> And thus we find how far worth and virtue depend on a knowledge of right and wrong and on a use of reason sufficient to secure a right application of the affections [. . .]. And thus if there be anything which

teaches men either treachery, ingratitude or cruelty [. . .] this is not nor ever can be virtue of any kind or in any sense but must remain still horrid depravity, notwithstanding any fashion, law, custom or religion which may be ill and vicious itself but can never alter *the eternal measures and immutable independent nature of worth and virtue.*

(Shaftesbury 1999: 175)

That final point, the one relevant here, Shaftesbury was kind enough to italicize for us: how, one might ask, could morality be the result of evolutionary, historical, and thus contingent processes, if the 'measures' of 'worth and virtue' are both eternal and immutable?

Shaftesbury is usually thought to be in the 'moral sense' school of moral philosophy, a school founded, or at least paradigmatically exemplified, by Francis Hutcheson. The view that Shaftesbury belongs to this school is based on his claims in the *Inquiry* that the rightness or wrongness of an action is perceived by observers, and that indeed we have a 'sense of right and wrong'.[14] This aspect of Shaftesbury's morality might separate him from the Smithian account, and even from the 'evolutionary' account Shaftesbury himself elsewhere gives, if it implies that what we do is merely observe or perceive antecedently existing moral truths, the way we observe light from an antecedently existing sun, as opposed to our generating moral truths that did not otherwise exist by interacting in certain specific historical contexts.

One might suspect that the problem I see here is not as acute as I would have it, since Shaftesbury's notion of 'polishing' would seem to presuppose something valuable underneath that needs only bringing out.[15] Thus perhaps Shaftesbury's view is that we are born with notions of right and wrong, in which case the 'polishing' does not create them whole cloth; and the 'marketplace of ideas' serves only to uncover or, to use a Platonic metaphor, recall them. I think this suggestion misunderstands Shaftesbury's 'polishing' metaphor, however. According to Shaftesbury, what gets 'polished' are our manners: not moral truths. Moral truth exists for Shaftesbury quite independently of our manners; they are, to repeat, 'eternal measures' (175), detectable by our 'sense of right and wrong', which we have from birth (179). What needs polishing, then, is not morality in itself, but rather our habits of judgment and behaviour. The question remains, then, how the eternally fixed standards of right and wrong and our evolutionary and historical method of molding our behaviour and judgments are connected.

I think one way of understanding Shaftesbury's claims about the intrinsic goodness or rightness of moral virtue that draws on his notion of a moral sense might bring him closer to the Smithian historical and evolutionary account. I base it in part on this passage from *Miscellany III*:

Our joint endeavour, therefore, must appear to be this: to show that nothing which is found charming or delightful in the polite world, nothing which is adopted as pleasure or entertainment of whatever kind can any way be accounted for, supported or established without the pre-establishment or supposition of a certain taste. Now a taste or judgment, it is supposed, can hardly come ready formed with us into the world. Whatever principles or materials of this kind we may possibly bring with us, whatever good faculties, senses or anticipating sensations and imaginations may be of nature's growth and arise properly of themselves without our art, promotion or assistance, the general idea which is formed of all this management and the clear notion we attain of what is preferable and principal in all these subjects of choice and estimation will not, as I imagine, by any person be taken for innate. Use, practice and culture must precede the understanding and wit of such an advanced size and growth as this. A legitimate and just taste can neither be begotten, made, conceived or produced without the antecedent labour and pains of criticism.

(Shaftesbury 1999: 408)

My suggestion is that the transcendence of goodness and virtue to which Shaftesbury appeals might be based not on an otherworldly standard but rather on the (relative) fixity of human nature. The faculties, senses, and anticipating sensations and imaginations that Shaftesbury mentions belong to us; that is, they are *our* faculties, senses, and so on. And if human nature is common and universal, as Shaftesbury, like most of the eighteenth-century Scots, probably believes, then a reconstruction of Shaftesbury's position might be this: All properly formed moral judgments will agree because they will issue from properly functioning instruments for perceiving the world as it truly is. What benefits people or harms them are matters of objective fact and must be empirically discovered through trial and error, and judgment and taste that can reliably distinguish the two must themselves be empirically tested. Some people's judgment will be demonstrably better than others'; only the former's will we call good judgment and good taste, and it can be achieved only through hard work under criticism by others and correction by the reality we face.[16]

This interpretation indexes Shaftesbury's 'eternal measures and immutable independent nature of worth and virtue' to a proper apprehension by human faculties of actual human experience. Although it therefore maintains a clear, and I believe plausible, way for such apprehensions to be objectively right or wrong, at the end of the day it may not capture the full spirit of Shaftesbury's adversion to a seemingly transcendentalist source of moral rectitude – even if it does comport better with Shaftesbury's own evolutionary accounts of morality elsewhere. As I have already suggested, in several other passages Shaftesbury's argument runs in the direction of this 'middle-way' interpretation. Here is one example, this one from the *Inquiry*:

If there be no real amiableness or deformity in moral acts, there is at least an imaginary one of full force. Though perhaps the thing itself should not be allowed in nature, the imagination or fancy of it must be allowed to be from nature alone.

(Shaftesbury 1999: 178)

This passage seems consistent with my suggestion of a relatively fixed human instrument – here, 'imagination or fancy'[17] – that apprehends or contemplates moral rectitude or depravity; and note that Shaftesbury emphasizes, tellingly, that moral judgments arrived at by this imagination or fancy would retain their 'full force'. And elsewhere in *Miscellany III* Shaftesbury writes, 'Thus, we see, after all, that it is not merely what we call *principle* but a *taste* which governs men' (413). Here Shaftesbury is discussing one explanation of moral failing, namely that people frequently follow their moral 'taste' or 'savour' rather than any high moral principle, even if the people themselves believe otherwise. But although Shaftesbury therefore has other purposes in mind here, my ascription of an evolutionary account can interpret a passage like this one as again suggesting an awareness of moral judgment being the joint product of (1) human nature and (2) human experience in the world.

I will not press this interpretation of Shaftesbury any more than I already have. Instead I will close this section with the speculation that a reconstruction like the one I have attempted might have struck a chord with the Scots of the eighteenth century, and with Adam Smith in particular, who was about to explore his own evolutionary account of human morality – and who may well have sensed this tension in Shaftesbury's account and come in time to resolve it by eschewing dependence on supernatural transcendence altogether.

Shaftesbury on Hobbesianism

Despite the one possible departure from Smithian social theory constituted by Shaftesbury's seeming commitment to transcendent, intrinsic, and perhaps even infallibly ascertainable moral goodness, significant similarities nevertheless remain. Before articulating those similarities and especially the correspondences between Shaftesbury and Adam Smith, however, let me take a moment to substantiate my claim that a principal target of Shaftesbury's – and perhaps via Shaftesbury of Smith's – was Hobbesianism.[18] Shaftesbury thought Hobbes got just about every part of his social philosophy wrong. Or rather, Hobbes got one central premise wrong, and thus the rest of the Hobbesian program that is built on its foundation falls. The crucial mistake Hobbes made was not in thinking that human beings were self-interested, but rather that they were only self-interested. On the contrary, according to Shaftesbury human beings have 'natural affection' for others as well, a fact that immediately deflates Hobbesian pretences.

Shaftesbury's attack on Hobbesianism has two aspects. The first can be seen when he addresses the Hobbesian argument in *Sensus Communis*:

But supposing one another to be by nature such very savages, we shall take care to come less in one another's power and, apprehending power to be insatiably coveted by all, we shall the better fence against the evil, not by giving all into one hand (as the champion of this cause would have us) but, on the contrary, by a right division and balance of power and by the restraint of good laws and limitations which may secure the public liberty.

(Shaftesbury 1999: 44)

Shaftesbury's argument here for decentralization of power may display his Whig political prejudices (Den Uyl 1998: 305–11; Klein 1994, chs 7 and 10), but it is not particularly telling against Hobbesianism unless Shaftesbury can explain why dividing state power 'secures public liberty' better than concentrating it does, and, perhaps more pressing, how good laws can 'better fence against the evil' when Hobbes has argued, 'And Covenants, without the Sword, are but Words, and of no strength to secure a man at all' (Hobbes 1991 [1651]: 117). According to Hobbes's familiar argument, because in the state of nature there is among mankind pervasive competition, diffidence, and the desire for glory, if there is no 'visible Power to keep them in awe, and tye them by feare of punishment to the performance of their Covenants', what ensues is war of all against all (Hobbes 1991 [1651]: 117). Shaftesbury's objection here to Hobbes is weak because it is not clear how, if Hobbes's conception of human nature is accurate, dividing the power of the sovereign would protect citizens better than concentrating it would. Hobbes would, and does, argue (Hobbes 1991 [1651], chs 18–20 and 29) that divided sovereignty is actually more unstable and more likely to lead to tyranny than the single overawing authority – because we can at least assassinate a single tyrant. Indeed, that is part of the justification for his argument for the necessity of a single supreme sovereign.

The main difference between Shaftesbury and Hobbes thus turns on their different conceptions of human nature, and more particularly on their different conceptions of natural human sociality. And it is on this natural human sociality that Shaftesbury bases the second, and central, aspect of his disagreement with Hobbesianism. The argument, in my reconstruction, is a simple modus tollens running like this: if people were as naturally antisocial as Hobbes claims, then there would be no society at all; but there is society; therefore people cannot be as naturally antisocial as Hobbes claims. Shaftesbury elaborates his argument by noting that human society is in fact all around us every day, and it is not enforced by a sword. In various ways, Shaftesbury's entire argument in the *Characteristics* is in support of this point. What is politeness, after all, if not uncoerced consideration of others' concerns, interests, and well-being? If Lawrence Klein is correct that politeness is the central virtue for Shaftesbury (see Klein's Introduction to Shaftesbury 1999, xii–xv; Klein 1994, chs 7–10), then this fundamental difference between Shaftesbury and Hobbesianism explains the entirely different trajectories their political and moral positions take. Shaftesbury summarizes his position, and thus his opposition to Hobbesianism, in Section Four of *Moralists*; he italicizes the text to emphasize its importance: '*In short, if generation be natural, if natural affection and the care and nurture of the offspring be natural, things standing as they do with man and the creature being of that form and constitution he now is, it follows that society must be also natural to him and that out of society and community he never did, nor ever can, subsist*' (287).[19] The crucial point is that for Shaftesbury politeness resulting from affection would be a 'natural' and genuine virtue, not a mere stratagem, as a Hobbesian might claim. In Shaftesbury's account, society and community are natural outgrowths of natural – and real – human affections, and thus Hobbes's internecine state of nature could never have obtained.

Shaftesbury and Smith

There are numerous intriguing similarities between Shaftesbury and Adam Smith – so many, in fact, that on reading the works side by side one might think that the later one simply adopted some of the ideas, arguments, and perhaps even phrasings of the earlier. The fact that these similarities exist is all the more intriguing given that when Smith mentions or speaks of Shaftesbury, it is usually with a measure of contempt. In his *Lectures on Rhetoric and Belles Lettres*, for example – the only extant place where Smith discusses Shaftesbury at any length – Smith sharply criticizes him. 'Shaftesbury himself, by what we can learn from his Letters, seems to have been of a very puny and weakly constitution, always either under some disorder or in dread of falling into one. [. . .] Abstract reasoning and deep searches are too fatiguing for persons of this delicate frame' (Smith 1983, LRBL i.139). He goes on to remark that Shaftesbury was 'no great reasoner, nor deeply skilled in the abstract sciences', though Smith does somewhat condescendingly allow that he 'had a very neice [*sic*] and just taste in the fine arts and all matters of that sort' (LRBL i.140). Nevertheless, 'Naturall philosophy he [Shaftesbury] does not seem to have been at all acquainted with, but on the other hand he shews a great ignorance of the advances it had then made and a contempt for its followers' (ibid.). On top of Shaftesbury's ignorance and weak reasoning abilities, Smith also castigates him for having developed his own peculiar style, thereby inexcusably flouting the rules of style Smith himself had laid out (LRBL i.148).

It is often difficult to demonstrate an actual historical influence between two authors, owing to the many difficulties inherent in trying to untangle the sources of any person's ideas. But we know that Smith read Shaftesbury carefully, and the similarities between Shaftesbury and Smith are striking.

When discussing the connection between individual goods and the good of the individual's community, Shaftesbury writes:

the thousandth part of those whose interests are concerned are scarce so much as known by sight. No visible band is formed, no strict alliance, but the conjunction is made with different persons, orders and ranks of men, not sensibly, but in idea, according to that general view or notion of a state or commonwealth. [. . .]

Thus the social aim is disturbed for want of certain scope. The close sympathy and conspiring virtue is apt to lose itself for want of direction in so wide a field.

(Shaftesbury 1999: 52)

Smith too will become quite interested in the 'sympathy' that can develop between people, even upon such a slender cause as their merely seeing one another with some fleeting regularity; Smith's 'desire for the mutual sympathy of sentiments' is arguably the single most important part of the theory developed in his TMS (Otteson 2002, ch.1). One also wonders about that phrase, 'no visible band'. I know of no evidence suggesting that it inspired the most famous phrase in all of Smith's writings, but it is tantalizingly close, and the passage overall has clear invisible-hand, or 'spontaneous order', suggestions. Finally, later in the same passage Shaftesbury speaks of the 'mutual succour' and 'common affection' that arises naturally when people come to count on each other in achieving their ends (Otteson 2002, ch.1).

Far more extensive are the similarities between Shaftesbury's and Smith's respective accounts of introspection. In *Soliloquy, or Advice to an Author*, Shaftesbury adopts the Montaignesque position that an author must look to himself – to his own behaviour, thoughts, instincts, and so on – if he wants to perceive what is 'natural' for human beings and to have any hope of portraying it realistically. The epigraph for *Soliloquy* is 'Nec te quaesiveris extra', 'Do not inquire outside yourself'. In elaborating his position, Shaftesbury develops a conception of observing oneself that is reminiscent of Smith's description in *The Theory of Moral Sentiments* of one's conscience and the creation of the impartial spectator's viewpoint. Smith writes, for example: 'When I endeavour to examine my own conduct, when I endeavour to pass sentence upon it, and either to approve or condemn it, it is evident that, in all such cases, I divide myself, as it were, into two persons; and that I, the examiner and judge, represent a different character from that other I, the person whose conduct is examined and judged of' (Smith 1976a, TMS III.1.6). Compare that passage with this from Shaftesbury's *Soliloquy:* ' "Mere quibble!", you will say, "for who can thus multiply himself into two persons and be his own subject?" [. . .] Go to the poets, and they will present you with many instances. Nothing is more common with them than this sort of soliloquy. [. . .] By virtue of this soliloquy, he ['a person of profound parts, or perhaps of ordinary capacity'] becomes two distinct persons. He is pupil and preceptor. He teaches and he learns' (72).

Shaftesbury goes so far as to claim that true virtue lies not just in acting in accord with virtue, but in observing one's own conduct and achieving an awareness that one's conduct is virtuous. It is for Shaftesbury a *dual* spectatorship: observing the behaviour of others and of oneself, *and* observing oneself making these observations. It is in the awareness that one is making moral choices – thus in the awareness that one is acting virtuously out of knowledge that it is virtuous behaviour – that one becomes truly virtuous. Here is Shaftesbury in the *Inquiry*:

> So that if a creature be generous, kind, constant, compassionate, yet if he cannot reflect on what he himself does or sees others do so as to take notice of what is worthy or honest and make that notice or conception of worth and honesty to be an object of his affection, he has not the character of being virtuous. For, thus and no otherwise, he is capable of having a sense of right or wrong, a sentiment or judgment of what is done through just, equal and good affection or the contrary.
>
> (Shaftesbury 1999: 173)

Elsewhere in *Soliloquy* Shaftesbury writes, 'Thus it may appear how far a lover by his own natural strength may reach the chief principle of philosophy and understand our doctrine of two persons in one individual self' (83). And in a passage that describes something strikingly close to Smith's theory of the impartial spectator, Shaftesbury writes:

> And here it is that our sovereign remedy and gymnastic method of soliloquy takes its rise when, by a certain powerful figure of inward rhetoric, the mind apostrophizes its own fancies, raises them in their proper shapes and personages and addresses them familiarly, without the least ceremony or respect. By this means, it will soon happen that two formed parties will erect themselves within. For the imaginations or fancies being thus roundly treated are forced to declare themselves and take party. Those on the side of the elder brother Appetite are strangely subtle and insinuating. They have always the faculty to speak by nods and winks. By this practice they conceal half their meaning and, like modern politicians, pass for deeply wise and adorn themselves with the finest pretexts and most specious glosses imaginable till, being confronted with their fellows of a plainer language and expression, they are forced to quit their mysterious manner and discover themselves mere sophisters and impostors, who have not the least to do with the party of reason and good sense.
>
> (Shaftesbury 1999: 85)

This passage is extraordinary for several reasons. Who is this fellow of 'plainer language and expression' who is not swept up in the fury of the appetites and who has rather 'to do with the party of reason and good sense'? One is tempted to see here the Smithian impartial spectator, who, Smith tells us, 'does not feel the solicitations of our present appetites. To him the pleasure which we are to enjoy a week hence, or a year hence, is just as interesting as that which we are to enjoy this moment' (TMS IV.2.8). Where Shaftesbury suggests that one's appetites find various ruses and deceptions to convince their possessor that they are justified, Smith writes, 'The passions, upon this account, as father Malebranche says, all justify themselves, and seem reasonable and proportioned to their objects, as long as we continue to feel them' (TMS III.4.3). Malebranche does indeed say this, and, as the editors of the Glasgow edition of TMS remind us, Hutcheson also quoted this line from Malebranche (TMS III.4.3, n). So perhaps that, not from Shaftesbury, is where Smith got it, although since Smith's teacher Hutcheson was himself deeply influenced by Shaftesbury, perhaps the connection is not so remote after all. Regardless, the correspondence to Shaftesbury's description and, moreover, the integration of that thought into a larger argument serving apparently the same purpose cannot be gainsaid.

The correspondence continues. Smith uses the remark he attributes to Malebranche as an introduction to the topic of self-deceit, which, Smith argues, issues from our frequent wish to see ourselves not as others would actually see us but rather as we might self-servingly wish others would see us. Smith writes, 'This self-deceit, this fatal weakness of mankind, is the source of half the disorders of human life. If we saw ourselves in the light in which others see us, or in which they would see us if they knew all' – this is Smith's adversion to the standard of the impartial spectator – 'a reformation would generally be unavoidable. We could not otherwise endure the sight' (TMS III.4.6). The lesson for Smith is that transparency is an important part of achieving perfect virtue, which would be perfect correspondence between our own sentiments and those of the impartial spectator. Perfect virtue is probably not possible for flawed creatures such as we are, but the more transparent we become to ourselves the better able we are to achieve sympathy with the impartial spectator. Now compare this passage from Shaftesbury: 'But whatever may be the proper effect or operation of religion, it is the known province of philosophy to teach us ourselves, keep us the self-same persons and so regulate our governing fancies, passions and humours as to make us comprehensible to ourselves and knowable by other features than those of a bare countenance' (127). There are several other, more isolated similarities between Shaftesbury and Smith that provoke no less intriguing questions, but we can leave those for another occasion.

There has been some scholarly attention paid to similarities between Shaftesbury and Smith, but not much. David Marshall has probably more than anyone else investigated the link between Shaftesbury and Smith on the former's notion of 'soliloquy' and the latter's notion of 'impartial spectator'. Marshall argues that the connection is in the 'theatricality' involved in being simultaneously an actor and a spectator of one's own actions (Marshall 1986, ch. 7).[20] Marshall contends that as Shaftesbury elaborates his conception of the soliloquy in which an author must engage, it becomes increasingly clear that in this view an author must adopt something like the imagined disinterested third-person perspective on himself that is embodied in Smith's impartial spectator. This dual role each individual plays – that is, as actor and spectator – lead Marshall to argue that theatricality is at the centre of moral wisdom for both Shaftesbury and Smith.[21]

Douglas J. Den Uyl also notes similarities to Smith, indeed several of them:

> Smith inherits a good deal from Shaftesbury. The inheritance includes Whig or liberal politics; the fascination with and incorporation of the Stoics into his doctrines; the centrality of rhetoric to both his own exposition and to the role it plays in shaping social opinion; the importance of beauty; the guiding force of sentiment; the process of spectating; the prioritizing of practical over speculative reason; and the recognition that the promotion of virtue is especially problematic in the modern world.
>
> (Den Uyl 1998: 314)

Den Uyl goes on to suggest that two further ideas of Smith's 'have the effect of being criticisms of Shaftesbury. The first is Smith's view that fortune can render moral norms inconsistent. The second is the separation of beauty from goodness' (Den Uyl 1998: 314). I have explored a few of these similarities here, but I note that, with the exception of the two 'criticisms' Smith makes of Shaftesbury, Den Uyl does not expand on or attempt to account for the similarities between Smith and Shaftesbury, nor does he make a claim about actual influence. Indeed, Den Uyl's language seems deliberately indefinite: 'even if Smith did not have Shaftesbury explicitly in mind when he formulated some of his doctrines [. . .]' (Den Uyl 1998: 314). This is not a criticism of Den Uyl: his work had other aims. But the similarities seem too great to be merely coincidental.

Conclusion

Let me now close by indicating the conclusions I draw from this investigation. First, Hobbesianism and the challenge it presented to natural human sociality formed a haunting spectre to much seventeenth- and eighteenth-century social thought, in particular to Shaftesbury's thought, and, both via Shaftesbury and generally, to the thought of Scots like Adam Smith. Second, Shaftesbury advocated to varying degrees and in disparate contexts several of the claims that would come to form pillars of the evolutionary spontaneous-order explanations of human social phenomena that Smith and other Scots would integrate and develop more systematically. Third, there were clear and striking similarities between Shaftesbury and Smith on the development of common moral judgments, on the role that local knowledge and individual liberty play in that development, and so on, despite at least one seeming difference – namely, that Shaftesbury claimed the existence of transcendent or intrinsic rightness about virtue, a claim hard to reconcile with the contingent, historical development of moral standards envisioned by Smith's system and seemingly implied by Shaftesbury himself elsewhere.

Finally, whatever other elements of Shaftesbury's writings – or politics, for that matter – that Smith or other Enlightenment Scots adopted, one crucial element missing from Shaftesbury's discussions is a full account of the mechanism connecting liberty and Shaftesburian politeness. Without an account of this mechanism, we cannot claim to have causal knowledge: all we have is, at best, awareness of a constant conjunction. And, adapting the lesson we were about to learn from Hume only a few decades later, for an account to be complete it must include a causal explanation; otherwise we have merely the story of our past experiences. Shaftesbury began, then, an evolutionary account of human social institutions, and he saw several of the central elements, though he did not complete the account. He thus laid the groundwork for Smith and other principals of the Scottish Enlightenment, and the gaps in his account may just be what led the Scots to think carefully about the matter and develop their own, more systematic evolutionary accounts of the origins and nature of human social institutions.

Acknowledgement

I would like to thank Douglas Den Uyl and an anonymous referee for numerous helpful suggestions on an earlier draft of this paper. Remaining errors are mine.

Notes

1 All references to Shaftesbury's work are to this edition, and all italics are in the original unless otherwise indicated. For more of Shaftesbury's own discussions of his methods, see also, for example, 350, 379–80, 393, and 395. I note that another excellent edition of Shaftesbury's *Characteristicks* has been published in three volumes by Liberty Fund in 2001. The Klein edition, which I use throughout here, has modernized the spelling and punctuation; the Liberty Fund edition retains original spellings and punctuation.
2 Stephen Darwall rightly claims that Shaftesbury's 'thought is pivotal for understanding the development of eighteenth-century ethics' (Darwall 1995: 176); yet he is also right when he says that 'Shaftesbury has been relatively ignored by philosophers of our time' (Darwall 1995: 176), his own study constituting an exception to that rule. See also Den Uyl (1998: 275–316); Klein (1994); Rykwert (1980, esp. ch. 6); and Schneewind (1998: 298–309).
3 Shaftesbury may have an Aristotelian notion of *phronesis,* and he may thus subscribe to an Aristotelian view that one's *phronesis* develops only through practice. I note that Shaftesbury does not refer to Aristotle here, though he does elsewhere. See, for example, *Soliloquy,* where Shaftesbury quotes extensively and favourably from the *Poetics* and refers to Aristotle as a 'master critic' and writes, 'So true a prophet as well as critic was this great man [viz., Aristotle]' (109, n.27 and 110, n.29, respectively).
4 See also 51–4, 167, 328, and 333. But elsewhere Shaftesbury makes the more rationalistic argument that virtue can only be the product of deliberate

ratiocination and depends on apprehension of *'eternal measures and [the] immutable independent nature of worth and virtue'* (175); and that a *'Sense of right and wrong'* is part of our natural constitution from birth and not the product of habit or education (179). I shall return to this issue.

5 See also 44.

6 See also 197 and 338.

7 See also 31–4, 43, 45, and 96. Note also the striking similarity between Shaftesbury's argument that those places that reached the highest points in civilization and learning were also the places where individuals were the freest, and the argument David Hume would later make: in his essay 'Of the Rise and the Progress of the Arts and Sciences', Hume reports that his 'first observation' concerning why some places achieve a level of politeness and learning above that of others is *'That it is impossible for the arts and sciences to arise, at first, among any people unless that people enjoy the blessing of a free government'* (Hume 1985: 115; Hume's italics). Adam Smith makes a similar argument in his *History of Astronomy* (Smith 1980, 'Astronomy' III.5: 51–2). See also Infantino (2003, esp. ch. 2).

8 See also 51–52, 167, 179, and 287.

9 Another passage demonstrates Shaftesbury's awareness of unintended beneficial macro-orders from micro-motives, this one from the *Inquiry*: 'But, notwithstanding the injury which the principle of virtue may possibly suffer by the increase of the selfish passion in the way we have been mentioning, it is certain, on the other side, that the principle of fear of future punishment and hope of future reward, how mercenary or servile soever it may be accounted, is yet in many circumstances a great advantage, security and support to virtue' (185). See Den Uyl (1998: 290, 311).

10 Cf. Smith's condemnation of the 'man of system' (TMS VI.ii.2.17: 233–4) and of legislators who suppose themselves wise enough to manage others' economic affairs (Smith 1976b, WN IV.ii.9–10: 456).

11 See also the final lines of *The Moralists:* ' "For everyone, of necessity, must reason concerning his own happiness, *what his good is and what his ill"* ' (338). A couple of pages earlier, philosophy had been defined as *'the study of happiness'* (336).

12 For further discussion of what this type of moral objectivity would be, see Max Hocutt (2000); and John Searle (1995). For discussion of Smith's version of a 'middle way' objectivity, see James R. Otteson (2005).

13 'I am sure the only way to save men's sense or preserve wit at all in the world is to give liberty to wit. Now wit can never have its liberty where the freedom of raillery is taken away, for against serious extravagances and splenetic humours there is no other remedy than this' (12). See also 31, 33, and 34.

14 See esp. *Inquiry* II.iii–iv, and III.i: 172–9.

15 I thank an anonymous reviewer for formulating this point for me.

16 Douglas Den Uyl made the intriguing suggestion to me that this might make Shaftesbury something of a Platonist after all, since this conception of morality bases it on a fixed and universal human nature. One difference might be that for Shaftesbury, unlike for Plato, the moral judgments generated by the evolutionary mechanism are just as real as, though no more real than, the relevant elements of human nature are. Thus Shaftesburian 'transcendence' would be across cultures or places, but still sublunary and dependent on this-worldly nature.

17 Shortly after the quoted passage, Shaftesbury writes, *'Sense of right and wrong therefore being as natural to us as natural affection itself [. . .]'* (179). Here he merely analogizes this sense to a natural affection; he elsewhere says it *is* a natural affection. See, for example, page 179 and, generally, *Inquiry* I.iii: 177–92.

18 This is not to suggest that Hobbes was Shaftesbury's only target, only one of his main ones. Locke was another principal target. I thank Douglas Den Uyl for clarification here.
19 See also *Sensus Communis*, III.ii: 51–3.
20 I note by way of contrast that Lawrence E. Klein's recent examination of Shaftesbury and his influence on the British and continental thinkers of the eighteenth century makes no mention of Smith or of most of the other principal figures in the Scottish Enlightenment, and makes only passing reference to Hume (Klein 1994: 53).
21 For other discussions of the 'theatrical' link between Shaftesbury and Smith, see Vivienne Brown (1994: 56–62) and Charles L. Griswold, Jr (1999, esp. 104–9). Brown says that 'the spectatorial metaphor for self-knowledge and moral judgment was well established by the time TMS was written' (59), and Griswold similarly claims that 'This theme was well established by Smith's time' (108, n.34). Most of the sources they mention, however, are ancient ones, like Epictetus, Cicero, and Marcus Aurelius. Aside from Shaftesbury, the other modern sources mentioned are Butler's 1726 *Sermons* (Brown, 63, n.31) and Hume's *Treatise* (T, 365; cited by Griswold, 105, n.28).

Bibliography

Brown, V. (1994) *Adam Smith's Discourse: Canonicity, Commerce and Conscience,* London: Routledge.
Darwall, S. (1995) *The British Moralists and the Internal 'Ought': 1640–1740,* Cambridge: Cambridge University Press.
Den Uyl, D.J. (1998) 'Shaftesbury and the modern problem of virtue', *Social Philosophy and Policy,*15: 275–316.
Griswold, C.L. Jr (1999) *Adam Smith and the Virtues of Enlightenment,* Cambridge: Cambridge University Press.
Hamowy, R. (1987) *The Scottish Enlightenment and the Theory of Spontaneous Order,* Carbondale, Ill.: Southern Illinois University Press.
Hobbes, T. (1991) [1651] *Leviathan,* R. Tuck (ed.), Cambridge: Cambridge University Press.
Hocutt, M. (2000) *Grounded Ethics: The Empirical Bases of Normative Judgments,* New Brunswick, NJ: Transaction.
Hume, D. (1985) 'Of the Rise and the Progress of the Arts and Sciences', in *Essays Moral, Political, and Literary,* E.F. Miller (ed.), Indianapolis, In.: Liberty Classics.
Infantino, L. (2003) *Ignorance and Liberty,* London: Routledge.
Klein, L.E. (1994) *Shaftesbury and the Culture of Politeness: Moral Discourse and Cultural Politics in Early Eighteenth-Century England,* Cambridge: Cambridge University Press.
Marshall, D. (1986) *The Figure of Theater: Shaftesbury, Defoe, Adam Smith, and George Eliot,* New York: Columbia University Press.
Otteson, J.R. (2002) *Adam Smith's Marketplace of Life,* Cambridge: Cambridge University Press.
—— (2005) 'Adam Smith und die Objektivität moralischer Urteile: Ein Mittelweg', in *Adam Smith als Moralphilosoph,* C. Fricke and H.-P. Schütt (eds), Berlin: DeGruyter.
Rousseau, J.-J. (1988) *On the Social Contract,* D.A. Cress (trans.), Indianapolis, In.: Hackett Press.

Rykwert, J. (1980) *The First Moderns: The Architects of the Eighteenth Century,* Cambridge, MA: MIT Press.

Schneewind, J.B. (1998) *The Invention of Autonomy: A History of Modern Moral Philosophy,* Cambridge: Cambridge University Press.

Searle, J. (1995) *The Construction of Social Reality,* New York: Free Press.

Shaftesbury, Third Earl of (Anthony Ashley Cooper) (1999) [1711] *Characteristics of Men, Manners, Opinions, Times,* L.E. Klein (ed.), Cambridge: Cambridge University Press.

Smith, A. (1976a) *The Theory of Moral Sentiments,* D.D. Raphael and A.L Macfie (eds), Oxford: Clarendon Press.

—— (1976b) *An Inquiry into the Nature and Causes of the Wealth of Nations,* R.H. Campbell and A.S. Skinner (eds), Oxford: Clarendon Press.

—— (1980) *Essays on Philosophical Subjects,* W.P.D. Wightman (ed.), Oxford: Clarendon Press.

—— (1983) *Lectures on Rhetoric and Belles Lettres,* J.C. Bryce (ed.), Oxford: Clarendon Press.

Montesquieu in Smith's method of 'theory and history'

Henry C. Clark

I Introduction

In the *Gazette Nationale* for 11 March 1790, eight months after the storming of the Bastille, an anonymous correspondent from England reported to the editor on the imminent appearance of a study of Charles de Secondat, Baron of La Brède and of Montesquieu's *Spirit of the Laws* (1748) by Adam Smith. The full notice read:

> It is claimed that the celebrated Mr. Smith, so favorably known through his treatise on the causes of the wealth of nations, is preparing and is going to publish a critical examination of The Spirit of the Laws. It is the result of many years of meditation, and what we have a right to expect from a head such as that of Mr. Smith is well-enough known. This book will be epoch-making in the history of politics and of philosophy; such, at least, is the judgment of well-informed men who are familiar with the fragments – which they speak of with enthusiasm for the most auspicious prospects.
>
> (Rae 1990: 431)

The expectation was not unreasonable. Already in the 1750s, Smith's lectures, as reported in a digest apparently made of a student's notes by his Glasgow colleague John Anderson, contained a substantial engagement with the recently published work of Montesquieu. His lectures on jurisprudence in the 1760s, dated notes of which were discovered and published in 1896 and 1978, show everywhere the pervasive influence of the Frenchman. In the 1770s, Smith's own epoch-making *Wealth of Nations* (WN) was permeated with reflections on the history of law and politics inspired by the Baron of La Brède. Then, in a 1785 letter to the duke of La Rochefoucauld, Smith described as 'a sort of theory and History of law and Government' one of the two 'great works upon the anvil' underway in his scholarly workshop (*Corr.* Letter 248, 1 Nov. 1785; also Ross 2004: 55). Finally, his 1790 edition of *The Theory of Moral Sentiments* (TMS) repeated a commitment he had made as early as 1759, namely to produce an 'account of the general principles of law and government, and of the different revolutions they have undergone in the different ages and periods of society' (TMS VII.iv.37).

This last comment is entirely redolent of the sort of approach to the study of law and politics that had become popular in the second half of the eighteenth century, and that was generally associated with the influence of Montesquieu in Scotland. Dugald Stewart (1753–1828), in reviewing this history, saw *Spirit of the Laws* as exposing the 'absurdity' of the natural-law universalism that had been prevalent in Scottish schools at that time, and as emancipating Scottish students from the 'insupportable dulness' of natural-law instruction. He acknowledged the work's lack of a coherent theoretical plan whose near relativism needed a course correction by later writers – especially by Adam Smith, whose *Wealth of Nations* 'judiciously and skilfully combined' the needed general principles with 'luminous sketches of *Theoretical History*'. But at bottom, he saw the Scottish Enlightenment as 'but a *reflection*, though with a far steadier and more concentrated force, from the scattered but brilliant sparks kindled by the genius of Montesquieu' (Stewart 1994, 1:193). An account of a law class at the University of Edinburgh in 1788 indicates that the professor 'endeavours to construct the science of the spirit of laws' (Ross 1995: 124), evidence of the enduring influence of Montesquieu. Smith's student John Millar, for his part, reported that he had 'had the benefit of hearing his [Smith's] lectures on the History of Civil Society, and of enjoying his unreserved conversation on the same subject. – The great Montesquieu pointed out the road. He was the Lord Bacon in this branch of philosophy. Dr. Smith is the Newton' (Millar 1803, 2: 429–30, note).

As this last, oft-quoted remark suggests, there were those who felt that WN itself offered an adequate response to the challenge posed to the Scottish Enlightenment enterprise by Montesquieu's work. Commentators on both sides of the Channel thought that, as Hugh Blair put it, 'since Montesquieu's *Esprit des Loix*, Europe has not received any Publication which tends so much to Enlarge and Rectify the ideas of mankind' (*Corr.* Letter 151, 3 Apr. 1776). A review in the semi-official *Mercure de France* of 22 March 1788 reported that this equation of Smith and Montesquieu was nearly universal in England. A letter to the *Journal de Paris* a few months before the meeting of the Estates-General (11 Oct. 1788) asserted that 'Great Britain, in bringing Smith into the world, has discharged its debt toward France, which has given birth to Montesquieu'. Even after the Revolution began, the *Spectateur national*, in reviewing the poet Jean-Antoine Roucher's French translation of WN, began by stating that 'The work of Smith must be epoch-making in the history of political science, like *The Spirit of the Laws*' (see Carpenter 2002: xlv, 74, 92). And of course, in the Advertisement of the sixth edition of TMS, Smith himself said of WN that 'I have partly executed' the commitment made in the 1759 edition, to produce 'an account of the general principles of law and government', 'at least so far as concerns police, revenue, and arms' (TMS Advertisement 2).

But even in the absence of his 1785 letter to La Rochefoucauld, and of his characterization of the unfinished jurisprudence part of his 1759 commitment as a 'great work', there would be good reason to doubt whether Smith himself would have considered his 1776 masterpiece to have provided the full-scale commentary and improvement upon Montesquieu's work promised in the 1790 *Moniteur* notice. As John Millar reported, Smith saw his moral philosophy program as consisting of separable sections on justice, on the one hand, and expediency on the other (D. Stewart, 'Account of the Life and Writings of Adam Smith, LL.D.', in EPS I.19; Raphael 1985: 14). The WN seems to have grown out of lectures mainly on the expediency part, but Smith would have been aware that Montesquieu's work is of fundamental importance also to the justice side of the equation. The purpose of this essay is to reassess the relationship between 'theory and history' in Smith's general intellectual method, and the significance of Montesquieu in its development.

II Montesquieu in recent Smith scholarship

Though the scholarship on Adam Smith over the past thirty years or so has been gratifyingly vast and eclectic, it has featured at least one marked shift in emphasis that deserves our present attention. In the 1970s, there was a remarkable flurry of studies in which the complex but critical relationship between Montesquieu and Smith was engaged at a high level of sophistication. Perhaps this trend was prepared by Ronald Meek's work in the 1960s and early 1970s, which emphasized the simultaneous invention of a theory of stadial history in the work of the Frenchman Anne-Robert-Jacques Turgot (1727–81) and of Scotsmen such as Adam Smith in the early 1750s (Meek 1971). The Glasgow edition of the works of Adam Smith, which began to appear in 1976 and of which Meek was one of the editors, gave significant emphasis to the French connection with Smith's writings, including the work of Montesquieu. In the companion volume of essays that appeared the year before that bicentennial event, W.P.D. Wightman embraced Stewart's term 'Conjectural History' as a description of the novel methods pursued before Adam Smith by Hume, d'Alembert (in the Preliminary Discourse to the *Encyclopédie* in 1751), and Montesquieu – and as illuminating not only Smith's two famous works, but also his more general intellectual method as revealed in the *First Formation of Languages* and the *History of Astronomy* (Wightman 1975: 49).

In the same volume, Andrew Skinner pointed out that conjectural history, which he saw Smith as teaching at the university as early as his lectures in 1748–51, was a species of scientific history, which Machiavelli, whom Smith admired, had pioneered. Conjectural history itself was exemplified not only in Montesquieu's *Spirit of the Laws*, furthermore, but in his 1734 *Considerations on the Causes of the Greatness and Decline of the Romans*, which Smith also owned and seems to have used. And Skinner points to the early influence of the Neapolitan Pietro Giannonne, of whom he rightly describes Montesquieu as a 'disciple' for his remarkable early work *The Civil History of the Kingdom of Naples* (1729) (see Montesquieu 1991: 446, 1690). Smith, for his part, ordered Giannone's book for the University Library at Glasgow when he was Quaestor there (Skinner 1975: 154, 171–4).

Duncan Forbes went further; emphasizing political theory rather than conjectural history, Forbes provides perhaps the most wide-ranging appreciation of the relationship between Smith's and Montesquieu's political ideas that we have. Both Smith and Montesquieu, it emerges, take liberty seriously, but both (along with Hume, of course) are 'sceptical' rather than 'vulgar' Whigs. Where Montesquieu (anticipating Burke) saw the aristocracy as a bulwark of liberty, Smith followed Hume in seeing hereditary aristocracy as mostly oppressive, and in preferring the middling ranks (a view that we will have occasion to revisit below). In short, Forbes agreed that Montesquieu's and Smith's methods were very similar, even if the details of their conclusions were often different (Forbes 1975: 185, 188–90, 192–3, 195–6).

Donald Winch's justly influential book *Adam Smith's Politics* is, among other things, a sort of culmination of the 1970s Cambridge-inspired redis-covery of the Montesquieu-Smith connection. Winch sees the Frenchman as a better reference point for understanding Smith's enterprise than nineteenth-century laissez-faire liberalism, particularly in understanding the prominently political roots of his economic thought. Taking his cue from John Pocock's notion of Montesquieu as the 'greatest practitioner' of a new 'sociology of civic ethics' (Pocock 1975: 14, esp. 484), Winch accurately notes that Montesquieu was the 'pivotal figure in the history of the eighteenth-century science of comparative politics', a science in which Smith and other Scots were keenly interested (Winch 1978: 36–7). Thus, he argues that like Adam Ferguson, whose 1766 *Essay on the History of Civil Society* contains perhaps the most fulsome encomium to the influence of Montesquieu to be found in the entire Scottish Enlightenment ('When I recollect what the President Montesquieu has written, I am at a loss to tell, why I should treat of human affairs' [Winch 1978: 38; Ferguson 1995: 66]), Smith adopted Montesquieu's division of powers into a war- and peace-making executive, a legislative and a judiciary, but that unlike the Highlander, Smith sought a dynamic and historical treatment of these powers (Winch 1978: 56; see also 159–61). Echoing Forbes, Winch sees Smith as relatively more likely than Montes-quieu to criticize feudal nobility as opposed to absolute monarchy (Winch 1978: 38, 95, 97, 157, 162). At bottom, Winch argues that the influence of Montesquieu on Smith, unlike that of his friend Hume, was 'diffuse rather than specific' (Winch 1978: 38) and indeed his own account detects such influence on everything from state debt to capital formation to the separation of powers.

In the thirty years or so since the flurry of Cambridge-inspired work by the likes of Pocock, Skinner, Forbes and Winch, the most influential works on Smith have moved markedly away from his affiliations with

Montesquieu (Winch 1996; Griswold 1999; Rothschild 2001; Fleischacker 2004). Sometimes this move has been accompanied by an attempt to depict Smith as Rousseauian in his general approach to the problems of modern society (Force 2003 and my review at Clark 2005). Even where the emphasis is placed upon the differences between Smith and Rousseau, however (see Rasmussen 2006a, 2006b), the absence of Montesquieu as a point of reference is striking. In short, this seems like an opportune moment to revisit the case for seeing Smith's engagement with Montesquieu as quite central to his intellectual enterprise as a whole.

III History in Smith's method

History was central to Smith's intellectual enterprise. In his 1785 letter to the Duke of La Rochefoucauld, both of the 'great works upon the anvil' on which he was supposedly labouring were histories: one a 'sort of Philosophical History' of philosophy and the art of language, the other a 'sort of theory and History of Law and Government' (*Corr.* Letter 248). According to Dugald Stewart, it was Montesquieu who first 'considered laws as originating chiefly from the circumstances of society'. This word 'circumstance' connotes a dynamic method of contextual and cross-disciplinary analysis that Stewart sees as informing every aspect of Smith's own intellectual career: his 'Dissertation on the Origin of Languages', his unfinished 'History of Astronomy', his lectures on jurisprudence, his treatment of the causes of economic growth in WN. Stewart reports that earlier in Smith's life, he had 'more than once' expressed his intention to treat 'the other sciences' on the same circumstantial and historical lines as in his astronomy essay. He asserts, too, that in Smith's 'social hours', he applied the same theoretical–historical view to more mundane topics; 'and the fanciful theories which, without the least affectation of ingenuity, he was continually starting upon all the common topics of discourse, gave to his conversation a novelty and variety that were quite inexhaustible' ('Account' in EPS II: 44, 50, 52, 54). Thus, it would appear that both Smith and Montesquieu were foxes rather than hedgehogs. Smith had learned from Montesquieu (as well as from Hume and others, no doubt) to replace a static natural-law approach with a dynamic historical one.

For both Smith and Montesquieu, of course, the relish of circumstance needed to be tempered by the discipline of theory. Montesquieu conveys some of the intellectual anxiety of this pursuit in the Preface to his great work when he remarks, 'Many times I began this work and many times abandoned it; a thousand times I cast to the winds the pages I had written; . . . But when I discovered my principles, all that I had sought came to me, and in the course of twenty years, I saw my work begin, grow, move ahead, and end' (Montesquieu 1989: xlv). Though he does not spell out what these 'principles' were, it seems reasonable to infer that they are the conceptual devices he resorts to repeatedly to provide order to his otherwise sprawling material: his novel regime typology, his concept of the 'general spirit' and its application to constitutions, his liberty standard, perhaps his theory of climate. By the 1750s already, Smith had developed at least two such conceptual devices that we find him using to reduce his own historical materials to some kind of theoretical order, namely the moral psychology of sympathy and the four-stages (or 'stadial') theory of history. He would develop other such devices later on, but their function would remain very similar: namely, to fit preexisting historical materials into some semblance of comprehensibility.

Smith himself is reported to have made this revealing comment to one of his classes at Glasgow, probably between 1753 and 1755: 'Monsieur de Montesquieu is one of the most singular Men that has ever been in the World for he possesses four Things which are never almost united. An excellent Judgment, a fine Imagination, great Wit, and vast Erudition' (Anderson 15; I use the original but for some of what follows, see also Meek 1977). It is also intriguing that the very next entry in Anderson's notebook alludes to what will in effect be the leading conceptual problem that Smith would inherit from Montesquieu: 'a Free government is the Intention of Nature', we read, but circumstance is of great importance too (Anderson 16). The relationship between the universal demands of human nature and the particular circumstances produced by history, all with liberty as a normative standard – these were central concerns for Montesquieu, and they were arguably among the most permanent conceptual problems in the career of Adam Smith.

How to characterize this new use of history? 'Reasoned history' or 'critical history' – in the way Diderot and d'Alembert's *Encyclopédie*, which began publication in 1751, was subtitled a *Dictionnaire raisonné* (literally, a 'reasoned dictionary') – would be helpful terms; Dugald Stewart's term 'conjectural history' is not inadequate either, provided it be remembered that the conjectures were not thought of as whimsies but as serious applications of the prevalent standards of critical reason to the necessarily fragmentary and confusing historical record. The implied alternative was always Scripture-based reconstruction. Indeed Etienne Bonnot, abbé de Condillac (1715–80), one of the most careful users of language in all of eighteenth-century Europe (many of whose works Smith owned), employed the French term '*conjecturer*' to describe his own attempts to fill in the gaps in the record of the history curriculum that he developed for the Prince of Parma (Condillac 1948).

IV Sympathy, stadialism and the law in Smith's early lectures

The lectures recorded in Anderson's notes already incorporate what would become a durable combination of Smith's characteristic preoccupations – especially a four-stages theory of history on the one hand, and a moral psychology of sympathy on the other – with insights and methods clearly derived from *The Spirit of the Laws*. Smith, as is well known, set great store on primal experiences of wonder and surprise as essential starting points for any kind of effective scientific inquiry (See 'Astronomy' in EPS, Intro. and I–III). That starting point is already visible in Anderson's notebook, applied to the crucial question of the origin of government. 'Nothing has appeared more surprising', we read, 'than the government of Nations because the few govern the many' (Anderson 296). Smith then attempted to apply his emerging moral psychology – derived partly from his reflections on Francis Hutcheson's moral philosophy lectures – to this question, explaining that society begins with independent families, that a 'union of families for safety' would then occur, and that the 'wisdom and wealth' of an individual would have been a natural basis on which such a community might choose its early leaders (Anderson 294; Meek 1977: 90).

His subsequent analysis consists of a complex three-cornered relationship involving an account of the legal institutions themselves, a moral psychology that aims to make sense of those institutions, and a stadial history that provides a general framework for their changes over time. Thus, to take one example of his method, Smith began a new section by observing, 'In order to judge the reasonableness and origin of different punishments, we must call to mind what a private person feels when injured' (Anderson 340; Meek 1977: 85).

Here, Smith states two principles of human nature that he sees as important in legal analysis – we may call them the principles of resentment and of sympathy. 'To deprive a Man of Life or Limbs or to give him pain is shocking to the rudest of our species when no Enmity or Grudge subsists, i.e., where no Punishment is due or danger apprehended. 2nd principle: We acquire a Liking for those Creatures or Things that we are much conversant with, to deprive one of them must give us Pain' (Anderson 368; Meek 1977: 81–82). This reasoning foreshadows Smith's later analysis in TMS of how justice arises out of resentment and sympathy (see as early as I.i.1.4, and esp. II.i.1–3; there are approximately 175 uses of the term 'resentment' in TMS).

To take a related case, Smith explains that the blood feud of clan relationships arises from a combination of three things: this universal psychology of resentment, the failure of primitive law to assure swift punishment, and the limited opportunities commerce affords to escape from crushing familial dependence. Likewise in assessing the propriety of punishments: thus, the Lex Talionis (Law of revenge), although ultimately and properly abolished as 'too cruel', had at least rested on the sound assumption that the victim's prior ignorance of 'what was to befall him' should help make the punishment at least equal in physical deprivation to the crime (Anderson 336–34).

So Smith attempts to apply his new moral psychology to a legal sociology inspired by Montesquieu. But as it happens, though the chief principle of the latter's analysis in Book 6 of the *Spirit of the Laws* was his regime typology, it contained a nascent moral–psychological approach not that far removed from what Smith would soon be using. For example, in discussing the effects of different punishments, Montesquieu wrote, 'Let us follow nature, which has given men shame for their scourge, and let the greatest part of the penalty be the infamy of suffering it' (Montesquieu 1989: 85; see also Montesquieu 1991: 1494). Honour and shame are general human reference points for Montesquieu's own analysis of the effectiveness of punishment. It is not impossible, therefore, that in addition to his teacher Hutcheson's discussion of resentment (see Hutcheson 2002: 18, 96, 190; and Hutcheson 2004: 106, 122, 143), which is the most obvious source of Smith's reflections on this subject, Montesquieu's analysis may also have stimulated Smith to attempt to develop a moral psychology of legal systems.

The two thinkers had disagreements in detail about where precisely to draw the line between the 'nature' of moral psychology and the 'circumstance' of history; they were not in fundamental disagreement about the method of relating these two domains or the need to do so. The only place where Smith disagrees with Montesquieu by name on this topic provides a good example: Montesquieu had argued that the Roman-law distinction between the punishment of manifest and non-manifest robbery arose from Lycurgus's desire to toughen Spartan youth in cunning and petty theft by severely punishing those caught at it. Smith instead appeals to the universal psychological fact that there is 'among all Nations' a 'greater Hatred against the criminal if taken immediately than if afterwards' (Anderson 330).

Slavery is another topic on which Smith seems to absorb Montesquieu in general while offering alternative examples of 'conjectural history' to improve upon him in detail. After arguing that slavery is not natural in any regime except perhaps despotism, Montesquieu had then highlighted two factors in the origin and abolition of slavery, one natural and the other circumstantial: climate and religion. Climate, he argues, can at least reduce the unnaturalness of slavery by reducing the incentives to free labour. And it was Christianity that abolished slavery in Europe (Montesquieu 1989, 15.1, 15.7–8: 246, 251–2). Already in the Anderson lectures, Smith was experimenting with an analysis of slavery focused also on nature and circumstance – but instead of climate and religion, it was his sympathy mechanism and its intersection with his stadial theory that he employed to solve Montesquieu's problem.

Distinguishing between primitive and polished stages of society, he argued that the virtue of 'humanity' was not developed in primitive society, so the treatment of debtors, prisoners of war and criminals was bound to be less refined than in civilized ages. Slaves were mostly recruited from these and similar categories of people. At the same time, Smith seems to have suggested that the condition of the slave was actually better in primitive than in polished society, again because of the sympathy mechanism: 'In the first State, the Slave ate and wrought with his Master and there subsisted an Intimacy between them. In the last State they were removed from the Sight of their Masters and therefore cruelly used' (Anderson 308; Meek 1977: 89).

The reason why slavery in the modern world is an atavistic institution – 'Slavery could not be introduced in a polished age', we read close by – is not because of the influence of Christianity but because the sympathy mechanism in an interdependent commercial society has so diffused the virtue of humanity as to make slavery broadly unthinkable. Where it already existed, however, that same sympathy mechanism made slavery worse. As for that part of historical circumstance accounted for by the differences in political constitution, Smith seems to be aware of Montesquieu's explanation based on his new regime typology. Thus, Anderson reports, 'To be a Slave in a despotic government is no worse than to be a freeman. See Montesquieu' (Anderson 308 and Montesquieu 1989, 15.1: 246; of course, it is conceivable here as elsewhere that Anderson himself may have interjected this note). But Smith seems to have chosen to replace this constitutional explanation with a stadial account. Or perhaps he simply had not developed a satisfactory regime typology of his own.

As for abolition, Smith again disagreed with the Frenchman on precisely which circumstance was decisive. We read that Smith expressly rejected Montesquieu's religious explanation for the decline of slavery: 'The common Law and not Christianity suppressed Slavery'. More interestingly, however, he is also quoted as rejecting what might be thought to be the implication of his own earlier invocation of sympathy by denying that it had any particular role in Europe's medieval abolition of slavery. Instead, if Anderson's report is accurate, he adopted a legal-institutional analysis focused on the feudal military. 'It was not abolished by Humanity or the Improvement of Manners – but as the Slaves were armed by their Lords and so dangerous to the Kings, the King abolished Slavery' (Anderson 306–304; Meek 1977: 89). This sort of approach, rich in historical irony, is redolent of Smith's famous 'trinkets and baubles' explanation (WN III.iv) of the unintended growth of commerce in medieval Europe. My claim that Montesquieu is Smith's chief interlocutor at this point seems to be bolstered by the fact that, like Montesquieu, Smith moves immediately from a discussion of the origins and abolition of slavery, to a discussion of mining conditions in modern Silesia (and, in Smith's case, Scotland as well) – exactly the transition that Montesquieu had made (1989, 15.8; for Smith, see Anderson 302, Meek 1977: 90).

V Montesquieu in the 1760s *Lectures*

As might be expected, the *Lectures on Jurisprudence* that Smith gave in Glasgow in the 1760s, whose records are fuller and more detailed than the Anderson notebooks from the 1750s but for our purposes remarkably consistent with them, again reveal him to be in entirely the same thought world as Montesquieu, while again drawing the boundaries between nature and circumstance somewhat differently. Some topics that he had already addressed in the Anderson lectures, such as the Spartan contrast between latent and manifest robbery, he repeats without significant change (LJA ii.150). But in general, a broader and more elaborate engagement with the Baron of La Brède is visible in these 1760s lectures. On the subject of divorce, for example, he parts company with prevailing opinion, restated by Montesquieu (Montesquieu 1989, 26.8: 502), that the infidelity of the two spouses should be treated unequally because of the unequal effects on the reproductive process. For Smith, the celibate ecclesiastics who developed medieval divorce law were less beholden to conflict of interest, and thus more psychologically likely to assume the role of impartial spectator, than the patriarchs of old Rome had been (LJA iii.16). Thus, where Montesquieu but not Smith saw medieval Christendom as abolishing slavery, it was Smith but not Montesquieu who saw the medieval Church as abolishing (or attempting to) the 'double standard' in divorce law. The method of conjectural history did not have a unitary or predictable effect on one's assessment of any given phenomenon, such as the formative influence of Christianity.

Perhaps the most interesting case in the LJ concerns the question of the naturalness of polygamy, a question which Pufendorf, after a lengthy survey of the subject, had left open (Pufendorf 2005, VI.I.xix: 573–9). Montesquieu offered what may have been the most searching analysis of the effects of that institution upon individual liberty in all of eighteenth-century Europe in his 1721 *Persian Letters*, where polygamy emerges as a powerful symbol of despotism itself, and where one of the leading victims of the practice (Roxana) ends up committing suicide rather than enduring such a denial of her natural liberty (Montesquieu 1964, Letter CLXI). But in *Spirit of the Laws*, Montesquieu added to the normative liberty standard by attempting to attribute the origins of polygamy to climatic differences. His argument was that these differences lead to different paces of sexual maturation, which in turn make polygamy a more rational option in southern countries than in northern ones (Montesquieu 1989, 16.2: 264).

In both the 1762–63 and the 1766 reports, Smith attacks this naturalistic argument and replaces it with an argument drawn more from a complex combination of his moral psychology (an argument from nature) and his general stadial theory (an argument from circumstance) – all informed, as with Montesquieu, by a liberty standard. The argument seems to run as follows: The natural mechanism of sympathy and the impartial spectator assures public approval of the sentiments of both spouses under monogamy. This tendency toward what might be called the 'simple and obvious system of natural liberty' in sexual matters – a liberty, it should be noted, that also supposes a high capacity for prudence, self-command and responsibility – is thwarted by history. Thus, he is reported in 1763 as saying that it is the 'incapacities which attend the want of marriage which alone *maintain* monogamy in any country', whereas the 'incapacities attending on illegitimacy are the only thing which *prevents* the introduction of polygamy into any country' (LJA iii.76; emphasis added).

In accounting for this superior prevalence of polygamy, Smith eschews Montesquieu's climatic explanation for a combination of stadial theory and his own liberty standard. In both 1763 and 1766, Smith is reported as attacking the Frenchman's claim, based on travellers' reports, that a vast imbalance of men and women exists in some countries (see Montesquieu 1989, 16.4 and 23.12: 266–7 and 434); in both reports, Smith cites 'the laws of nature' on the roughly equal balance of the sexes in all countries. In 1763, his explanation of the ubiquitousness of polygamy falls mainly on the stadial side: 'The conquests of barbarous and savage nations is what has given rise to this [polygamy] in all nations where it is practiced' (LJA iii.41). In the 1766 report, it is the liberty vs. despotism dichotomy that seems to predominate: 'Polygamy takes place under despotic governments', and conversely, 'despotism is always favourable to polygamy' (LJB 114, 115). Of course, since the overlap between despotism and barbarism is large, there is broad compatibility in the two accounts.

But regardless of whether his intention was to emphasize the descriptive and stadial or the normative and liberal, what is clear is that Smith finds it convenient in both places to appeal to a substantive argument one normally associates with Montesquieu. For in both reports, a key disadvantage of polygamy is that it prevents the emergence of an hereditary nobility. Since, as we saw above, it has sometimes been denied that Smith shared with Montesquieu and Burke a positive view of the importance of hereditary nobility for liberty, it is useful to underscore not only that he does so here, but that he does so in ways that offer a revealing example of both the extent and the limits of his methodological and normative convergence with Montesquieu, and one to which Smith would return in an important way toward the end of his life, as we will see (Section VII below).

Thus, in both the 1763 and 1766 reports, Smith offers at least three different reasons why the prevention of the rise of a nobility under a regime of polygamy is unhealthy for any society. First, polygamy disrupts the flow of natural sympathy and mutual trust among heads of families. This development, which may be looked upon as a further elaboration of his analysis of the natural sympathy of subordinates for their superiors in TMS (I.iii.2), is a bad thing in itself, since 'prevent[ing] all associations and friendship' must be harmful to any civilized order.

Secondly, however, the absence of such trust, friendship and association prevents the leading citizens from collaborating to resist the oppressive inclinations of the monarchy – inclinations which Smith, like Montesquieu, sees as always tending toward despotism if unchecked. This is important not only for the nobility but for society at large. Thus, it is the 'liberty and freedom of the people' that suffer when leading families are unable to band together to 'make head against the oppressions of the king' (LJA iii.41, 43). In the 1766 report, the domestic political reference is made even clearer: 'Now hereditary nobility is the great security of the people's liberty. Being in every corner of the country, whenever the subjects are oppressed they fly to him as their head' (LJB 116).

Thirdly, there is the matter of national independence, for it is the hereditary nobility who are most likely to be 'head[ing] the people when they are in danger of being oppressed by foreign invaders'. The statement in 1766 is nearly identical, if not stronger: 'Wherever there is a hereditary nobility the country cannot easily be conquered, or rather not at all. They may be beat once or twice, but they still recover under their natural heads' (LJB 116). That Smith intends a roughly Montesquieuan argument here is highlighted by his further claim that 'Both these ends [that is, combating domestic oppression and resisting foreign invasion] we see have been answered by the nobility in France and England'. Thus, Smith is not merely alluding to the happy outcome of the Jacobite rising of 1745. He is echoing Montesquieu's wider argument for intermediate powers between ruler and people (Montesquieu 1989, 2.4: 17–18), in which the existence of the nobility is depicted as the very difference between despotism and liberty under any monarchy. It is curious that Smith chooses to articulate this important area of agreement with Montesquieu in the context of a particular topic – polygamy – on which he expressly states his disagreement with the Frenchman. It is not the only time that he appears to be, as it were, using Montesquieu against himself.

It is also curious that on the very next day (8 Feb. 1763), in a different course, Smith is reported to have made the similarly Montesquieuan argument that the separation of executive and judicial powers is 'one of the most happy parts of the British Constitution', although he is careful to offer non-Whiggish explanations of this development: it is a function of the modern division of labour, which provided different functions to different members of government, and it was introduced into England not by design but as a result of circumstance, or as he put it, 'merely by chance' (LRLB ii.203).

VI Montesquieu in the *Wealth of Nations*

The year 1776 saw the publication of two works destined to be important in the history of economic thought. Shortly before Smith's work, abbé Condillac brought out *Commerce and government, considered in their mutual relationship*. Although both books were written under the shadow of the Physiocrats, the method informing them is entirely different. Condillac's deductive approach proceeds as one might expect a philosopher of the mind and of knowledge to proceed (for a defence, see Klein 1985: 54–62). He begins by constructing a thought experiment around a hypothetical tribe, and his entire exposition of economic and policy theory centers rigorously around the logical inferences one can make about the development of that tribe, based on a proper understanding both of human nature and of the principles of liberty and of political economy. His main purpose, he writes at the outset, is to fix the language of this new science, the better to generate further incremental discoveries in future (Condillac 1997: 78).

Smith's method is entirely different. He does not begin the WN by claiming scientific status for the work, or by promising to fix the language of political economy. The only times he treats his subject matter in a scientific context, in fact, his purpose is precisely to affirm that political economy, far from being an autonomous science, is rather a 'branch' of the 'science of a statesman or legislator' (WN IV.Intro.1, IV.ii.39). This move squarely places his enterprise in a framework fashioned at first by natural-law theory, and then by Montesquieu. In his standard account, Knud Haakonssen (1981) places the emphasis upon the former, but the shadow of the Frenchman is present in Smith's distinctly Montesquieuan practice of giving central importance to the role of circumstance in explaining prosperity. Indeed, 'circumstance' is if anything an even more pervasive concept in the WN than it had been in his earlier work, the term itself appearing something like a hundred times.

The principles of the division of labour and the extent of the market are, of course, the essential ideas informing the welter of material that appears in the WN. But Smith offers another way of introducing his material, often overlooked, that does more to highlight the essentially contextual, circumstantial method of his work. National wealth, he says, depends upon 'two different circumstances', namely the 'skill, dexterity and judgment' of labour, and the ratio of productive to unproductive labour in a particular society. The logic of WN's organization actually proceeds from this dual consideration of circumstance: since labour produces value, the first Book treats labour; since labour is a function of capital investment, Book two turns to that theme. Even in these two Books, Smith's entire method is anchored – like Montesquieu's but very unlike that of Condillac or the Physiocrats – in the messy details of history, what Smith calls the 'policy of Europe' 'since the downfall of the Roman Empire' (WN Intro.7; for a different view of the organization of WN, see Ross 1995: xxiv, 279–80).

Then, Book three is entirely devoted to what Smith calls the 'circumstances which seem to have introduced and established this policy'. The fourth Book, likewise, is conceived as a further broadening of the historical analysis of Book three. In it, Smith surveys the different 'plans' by which different governments in different countries have managed their respective economies. The perspective of 'different ages and nations', we are told, has informed the first four Books as a whole. Book five, on government, is presented as mixing the normative ('which of those expences ought to be defrayed by the general contribution of the whole society') and the descriptive (the 'causes which have induced almost all modern governments' to incur debt), but either way, it continues to be resolutely comparative and historical in approach (WN Intro.1–9). In his eclectic and wide-ranging scope, in his combination of laws, institutions, even manners and mores, in his juxtaposition of normative and descriptive considerations, in short in his mixture of history and theory,

Smith's *magnum opus* is much more the heir of Montesquieu's *Spirit of the Laws* than of the recent French school typified by the Physiocrats or by Condillac.

There is also more convergence in the origin and subject matter of these two works than is often appreciated. Thus, Smith's work seems to have originated in the 1760s out of the expediency section of his curriculum on moral philosophy, just as the lectures on jurisprudence originated in the justice section. For his part, conversely, Montesquieu's masterpiece also contained to a surprising degree the elements of what some contemporaries called a 'science of commerce' (see Cheney 2002); according to one account, something like a sixth of the content of *The Spirit of the Laws* treats 'commerce' and related subjects (Morilhat 1996: 6). The convergence in the two men's thinking on these themes is at times remarkable. Just as Montesquieu wrote that 'at bottom, everything is exchange' (Montesquieu 1991: 1694), so too Smith famously declared that 'Every man . . . lives by exchanging, . . . and the society itself grows to be what is properly a commercial society' (WN I.iv.1). In his diary, Montesquieu had written, 'virtually all the arts are connected; a needle is the result of many arts', just as Smith chose the pin factory to illustrate the division of labour (Montesquieu 1991, 206: 242; WN I.i.3). At the outset of his treatise, Montesquieu defined his purpose as relating the laws 'to the *physical aspect* of the country; to the climate . . .; to the way of life of the people, be they plowmen, hunters, or herdsmen; . . . to the degree of liberty that the constitution can sustain, to the religion of the inhabitants, their inclinations, their wealth, their number, their commerce, their mores and their manners' (Montesquieu 1989, 1.3: 9). And Smith early on in his career expressed his interest in the 'slow progress and gradual development of all the talents, habits and arts which fit men to live together in society' ('A Letter to the *Edinburgh Review*' in EPS, 11). It was the abiding concern of both thinkers to develop a 'theory and history', as it were, that would encompass all of these dimensions of human collective life, and this commitment, far from disappearing, continued strongly in WN.

There is convergence, too, in their sanguine views of the capacity of private prudence in civil society to overcome the myriad follies of their respective governments in the long run. Thus, Smith surveyed the material condition of the British Isles since Caesar and concluded that 'though the profusion of government must, undoubtedly, have retarded the natural progress of England towards wealth and improvement, it has not been able to stop it' (WN II.iii.35). Montesquieu, for his part, had noted in his diary the 'extraordinary facility with which [France] has always recovered from her losses, her maladies, her depopulations, and with what resourcefulness she has always endured or even surmounted the internal vices of her various governments' (Montesquieu 1991, 1302: 440).

In the remaining pages of this essay, I will attempt to demonstrate that, just as Smith's four-stages theory has the effect, if not the intention, of imparting order and intelligibility to Montesquieu's ingenious though scattered forays into conjectural history, so too can Smith's vigorous application of market reasoning be interpreted as an attempt to refine Montesquieu's enterprise by providing more of the 'general principles' Dugald Stewart thought missing from the Frenchman's great work.

Take, for example, their treatment of the law of Sesostris in ancient Egypt, which decreed that every man remain in his profession and pass it down to his children. Montesquieu views this law as distinctive of a particular type of regime, namely despotism, and suggests that its chief effect was social in nature, namely to dry up the natural emulation that leads one to excel in a profession – for in a despotism, 'none can or should be rivals' (Montesquieu 1989, 20.22: 350–1). Smith, however, considers the same law as a function not of the political regime per se but of the religion of Egypt, and he discusses it for its effect upon wages and profits, rather than its effect on the social psychology of the people. Nonetheless, Smith follows Montesquieu in condemning the Egyptian policy as 'violent' on 'natural-liberty' grounds, even if his reference point was more economic and less social or political than that of Montesquieu (WN I.vii.31). A similar lineage is visible on questions such as Chinese economic development and Islamic interest rates. On China, Smith eschews Montesquieu's climatic explanation but follows him in emphasizing the effects of the 'laws and institutions' of the country on the trustworthiness of Chinese trade (see Montesquieu 1989, 19.10, 19.20: 313–14, 321; WN I.ix.15). On Islam, Smith embraces Montesquieu's argument that interest rates are high there because of the laws against usury and the insecurity of property (Montesquieu 1989, 22.19: 420–1). But he then offers a more elaborate market analysis of the factors determining rate of interest (WN I.ix.15–21). In each of these cases, then, market reasoning grows out of Smith's general acceptance of Montesquieu's historical–legal–institutional framework.

Likewise, the dialogue with Montesquieu on slave labour, which we saw Smith engaging in as early as his 1750s lectures in Glasgow, is continued and deepened in WN. Montesquieu's treatment of the subject, it must be emphasized, was not lacking an economic dimension: thus, he distinguishes between slave and free labour in a wide-ranging book (Bk. 15) whose ostensible topic is the effect of climate on the slavery laws. But the case of mining seems to suggest to the author that even the most arduous work can, with adequate economic incentives, be performed by freemen. Thus, on his visits to the mines of Hartz and Hungary nearly two decades earlier, Montesquieu had been struck by how much more productive they were than the Turkish mines in Timisuara just a short distance away. He also draws an explicit connection between the growth of technology and the decline of slave labour, writing, 'With the convenience of machines invented or applied by art, one can replace the forced labour that elsewhere is done by slaves'. By the time he comes to the end of the chapter, he finds himself admitting, 'I don't know if my mind or my heart dictates this point. Perhaps there is no climate on earth where one could not engage freemen to work' (Montesquieu 1989, 15.8: 252–3; my trans.). Montesquieu's multi-faceted, open-ended, non-dogmatic approach is seldom on better display as he ends up replacing a climatic explanation with an institutional one informed by a lively sense of the power of liberty – this time, in the form of free labour.

Smith had treated the identical difference between Hungarian and Turkish mining in numerous lectures starting in the 1750s (see Anderson 302; LJB 299–300). He does so again in WN, but with a difference. Here, he silently omits the climate factor, adopts intact the Frenchman's general argument on the difference between free and slave labour, and elaborates upon two specific economic aspects of the issue – namely, the incidence of technical invention by slave labourers, and the contrast between ancient and modern labour costs as a function of the freedom and technical ingenuity of ancient and modern labourers. Again, therefore, a market analysis is rooted firmly in an ongoing discussion of laws and institutions (WN IV.ix.47).

If Smith's 'nature' was often more likely to concern self-interested individuals in the marketplace than the constraints of climate, his 'circumstance' tended to be shaped more by his four-stages theory than by Montesquieu's regime typology. Each approach is powerfully animated by a sense of both the naturalness and the normative force of liberty. For Smith is as ready to detect a correlation between commerce and natural liberty as Montesquieu had been to see English political liberty as paradigmatic of the differences between ancients and moderns. (On this theme, see Rahe 2005.) But repeatedly, we see Smith's stadial analysis brought in to do conceptual work that is very similar to what the Frenchman had done with his analysis of constitutional forms. Three examples, taken from a characteristically eclectic range of topics, will suffice to illustrate this broader theme: judicial bribery, methods of taxation, and musical education.

Whereas Pufendorf had treated the topic of judicial bribery in moral and a-historical terms – writing simply that 'a Judge ought not to sell that Justice which he should administer *gratis*' (Pufendorf 2005 [1729] V.i.5: 462) – both Montesquieu and Smith subjected the phenomenon of judicial bribery to wide-ranging historical analysis. Montesquieu treats it squarely as a function of his three polities. 'In despotic countries', he writes, 'the custom is that one does not approach a superior, even a king, without giving him a gift'. But 'Gifts are an odious thing in a republic because virtue has no need of them. In a monarchy, honour is a stronger motive than gifts' (Montesquieu 1989, 5.17: 67; my trans.). Thus, a comparative analysis is undergirded by an implied condemnation of despotism as a constitutional type.

For Smith, on the other hand, judicial bribery is a function not of political regime but of stadial development. As soon as class differences emerged, namely in the second stage of human evolution (the 'age of shepherds'), regular government arose to defend the property of the haves against the have-nots. As such, the dispensing of justice brought revenue rather than expense, throughout the pastoral age and into the agricultural one, as early medieval Europe shows.

Smith's approach softens Montesquieu's account in one way and sharpens it in another. On the one hand, far from being a touchstone for distinguishing despotism from liberty, Smith views judicial bribery as a function of the broad rise of civil government itself, and of the sovereign's need to raise revenue in still-primitive societies. While he and Montesquieu agree that corruption is wrong, Smith sees it as merely 'productive of several very gross abuses' rather than as constitutive of despotism itself. On the other hand, Smith's economic perspective on the justice system leads him to an overall verdict that is more jaundiced than that of the ex-President of the Bordeaux Parlement. Citing not only the taxes needed for judicial salaries but the fees paid to lawyers and attorneys, Smith concludes that 'Justice . . . never was in reality administered gratis in any country' (WN V.i.b.12–14, 17–18).

Secondly, the question of the methods of taxation was another stock subject for natural-law writers and for Montesquieu, and it is again out of that tradition that Smith's position mainly emerges. Pufendorf had concluded, mostly on grounds of equity and practicality, that a consumption tax was preferable to an income or property tax (Pufendorf 2005 [1729] VIII.v.6: 828–9). Montesquieu, however, applying his regime typology with its implied liberty standard to the same question, came to a similar conclusion by a very different route. 'The tax by head', he writes categorically in the first line of his chapter on the subject, 'is more natural to servitude; the tax on merchandise is more natural to liberty, because it is related in a less direct manner to the person' (Montesquieu 1989, 13.14: 222). Thus, a comparative framework again suggests a normative conclusion because of the sharp dichotomy between despotism and liberty.

Smith accepts Montesquieu's decision to regard this question in liberty terms, unlike Pufendorf, but both his stadial theory and his market analysis have the effect of refining the Frenchman's conclusions significantly. While elaborating upon the 'wretched' economic effects of the personal tax on French farming, where the incentive is to hide any sign of prosperity, and while acknowledging that poll taxes or personal taxes used to be common for all bondmen throughout Europe (and still were in Russia), he nonetheless situates the issue in broader historical terms – observing, in what seems virtually like a response to Montesquieu: 'Every tax . . . is to the person who pays it a badge, not of slavery, but of liberty. It denotes that he is subject to government, indeed, but that, as he has some property, he cannot himself be the property of a master' (WN V.ii.g.11).

A subcategory of the question of direct vs. indirect, personal vs. consumption taxes, is the role of domiciliary visits in their collection. This topic appeared barely if at all in Pufendorf's lengthy discussion of the taxation issue, but for Montesquieu, it was fundamental. Thus, he concludes his condemnation of direct personal taxation emphatically by writing, 'in order that the citizen pay, his house must be perpetually searched. Nothing is more contrary to liberty. . . .' (Montesquieu 1989, 13.7: 218; my trans.). Domiciliary visitation is thus an ultimate proof of the failure of direct taxation to meet the liberty standard.

Like Montesquieu but unlike Pufendorf, Adam Smith gives considerable attention to the question of house visits. In his lengthy discussion of revenue-raising mechanisms, Smith cautions the legislator that there are four ways in which taxes might 'take out or keep out of the pockets of the people a great deal more than it brings into the publick treasury'. One of these is that, 'by subjecting the people to the frequent visits, and the odious examination of the tax-gatherers, it may expose them to much unnecessary trouble, vexation, and oppression'. He therefore agrees with Montesquieu that domiciliary visits can bring an affront to liberty, a point he repeats elsewhere in his criticism of the taxation of interest as opposed to landed property, where he intones, 'An inquisition into every man's private circumstances, and an inquisition which, in order to accommodate the tax to them, watched over all the fluctuations of his fortune, would be a source of such continual and endless vexation as no people could support' (WN V.ii.f.5).

But Smith adds to his remark on vexation and oppression an observation that is as economic as it is political, arguing that 'though vexation is not, strictly speaking, expence, it is certainly equivalent to the expence at which every man would be willing to redeem himself from it' (WN V.ii.b.6). This rather odd locution, which has the air of a modern cost-benefit analysis, signals again Smith's view that Montesquieu's liberty-despotism dichotomy, which he accepts in broad outline, must be supplemented by a market-reasoning analysis that is sometimes as much quantitative as qualitative. The conclusion reached by this particular Smithian analysis is that house visits are one injustice among many, and one of many factors that make the raising of revenues by these methods wasteful and even counterproductive.

A third example of Smith's reworking of Montesquieu's conjectural history concerns the role of music in Greek education. The Baron of La Brède had posed a paradox: why would Polybius, Plato, Aristotle, Theophrastus, Plutarch, Strabo – some of the luminaries of antiquity, who often agreed about little else – all agree that music was nothing less than an essential part of the constitution of Greek city-states? His explanation was that, due to the prevailing prejudices against the supposedly mean occupations of commerce, industry, even agriculture, Greek citizens had only the rough activities of gymnastics and military exercises to educate them. Music was thus intro-duced as a counterweight against this imbalance, and it was successful: it 'curbed the effect of the ferocity of the founding and gave the soul a part in education that it would not otherwise have had'. The Frenchman's explana-tion also contained an implied contrast between the harder dispositions of 'roughness, anger, and cruelty' and softer dispositions such as 'pity, tenderness, and sweet pleasure' – redolent of Smith's own guiding distinction between the virtues of self-command and of humanity in TMS (Montesquieu 1989, 4.8: 39–41, my trans.; for one treatment of the latter, see Clark 1993).

Nonetheless, Smith was having none of this explanation, and it is instructive to see why. He clearly takes Montesquieu as his starting point, citing him by name, and indeed introduces his general contrast of ancient and modern educational systems with the specific question of Greek music. But he begins his analysis by broadening Montesquieu's frame of reference from the Greeks to the Greeks and Romans. Then he applies a more specific standard by which to judge the success of Greek and Roman education, a standard suggested by Montesquieu himself throughout *Spirit of the Laws*, namely the 'moderation of contending factions'. This moderation, he asserts, is 'the most essential circumstance in the publick morals of a free people'. Having redefined the contrast, and having established a modified standard, he then feels able to demonstrate that the Romans, who did not adopt music in their civic education, enjoyed more success in imparting their public morals than the Greeks.

But this was not all. Having partially extended the frame of reference within the ancient West, Smith now broadens it further with the help of his stadial theory to include evidence from beyond classical antiquity. Thus, ranging widely from African tribal peoples to the ancient Celts to the early medieval Scandinavians, he states that 'Musick and dancing are the great amusements of almost all barbarous nations'. The Greek republics, therefore, were simply further historical developments of Greek tribal culture – in no essential way dissimilar to other barbarous communities. The respectable accounts of the institution of music by Polybius, Plato, and others emerge, in Smith's telling, simply as philosophical rationalizations bred of a quite natural respect for one's ancestral customs (WN V.i.f.39–41).

Thus, it was in one sense Smith's stadial account of universal history that enabled him to offer an entirely different framework for understanding the role of music in Greek education. In another sense, however, he uses Montesquieu against himself, as we also saw him doing on the polygamy question above. Specifically, by taking seriously the claims to liberty of the Greek republics, and by applying a moderation standard made most famous by Montesquieu himself (see Montesquieu 1989, 3.4, 5.6, 5.8, 9.2 and esp. 29.1; and Cohler 1988) to the assessment of Greek and Roman success at nurturing liberty, Smith arrived at conclusions that were markedly different in interpretive detail from those of his French interlocutor – even though the conceptual raw materials of legal and institutional sensitivity, conjectural history, and the ready application of a liberty standard to culturally diverse cases were broadly the same.

VII Montesquieu and the 1790 edition of TMS

A greater awareness of Smith's Montesquieuan connections also sheds light on a contested issue, namely whether his new Part six in the 1790 edition of TMS intended to offer commentary on the early events of the French Revolution. The 'spirit of system' or 'man of system' section (VI.ii.2.13–18) has been seen to refer to everyone from the radical Whig Richard Price to the Stuart King James II, even Frederick the Great of Prussia (TMS VI.ii.2.4, n.2; Ross 1995: 391–4; Rothschild 2001: 55, 272 n.31). This sort of exercise is as inconclusive as it is irresistible. Thus, I will begin by outlining my own very tentative speculation about what Smith may have had in mind in the paragraphs in question, then will make a larger point about the whole section in which the contested paragraphs appear.

My speculation is that Smith was making an oblique contrast between George Washington, on the one hand (as Ian Ross has suggested), and some of the leaders of the French Revolution on the other, by way of offering broader words of caution over the direction of events in France. Thus, he begins by noting that, though it is harder for a factional leader to achieve the 'universal gratitude' (TMS VI.ii.2.13) of his people than it is for the leader in a foreign war, the factional leader who achieves his ends while tempering and moderating the actions of his confederates – a characterization that would seem to apply to George Washington (see Ross 1995: 393) – may emerge as the 'reformer and legislator of a great state' (TMS VI.ii.2.14). From this positive prospect, Smith moves to the contrasting picture of the 'spirit of system' (TMS VI.ii.2.15) that arises in times of trouble. Here, as others have argued, Smith's comment about the 'subjects of a great empire [who] have enjoyed, perhaps, peace, security, and even glory' (TMS VI.ii.2.15) for centuries would seem clearly to refer to the French. What Smith seems particularly concerned about, however, is the way in which leaders in such circumstances often get swept along by the popular passions in spite of their better judgment. His specific comment that such leaders 'originally may have meant nothing but their own aggrandisement' (TMS VI.ii.2.15) could refer to someone like the flamboyant aristocrat and popular leader Mirabeau. But other allusions, such as to the 'public spirit which is founded upon the love of humanity' (TMS VI.ii.2.15), are more redolent of the role of a figure like the Marquis de Lafayette. In the immediate aftermath of the fall of the Bastille (17 July 1789), Lafayette, as vice-president of the National Assembly, was obliged to mediate between Louis XVI and the new masters of Paris. And on 5–6 Oct. 1789, Lafayette found himself at the head of a turbulent crowd of mainly market women from Paris who marched to Versailles and pressured the royal family into returning with them to the capital. These exercises in political improvisation would seem to be more consistent with Smith's claim that such leaders become 'dupes of their own sophistry' (TMS VI.ii.2.15).

That Lafayette served with Washington in America in his young manhood, idolized him, perhaps saw himself as the French version of the great American general, and was celebrated as the 'hero of two worlds' as early as 1778, adds piquancy to this interpretive possibility. And he was already associated in the public mind with the 'dazzling colours' of revolutionary 'eloquence' (TMS VI.ii.2.15) that Smith evokes. His dictum, 'For a nation to be free, it is sufficient that she wills it', was cited approvingly by Paine in his polemic against Burke in 1791, and was still remembered in Scotland as late as the August 1832 celebrations of the Great Reform Bill by the Edinburgh Trades Union Council at Bruntsfield Links (Meikle 1912: 62, 238).[1]

But this, and every, specific interpretation of the 'spirit of system' section is speculative, and is ultimately beside the point. For in this part of TMS, Smith was writing as a theorist of moral sentiments, even a philosopher, and the clear purpose of Sections one and two of Part six was to restate certain perennial themes in his career for the new circumstances, however he may have viewed them. Smith was among a certain strand of Enlightenment thinkers who would have been most unlikely to choose sides in a factional controversy. As his friend David Hume suggested in his criticism of the Whigs of his day, a philosopher who has 'embraced a party' is likely engaging in 'a contradiction in terms' ('Of the Original Contract' in Hume 1987: 469). The detachment, even elusiveness, that one finds in the 'spirit of system' section is almost certainly a result of a similar diffidence.

Accordingly, what is more certain and more important about these controversial passages is the general framework within which they appear. And here, the continuing resonance of Montesquieu for Smith's method of history and theory is clear and unmistakable. The general framework itself, it must be observed, is very carefully and coherently assembled. The entirety of sections one and two seem calculated, for one thing, to promote a Montesquieuan conception of a constitution at a time when the creation of a new constitution was a central preoccupation both in France and in America. As Keith M. Baker has pointed out, it was Montesquieu's *Spirit of the Laws* that gave the political concept of the constitution a 'new centrality' in eighteenth-century thought, but it did so by emphasizing a more Aristotelian 'order of existence' connotation rather than an active 'establishment or institution' connotation associated with Rousseau (Baker 1990: 254–5, cited in Ross 1995: 392; Rousseau's voluntaristic notion appears at III.13 of *The Social Contract*).

Smith frames the discussion with a pointed reference to just this conception of a constitution, writing, 'Upon the manner in which any state is divided into the different orders and societies which compose it, and upon the particular distribution which has been made of their respective powers, privileges, and immunities, depends, what is called, the constitution of that particular state' (TMS VI.ii.2.8). Then, in successive paragraphs, he contrasts the good reformer, who merely attempts to 're-establish and improve the constitution', with the zealous party leaders who are out to 'new-model the constitution', a rhetorical dichotomy that would have been readily recognizable to English-speaking readers who remembered Cromwell's ill-fated experiment. The plain purpose here is to validate the actually existing rights and privileges of even an imperfectly organized society against the threat of violence, which would undo what Smith twice calls the 'divine maxim of Plato' – i.e., 'never to use violence to his country no more than to his parents'

(TMS VI.ii.2.16). The 'divine maxim' passage, in turn, is a carefully calibrated echo of a passage at the very beginning of the whole section on the individual's relationships with others (TMS VI.ii.intro.2), in which Smith cites the 'sacred and religious regard not to hurt or disturb in any respect the happiness of our neighbour'. Violence, then, is a bright line that even the most righteous reformer must not cross.

Alongside the term 'constitution', moreover, Smith uses the term 'moderation' in equally significant ways. Thus, he contrasts the 'proper temper and moderation' of the good factional leader – the George Washington reference, as it were – with the factional violence of the bad leaders whose lack of 'moderation' squanders a chance at gradual or partial reform (TMS VI.ii.2.14–15). At the same time, he gives moral weight to this Montesquieuan political point by depicting moderation as the truest expression of 'humanity' and 'benevolence' – two terms which, alongside 'constitution', Smith uses to frame the whole discussion (see TMS VI.ii.intro.2, VI.ii.2.16), and whose place in his larger moral system had been made clear in the first five parts of the work. Indeed, 'humanity' and 'benevolence' emerge as nothing less than the proper standard for discerning true public spirit.

In placing such calculated emphasis upon 'moderation' and upon the 'constitution' thus defined, Smith was doing nothing more than restating and reapplying principles to which he had long subscribed. I have counted sixty-six uses of the term 'constitution' in the modern edition of LJ, for example, not one of which contains a hint of Rousseau's voluntaristic notion of 'fixing' the constitution. Instead, on the rare occasions when he uses the term in a recognizably political way, it is in a Montesquieuan fashion, as in his allusions to the 'feudall constitution' or to the 'constitution of England' (see the entries for 21 Jan., 3 Mar. and 4 Mar., 1763, among others; see also WN I.viii.26, TMS IV.i.11, and LRLB ii.203 for similar usages, as well as Alvey 2003: 137–8). As for 'moderation', we have already seen Smith's distinctly Montesquieuan application of this concept as recently as the WN, where he actually uses it against Montesquieu himself in the discussion of Greek musical education.

Revisionist scholars are not wrong, in my view, in insisting upon Smith's reformist credentials and even in keeping open the question of his engagement with the French Revolution. He did, after all, conspicuously pass up the opportunity to rail against some of the episodes in 1789 that attracted the shock and ire of his friend Edmund Burke, among others. He also slid rather quickly from his criticism of the factional leader's 'spirit of system' to his categorical claim that 'sovereign princes are by far the most dangerous' embodiments of that spirit of system (TMS VI.ii.2.18). And he expressly declined to pass judgment on whether 'political wisdom' would support 'innovation' or 're-establish[ment]' in such unsettled times as the ones to which he seemed to be alluding (TMS VI.ii.2.12). But his deep appreciation of the complex and multifaceted place of circumstance in human social existence, and of the fragility of the manners, laws, customs and institutions that hold societies together, which he shared with and partly learned from Montesquieu, led him to regard with caution and scepticism the kind of merely political 'discourse of will' then becoming prominent in France (see Baker 1990: 25–7, 105–6). It was for this reason, and not for lack of compassion, that he explicitly stated that 'the peace and order of society, is of more importance than even the relief of the miserable' (TMS VI.ii.1.20).

Even his critique of absolute monarchy itself repeats an entirely Montesquieuan indictment of what precisely is so dangerous about it, an indictment that had appeared already in LJ, as we saw above: namely, that absolute monarchs seek to remove all obstacles to their own arbitrary will; that they seek to 'reduce the authority of the nobility; to take away the privileges of cities and provinces, and to render both the greatest individuals and the greatest orders of the state, as incapable of opposing their commands, as the weakest and most insignificant' (TMS VI.ii.2.18). Montesquieu himself sometimes came to be vilified as a reactionary and an 'aristocrat' as the Revolution took an increasingly radical course (Hampson 1983); it is easy to imagine Smith experiencing a similar fate had the 'circumstances' of his own life and death been somewhat different.

Conclusion

Smith's engagement with the standards of theory and history set in Montesquieu's *Spirit of the Laws* was therefore various. Though they both had robust conceptions of nature and circumstance, which they were constantly attempting to adjust into a coherent framework, nature and circumstance did not mean precisely the same thing to the two thinkers. There was more climate in Montesquieu's 'nature' and more moral psychology and market incentive in Smith's. Montesquieu's 'circumstance' hinged more on his regime typology, Smith's on his stadial explanation. Sometimes, as with the Spartan *fur manifestus*, Smith applied a natural standard (the sympathy mechanism) to a problem on which Montesquieu had offered a more circumstantial analysis. Other times, as with house visits in tax collection, it was Montesquieu whose implied standard of natural liberty Smith forewent in favour of more circumstantial considerations drawn from stadial theory. These divergences can easily be exaggerated, as we have seen: the Frenchman was keenly sensitive to moral-psychological factors and to variations in historical epoch; the Scot clearly meant to integrate some sort of regime typology into his overall analysis, as some contemporaries appreciated. And in the crisis of 1789, it was long-held ideas on moderation and on the nature of a constitution – ideas associated distinctively, though of course not uniquely, with Montesquieu – that Smith reverted to in making sense of unfolding events.

One obvious difference between them is that Montesquieu finished his 'history and theory' and Adam Smith did not. The historic success of WN as an economic treatise can easily obscure this fact, but specialists know how problematic is this question: why did Smith never complete the 'sort of theory and History' (*Corr.* Letter 248, 1 Nov. 1785) that he had planned? To a certain extent, the answer is that Smith, like other eighteenth-century thinkers, had interests that were too diffuse to accommodate the sort of focus that such an ambitious project would have required. Thus, after completing his work on WN, he may have been as preoccupied by botany in the 1770s and especially by the imitative arts in the 1780s (see Smith 1980, EPS) as he was by his comparative history and theory of law and government. (See Ross 1995: 305, 338, 345, 351, 380 on the arts, and 227 on botany.)

These considerations aside, my own tentative suggestion is that Smith would have wanted his 'theory and History' to include not only the encyclopedic coverage contained in Montesquieu's work (such coverage was already a feature of WN, after all), but also a fresh approach to regime typology that would fully incorporate the moral–psychology of his sympathy theory and the metahistory of his stadial theory – both of which were early innovations in his career, mostly absent in Montesquieu – and that he found it impossible to digest and master these disparate agendas in a way that would have satisfied his finicky perfectionism. The Baron of La Brède had set the bar high on any attempt at the kind of study Smith would have wanted to do. This is perhaps one reason why his deep and lasting influence on Smith has not always gotten the recognition that it deserves.

Acknowledgement

I am grateful to Douglas J. Den Uyl for inviting me to participate in this feature, and to the editor of *The Adam Smith Review* and its outside reviewers for their assistance and helpful suggestions.

Note

1   While the recent essay by F.P. Lock (2007) deserves more attention that is possible here, it does prompt one elaboration of the foregoing argument: the final lines of VI.ii.2.18, which Prof. Lock sees as an attack on Joseph II, seem to me more likely a reference to Louis XIV (1643–1715), standard exemplar of those 'sovereign princes' who 'consider the state as made for themselves'. This reading has Smith apportioning blame for France's current troubles between the absolute monarchy (and its current heirs and defenders in the royal 'party') and a patriot 'party' unwittingly guilty of the same spirit of heedless innovation – an exercise in intellectual balance and mediation entirely consistent with Smith's style of thought.

Bibliography

Alvey, J. (2003) *Adam Smith: Optimist or Pessimist? A New Problem Concerning the Teleological Basis of Commercial Society*, Burlington: Ashgate.

Anderson, J. *Commonplace Book*, Anderson MSS, Anderson Library, Strathclyde University, MS 35.1: 1–21, 368–292.

Baker, K. (1990) *Inventing the French Revolution: Essays on French Political Culture in the Eighteenth Century*, Cambridge: Cambridge University Press.

156 *Henry C. Clark*

Carpenter, K.E. (2002) *The Dissemination of the* Wealth of Nations *in French and in France: 1776–1843*, New York: The Bibliographical Society of America.

Cheney, P. (2002) 'The history and science of commerce in the century of enlightenment: France, 1713–89', Ph.D., Columbia University.

Clark, H. (1993) 'Women and humanity in Scottish Enlightenment social thought: the case of Adam Smith', *Historical Reflections/Réflexions Historiques*, 19: 335–61.

—— (2005) Review of Pierre Force, *Self-interest before Adam Smith*, in *New Perspectives on the Eighteenth Century*, 2: 63–5.

Cohler, A. (1988) *Montesquieu's Comparative Politics and the Spirit of American Constitutionalism*, Manhattan: University of Kansas Press.

Condillac, E. (1948) 'Cours d'étude', in vol. 2 of *Œuvres philosophiques*, 3 vols., G. Le Roy, (ed.) Paris: Presses Universitaires de France.

—— (1997) *Commerce and Government: Considered in their Mutual Relationship*, S. Eltis (trans.), S. Eltis and W. Eltis (eds), Cheltenham: Edward Elgar.

Ferguson, A. (1995) *An Essay on the History of Civil Society*, F. Oz-Salzberger (ed.), Cambridge: Cambridge University Press.

Fleischacker, S. (2004) *On Adam Smith's* Wealth of Nations: *A Philosophical Companion*, Princeton: Princeton University Press.

Forbes, D. (1975) 'Sceptical whiggism, commerce, and liberty', in *Essays on Adam Smith*, 179–201, A.S. Skinner and T. Wilson (eds), Oxford: Clarendon Press.

Force, P. (2003) *Self-interest before Adam Smith: A Genealogy of Economic Science*, Cambridge: Cambridge University Press

Griswold, C.L., Jr (1999) *Adam Smith and the Virtues of Enlightenment*, Cambridge: Cambridge University Press.

Haakonssen, K. (1981) *The Science of a Legislator: The Natural Jurisprudence of David Hume and Adam Smith*, Cambridge: Cambridge University Press.

Hampson, N. (1983) *Will and Circumstance: Montesquieu, Rousseau, and the French Revolution*, Norman: University of Oklahoma Press.

Hume, D. (1987) *Essays Moral, Political, and Literary*, E.F. Miller (ed.), Indianapolis: Liberty Fund.

Hutcheson, F. (2002) [1728] *An Essay on the Nature and Conduct of the Passions and Affections with Illustrations of the Moral Sense*, A. Garrett (ed. and intro.), Indianapolis: Liberty Fund.

—— (2004) [1725] *An Inquiry into the Original of Our Ideas of Beauty and Virtue*, W. Leidhold (ed. and intro.), Indianapolis: Liberty Fund.

Klein, D. (1985) 'Deductive economic methodology in the French Enlightenment: Condillac and Destutt de Tracy', *History of Political Economy*, 17: 51–71.

Lock, F.P. (2007) 'Adam Smith and "the man of system": interpreting *The Theory of Moral Sentiments, VI.ii.2.12–18*', in *The Adam Smith Review*, 3:37–48, London and New York: Routledge.

Meek, R. (1971) 'Smith, Turgot, and the "four-stages" theory', *History of Political Economy*, 3: 9–27.

—— (1977) *Smith, Marx, and After: Ten Essays in the Development of Economic Thought*, London: Chapman & Hall.

Meikle, H. (1912) *Scotland and the French Revolution*, Glasgow: Maclehose.

Millar, J. (1803) *An Historical View of the English Government*, 4 vols., London: Mawman.

Montesquieu, C. (1964) *The Persian Letters*, G.R. Healy (trans.), Indianapolis: Hackett; repr. 1999.

—— (1989) *The Spirit of the Laws*, A. Cohler, B. Miller, and H. Stone (eds), Cambridge: Cambridge University Press.

—— (1991) *Pensées, Le Spicilège,* L. Desgraves (ed.), Paris: Robert Laffont.

Morilhat, C. (1996) *Montesquieu: politique et richesses,* Paris: Presses Universitaires de France.

Pocock, J.G.A. (1975) *The Machiavellian Moment: Florentine Political Thought and the Atlantic Republican Tradition,* Princeton: Princeton University Press.

Pufendorf, S. (2005) [1729] *Of the Law of Nature and Nations: Eight Books,* 4th edn, B. Kennett (trans.), Clark, N.J.: Lawbook Exchange.

Rae, J. (1990) [1895] *Life of Adam Smith,* Bristol: Thoemmes.

Rahe, P. (2005) 'The book that never was: Montesquieu's *Considerations on the Romans* in Historical Context', *History of Political Thought,* 26: 43–89.

Raphael, D.D. (1985) *Adam Smith,* Oxford: Oxford University Press.

Rasmussen, D. (2006a) 'Does "bettering our condition" really make us better off? Adam Smith on progress and happiness', *American Political Science Review,* 100: 309–18.

—— (2006b) 'Rousseau's "philosophical chemistry" and the foundations of Adam Smith's thought', *History of Political Thought,* 27: 620–41.

Ross, I.S. (1995) *The Life of Adam Smith.* Oxford: Clarendon Press.

—— (2004) ' "Great works upon the anvil" in 1785: Adam Smith's projected corpus of philosophy', *The Adam Smith Review,* 1: 40–59, London and New York: Routledge.

Rothschild, E. (2001) *Economic Sentiments: Adam Smith, Condorcet, and the Enlightenment,* Cambridge: Harvard University Press.

Skinner, A.S. (1975) 'Adam Smith: an economic interpretation of history', in *Essays on Adam Smith,* 154–78, A.S. Skinner and T. Wilson (eds), Oxford: Clarendon Press.

Smith, A. (1976a) *The Theory of Moral Sentiments,* D.D. Raphael and A.L. Macfie (eds), Oxford: Clarendon Press; reprinted, Liberty Press (1982).

—— (1976b) *An Inquiry into the Nature and Causes of the Wealth of Nations,* 2 vols., W.B. Todd (ed.), Oxford: Clarendon Press; reprinted, Liberty Press (1981).

—— (1977) *Correspondence of Adam Smith,* E.C. Mossner and I.S. Ross (eds), 2nd edn, Oxford: Clarendon Press; reprinted, Liberty Press (1987).

—— (1978) *Lectures on Jurisprudence,* R.L. Meek, D.D. Raphael, and P.G. Stein (eds), Oxford: Clarendon Press; reprinted, Liberty Press (1982).

—— (1980) *Essays on Philosophical Subjects,* W.P.D. Wightman (ed.), Oxford: Clarendon Press; reprinted, Liberty Press (1982).

—— (1983) *Lectures on Rhetoric and Belles Lettres,* J.C. Bryce (ed.), Oxford: Clarendon Press; reprinted, Liberty Press (1985).

Stewart, D. (1994) [1815] 'Dissertation: exhibiting the progress of metaphysical, ethical, and political philosophy, since the revival of letters in Europe', in *The Collected Works of Dugald Stewart,* 11 vols., Sir W. Hamilton (ed.), introduction by K. Haakonssen, London: Thoemmes.

—— (1980) [1794] 'Account of the Life and Writings of Adam Smith, LL.D.', in A. Smith, *Essays on Philosophical Subjects,* W.P.D. Wightman (ed.), Oxford: Clarendon Press; reprinted, Liberty Press (1982).

Vivenza, G. (2001) *Adam Smith and the Classics: the Classical Heritage in Adam Smith's Thought,* Oxford: Oxford University Press.

Wightman, W.P.D. (1975) 'Adam Smith and the history of ideas', in *Essays on Adam Smith,* 44–67, A.S. Skinner and T. Wilson (eds), Oxford: Clarendon Press.

Winch, D. (1978) *Adam Smith's Politics: An Essay in Historiographic Revision,* Cambridge: Cambridge University Press.

—— (1996) *Riches and Poverty: An Intellectual History of Political Economy in Britain, 1750–1834,* Cambridge: Cambridge University Press.

Adam Smith's moral philosophy in the context of eighteenth-century French fiction

Neven Brady Leddy

Adam Smith was a professional British philosopher engaged with the stoic tradition as well as a European Enlightenment figure who drew on sources beyond his immediate national and disciplinary contexts. In particular, Smith identified the fiction of Pierre Marivaux (1688–1763), Crébillon *fils* (1707–1777), and Marie-Jeanne Riccoboni (1713–1792) as an appropriate corpus of ethical theory with which to complement stoic teachings. These novelists answered the reductive view of human nature in which all human action is necessarily determined by the single principle of *amour-propre* by emphasizing the countervailing process of sympathetic love. In varying degrees their work can be seen as a response to La Rochefoucauld's *Maximes* (1665–1678), challenging first his reductive claim, and then his deterministic assertion of universality. Sympathetic love as an alternative to *amour-propre* was presented in an equally deterministic manner, but the *romanciers* worked autonomy back into the process in the form of *générosité*, an other-regarding aspect of love outside the deterministic process of the *coup de sympathie*. Smith took up their alternatives to La Rochefoucauld's model, and supplemented the idea of sympathy with an informed Impartial Spectator.

Our understanding of Adam Smith's moral philosophy owes a great deal to D.D. Raphael and A.L. Macfie's 1976 edition of *The Theory of Moral Sentiments* (TMS) in the Glasgow Edition of the Works and Correspondence of Adam Smith. Their influential presentation of Smith emphasizes the stoic elements in the TMS, and locates that work in the British philosophical tradition of Francis Hutcheson and of David Hume. In this paradigm, they prioritize Smith's response to Mandeville's *Fable of the Bees* (1714) to the exclusion of his mediated response to La Rochefoucauld. I hope to re-open some of the questions that this presentation glosses over by a broader contextualization of Smith's moral theory.

Raphael and Macfie grant that Smith read widely across languages and disciplines, but they are curiously blind to the 'interdisciplinary' nature of Smith's eighteenth-century mind, so that they privilege his reading of philosophical texts over his philosophical reading of literary texts:

Smith was well informed about ancient philosophy, keenly interested in the history of science and the evolution of society, and widely read in the culture of his own time, especially its literature, history, and nascent social science. He was anything but insular: his reading of recent books was almost as extensive in French as in English, and it was not negligible in Italian. Yet he was not closely acquainted with the ethical theory of the eighteenth century.

(Raphael and Macfie 1976: 10)

This implies a distinct view of 'ethical theory' that Raphael and Macfie impose on Smith's French-language reading. At no point do they refer to the novels that Smith himself offered as an alternative to ethical theory narrowly defined. Even within this already limited framework, Raphael and Macfie further restrict the scope of Smith's engagement with moral philosophy:

Faint echoes of Mandeville and of Rousseau can be heard in the passages about the deception of nature. But all these are nothing to the echoes of Stoicism and Hume that appear so often in both the language and the doctrine of TMS. . . . Apart from Hutcheson, the only contemporary philosopher who is considered at length is Mandeville in VII.ii.4. (In editions 1–5 his name was coupled with that of La Rochefoucauld, but Smith's actual exposition and criticism of 'licentious systems' in this chapter were always confined to the work of Mandeville.)

(Raphael and Macfie 1976: 11)

While there is no doubt that Smith responded to Mandeville, his appeal to French literature published prior to the penetration of Mandeville's ideas in France presents a historical problem that is not addressed by Raphael and Macfie. Likewise their strict reading of what constitutes 'ethical theory' divorces their interpretation from the internal evidence in the text they present.

The more general role of fiction in the Scottish Enlightenment has been addressed by a number of scholars, who are uneasy about the separation of literature from the history of ideas. John Mullan has examined the complementary role of literature to the philosophy of sentiment in the Scottish Enlightenment (Mullan 1987, 1988). Pierre Carboni has argued for the importance of the place of *belles-lettres* among other areas of endeavour (Carboni 1997). As with the others, John Dwyer has picked up on the relationship of Henry Mackenzie to Smith, and greatly contributed to our understanding of the influence of the TMS on subsequent literature (Dwyer 1993, 1998). Their tendency has been to work from the more formal philosophy of Hume and Smith, outwards. My contribution is intended as a complement to this scholarship, working from literature to philosophy. In this framework I am following a path identified by Dierdre Dawson in her

1991 article 'Is sympathy so surprising? Adam Smith and the French fictions of sympathy'.

Adam Smith was born into an appreciation of French letters which he further developed on his own terms, very likely with special intensity during his time at Oxford. From his father's editions of Molière and Fénelon in his boyhood home (Ross 1995: 3), to his practice of translating from the French (Stewart 1980, I.9), and his later travels in France, Smith was well grounded in French letters and culture. Of the contemporary authors with whom Smith was familiar, he made it clear that he found the French to be the most vibrant. In an illuminating discussion of the 'science of man' project in his 'Letter to the Edinburgh Review' (1755), Smith explained how, and where, the project stood:

> The original and inventive genius of the English has not only discovered itself in natural philosophy, but in morals, metaphysics, and part of the abstract sciences . . . Mr. Hobbs, Mr. Lock, and Dr. Mandevil, Lord Shaftsbury, Dr. Butler, Dr. Clarke, and Mr. Hutcheson have all of them according to their different and inconsistent systems, endeavoured at least to be, in some measure original . . . This branch of the English philosophy, which now seems to be intirely neglected by the English themselves, has of late been transported into France.
>
> ('Letter to the Edinburgh Review',
> para. 10, in Smith 1980)

Much of this discussion of moral philosophy consisted of a response to La Rochefoucauld in the *roman d'analyse* of the 1710s, 1720s and 1730s and later, if less immediately, in the works of Riccoboni.

This genre of fiction provoked one of the more risibly reactionary episodes of the Scottish Enlightenment when David Hume was censured for his acquisition of 'unworthy' French books, specifically Crébillon's *L'Ecumoire*, and two others. This episode has attracted the attention of scholars for Hume's response – effectively resigning – to the removal of these books from the Advocate's Library.[1] It is noteworthy that Hume purchased Marivaux's *La Vie de Marianne* for the Advocate's in the same order and his successors continued to expand the Advocate's holdings of contemporary French fiction. A document dated August 1779 headed 'Note of Books to be got immediately by order of the Curator, for the Advocate's Library' (NLS Fr 339r2), includes the 'Œuvres' of both Crébillon and Riccoboni, which were duly acquired, and appear in the 1787 appendix to the catalogue of the Advocate's.

La Rochefoucauld's widely-read collection offered what must have been, to the eighteenth-century mind, a maddeningly coherent and highly accessible reductive interpretation of human nature; that every human action was prompted by *amour-propre*. It was a view that was not shared by early eighteenth-century men of letters such as Pierre Marivaux and Claude Crébillon, and was given a gendered modulation by Marie-Jeanne *dit*

Madame Riccoboni. While there was too much self-evident truth in La Rochefoucauld's theory to contradict it outright, the eighteenth-century *romanciers* were keen to demonstrate that La Rochefoucauld was only partially correct. In their novels of sentiment, Marivaux, Crébillon, and Riccoboni offered myriad examples of a counter-tendency that was every bit the equal of La Rochefoucauld's *amour-propre*: the spontaneous compulsion of sympathy.

The problem for the eighteenth-century opponents of La Rochefoucauld was his reductionism, and their response thereto opened up the secondary problem of his determinism. La Rochefoucauld's reductive argument was that *amour-propre* was the sole principle guiding human conduct, calculating at the higher level, and sub-conscious in other cases; in the present discussion it is the calculating aspect of this view that is primarily at issue. His deterministic argument was that there was no way to opt out of this framework. La Rochefoucauld's preferred vocabulary for this discussion was one of vice and virtue, passion and interest, but also of sympathy, utility, and always of hypocrisy.

For the present purpose, La Rochefoucauld's maxims on altruism and love are the most salient. To begin with, La Rochefoucauld explicitly denied the possibility of disinterested action:

> When we work for the benefit of others it would appear that our self love is tricked by kindness and forgets itself; and yet this is the most certain way to achieve our ends, for it is lending at interest while pretending to give, in fact a way of getting everybody on our own side by subtle and delicate means.
>
> (La Rochefoucauld 1976: #236/p. 83)[2]

The response to this might be: but what of love? And here too La Rochefoucauld anticipated such an objection and reduced even love to a kind of acquisition:

> It is difficult to define love; what can be said is that in the soul it is a passion to dominate another, in the mind it is mutual understanding [sympathie], whilst in the body it is simply a delicately veiled desire to possess the beloved after many rites and mysteries.
>
> (La Rochefoucauld 1976: #68/p. 55)[3]

In terms of the eighteenth-century development of moral theory, this might be the most important maxim of all. While for the first and third terms of the maxim – the soul and the body – love is a species of domination or possession respectively; for the middle term – the intellect – La Rochefoucauld allowed that it was a kind of sympathy.

The evolution of the term 'sympathy' lagged somewhat behind the process traced here, until it came ultimately to be defined as spontaneous, uncalculating identification, in our current usage. In the first available definition, sympathy had only the slightest inkling of this future development: 'Of the affinity of relation of humours and inclinations. *Great, powerful sympathy, nothing binds two friends together as much as sympathy*' (*Dictionnaire de L'Académie française*,1694).[4] If La Rochefoucauld had allowed that this was the intellectual aspect of love, there would be an argument for a certain, if limited, continuity with the eighteenth-century theories of sentiment. In the very next maxim, however, La Rochefoucauld seemed to claw back this identification through the process of love, when he wrote: 'If pure love exists, free from the dross of our other passions, it lies hidden in the depths of our hearts and unknown even to ourselves (La Rochefoucauld 1976: #69/p. 55).[5] With this La Rochefoucauld buried the possibility of sympathy in the sub-conscious. Given that La Rochefoucauld also explicitly denied the possibility of altruism (#236 above), this presented a difficult challenge to anyone seeking to move beyond his reductive system, but this is precisely what the eighteenth-century *romanciers* did, and they did it on La Rochefoucauld's terms.

The first challenge in the rehabilitation of human nature as undertaken by Marivaux and Crébillon was to demonstrate that sympathy could operate beneath the level of conscious calculation – in short, to frame the concept in an anti-rational manner. The second was to demonstrate that love was not a question of interest, or at least not always. The effect was not so much to completely overturn La Rochefoucauld's system, but rather to establish exceptions – to poke holes in La Rochefoucauld's universal pretensions.

The strength of La Rochefoucauld's argument was such that it could not be easily dismissed or flatly contradicted. His presentation of *amour-propre* could not be met head on, nor did the eighteenth-century *romanciers* suggest that his interpretation of the working of *amour-propre* was inaccurate. In fact it was the very success with which La Rochefoucauld made his case that exposed his theory to a much-needed correction. La Rochefoucauld's system was a hermetic moral vacuum which collapsed the range of human motivations to a single principle of *amour-propre*. As in the literal sense, of an airtight and airless system, all that was necessary to re-inflate human psychology was to puncture La Rochefoucauld's system once for air to return to the vacuum and for the range of human psychology to reassert itself. In other words, Crébillon and Marivaux needed only to prove that any other principle than *amour-propre* was genuinely at play in order to explode the universal reductive pretension of La Rochefoucauld's psychology. Once the exclusivity of self-interest was undone, it would be only one among other motivations, even if it remained privileged over the others.

There can be no doubt that Crébillon and Marivaux shared a view of human nature that was, to some extent, calculating and self-interested. In this Crébillon was perhaps more explicit than Marivaux, and certainly more cynical, particularly in *Les égarements du cœur et de l'esprit*,[6] which was a fully developed libertine *bildungsroman*. *Les égarements* is the story of the seventeen-year-old Melicour's philosophical education and sexual socialization. He is mentored in this process, sexually, by Mme Lursay (in her mid-forties), and on a more philosophical level by M. Versac.

In the very beginning of the novel Melicour sets out his immature reductive view of love:

> What both sexes called love was a form of interaction [commerce] that one engaged in often without any real inclination [sans gout], in which agreeability [commodité] was always preferred to sympathy, interest to pleasure, and vice to sensibility [sentiment].
>
> (Crébillon 1993: 24)[7]

From this initial reductionist position, Melicour is tutored in the power of sentiment over intellect, with special reference to his youth and inexperience:

> Sentimentality, for example, is an outlook that won't lead you astray; it is not a judgement of the head but of the heart and matters of interest engage both limited and developed intellects.
>
> (Crébillon 1993: 29)[8]

Here we have the first of many examples in which a thinking and a feeling faculty are opposed, beginning from the premise of reductive self-interest and developing towards an understanding of the power of sentiment beyond self-interest. At this point in Melicour's development, Crébillon continued operating in an untranscended Rochefoucauldian paradigm in which both faculties might be collapsed to *amour-propre*. It was not until Crébillon introduced the *coup de sympathie* that La Rochefoucauld was left behind, and even then, not by much.

In this particular case, Crébillon was more interested in making a point about women than about sympathy, but the result was nevertheless to further limit the scope of La Rochefoucauld's *amour-propre*. Versac explains to Melicour women's capacity for rationalizing their own seduction:

> A woman gazes, is enthralled and taken unawares, and because she declines to reflect, is convinced that it is your charm that doesn't leave her the time to do so. If she happens to think of the resistance she might offer, it is only to better convince herself that it would be futile in the face of a thing so forceful, so unforeseen, so extraordinary as a *coup de sympathie*.
>
> (Crébillon 1993: 137)[9]

This passage is typical of Crébillon's double-edged moralist/libertine style. On the one hand a belief that one is struck by a *coup de sympathie* is self-serving, and in that sense, might be reduced to *amour-propre*; on the occasion of a genuine *coup de sympathie*, on the other hand, there is clearly no room for calculation, or any psychological response whatsoever. On the second reading of the *coup de sympathie* La Rochefoucauld's system starts to destabilize, although Crébillon's intention to that effect remains ambiguous.

The *coup de sympathie* was presented as an uncalculating compulsion which challenged La Rochefoucauld's reduction of all actions to *amour-propre*. That this sympathy was itself deterministic pitted one aspect of La Rochefoucauld's system against another, but Crébillon went further to undermine this strict determinism by invoking questions of difficulty and occasion. *Les égarements* can be read as a young man's initiation in a corrupt world, where the degree of difficulty in achieving virtue seemed absurd (Dornier 1993). Crébillon discussed this in terms of an opposition between *le monde* and *la morale*; Versac explains to Melicour that they were often incompatible: 'Social and ethical life are not always consistent with each other, and as you know we often succeed in one at the expense of the other' (Crébillon 1993: 138).[10] Crébillon presented a curious relationship to La Rochefoucauld's reductionism, where he seemed to suggest that we are capable of virtuous behaviour, but that we opt for lesser conduct. While this was ambiguous in relation to reductionism, it was very clearly anti-deterministic, which suggests the second area in which the eighteenth-century *romanciers* departed from La Rochefoucauld.

Marivaux's development of sympathy as a transcendence of La Rochefoucauld's *amour-propre* emphasized the distinction between the two to a greater extent than Crébillon. Yet Marivaux, too, retained the element of calculation in human motivation. In his novels, Marivaux depicted an opposition between a thinking faculty and a feeling faculty that together defined the human self, suggesting that sentiment might be more effective than reason in achieving a calculated response; the extent to which sympathy might involve calculation remained open. This topic has not been neglected in the secondary literature on Marivaux (Culpin 1987, 1996; Munro 1996). The role of reason, in particular, has been investigated in relation to action, but I am not convinced that Marivaux intended a resolution to this tension. He had moved beyond the framework of La Rochefoucauld, where all human actions might be reduced to a single motor, be it *amour-propre* or sympathy. He accepted that self-interested calculation was a common motive, without feeling obliged to offer a blanket condemnation thereof, but he also expanded the realm of motivation to include other, unthinking, anti-rational alternatives.

The eponymous heroine of the *Vie de Marianne* explains how the immediacy of sentiment has clearly triumphed over the intellectual hesitation of calculation in her first experience of love: 'Between two people who love one another there are basic sentiments that the intellect might take notice of, if it wanted to, but which it allows to pass unnoticed for the sake of the heart' (Marivaux 1997: 130).[11] In another context, she rejects the necessity of calculation in the face of good-heartedness; and again the emphasis is on the spontaneity of such a response: 'We are immediately linked to good-hearted people, whoever they are; they're like friends that we have in every walk of life' (Marivaux 1997: 530).[12] This opposition between the thinking and the feeling faculties runs throughout Marivaux's fiction. These faculties were contrasted in a range of formulations; the reasoning faculty was usually defined as *esprit*, and the feeling faculty variously, as *sentiment*, *cœur*, or *âme*.

Marivaux offered this view in a reflection that was ripe with significance for Smith's development of this tension: 'Excessively good souls are willingly imprudent from an excess of goodness, the flip-side of which is that prudent souls are fairly rarely good' (Marivaux 1981: 143).[13] The use of 'prudence' in this passage suggests that calculation might be eclipsed by *bonté*, and even that the essence of *bonté* is the absence of calculation. He drove this home by suggesting that *esprit* or intelligence actively thwarts the tendency to benevolence, both on the part of the actor and on the part of the beneficiary; he explained that La Rochefoucauld's reductive view is so common that a beneficiary is likely to suspect the motive of an intelligent person. Significantly this discussion unfolds in language not far removed from Smith's discussion of prudence and benevolence. As with Crébillon, Marivaux has turned determinism against reductionism and then sought an escape from this corrosive aspect of sympathy (Marivaux 1997: 278–9).

In the appropriately-titled *Les effets surprenants de la sympathie*, Marivaux explored the nature of love in two aspects: sympathy and generosity. It is impossible to encapsulate the plot of this novel, if such a thing can even be said to exist; it is an engaging, multi-layered shaggy-dog story of seven intertwining narratives. In one of these narratives we are presented with a collapsing love triangle, involving the intrepid hero Clorante, his jilted lover Clarice, and his current love Caliste. Ex-lover Clarice is presented in this situation as an *âme généreuse* who stands outside of the determinism of thwarted love; even though she experiences the emotional consequences of that love she is not compelled by it:

> She does not feel that awful jealousy, which nearly all unhappy lovers feel towards a rival. These surges of jealousy bring with them a stubborn antipathy which makes them capable of anything: this type of jealous person is necessarily cruel and mean, which justifies our subsequent disgust with them. Truly magnanimous [généreux] hearts have these feelings in the first instance, over which they have no control, but an overriding virtuousness quickly restores them to that greatness of character from which they were shaken.
>
> (Marivaux 1972: 103–4)[14]

Clorante, our hero, is in his turn compelled by his love – but not for Clarice. He recognizes his debt to her, which tempers his love of Caliste, but does not thwart it:

Clorante is grateful, it is true, and that gratitude diminishes his pleasure in giving himself over to his love [of Caliste] without undermining the determinism [nécessité] which forces him to love Caliste. Love, in a good-hearted person does not extinguish all sentiment of magnanimity [générosité]; this sentiment is the result of virtue which reveals to them what they owe one another, without empowering then to pay that debt in full.

(Marivaux 1972: 108)[15]

With this Marivaux offered an opposition between *générosité* and sympathetic love in which, for women at least, love need not be deterministic.

For Marie-Jeanne Riccoboni, the proper response to La Rochefoucauld's brand of reductive and deterministic *amour-propre* was equally a comment on gender: that while the actions of men are certainly determined by their passions, those of women are otherwise conditioned. As with Marivaux, and possibly under his influence, Riccoboni invoked the vocabulary of generosity and prudence. Her earliest novel set the tone for Riccoboni's career-long investigation into all aspects of love. Beginning with *Lettres de Mistress Fanni Butlerd* (1757), Riccoboni set out the irresistibility of love, in a manner akin to the *coup de sympathie* of Marivaux and Crébillon. She explained that love undermines free will but allowed for a different variety of freedom, which is in no case a rational freedom of choice. Reason is locked out of the experience: 'Love itself, that most insinuating of sentiments, binds us with unseen shackles'; 'The intellect does not speak to the heart, it does not speak like the heart' (Riccoboni 1979: ##64, 65).[16] And love is certainly meant as an affair of the heart. Since she always equated love with dis-interest there can be no question of an interest calculation in this process.

In *Lettres de Milady Juliette Catesby* (1758), Riccoboni took this idea of deterministic love further, and used a striking vocabulary to describe the process as it is experienced by Juliette in all its bitter glory: 'It seemed to me, as I finished the letter, that an invisible hand pushed into an abyss and destroyed my will to live' (Riccoboni 1983: #14).[17] The distinction that Riccoboni often made in her discussion of irresistible eros was that for women it was a question of love, while for men more often than not it was lust, but common to both genders was the futility of rational self-command in these situations, though women might command their lust – but not every woman, and not in every instance. The example of Milord d'Ossery's unwilled lapse in *Lettres de Milady Juliette Catesby* provides an excellent example, particularly as Ossery is one of Riccoboni's more upstanding male characters. He describes the psychology of transportation as he betrays Juliette with the sister of a friend after a night of drunken revelry:

. . . she began to laugh with such good-heartedness, that her gaiety provoked my own . . . Her excessive enjoyment made an extraordinary impression on me – it made me bold: The loss of my reason set my heart alight. Delivered entirely to sensuality, I forgot my love, my integrity ... A respectable girl seemed to me at that moment, nothing but a vehicle for my desire, for that vulgar passion which activates our one instinct.

(Riccoboni 1983: #35)[18]

For Riccoboni this was an expression of masculine nature, and even when it leads to betrayals as it so often does in her fiction, these men are excused because they are understood to be conditioned by their nature. It is the double standard by which women are not allowed the same leeway that so infuriated Riccoboni.

It needs also to be said that Riccoboni's was not a naïve view of love, nor were her characters as one-dimensional as they sometimes come across. In the *Histoire de M. le Marquis de Cressy*, in particular, Riccoboni complicated her presentation of love. The Marquis de Cressy and Hortense de Berneil have been linked to the later development of sexual psychology in Sade, but they are equally related to La Rochefoucauld's view of love as a desire for domination. Hortense, 20, is the ward of Cressy who matches his cynicism in erotic matters, and wilfully engages in a manipulative sexual relationship with him during his courtship of Adélaïde. Riccoboni explains the psychology of their mutual seduction as follows:

Mademoiselle de Berneil, in reciprocating the passion of the Marquis, yielded perhaps less to her lover than to the curiosity to know if that passion would provide for her all the happiness she had always been assured followed from it. She wanted the pleasures and didn't worry about the subtleties. The more she thought she had sacrificed in acceding to the wishes of her lover, the more she demanded his gratitude. The sentiment which guided her was not the sincere attachment of Adélaïde nor the tender and gentle love of the Marquise; it was a hedonistic urge – it was the pleasure of dominating and in turn submitting to the caprice of another's heart.

(Riccoboni 1989: 88)[19]

With this we are no doubt some way from Smith's use of Riccoboni as a corrective to stoic apathy, and yet this searching analysis of the process of love at the heart of her sentimental framework opens out onto a very specific discussion of philosophy.

In her most explicitly philosophical novel, *Lettres de Mylord Rivers* (1777), Riccoboni offered a gendered reading of stoicism, in the aspect of self-command so dear to Smith. Riccoboni approaches stoic self-control as a masculine prerogative, which she undermines with the claim that it is women and not men who are better able to control their passions. In this presentation the stoic figure moves from caricature to liar to delusional:

I am a man it is true. But man is a feeble creature, less able than you perhaps to resist the compulsion of his senses, of thwarting the provocation of his desires. A fair-minded disposition, the accumulation of learning, sound consideration, the feeling that it is necessary to be at peace with oneself, the laudable ambition of merited approbation, gives us like you the power to moderate our violent passions, to repress them, to subjugate them to duty, but never the power not to suffer by such a severe constraint.

Yes, no doubt *stoicism is a lie*, but equally sure is that there are no real stoics, and never can be. Let them talk and write, these enthusiasts, whose cold hearts and exalted spirits describe a humanity in which men do not recognize themselves. To describe an unattainable human nature does not raise the spirit, but discourages it.

(Riccoboni 1992: #10)[20]

This question of gender and self-command is present in all of Riccoboni's works, and might even be said to be her principal preoccupation.

In her earlier novels in particular Riccoboni's male characters display very little in the way of self-command. Riccoboni demonstrated the distinctly gendered processes of desire and self-command in her most odious male character, the Marquis de Cressy and his young fiancée, Adélaïde du Bugei. Riccoboni sets the scene of their late-night rendez-vous in an isolated garden court. The setting, scent of the flowers, the silence of the place, and not least the gentle breeze that pulled at Adélaïde's light and low-cut dress, provoked arousal in Cressy. Riccoboni's description of this process and Adélaïde's response are foundational to her view of human nature and gender. She describes Cressy's arousal in terms of 'those impetuous ardent desires so difficult to repress when the opportunity to satisfy them further augments the power of the senses over reason'. She describes how Cressy, taking Adélaïde in his arms, 'holding her tenderly planted on her lips one of those fiery kisses whose pleasant murmur awakes love and desire'. Here we have a depiction of masculine desire feeding off itself and the occasion, to which she contrasts feminine desire and self-mastery:

Adélaïde was surprised and ceded for a moment to the temptation of an unfamiliar pleasure. She felt the first stirring of that insinuating feeling that beguiles our reason, and by which nature eclipsing all our constraints returns us to our happy simplicity. It was brief this beguilment.

(Riccoboni 1989: 67–8)[21]

Riccoboni characterizes Adélaïde as 'revenant à elle-même' – getting hold of herself – to exercise the self-command that was required to protect her social virtue prior to her wedding; it is the 16 year-old girl – innocent in the ways of the world – who demonstrates a greater self-command than the twenty-eight year old military figure Cressy. Riccoboni further developed this idea into a scathing critical sociology of gender in her increasingly philosophical 'love stories'.

These *romanciers* were caught in an awkward dilemma of their own making; because they used sympathy to explode La Rochefoucauld's reductionist vacuum, they seemed to give credence to his determinism, locating a stress in the relationship of love to sympathy to necessity. These analytical novels of sentiment dealt primarily with love, which operated as sympathy, and seemed to leave no room for choice. It seemed impossible in this framework not to love when faced with the workings of sympathy, and so the novelists sought another way to work autonomy back into their system, in the form of *générosité*. In this, as elsewhere, Marivaux was more effective in transcending La Rochefoucauld than was Crébillon, whereas Riccoboni offered a gendered response to La Rochefoucauld that exempted women from his analysis.

It must be noted that the argument I have distilled from these texts was intended to be so gleaned. Both Crébillon and especially Marivaux were keen to emphasize that they wrote as much for didactic as for literary purposes. Not one of their novels lacks a preface containing a direct and explicit plea to the reader to balance the content and the form of the novels. Crébillon argued, in the preface to *Les égarements*, that fiction served one of two purposes, but that to serve both was particularly difficult: 'Any man who writes can have but two objectives – the useful and the amusing. Few authors have managed to reconcile the two' (Crébillon 1993: 19).[22]

The other challenge for Crébillon was to depict the human condition accurately, without producing a scandalous, but ultimately vapid *roman à clef* (Crébillon 1993: 20). Nor were academic treatises on morality a useful tool for Crébillon's purpose. He explained his mission, and the difficulties in reaching a broad audience in the preface to *Le sopha*:

> It is only to the truly enlightened, above prejudice, knowing the futility of science, who understand how much esteem and even veneration we owe to those who can write novels – and who have the will power to devote themselves to the task despite the reputation for frivolity that pride and ignorance attach to the genre. The important lessons contained in these stories, the grand sweep of imagination which we so frequently encounter and the humourous ideas of which they are always full take nothing from the vulgar, whose esteem one can only earn by presenting them with that which they never understand, but they would do well to learn.

> (Crébillon 1995: 29–30)[23]

The difficulty that Crébillon identified was pedagogical: how to deliver a moral lesson to a broad audience without seeming to moralize.

Unlike Crébillon, Marivaux was fond of the reflection as a literary device. He drew attention to the reflections in the preface to each of his novels. In the *avertissement* to the second part of *Marianne* he explained how the reflections were meant as pedagogical tools:

> The first part of *Vie de Marianne* seems to have pleased many readers who particularly enjoyed the frequent reflections. Others have said that there were too many, and it is to these that this advertisement is addressed.
> If we gave them a book entitled *Reflections on Man*, would they not willingly read it if the reflections were good? We have a great number of such works, of which some are well thought of – why then do reflections displease them, unless then have something against reflections? . . .
> If you look at the *Vie de Marianne* as a novel, you're right, your criticism is valid: there are too many reflections, which is unusual for a novel or stories told for entertainment. But Marianne did not set out to write a novel.
>
> (Marivaux 1997: 109)[24]

These digressions or *réflexions* which Marivaux here defended by hiding behind his protagonist were his didactic asides, and read like philosophical maxims in the tradition of La Rochefoucauld, to whom they were often a response.[25]

Marivaux elaborated the difficulties of reconciling literature and philosophy in *Réflexions sur l'esprit humain à l'occasion de Corneille et de Racine*, where he bemoaned the valorization of philosophers over men of letters: 'In relation to other great men, why do we assign them a lesser rank? Why do we not have the same view of their capacities?' (Marivaux 2001: 472).[26] Marivaux explained that the novelists' effectiveness was often overlooked because of its subtlety:

> the beauties they impart to us don't strike us as new, since we always think we recognize them – we had only glimpsed them, but until the novelists we had left it at that, and hadn't looked carefully enough to express them for ourselves.
>
> (Marivaux 2001: 473)[27]

In the first instance Marivaux and Crébillon seemed to demand recognition of their philosophical fiction as 'ethical theory' and in the second Marivaux seemed to claim for the romanciers the status if not of *philosophe*, then at least of *génie*.

It is equally certain that Smith recognized that these novels were to some extent just such vehicles of 'ethical theory'. In the twentieth of the lectures collected as LRBL (Smith 1983), Smith compared the *romanciers* to Tacitus, and identified him as a forerunner of his own philosophy of human nature:

Marivaux and Crebillon resemble Tacitus as much as we can well imagine in works of so conterary a nature. They are Allways at great pains to account for every event by the temper and internall disposition of the several actors in disquisitions that approach near to metaphysicall ones.

(LRBL ii.64)

On this point it seems fair to let Smith's interpretation of what constitutes 'ethical theory' supercede that of Raphael and Macfie.

The historical difficulty with the Raphael/Macfie argument that Smith responded to Mandeville but not La Rochefoucauld has surprisingly not arisen in the secondary literature. In the Raphael/Macfie paradigm, Mandeville would be substituted for La Rochefoucauld in the present analysis, so that Smith would be said to have drawn on the *romanciers* in order to refute Mandeville; this is valid to an extent, but it fails to take into consideration that Marivaux and Crébillon were unfamiliar with Mandeville during the gestation and composition of the works in question here. Marivaux's *Les effets surprenants de la sympathie* (1712), *Le paysan parvenu* (1734–1735) and *La vie de Marianne* (1727–1741) and Crébillon's *Les égarements du cœur et de l'esprit* (1736–38) all pre-date the vogue for Mandeville in France, which is generally dated from the translation of the *Fable* in 1740.[28] In historical terms they must be understood as responding to La Rochefoucauld, and no doubt to broader currents of Augustinianism more generally. The most generous correction of the Raphael/Macfie presentation of this process, then, would be that Smith transposed a response to La Rochefoucauld for use against Mandeville, but to my mind this remains too anglocentric to do Smith justice.[29]

Smith echoed the *romanciers'* recalibration of the relationship of sympathy to self-interest in his discussion of anticipation, based on the acceptance that we calculate in order to provoke sympathy. This calculation of sympathy-to-be-achieved was one of the major motivations for commanding one's behaviour:

He fixes his thoughts, therefore, upon those [circumstances] only which are agreeable, the applause and admiration which he is about to deserve by the heroic magnanimity of his behaviour. To feel that he is capable of so noble and generous an effort, to feel that in this dreadful situation he can still act as he would desire to act, animates and transports him with joy, and enables him to support that triumphant gaiety which seem to exult in the victory he thus gains over his misfortunes.

(TMS I.iii.1.15)

Smith further develops this idea in the third book, as an example of how the process of sympathy tends to a transcendence of La Rochefoucauld's determinism. This idea was predicated on the balanced observation of the abstract Impartial Spectator, to suggest that one anticipated an objective and informed interpretation of one's actions:

> He anticipates the applause and admiration which in this case would be bestowed upon him, and he applauds and admires himself by sympathy with sentiments, which do not indeed actually take place, but which the ignorance of the public alone hinder form taking place, which he knows are the natural and ordinary effects of such conduct, which his imagination strongly connects with it, and which he has acquired a habit of conceiving as something that naturally and in propriety ought to follow from it.
>
> (TMS III.2.5)

For La Rochefoucauld or the *romanciers*, this kind of calculation was condemnable, but Smith's formulation was more nuanced. He allowed that calculation to achieve sympathy was a neutral and acceptable aspect of human nature – yet it remained problematically deterministic.

This difficulty was that sympathy had been established as instantaneous, and uncalculating. In the calculation to achieve sympathy, Smith distinguished between vanity and pride. He suggested that pride, dismissed by La Rochefoucauld and the *romanciers* as an embodiment of *amour-propre*, might occasion sympathy in just such a manner as uncalculating *bonté*:

> We frequently, not only pardon, but thoroughly enter into and sympathize with the excessive self-estimation of those splendid characters in which we observe a great and distinguished superiority above the common level of mankind. [. . .] But we cannot enter into and sympathize with the excessive self-estimation of those characters in which we can discern no such distinguished superiority.
>
> (TMS VI.iii.33)

The difference, according to Smith was based on sincerity:

> The proud man is sincere, and, in the bottom of his heart, is convinced of his own superiority. [. . .] He disdains to court your esteem.
>
> The vain man is not sincere, and in the bottom of his heart, is very seldom convinced of that superiority which he wishes you to ascribe to him. [. . .] He flatters in order to be flattered. He studies to please, and endeavours to bribe you into a good opinion of him by politeness and complaissance, and sometimes even by real and essential good offices, though often displayed, perhaps with unnecessary ostentation.
>
> (TMS VI.iii.35–6)

As much as one might calculate to win sympathy, Smith argued that such sympathy was not a prize to be won; that our estimation of vanity or sincerity would determine our response – a proud man might provoke sympathy, but a vain man would not.

The distinction between vanity and pride was based on the informedness of the observer, which Smith had identified as a necessary aspect of the process of sympathy in the first instance: 'Whatever is the passion which arises from any object in the person principally concerned, an analogous emotion springs up, at the thought of his situation, in the breast of every attentive spectator' (TMS I.i.1.4). To suggest that attentiveness and informedness are interchangeable would do violence to the text, but the one is at least a precondition of the other. With this, we can see how Smith identified a manifestation of sympathy that was sincere and even uncalculating, and in so doing freed the 'science of man' of the hangover of La Rochefoucauld that remained in the *romanciers*. Smith transcended the zero-sum-game of the opposition between *bonté* and calculation.

Smith's response to Riccoboni's gendered adaptation of La Rochefoucauld is less a question of influence than a dialogue. Unlike Marivaux and Crébillon who were on Smith's mind in the 1750s, Riccoboni was not mentioned until the sixth edition of TMS in 1790. We know that Smith had a personal relationship with Riccoboni in Paris, but by that time he had already published his thoughts on gender and virtue in the 1759 TMS. It is purely speculation on my part to suggest that Smith may have influenced Riccoboni, especially the 1777 novel *Rivers*, which seems to respond specifically to Smith, to which Smith himself may have responded in 1790. This remains speculation; more concretely, we can see how Smith's view of love hardened in the sixth edition regardless of whether or not it was in response to Riccoboni.

Throughout TMS Smith worked with two general types of virtues, which he laid out in the first part, and then gendered in Part IV. In I.1.5, 'Of the amiable and respectable virtues', Smith set up the initial distinction between the kinds of virtues:

> The soft, the gentle, the amiable virtues, the virtues of candid condescension and indulgent humanity, are founded upon the one: the great, the awful and respectable, the virtues of self-denial, of self-government, of that command of the passions which subjects all the movements of our nature to what our own dignity and honour, and the propriety of our own conduct require, take their origin from the other.
>
> (TMS I.i.5.1)

Smith returned to this classification, and established a gendered distinction between generosity and humanity based on self-command:

> Generosity is different from humanity. Those two qualities, which at first sight seem so nearly allied, do not always belong to the same person. Humanity is the virtue of a woman, generosity of a man. . . . Humanity

consists merely in the exquisite fellow-feeling which the spectator entertains with the sentiments of the persons principally concerned, so as to grieve for their sufferings, to resent their injuries, and to rejoice at their good fortune. The most humane actions require no self-denial, no self-command, no great exertion of the sense of propriety. They consist only in doing what this exquisite sympathy would of its own accord prompt us to do. But it is otherwise with generosity. We never are generous except when in some respect we prefer some other person to ourselves, and sacrifice some great and important interest of our own to an equal interest of a friend or of a superior.

(TMS IV.2.10)

Both of these passages were original to the first edition of TMS, and Smith certainly did not feel obliged to update his view of gender in later editions. As we have seen above, Riccoboni reversed this formulation.

Smith and Riccoboni remained equally unreconciled as to the nature of love. For Smith it was a ridiculous experience that grew out of an imaginative process, which was best avoided altogether. In I.ii.2, 'Of those Passions which take their origin from a particular turn or habit of the Imagination', Smith discussed the ridiculous nature of love, based on his view that it was a closed process:

The imaginations of mankind, not having acquired that particular turn, cannot enter into them; and such passions, though they may be allowed to be almost unavoidable in some part of life, are always in some measure, ridiculous. This is the case with that strong attachment which naturally grows up between two persons of different sexes, who have long fixed their thoughts upon one another. Our imagination not having run in the same channel with that of the lover, we cannot enter into the eagerness of his emotions.

(TMS I.ii.2.1)

Smith went on to draw an analogy between love and bad theatre; the only manner in which love can be presented on the stage, Smith argued, was if misadventure was lurking around the corner. In the sixth edition, Smith suggested a Platonic model of love among men of virtue as the proper realm in which to experience love:

Such friendships, arising not from a constrained sympathy, not from a sympathy which has been assumed and rendered habitual for the sake of conveniency and accommodation; but from a natural sympathy, from any involuntary feeling that the persons to whom we attach ourselves as the natural and proper objects of esteem and approbation; can exist only among men of virtue. [. . .] They who would confine friendship to two persons, seem to confound the wise security of friendship with the foolish jealousies of love.

(TMS VI.ii.1.18)

This very clubbable model of love would suggest that Smith had even less regard for the experience of romantic love than he had in 1759.

Where Smith referred to love in relation to stoicism, it was always love as represented in literature, and never from lived experience.[30] To the comment about the ridiculous nature of a scene consisting of 'two lovers, in a scene of perfect security, expressing their mutual fondness for one another' (TMS I.ii.2.3), can be added his comments equating love to kingship as the highest emotional and political states of humanity. In I.iii.2, 'On the origin of Ambition, and the distinction of Ranks', Smith returned to the theatre to explain the kinship of love and kingship:

It is the misfortunes of Kings only which afford the proper subjects for tragedy. They resemble, in this respect, the misfortunes of lovers. Those two situations are the chief which interest us upon the theatre; because, in spite of all that reason and experience can tell us to the contrary, the prejudices of the imagination attach to these two states a happiness superior to any other.

(TMS I.iii.2.2)

It should come as no surprise, then, that the one remaining reference to La Rochefoucauld in the sixth edition should come in the same section where Smith warned that love rarely succeeds ambition (TMS I.iii.2.2, echoing #490). Implicit in this view is that the fate of lovers in the absence of menace was appropriate only for comedy – that love did not merit serious consideration in and of itself. This is the most fundamental difference in the intellectual frameworks of Smith and Riccoboni; for Smith love was 'perhaps unavoidable' but was to be minimized at every occasion – for Riccoboni, love was the stuff of life, to be analyzed, explored and celebrated.

Smith's *Theory of Moral Sentiments* is a work of such gravity that it seems to have drawn in elements from far beyond the society of lowland Scotland or Great Britain. The extent to which Smith's project developed in response to his experience in France is not at issue here, but rather the extent to which his mature work reflects his life-long immersion in French literature. The evolution of TMS would suggest that by 1790 Smith has settled on an 'asymmetrical stoicism'[31] in which self-command shared primacy with sympathy as the cardinal principles of his system. On this approach, Smith's system is the end-product of his engagement with the reductive and deterministic *Maximes* of La Rochefoucauld, mediated through the novels of Marivaux, Crébillon and Riccoboni. That he then translated this engagement into an attack on Mandeville does not mitigate the importance of Smith's French-language reading.

Beyond the issues of national and linguistic contexts for Smith's *Theory of Moral Sentiments* I hope to have demonstrated the limitations of approaching Smith through our own academic disciplines – so carefully guarded and territorially delineated. If we follow the evidence that Smith provided regarding his own sources and his development of those sources we are inevitably led beyond our disciplinary comfort zones to the limits of our competences as philosophers, economists, political theorists or historians. This investigation of Smith's borrowings from the field of *Lettres* demonstrates that he was comfortable with such an approach. Smith's conception of sympathy as one of the two pillars of his system was evidently informed by his reading of eighteenth-century French fiction, and he presented that fiction as a necessary complement to an overly philosophical ethical system, as exemplified by stoics ancient and modern. The case I have presented in this paper is perhaps the most obvious instance of Smith's engagement with literature as ethical theory but there are undoubtedly others relating to his development of the role of sympathy, and very likely other aspects of his thought, that would reward further investigation.[32]

Notes

1 The document indicating the removal is an order list dated 4 April 1754 that has been reproduced by Dickson (1932) and Hillyard (1989), and is now missing from the NLS. Perhaps not co-incidentally, another of Crébillon's works *Lettres de la Marquise de Mxxx* was sent for binding on 17 April 1754, and was presumably not on the shelves during the inspection of 27 June 1754. See NLS FR 339e(i)/16.
2 Matching English translations by Leonard Tancock (London: Penguin, 1959). Page numbers refer to the French edition: 'Il semble que l'amour-propre soit la dupe de la bonté et qu'il s'oublie lui-même lorsque nous travaillons pour l'avantage des autres. Cependant c'est prendre le chemin le plus assuré pour arriver à ses fins; c'est prêter à usure sous prétexte de donner; c'est enfin s'acquérir tout le monde par un moyen subtil et délicat.'
3 La Rochefoucauld, *Maximes*, #68/p. 55: 'Il est difficile de définir l'amour. Ce qu'on peut dire est que dans l'âme c'est une passion de régner, dans les esprits c'est une sympathie, et dans le corps ce n'est qu'une envie cachée et délicate de posséder ce que l'on aime après beaucoup de mystères.'
4 'De la convenance du rapport d'humeurs & d'inclinations. Grande, forte sympathie, rien n'unit plus estroitement deux amis que la sympathie.'
5 'S'il y a un amour pur et exempt du mélange de nos autres passions, c'est celui qui est caché au fond du cœur, et que nous ignorons nous-mêmes.'
6 Where Smith refers to these authors he does not indicate specific works. Neither Marivaux nor Riccoboni appear in Mizuta's (2000) catalogue of Smith's library; in the case of Crébillon, *Les égarements* appears as a separate entry from the complete works.
7 'Ce qu'alors les deux sexes nommaient amour était une sorte de commerce où l'on s'engageait, souvent même sans gout, où la commodité était toujours préférée à la sympathie, l'intérêt au plaisir, et le vice au sentiment.'
8 'Le sentiment par exemple en est une [résolution] sur laquelle on ne se trompe point: ce n'est pas l'esprit qui le juge, c'est le cœur; et les choses intéressantes remuent également les gens bornés et ceux qui on plus de lumières.'

9 'Une femme admire, s'étonne, s'enchante, et parce qu'elle se refuse à la réflexion, croit que ce sont vos charmes qui ne lui en laissent pas le temps. Si par hazard elle songe à la résistance qu'elle pourrait vous faire, ce n'est que pour mieux se persuader qu'elle serait inutile et qu'on n'en doit point employer contre quelque chose d'aussi fort, d'aussi imprévu, d'aussi extraordinaire enfin, qu'un coup de sympathie.'

10 'Le monde et elle [la morale] ne s'accordent pas toujours, et vous éprouves que le plus souvent, on ne réussit dans l'un qu'aux dépens de l'autre.'

11 'Entre deux personnes qui s'aiment, ce sont là de ces simplicités de sentiment que peut-être l'esprit remarquerait bien un peu s'il voulait, mais qu'il laisse bonnement passer au profit du cœur.'

12 'On est tout d'un coup lié avec les gens qui ont le cœur bon, quels qu'ils soient; ce sont comme des amis que vous avez dans tous les états.'

13 'Les âmes excessivement bonnes sont volontiers imprudentes par excès de bonté même, et d'un autre côté, les âmes prudentes sont assez rarement bonnes.'

14 'Elle ne ressentit point cette affreuse jalousie, à laquelle presque tous les amants malheureux se déterminent à la vue d'un objet qu'on leur profère. Ces mouvements jaloux emportent avec eux une aversion opiniâtre qui rend capable de tout: les jaloux de cette sorte sont nécessairement cruels et méchants, et justifient dans les suites l'indifférence qu'on a pour eux. Les cœurs veritablement généreux ont leurs sentiments dans un premier instant, dont ils ne sont pas les maîtres, bientôt un caractère de vertu qui domine les ramène à cette grandeur de sentiments dont un premier mouvement les avait tirés.'

15 'Clorante est reconnaissant, il est vrai; et cette reconnaissance diminue le plaisir qu'il a de se livrer à son amour, sans diminuer la nécessité qui le force à aimer cette inconnue [Caliste]. L'amour dans les belles âmes n'éteint pas tout sentiment de générosité: mais ce sentiment est un effet de la vertu, qui leur peint ce qu'ils doivent à un autre, sans les mettre au pouvoir de le payer du retour qu'il mérite.'

16 'L'amour même, le sentiment le plus flatteur de tous, qui nous enchaîne par des liens dont le tissu se cache sous des fleurs'; 'L'esprit ne parle pas au cœur, il ne parle pas comme le cœur.'

17 'Il me sembla, en la finissant [la lettre], qu'une invisible main me précipitait dans un abîme et détruisait en moi le principe de ma vie.'

18 '. . . elle se mit à rire de si bon cœur que sa gaîté excita la mienne. . . . L'excès de son enjouement me fit une impression extraordinaire; il m'enhardit: l'égarement de ma raison passa jusqu'à mon cœur. Livré tout entier à mes sens, j'oubliai mon amour, ma probité . . . Une fille respectable ne me parut dans cet instant qu'une femme offerte à mes désirs, à cette passion grossière qu'allume le seul instinct.'

19 'Mademoiselle de Berneil, en payant de retour la passion du marquis, cédoit peut-être moins à son amour, qu'au desir curieux d'éprouver si cette passion procuroit tout le bonheur dont on l'avoit assurée qu'elle étoit la source; elle en cherchoit les plaisirs, et n'en donnoit pas les douceurs; plus elle pensoit avoir sacrifié en comblant les vœux de son amant, plus elle exigeoit de sa reconnoissance. L'espèce de sentiment qui la conduisoit, n'étoit pas cet attachement sincère d'Adélaïde, ni cet amour tendre et delicat de la marquise; c'étoit un mouvement voluptueux, c'étoit le plaisir de dominer et de soumettre un cœur à tous ses caprices.'

20 'Je suis homme, il est vrai. Mais un homme est une foible créature, moins capable, que vous, peut-être, de résister à l'impulsion de ses sens, d'arrêter la fougue de ses desirs. Un esprit juste, des lumières acquises, de solides réflexions; la nécessité sentie d'être en paix avec nous-mêmes, la louable ambition de mériter l'approbation des autres, nous donnent comme à vous, la force de modérer des passions violentes, de les réprimer, de les immoler à nos devoirs, mais jamais le pouvoir de ne pas soufrir en leur imposant une sévère contrainte.'

21 '[La parure d'Adélaïdeet les charmes du lieu] élevèrent peu-à-peu dans l'ame du marquis ces desirs ardens, impétueux, si difficiles à réprimer, quand l'occasion de les satisfaire augmente encore l'empire que les sens prennent sur la raison. . . . Il prit Adélaïde dans ses bras; et la serrant tendrement, il imprima sur ses lèvres un de ces baisers de feu, dont le mumure aimable éveille l'amour et la volupté. Adélaïde surprise, céda pour un instant l'attrait d'un plaisir inconnu; elle sentit la première atteinte de cette sensation flatteuse, qui conduit ce doux égarement, où la nature, par l'oubli de tout ce qui contraint ses mouvements, semble nous ramener à son heureuse simplicité. Il fut court cet oubli; . . .'

22 'L'homme qui écrit ne peut avoir que deux objets: l'utile et l'amusant. Peu d'auteurs sont parvenus à les réunir.'

23 'Il n'y a que les personnes vraiment éclairées, au-dessus des préjugés, et qui connaissent le vide des Sciences, qui sachent combien l'on doit d'estime, et même de vénération aux gens qui ont assez de génie pour en faire, et assez de force dans d'esprit pour s'y dévouer, malgré l'idée de frivolité que l'orgueil et l'ignorance ont attachée à ce genre. Les importantes leçons que les contes renferment, les grands traits d'imagination qu'on y rencontre si fréquemment, et les idées riantes dont ils sont toujours remplis, ne prennent rien sur le vulgaire de qui l'on ne peut acquérir l'estime, qu'en lui donnant des choses qu'il n'entend jamais; mais qu'il puisse se faire honneur d'entendre.'

24 'La première partie de la Vie de Marianne a paru faire plaisir à bien de gens; ils en ont surtout aimé les réflexions qui y sont semées. D'autres lecteurs ont dit qu'il y en avait trop; et c'est à ces derniers à qui ce petit Avertissement s'adresse.

Si on leur donnait un livre intitulé *Réflexions sur l'Homme*, ne le liraient-ils pas volontiers, si les réflexions en étaient bonnes? Nous en avons même beaucoup, de ces livres, et dont quelques-uns sont fort estimés; pourquoi donc les réflexions leur déplaisent-elles, en cas qu'elles n'aient contre elles que d'être des reflexions? . . .

A celà voici ce qu'on leur répond. Si vous regradez la *Vie de Marianne* comme un roman, vous avez raison, votre critique est juste; il y a trop de réflexions, et ce n'est pas là la forme ordinaire des romans, ou des histoires faites simplement pour divertir. Mais Marianne n'a point songé à faire un roman non plus.'

25 Coulet (1981: 19) has determined that in the first two parts of *Marianne* these *réflexions* are 19% of the text.

26 'À l'égard des autres grands génies, pourquoi les met-on dans un ordre inférieur? Pourquoi n'a-t-on pas la même idée de la capacité dont ils ont besoin?'

27 'Les belles choses qu'ils nous disent ne nous frappent pas même comme nouvelles; on croit toujours les reconnaître, on les avait déjà entrevues, mais jusqu'à eux on en était resté là, et jamais on ne les avait vue d'assez près, ni assez fixement pour pouvoir les dire.'

28 Although it is possible that the *romanciers* were familiar with the content of the *Fable* from the extensive reviews published in 1729 and 1733; see Hundert (1994: 102–4).

29 When the relationship of Mandeville to La Rochefoucauld has been examined it has revealed a different historical problem. Hundert (1994) offers an interpretation of La Rochefoucauld that muddies the genealogy I have outlined running from La Rochefoucauld, via the French *romanciers* to Smith. He imposes a class-based distinction between La Rochefoucauld and Mandeville, which suggests that they would not have garnered the same response: 'Mandeville had only a passing interest in the rigorously exclusive social arena of court society, whose threatened habits of life was the compelling subject of La Rochefoucauld and his contemporaries. [. . .] La Rochefoucauld, Pascal and Nicole sought to desanctify *all* pretensions to human greatness; but their recurring subject remained the ideal actor of their own tradition – the honoured warrior capable of remarkable fortitude in the face of

shifting fortune – and thus their critique did not extend to society at large' (Hundert 1994: 33). While this may be a valid interpretation of La Rochefoucauld and Mandeville, it tells us nothing about the reception of these texts. Moreover, it does not seem to be based on any internal evidence. La Rochefoucauld speaks in quasi-universals, and never limits the scope of his observations in this manner. For our purposes here, this interpretation is anachronistic.

30 'The poets and romance writers, who best paint the refinements and delicacies of love and friendship, and of all other private and domestic affections, Racine and Voltaire; Richardson and Maurivaux, and Riccoboni; are in such cases, much better instructors than Zeno, Chrysippus, or Epictetus' (TMS III.3.14/p. 143).

31 The term is Martha Nussbaum's from a conference paper delivered to the Hume Society in Toronto in 2005.

32 My Oxford D.Phil in progress deals with some of these other engagements – particularly with Rousseau and the *Encyclopédie*.

Bibliography

Archives

National Library of Scotland Faculty Records (NLS).

Primary works

Crébillon, C.P.J. de. (1993) [1736–38] *Les égarements du cœur et de l'esprit*, in *Romans libertins du XVIIIe siècle*, R. Trousson (ed.), Paris: Éditions Robert Laffont.

—— (1995) [1742] *Le Sopha*, F. Juranville (ed.), Paris: Flammarion.

Dictionnaire de L'Académie française (1694) 1st edn, ARTFL database, www.lib. uchicago.edu/efts/ARTFL/projects/dicos/

La Rochefoucauld, F. VI, Duc de (1976) [1665–1678] *Maximes et Réflexions diverses*, J. Lafond (ed.), Paris: Gallimard.

—— (1959) *Maximes et Réflexions diverses*, L. Tancock (trans.), Harmondsworth: Penguin.

Marivaux, P. de Carlet de (1972) [1712] *Les effect surprenants de la sympathie*, in *Œuvres de jeunesses*, F. Deloffre et C. Rigault (eds), Paris: Gallimard.

—— (1981) [1734–38] *Le paysan parvenu*, H. Coulet (ed.), Paris: Gallimard.

—— (1997) [1727–41] *La vie de Marianne*, J. Dagen (ed.), Paris: Gallimard, Folio Classique.

—— (2001) [1744] 'Réflexions sur l'esprit humain à l'occasion de Corneille et de Racine', in *Journaux et Œuvres diverses*, F. Deloffre and M. Gilot (eds), Paris: Classiques Garnier.

Riccoboni, M.-J. (1979) [1757] *Lettres de Mistress Fanni Butlerd,* J.H. Steward (ed.), Genève: Droz.

—— (1983) [1758] *Lettres de Milady Juliette Catesby*, Paris: Desjonquères.

—— (1989) [1758] *Histoire du Marquis de Cressy,* O. Cragg (ed.), *SVEC* 266.

—— (1992) [1777] *Lettres de Mylord Rivers à Sir Charles Cardigan*, O. Cragg (ed.), Genève: Droz.

Smith, A. (1976) [1759–90] *The Theory of Moral Sentiments*, D.D. Raphael and A.L. Macfie (eds), The Glasgow Edition of the Works and Correspondence of Adam Smith Vol. 1, Oxford: Clarendon Press; reprinted Liberty Press (1982).

—— (1980) *Essays on Philosophical Subjects*, W.P.D. Wightman (ed.), The Glasgow Edition of the Works and Correspondence of Adam Smith, Vol. 3, Oxford: Clarendon Press; reprinted, Liberty Press (1983).
—— (1983) [delivered 1748–1763] *Lectures on Rhetoric and Belles Lettres*, J.C. Bryce (ed.), The Glasgow Edition of the Works and Correspondence of Adam Smith Vol. 4, Oxford: Clarendon Press; reprinted, Liberty Press (1985).

Secondary works

Carboni, P. (1997) 'Les penseurs écossais des belles-lettres', in *Écosse des Lumières: Le XVIIIe siècle autrement*, P. Morère (ed.), Grenoble: Ellug.
Coulet, H. (1981) 'Préface', *Le Paysan parvenu*, H. Coulet (ed.), Paris: Gallimard Collection Folio Classique.
Culpin, D. (1987) 'Morale et raison dans la pensée de Marivaux', *Revue d'Histoire littéraire de la France*, 87: 627–37.
—— (1996) 'La morale mondaine de Marivaux', in *Marivaux et les lumières: L'Éthique d'un romancier*, Actes du colloque à Aix-en-Provence les 4,5,6 juin 1992, Publication de l'Université de Provence.
Dawson, D. (1991) 'Is Sympathy so surprising? Adam Smith and the French fictions of sympathy', *Eighteenth-Century Life*, 15: 147–62.
Dickson, W.K. (1932) *David Hume and the Advocate's Library*, Edinburgh: W. Green and Son; originally published in the *Juridical Review*, March 1932.
Dornier, C. (1993) 'Le traité de mondanité d'un mentor libertin', in *L'honnête homme et le dandy*, A. Montandon (ed.), Tubingen: Verlag.
Dwyer, J. (1993) 'Enlightened spectators and classical moralists: sympathetic relations in eighteenth-century Scotland', in *Sociability and Society in Eighteenth-Century Scotland*, J. Dwyer and R.B. Sher (eds), Edinburgh: The Mercat Press.
—— (1998) *The Age of the Passions: An Interpretation of Adam Smith and Scottish Enlightenment Culture*, East Lothian: Tuckwell Press.
Hillyard, B. (1989) 'The keepership of David Hume', in *For the Encouragement of Learning: Scotland's National Library 1689–1989*, P. Cadell and A. Matheson (eds.), Edinburgh: HMSO, 103–9.
Hundert, E.J. (1994) *The Enlightenment's Fable: Bernard Mandeville and the Discovery of Society*, Cambridge: Cambridge University Press.
Mizuta, H. (2000) *Adam Smith's Library: A Catalogue*, Oxford: Clarendon Press.
Mullen, J. (1987) 'The language of sentiment: Hume, Smith and Henry Mackenzie', in *The History of Scottish Literature, Vol. 2, 1660–1800*, A. Hook (ed.), Aberdeen University Press.
—— (1988) *Sentiment and Sociability: The Language of Feeling in the Eighteenth Century*, Oxford: Clarendon Press.
Munro, J. (1996) 'Le Rationel et l'irrationel chez Marivaux', in *Marivaux et les lumières: L'Éthique d'un romancier*, Actes du colloque à Aix-en-Provence les 4,5,6 juin 1992, Publication de l'Université de Provence.
Raphael, D.D. and A.L. Macfie (1976) 'Introduction' to Adam Smith, *The Theory of Moral Sentiments*, Oxford: Clarendon Press.
Ross, I.S. (1995) *The Life of Adam Smith*, Oxford: Clarendon Press.
Stewart, D. (1980) 'Account of the Life and Writings of Adam Smith, LL.D', in Adam Smith, *Essays on Philosophical Subjects*, W.P.D. Wightman (ed.), The Glasgow Edition of the Works and Correspondence of Adam Smith, Vol. 3. Oxford: Clarendon Press; reprinted Liberty Press (1983).

Pins and needles

Adam Smith and the sources of the *Encyclopédie*

Robert Mankin

Car en quelque matière que ce soit, on n'a parcouru tout l'espace qu'on avait à parcourir, que quand on est arrivé à un principe qu'on ne peut ni prouver, ni définir, ni éclaircir, ni obscurcir, ni nier, sans perdre une partie du jour dont on était éclairé, & faire un pas vers des ténèbres qui finiraient par devenir très-profondes, si on ne mettait aucune borne à l'argumentation.

(Diderot art. *Encyclopédie*)[1]

In 1754 Adam Smith had not yet published a work of argument, but in that year he delivered his first oration. The occasion was the founding of the Select Society of Edinburgh, a society intended to promote 'philosophical inquiry, and the improvement of the members in the art of speaking'.[2] The fifteen original members of the Society did not mean entirely to keep among themselves. Along with schedules for admitting new members, organizing debates and presenting prizes for schemes of improvement in different fields of Scottish life, there was also a publishing project. At the suggestion of Alexander Wedderburn, some of the founders secretly agreed to produce a new magazine for the general public. The authorship of texts was to be kept anonymous and thus unrelated to the activities of the Society and its public voice. What is more, the editorial project was itself kept secret from one of the Society's founders, David Hume, presumably so as to avoid his participation and the polemical reactions that might thereby be aroused in the public. This paper on Smith's sources sets out from his formal (though anonymous) beginnings as an author in the pages of that magazine, the *Edinburgh Review*, in 1755 and 1756. It looks inside the world of Smith's intellectual experience, towards one of those essays in particular and then at the opening of the *Wealth of Nations*, in order to gauge the way in which Smith turned the occasion into a creative experience. Smith belonged to a variety of clubs, he was a practised lecturer, but it is here that his writing career began.

The 1750s and 1760s in Smith's life are a time of very heterogeneous production, which the two essays in the *Edinburgh Review* perhaps initiate but to which they do not altogether belong. During this period he was engaged in a great many forms of what might be called local or isolated writing. These include dictated versions of his university lectures for Glasgow (corresponding to the curricula he was assigned to teach) and other exploratory studies which are often difficult to date, including an early draft (ED) of the opening of the *Wealth of Nations* and a series of more or less finished pieces on an unusual array of subjects. Although many of these texts bear on the most general issues of science, philosophy and knowledge, they can be considered as 'local' for two different kinds of reasons. On the one hand, the texts rarely connect or build on each other explicitly; the most strikingly enigmatic case is no doubt ED, which is presented as 'Chap. 2' – whereas we are in the dark about what would have been Chapter 1 (Smith 1978, ED 1). Nor, on the other hand, did Smith publish or deliver any of these explorations before an audience during this early period. Clearly *The Theory of Moral Sentiments* (TMS) broke with this local purview when the book was published in Edinburgh but also in London in 1759. (In addition, TMS was signed.) And it is likewise clear that late in life, after the *Wealth of Nations* (WN), Smith wished to return to many of his early projects in order to provide a synthetic account of philosophy and the sciences. Instead of preliminary explorations that either led nowhere or else helped to bring him to the writing of TMS or WN, he now recognized these essays as 'a fragment' of 'a great work' he would have wished to produce (*Corr.* No. 137 to Hume, 16 Apr. 1773). Although he died before he could achieve his goal, he made provisions for a part – apparently a small part – of his manuscripts to survive him. Most of the texts collected in the 1795 edition of *Essays on Philosophical Subjects* were those of the 1750s and 1760s, and they were meant to indicate the system that might have emerged. The fact that they were early, and his intention was late, is usually taken as irrelevant.

It is worth pointing out, by way of contrast, that the essays in the *Edinburgh Review* did not form part of the 1795 volume. Perhaps Smith or his posthumous editors Joseph Black and James Hutton felt that previously published pieces did not need to be collected. But perhaps also Smith felt that there was something inappropriate for his larger view in the approach or the subject or even the style of the two short essays. By somewhat tacitly including them in the Glasgow edition of *Essays on Philosophical Subjects* (Smith 1980, EPS), Smith's twentieth-century editors have blurred the contours of the original volume and slightly obscured the fact that until 1967 the English-speaking world seems to have shown no particular interest in viewing these pieces as part of Smith's opus.[3] If one were to assign a stylistic reason for this neglect, it might be that by the end of Smith's life, the pedagogical concerns of 1755 were no longer relevant. If there is a disciplinary reason, it is surely that Smith needed to be read and touted only as an economist. Perhaps, too, these occasional writings could not be assigned to any one academic discipline and, in addition, the sciences of mid-century France had been improved upon. But if there is also an intellectual reason for this neglect, it might be that the essays introduce a complication in what Black and Hutton called Smith's 'plan' for 'a connected history of the liberal sciences and elegant arts' ('Astronomy', Advertisement, in EPS): the complication involves what we mean by the fact that it was Smith's.

My concern in this paper is not directly with Smith's late period and its attempt at a system but with his first formal articulation, in 1755–6, of the need for a connected history, and one or two aftershocks that articulation may have had in his writing. I will contend that his understanding of connected history was fuelled in part by the sources he encountered in reading the French authors that he described in the *Edinburgh Review*. In addition, I will suggest that by reflecting on those sources, Smith discovered a way to become his own source and thereby to launch his intellectual career. Smith's intellectual identity is in large part, and at various levels, related to his characteristically eighteenth-century sense of how deeply socialized man is. What I describe in the following pages shows the meaning he assigned to the fact that man is so social an animal that he confuses some of his deepest impulses, taking them for private when they are in fact the result of public resources.

Given its diversity and philosophical seriousness, what I have called the early period in Smith's thought invites the idea of the *Encyclopédie*. To begin with, there are obvious affinities between d'Alembert's *Discours prélimin-aire* and contemporaneous arguments in Smith. For example, 'The History of Astronomy' (presumed to have been written before 1758; EPS 7–8, 'Astronomy' IV.74) calls for a unified history of the sciences and attributes the name 'philosophy' to that perspective: 'Philosophy', Smith writes, 'is the science of the connecting principles of nature' ('Astronomy' II.12). The encyclopaedic family tree, or '*arbre des connaissances*', is being recast in a more abstract vocabulary and related in particular to the faculty of the imagination. In a different vein, the relation between Smith's early thinking about economics and the first major texts of the *Encyclopédie* devoted to economics, Turgot's article 'Fermiers' for example, not only intrigues readers today: it also did at the time. Smith's first biographer Dugald Stewart felt obliged to deny that the thinker had been deeply influenced by the French but he went further and defended Smith against the charge of plagiarism as well (Stewart 1980 [1794] IV.23). The defence is clear (a matter of dates) but also circuitous: Stewart invokes Hume, arguing that though Hume instructed Smith, Smith understood better because he performed a 'compre-hensive survey of the whole field of discussion' (Stewart 1980, IV.24), whereas Hume clearly was of more direct use to Turgot because Turgot was a narrower thinker. It would follow that whatever Smith learned from Turgot, he already knew, and so he didn't exactly learn anything . . . We shall return to this strained reasoning later in the paper. Suffice it to say for now that, beyond specific areas of correspondence and some ambiguous areas of overlap, the most impressive similarity between Smith and the *Encyclopédie* lies in that general sense of comprehensiveness. Given the breadth of Smith's thinking in questions of morals, economy, jurisprudence and much else, it is easy to conclude that his thought and culture are so trans-disciplinary that we have no choice *but* to use a term like 'encyclopaedic'. This semantic necessity is enough to link Smith to the *Encyclopédie*, even as it is clear that no one acquires an encyclopaedic mind just by reading encyclopaedias. So we are thrown back on the world that produced such enterprises. Luckily, there are two moments of intersection, two concrete and limited cases in which the *Encyclopédie* figures in Smith's work, and in which he takes the measure of the French project and also considers how he himself measures up to it.

*   *   *

The first moment occurs in 1755–6 when Smith had already advanced in his teaching career by moving from Edinburgh, where he lectured primarily on rhetoric and belles-lettres, to Glasgow, where he occupied the chair of logic and then of moral philosophy. But the encounters in the *Edinburgh Review* are less academic than civic. In 1755 an essay entitled 'Review of Johnson's Dictionary' hailed the publication at long last of a true dictionary of the English language. Six months later, in 1756, he posed as a learned member of the general public and wrote a 'Letter to the Edinburgh Review' concerning noteworthy publications from the continent, especially France. The first five volumes of the *Encyclopédie* are among the works discussed in this long essay (today we would call it a review essay), and Smith speaks with some admiration of the project.

Before going briefly into details of Smith's 'letter', it will be useful to put his admiration in perspective. In 1952, the Enlightenment scholar John Lough paid tribute to this untitled text as 'undoubtedly the most eulogistic account of the *Encyclopédie* to be published in this country in the eighteenth century' (Lough 1970: 14). But Lough's mini-panegyric is curiously hollow, as (to some extent) is Smith's. To begin with, it is impossible to know what exactly Smith had read of the five volumes he had under review. Not only did he not own the *Encyclopédie*,[4] he himself is perfectly unhelpful on the matter. Only once does he cite the text of an article (the *Discours préliminaire*) but without acknowledging it as a literal citation.[5] In contrast, it takes very little reading between the lines to see that Smith has some reservations about the *Encyclopédie*.[6] He does not hail it as an eternal monument or as, at long last, the powerful synthesis of ideas and practices we have all been waiting for, but rather as a work that promises to be of great interest *for a while*. The value of such performances is a matter of time and chance: they 'have yet a chance to be remembered for thirty or forty years to come' ('Letter' 2) rather than to be the talk of the town, as it were, for a short time, like an article in a newspaper.[7] The *Encyclopédie* is ephemeral literature, Smith seems to be suggesting, but of the nobler sort: more like Addison and Steele's *Spectator*, where the contingency of individual sheets made the quantum leap into book format, than like the *Edinburgh Review*, which was not the work of committed journalists and which soon went out of business. It must be added that Smith's praise has to seem a bit biased. Part of his interest in the *Encyclopédie* resides expressly in the fact that its authors had broken with Cartesian philosophy, making their work a vehicle for English thought. Nevertheless, this bias does not help Smith in any immediate way to appreciate the *Discours préliminaire*, which he takes as a simple reformulation of Bacon ('Letter' 6).[8] Nor does he take time to recall that the *Encyclopédie* as a whole was inspired by the *Cyclopaedia* (1728) of an Englishman, Ephraim Chambers. In addition, he complains that certain articles are too declamatory.[9] The only article he explicitly names, 'Amour' by Abbé Claude Yvon, receives a pique or two precisely because it is one of the offenders.[10] Smith thus appears torn between a sense of wonder at an educational project of amazing comprehensiveness – 'Scarce anything seems to be omitted' ('Letter' 6) – and a certain irritation about some of the rhetoric ('Letter' 7). In short, the *Encyclopédie* deserves to be read, in spite of certain failings, because it is serious, credible and, to use a word he repeats again and again, extraordinarily 'compleat'. He recommends the work not only because readers can learn a great deal from the different articles, but also because even the weakness of some articles will provide healthy food for thought.

The *Encyclopédie* has not been put on a pedestal. And the reader will be confirmed in that sense merely by continuing to read, for Smith goes on to review a number of other publications. Even more than our review essays, this 'letter' on the state of learning and the arts in Europe refers to thousands of pages of learned writing. The reader too will want to gasp 'scarce anything seems to be omitted', and perhaps also to wonder how Smith read it all. After his brief account of 'the new French Encyclopedia' ('Letter' 5), Smith hails the publication of still other encyclopaedic works, including the five volumes of Buffon's and Daubenton's *Description du Cabinet du Roi*, and the eight volumes of 'Mr Réaumur's history of insects' ('Letter' 8–9). In regard to each of these different undertakings, Smith notes with satisfaction that further volumes are forthcoming. And after all of this, he ends with several pages on an author he takes to be a disciple of Bernard Mandeville, Jean-Jacques Rousseau. Thus, though the *Encyclopédie* gets a positive nod, Smith's discussion of it makes neither for the longest nor for the most approving part of his essay.[11] Réaumur's *Mémoires pour servir à l'histoire des insectes* arouse his enthusiasm, and in terms that make it impossible to guess whether he knew about the strained relations between Réaumur and Diderot. Quite unexpectedly, it is Voltaire who returns at the end of the essay and, as it were, steals the show: Smith hails him as a 'universal genius' ('Letter' 17) and a master of every style. By the end of the essay, in other words, the reader may suspect that Smith was out to praise the genre or the ambition of encyclopaedic writing as such, rather than to promote Diderot and d'Alembert in particular, or to give pride of place to Rousseau.

These suspicions are helpful, because they throw light on the peculiar nature of the young professor's first publications. It would appear a curiously incomplete or uncomfortable undertaking for a Scot to be writing in the public sphere: since the Revolution of 1688 and even more since the Union of 1707 and the 1745 Jacobite rising, the lines of communication were down. Although modern scholarship has amply demonstrated the solid development of intellectual life in Scotland in the first half of the eighteenth century, notably in the universities, that is more our retrospective conclusion than Smith's contemporary impression. In the university one could give lectures; in select company, there could be debates. But Lowland Scottish society had not yet discovered progress. In 1755–6, Smith implies that Scotland has not yet found its own resources but needs to look elsewhere, whether in terms of 'its' language, English,[12] or its general culture. Both language and culture are being advanced as more specifically Scottish than English preoccupations. As strange as it sounds, we know that the same problem obtrudes in Hume's sense that, as a Scot, he was in the best position possible both to write English history and to encourage his fellow Scots to be interested in it (Pocock 1999). This specific concern helps us to see the ambiguity of John Lough's phrase 'in this country'. Lough's essay is entitled 'The *Encyclopédie* in 18th-century England' and so Smith should not really be involved at all, not even as a Briton. For in his essay Smith recognizes in passing that the Scots are not yet, or not exactly, 'Briton[s]'. Speaking of Bacon, Boyle and Newton, Smith writes:

> As, since the union, we are apt to regard ourselves *in some measure* as the countrymen of those great men, it flattered my vanity, as a Briton, to observe the superiority of the English philosophy thus acknowledged by their rival nation.
>
> ('Letter' 5; my italics)

Being a Briton, or becoming one, is almost Smith's point in writing. Fifty years after the union, this is a problem requiring pedagogical attention, both from the universities and at another, more general level. It might be said that the prescription delivered in both of Smith's texts from the *Edinburgh Review*, shortly before it ceased to exist, tends to confirm the gravity of the disorder. Accordingly, the Scottish public is being recommended regular heavy doses of encyclopaedic literature.

Thus, Smith's 'eulogistic account' of the *Encyclopédie* is not only *not* English and uncritical, but it belongs to a specific Scottish and British context. At the start of his review essay of 1756, Smith maintains that to develop Scottish society, it is not enough to resort to English letters only, as he himself had done with Johnson a few months earlier: European letters must also be employed, less for the scope of 'connected history' than for the comprehensiveness of style. A brief review of the situation in Western Europe demonstrates that there are Academies of considerable interest in the less eminent countries, whereas in the most advanced, individuals count more than collective structures.[13] In England and France, the talents are not only individual but easily described: 'Imagination, genius and invention, seem to be the talents of the English; taste, judgment, propriety and order, of the French' ('Letter' 4). There is nothing particularly original about this vision, even if it is striking how Smith insists on its clarity.[14] And he goes on next to frame a commonplace of eighteenth-century Anglophilia: 'almost all' the great scientific advances of the period are the result of the English:

> In natural philosophy, the science which in modern times has been most happily cultivated, almost all the great discoveries, which have not come from Italy or Germany, have been made in England. France has scarcely produced any thing very considerable in that way.
>
> ('Letter' 5)

Intellectual modernity itself, whereby science and culture advance hand in hand, was likewise invented by the English: 'The English seem to have employed themselves entirely in inventing, and to have disdained the more inglorious but not less useful labour of arranging and methodizing their discoveries [. . .]' ('Letter' 5). All the English seem to know how to do is invent, or rather that is all they used to know how to do. For Smith now adds a third and less canonical element to his vision. 'The greatest passion for the science and learning of England' no longer belongs to the English. Despite a glorious past, they have sunk into a state of discouragement, close to intellectual bankruptcy ('Letter' 5). Smith shared this feeling with Hume,[15] but he draws a different conclusion: the real passion for English achievement now resides in France, and so it is that the *Encyclopédie* should not be considered as a new spirit taking over in philosophy (hence his lukewarm response to the *Discours préliminaire*) but rather as an appropriate vehicle on account of style:

> [. . .] and it is with pleasure that I observe in the new French Encyclopedia the ideas of Bacon, Boyle, and Newton, explained with that order, perspicuity and good judgment, which distinguish all the eminent writers of that nation.
>
> ('Letter' 5)

Given Smith's sense of the deficiencies of English culture, we may surmise that his pleasure is less chauvinistic than aesthetic. A French style of exposition, he notes, 'entertains the mind with a regular succession of agreeable, interesting and connected objects' ('Letter' 4). This kind of appreciation may seem hollow and a little disdainful, but it may also reflect rhetoric in the best sense of the term – not flowery declamation but an art of writing in which the organization of thought is paramount. Describing such an art was one aim of Smith's own lectures on rhetoric as we know them from 1762–3 (Smith 1983, LRBL, Lectures 5, 8 and passim), and presumably from his earlier teaching of rhetoric in Edinburgh as well. In any case, though,

Scottish culture is being led to a curious fork in the road, if English genius henceforth is expressed through the 'taste' and 'propriety' of French culture. What about the British? Or to put the matter differently, how should the Scots now write in English?

Having insisted on the specific motivation behind Smith's vision, we must recall something that is vexing about this story and almost never challenged. John Lough's tribute so easily tends towards hyperbole, because the major figures of English culture at the time clearly do *not* see the *Encyclopédie* as an occasion for panegyric. Whether for political or philosophical reasons, they do not acknowledge the project, at least with pleasure. After finishing his Dictionary, Samuel Johnson thought about producing a new updated edition of Chambers's *Cyclopaedia*, but nowhere in Boswell's account of him do we ever find Johnson discussing or even pronouncing the name of the French Encyclopaedia. Yet we know from other sources that he owned seven volumes of it (Lough 1970: 13). Incensed in his youth by the role assigned to memory in the *Discours préliminaire*, Edward Gibbon claimed to have written his first book, the *Essai sur l'étude de la littérature* (1761), to refute d'Alembert's philosophical animus against history. But in the great work of his maturity, *The Decline and Fall of the Roman Empire* (1776–88), Gibbon almost never refers to the *Encyclopédie*, preferring instead to look back to Pierre Bayle or to the learned articles collected in the transactions of the Parisian Académie des Inscriptions. In the absence of favourable notice from such towering figures of English intellectual life, we are obliged to fall back on an Irishman, Edmund Burke, who as early as 1790 claimed to see through the French Revolution and to blame it in part on a class of people he called 'political Men of Letters' who were quite naturally involved in the 'the vast undertaking of the Encyclopaedia' (Burke 1968: 211; cf. TMS III.2.22–3). For Burke, the *Encyclopédie* was not aimed at promoting polite society, or improving Scotland, or taking its place as an object of learned discussion in the university: it was a subversive tool aimed at the violent transformation of society. This is aggrandizement, without a doubt, but far from panegyric.

Perhaps the most startling silence of all is David Hume's. In the 1740s Hume put forth the idea that the French monarchy had reached a point where it allowed for as much social progress as the mixed system of British government.[16] Furthermore, Hume respected and corresponded with Montesquieu; he later tried to befriend Rousseau, and if nothing else, the disaster of that attempt boosted his friendship with d'Alembert, to whom he even left money in his will. The volumes of the *Encyclopédie* that Smith consulted for his review essay were probably the ones Hume had ordered for the Advocates' Library of Edinburgh.[17] In other words, many factors were in favour of a strong tie between Hume and the *Encyclopédie*, even from Smith's point of view. Hume was not just an English, but a British, source; he is quoted in certain articles; it would seem natural for him to take an interest in the project. And yet to my knowledge, the philosopher never mentions the articles or even the undertaking, whether in his writings or his letters.

With this backdrop of Anglo-British indifference, Smith's compliments and his quasi-psychological hypotheses in the *Edinburgh Review* (unbeknownst to Hume!) take on added meaning. Was it because the English were demobilized by their glorious past that they could no longer recognize themselves in the project of the *Encyclopédie* and its culture of Anglophilia? Or were English genius and invention hampered by the felicitous arrangement of words in sentences? For a Scot who was concerned to educate the public, the *encyclopédistes*' socialization of knowledge clearly had pedagogical virtues: bartering a little genius against a lot of politeness could look like a very good deal. For an Englishman, in contrast, who had a more exclusive idea of invention or erudition, the encyclopaedic project might well seem frivolous. Smith, in other words, was not only eulogistic but unusual. Or had he simply taken to heart the ideal of public speaking and of political action that the Select Society was trying to embody,[18] even as he transported it into writing?

* * *

This rapid sketch of cloistered worlds will allow us to move on to what I called Smith's second moment of intersection with the *Encyclopédie*. This time the story is more cryptic. Everything hangs on a small detail contained in the presentation of the division of labour in the first chapter of the *Wealth of Nations* [1776]. After two short paragraphs introducing this key phenomenon in the history of human productivity, Smith hastily turns to an example which he derives from a 'very trifling manufacture', the fabrication of pins (Smith 1976, WN I.i.3). The job is indeed *very* trifling, because pins are themselves small and also because they do not occupy a very considerable, or noble, place in human life – nor in a book of serious reasoning. If aesthetics is again invoked, we would have to confess that the *Wealth of Nations* opens on a highly indecorous note and that Smith knew it: in ED, he successively calls the making of pins 'this frivolous manufacture' and 'this frivolous instance' of the division of labour (Smith 1978, ED 8, 10). From the standpoint of philosophy, one might even argue that he had chosen to involve himself too much in one of those 'indifferent things' that his Stoic authors found all too often in their way as they sought to live a life of virtue.[19] But the poor decorum of pins is amply supplied by the consequences of Smith's argument. The division of labour multiplies the number of people involved in production, and so the gain is enormous, almost fantastical. One man, Smith says, 'could scarce, perhaps, with his utmost industry, make one pin a day, and certainly could not make twenty' (WN I.i.3) and he repeats the assertion a page later, as if hypnotically, when it comes to assessing a group of men who divide their labour:

[Ten men in association] could make among them upwards of forty-eight thousand pins in a day. Each person, therefore, making a tenth part of forty-eight thousand pins, might be considered as making four thousand eight hundred pins in a day. But if they had all wrought separately and independently, and without any of them having been educated to this peculiar business, they certainly could not each of them have made twenty, perhaps not one pin in a day; that is, certainly, not the two hundred and fortieth, perhaps not the four thousand eight hundredth part of what they are at present capable of performing, in consequence of a proper division and combination of their different operations.

(WN I.i.3)

It is interesting to wonder how, with what kind of metaphors, an eighteenth-century writer could articulate so dizzying a difference. Smith's mind does not take any of the avenues we might expect. He does not simply affirm the benefits of dividing labour, as did his predecessors on the subject (Petty, Mandeville, Hutcheson). Nor does he associate these vertiginous gains with the moneyed men of his world, the wild ups and downs of a stock exchange, a cut-and-dried opposition between haves and have-nots, brazen luxury and mere subsistence, or even with magic. Smith's logic of frivolity and fable is placed at the service of a highly beneficial project, production, but it is also reasonable and good in itself.

More than just the materialistic credo of capitalism, the division of labour betokens an intellectual progress. As such, pins have more than a little in common with collective enterprises like encyclopaedias. Compare the pin factory with the literary workshop, in light of the vast numbers of entries ('that vast collection of every sort of literature'; 'Letter' 5), the writer's valorization of the slightest objects by dint of intellectual work, and the resultant capacity to arrange materials so that the most serious and the most frivolous stand side by side. The end of the article 'Épingle' (Pin) makes this last aspect explicit. A propos of the article's presumed author, M. Delaire, a note adds that he:

described the fabrication of pins from within the workshops themselves, at our request, even as he published his analysis of the sublime and profound philosophy of Lord Chancellor Bacon, in Paris. Along with the previous description, that volume will prove that a good mind can sometimes, with equal success, rise to the highest contemplations of Philosophy and descend into the slightest details of the mechanic arts.[20]

Even when the subject is low, high seriousness emerges as the winner. The *encyclopédistes* recognized this challenge in the very organization of their enterprise. They knew, for instance, that when it came to presentation, the tree of knowledge had to be sacrificed to alphabetical order, even as the slightly surreal dimension introduced by the latter needed to be overcome.[21]

Likewise, the declamatory register and the endless stream of words had to be kept under control. If not, knowledge would become pure, lifeless metonymy or frivolous babble. In this sense too, the *encyclopédistes* were interested not just in enlightenment but in making a go of the business of enlightenment.

Smith too belongs to a world concerned not only with business, but with giving a foundation to knowledge, and so there is a casual touch of irony in his summary of all the steps needed in the fabrication of a pin: 'and the important business of making a pin is, in this manner, divided into about eighteen distinct operations' (WN I.i.3). Of course he means: it's not important, but yes it certainly is. The editors of the Glasgow edition of Smith's works explain in a footnote to this sentence that the idea of 'eighteen distinct operations' corresponds to the detailed presentation to be found in the article 'Épingle' from the *Encyclopédie*. There are no good reasons to doubt the claim, even though the reference is at best oblique, and to that obliqueness the word 'about' adds a further note of casualness. In any case, Smith justifies his choice of example by emphasizing that the pin is familiar from other texts. The first words of the paragraph put this intertextuality front and centre: 'To take an example, therefore, from a very trifling manufacture, but one in which the division of labour has been very often taken notice of . . .' (WN I.i.3). Apart from the *Encyclopédie*, the most obvious written source for information on pins was probably the entry 'Pin' from Ephraim Chambers's *Cyclopaedia*, and here again Smith's editors can hardly be wrong in noting that that article refers, very briefly and in passing, to twenty-five operations.[22] The *Cyclopaedia* reads: 'They reckon twenty-five workmen successively employed in each pin, between the drawing of the brass-wire, and the sticking of the *pin* in the paper' (Chambers, 1728: q.v. 'PIN'; his italics). Smith's library contained an edition of the *Cyclopaedia*, but from a later period; it is highly probable, however, that he had consulted the entry in Chambers elsewhere. Long before publishing the *Wealth of Nations*, Smith had himself often 'taken notice of' the subject, expounding and reworking the example of the pin in his lectures. And each time he gives the figure of eighteen or 'about eighteen' operations. In 1776, for the first time, he also mentions having personally visited a pin factory to observe manufacturing techniques (WN I.i.3). On that occasion, he observed only ten workers on the assembly line. But he did not change his mind: the ten men were clearly executing the eighteen, rather than the twenty-five, operations that go into making a pin.

Smith's university lectures and manuscript drafts suggest that the division of labour, and more specifically the example of pins – the '*proper division and combination of their different operations*' (WN I.i.3; my italics) – constitutes the *omphalos* or narrative origin of the *Wealth of Nations*.[23] We have seen something of how Smith's editors identify his choice of the French source for the example, rather than the source of the source, in Chambers. One might think that Smith had learned to temper the patriotic satisfaction he had shown in 1756 concerning Newton and Bacon as compared to Descartes. Indeed, a variety of passages in his subsequent work ('Astronomy' IV.61–7; LRBL ii.134) suggest that Smith was learning just such a lesson. But even more importantly, as Diderot remarks in the epigraph to the present paper, origins are always complex. In regard to the *Wealth of Nations*, we might say that Smith uses his allusion to highlight intellectual even more than technical progress. The authority of the *Encyclopédie*, the clarity and intellectual seriousness of the project, rely on the possibility of eliminating frivolity or transforming it into value. In the end, the figure Smith chooses is simply arbitrary ('about eighteen') and what is more, he seems never to have seen eighteen men doing the job in real life. What counts very much more is the fact that, as early as 1756, Smith had recognized the abilities of the French when it came to ordering things.[24] Nevertheless, the editors of the Glasgow edition are inexact when they insinuate that Smith chose the analysis provided by the *Encyclopédie* over that of Chambers. Smith was probably more interested by Chambers's book than meets the eye: there is a good chance that some of the observations published in the *Edinburgh Review* were inspired or adapted from the Preface of the *Cyclopaedia*, or at least were expressions of a very similar sensibility. Each of these observations concerns the encyclopaedic genre as such, as if the very same criteria of interpretation could be applied to Johnson, Diderot and Chambers. The French achievement would then need to be considered only as a slightly vaster and more finished product stemming from a form of activity common and in fact widespread in France, England, and in the Academies of Europe. As such, the *Encyclopédie* would be no more and no less than another contribution to an ongoing process of cultural dialogue.

There is of course another reason why it makes sense to discuss the theme of encyclopaedias in relation to Smith. The *Encyclopédie* is not only based on a division of literary labour, but that basis is made into one of its explicit themes. As such, the project differs from those of Chambers and Johnson. The two English dictionaries are distinct, individual creations, about which we never stop to query attributions, as sometimes happens for the articles of the *Encyclopédie*. The English works thus deserve to be considered as 'performances which a man's whole life is scarcely equal to' (as Chambers says, referring to himself), or as performances that required 'a longer time in the composition, than the life of a single person could well have afforded' (as Smith says, speaking of Johnson; 'Review' 1).[25] Such works roll back the limitations of the individual and in doing so define what the eighteenth century was beginning to call 'genius'. But curiously, this is where Smith may begin to seem 'French', as he sets about insisting – in a different manner from Shaftesbury, for example – on the necessity of socializing genius. That affirmation of socialized genius may even help us to understand the only real criticism that Smith makes of Johnson:

The merit of Johnson's dictionary is so great, that it cannot detract from it to take notice of some defects [. . .] Those defects consist chiefly in the plan, which appears to us not to be sufficiently grammatical. The different significations of a word are indeed collected; but they are seldom digested into general classes.

('Review' 1; cf. 'Letter' 7)

Johnson's definitions may be creative and pertinent, but they lack that 'judgment, propriety and order' in things semantic that he calls grammar.[26] Johnson does not, as it were, socialize words by fitting them into 'general classes'.

Smith's account of the division of labour affirms that social dimension in experience, and does so in the same terms as a collective undertaking like the *Encyclopédie*. Here at last, we might say, we have found the reason why it made such good sense to privilege the French example of pins over that given by Chambers. But there is still a problem. The entry on the 'Pin' in Chambers makes for very interesting reading, and it reflects a mind that is very different from that of the *Encyclopédie*, a mind that is closer to the empirical details of ordinary life, freer in its movements, and far less orderly. The comparison between these two turns of mind would necessarily be fascinating – except that it would probably lead us even farther astray in our sense of how to define French and English so as then to situate Smith, Scotland and Britain. For the article 'Pin' is not exactly the work of Chambers. The text of his article is in fact the wholesale translation of a passage from another dictionary, the *Dictionnaire universel de commerce* (1723) of Jacques Savary des Brulons.[27] Chambers displays the talents of the solitary lexicographer, the experienced compiler and the graceful translator in this case, masterfully reducing Savary's article 'Épingle' in such a way that after the opening passage, there are scarcely a dozen words that can be attributed to the English author.[28] To my knowledge, this felicitous gleaning has never been remarked by historians and modern analysts, even though they regularly cite the case of the pin. But it is perfectly clear that Diderot knew about it:

Chambers's encyclopedia [. . .] would perhaps never have been produced if, prior to its publication in English, we had not had works in our language from which Chambers endlessly and indiscriminately drew the lion's share of what makes up his dictionary. What would our French readers have thought of a simple translation?[29]

This passage from the 1750 'Prospectus' was incorporated into the *Discours préliminaire*, to justify the editors' decision to abandon their original intention; as we all know, the *Encyclopédie* began as a project simply to translate Chambers into French. At the same time, Diderot introduces the example of Chambers in a larger polemic about the use and abuse of erudition. But what matters more to us here is that the division of labour can be found in places where it was hardly suspected. On the basis of Chambers's talents as a compiler, and in light of his own experience during ten years of work as a writer and editor for the *Encyclopédie*, Diderot went on to affirm his own character in language we may find surprising. In the article 'Encyclopédie', from 1755, he writes:

> Why is the encyclopaedic order so perfect and regular in the English author [Chambers]? Because in limiting himself to compiling from our dictionaries and to analyzing a small number of works, without inventing anything, but instead sticking carefully to things that were known, everything was equally interesting and indifferent to him [. . .] Chambers's articles are rather regularly laid out; but they are empty. Ours are full, but irregular. If Chambers had filled his, I am sure the order would have suffered.
>
> (Diderot 1999, art. 'Encyclopédie')[30]

Diderot affirms that the 'order' in Chambers is perfect but not good; or to apply Smith's language, perfect but not 'proper'. It lacks the reflexive, synthetic quality of a real encyclopaedic effort – and we might add, of real philosophic labour. That quality does not arise from the felicitous arrangement of words, but from invention. So the tables are turned: Chambers is the author who specializes in monotonous regularity and a more or less empty compilation. The assertion is of course arguable, but it is Diderot's ambition that matters to us here. For 'the new French Encyclopedia' may now be presented as a very English work that can correct the deficiencies of an English work that is (in more ways than one) not a little French.

Here we must return to Smith, whom we have been taking as both 'French' and 'Scottish' on account of his interest in an orderly description of the collective reality of labour. Specifically, it is time to look a bit closer at the 'Early Draft' of the *Wealth of Nations*, which dates to the 1760s. After presenting the division of labour in the fabrication of pins, in a near definitive version, Smith makes a series of remarks which are not all carried over in the final text. Several of these deserve mention in relation to his thoughts on intellectual labour. In view of the modernity of the techniques, and society's growing influence on the life of individuals, Smith accepts the idea that there is nothing absolute about the role of the individual; all of us are exposed to influences, and inventions, coming from many different parts of society. The philosopher, for instance, may seem utterly distinct from a porter, belonging to a different class, but in fact they cooperate; each owes something to the other and each has a beneficial effect on the other. In such a world, the philosopher rediscovers a Socratic role for himself. Instead of knowing that he doesn't know, he will know how little he knows strictly on his own. A social animal, he will understand that most everything he knows also belongs to others to know, and is more often than not derived from the labour of others. In addition, that labour is very often bookish. As Smith says of the readers of the *Encyclopédie*:

> There are few men so learned in the science which they have peculiarly cultivated, as not to find in this work something even with regard to it which will both instruct and entertain them; and with regard to every other, they will seldom fail of finding all the satisfaction which they could desire.
>
> ('Letter' 6)[31]

The role of the philosopher – and we may well want to use the French word and speak here of the *philosophe* – is to keep this circular relation going. His job will be to use common language to comprehend the reality that is served up to him by other men, and to deliver it back to them as an object not only of instruction and entertainment, but even of consumption and invention. In other words, the *philosophe* will be an *encyclopédiste*, and both will be inventors of sorts. Smith had not left this sphere of concern when he wrote 'First Fragment on the Division of Labour' (in Smith 1978):

> If the speculations of the philosopher have been turned towards the improvement of the mechanic arts, the benefit of them may evidently descend to the meanest of the people. Whoever burns coals has them at a better bargain by means of the inventer of the fire-engine. [. . .] Even the speculations of those who neither invent nor improve any thing are not altogether useless. They serve, at least, to keep alive and deliver down to posterity the inventions and improvements which have been made before them. They explain the grounds and reasons upon which those discoveries were founded and do not suffer the quantity of useful science to diminish.
>
> ('First Fragment' 1)

To put it somewhat paradoxically, what makes the *philosophe* original and synthetic is sometimes the commonness of his vision. And when he goes to the workshop to see for himself, he is (in one sense) merely switching from one scene of the division of labour, that of books, to another.

If we follow this intuition through, the landscape of intellectual history begins to shift before our eyes, with a speed that would be deeply disconcerting if only we did not already know what we are beginning to see. Smith's perspective forces us to account differently for some well-known facts. Chambers's dictionary, for instance, was an impressive achievement for 'a single person's experience', except that his writing was in fact the product of a cottage industry. Chambers was a genial author – who worked with assistants and other texts. Beyond all of his hard work, one might almost conclude that what mattered, and what was really the stuff of genius, was his desire to sign and appropriate the finished work. As for his assistants, one figure must be of particular interest, because Alexander McBean later became the secretary for Samuel Johnson as he set about writing his dictionary of the language. McBean's presence helps to explain how it was that Johnson borrowed so extensively from Chambers's definitions, a fact that was noted at the time and considered by some as a flaw. And yet Johnson too signed his work and was celebrated for a hallmark achievement both in respect to our language and to the overthrow of literary patronage. The question of originality is obviously central here, but a further example shows how far this problem is from being simply one of plagiarism. In 1755 Malachy Postlethwayt published a translation of Savary's *Dictionnaire économique* that proved an immediate success. How could he do so and not immediately discredit Chambers, for example, by revealing the source of the article 'Pin'? The answer is that Postlethwayt selected which passages of Savary he wished to include, even though he presents his work as 'translated from the French of the Celebrated Monsieur SAVARY, INSPECTOR-GENERAL of the MANUFACTURES for the King, at the Custom-House of Paris, with large Additions and Improvements incorporated through-out the whole work' (Postlethwayt 1766, title page). Authorship is achieved here by translating, or *badly* translating, an author. In light of his sales, Postlethwayt was encouraged in subsequent editions to announce that his book was only just based on Savary's dictionary, and that it adapted the latter's subjects to the reality of Great Britain.[32]

At this point, the English genius that was being admired from a French perspective will have to seem tarnished, as will the authority of the author as such. Indeed, we may be tempted to conclude that this is all just a story of the book trade, a straightforward and rather crude application of the rules of the division of labour – that is, the laws of the capitalist marketplace. In fact, complaints of this kind were already being made at the time, and in England to boot. One critic of Johnson's dictionary saw it as the confirmation of an unfortunate truth. The encyclopaedic ambition had not been harnessed in the service of politeness and the education of peoples; it was just a commercial trick. Johnson's dictionary is thus full of:

> those monstrous words from the things called Dictionaries such as adespotick, amnicolist, androtomy &c. words, if they may be called words, merely coined to fill up their books and which never were used by any who pretended to talk or write English [. . .] In its present condition it is, as most books lately published seem to be, nothing but a bookseller's job.
>
> (cited in Clifford 1979: 141)

This critique of the publishing market was penned by a Whig, a certain Thomas Edwards, whom we would have to style a vulgar Whig according to the going nomenclature. It hardly matters that Smith himself may have similar reservations about some of the words Johnson thought it appropriate to include: 'Most words, we believe, are to be found in the dictionary that ever were *almost suspected* to be English' ('Review' 1; my italics).

* * *

If the treatment of the *Encyclopédie* in the *Edinburgh Review* looked particularly towards questions of education and politeness, our consideration of pins and their multiple relations with encyclopaedic works has led us towards a more philosophical perspective. Intelligence is there the power to assimilate and represent a shared world. Still, we may almost feel relief that Smith does not reduce philosophy to the labours of the *philosophes* or to Grub Street. Part of the 'Early Draft' that largely disappears in the published text of the *Wealth of Nations* enters the idea of another figure whom Smith is tempted to call a philosopher. Everything we know comes from somewhere else, but there is a chance that the philosopher is someone who has genius but not skill, not even the skill of an encyclopaedia writer. A philosopher is thus no *philosophe* but rather:

> one of those people whose trade it is not to do any thing but to observe every thing, and who are upon that account capable of combining together the powers of the most opposite and distant objects. To apply in the most advantagious manner those powers which are allready known and which have already been applyed to a particular purpose, does not exceed the capacity of an ingenious artist. But to think of the application of new powers, which are altogether unknown and which have never before been applied to any similar purpose, belongs to those only who have a greater range of thought and more extensive views of things than naturally fall to the share of a meer artist.
>
> (ED 19)

Although he is unspecialized, this philosopher does not aim at a very 'compleat' description of reality. His place is not in the heart of society, in a world of applications, where one's role would be to perform a labour of style or commonality. The philosopher instead becomes the emblem of a certain idea of invention and genius – that Smith may still have wanted to call English. This philosopher is someone who finds ways to transform, if not to break out of, the world of style and socialized knowledge. His 'thought' has powerful material effects: as Smith famously allows in the same passage, an artisan of genius merits the title of philosopher. For his discovery enables him to transform the division of labour.

Although this conception of philosophy becomes more muted in WN, it may represent an important step in the evolution of Smith's ideas. We can develop and directly link it to him by a brief look at one other acknowledged source of the *Encyclopédie*, Francis Bacon. Whether or not d'Alembert and Diderot manage fully to connect Baconian natural history with a science of general axioms (Malherbe 1996: 86f.),[33] there can be little doubt that the *Encyclopédie* and Smith draw an important lesson from Bacon's under-standing of invention. Certainly Bacon is not a polite author who could be recommended for pedagogical purposes, and we have already mentioned how in 1756 Smith felt the *Encyclopédie*'s style had served simply and somewhat flatly to restate Baconian principles. But it may be that in the late 1750s Smith found new reasons to think about Bacon's idea of invention:

> INVENTION is of two kindes, much differing; The one of ARTS and SCIENCES, and the other of SPEECH and ARGUMENTS. The former of these, I doe report deficient: which seemeth to me to be such a deficience, as if in the making of an Inventorie, touching the State of a defunct, it should be set downe, *That there is no readie money*. For as money will fetch all other commodities; so this knowledge is that which should purchase all the rest. And like as the *West Indies* had never been discovered, if the use of the Mariners Needle had not been first discovered; though the one bee vast Regions, and the other a small Motion: So it cannot be found strange, if Sciences bee no further discovered, if the Art it selfe of Invention and Discoverie, hath been passed over.

(Bacon 2000: 107f.)

In the *Advancement of Learning* [1605], which is both an uncouth and a genial book, invention is a complex and even enigmatic activity. It corres-ponds to no philosophical logic of discovery but to a practice of induction which as easily involves animals and artisans as thinkers. In the passage cited here, invention or discovery is not a matter of discursive 'arts and sciences' or of method only, but is based on a capital of previous inventions and the management of that capital. Thus, small can produce large. An invention can lead to the discovery of whole 'Sciences', and magnetizing 'an iron nail'[34] or a needle can lead to a vast New World. From an eighteenth-century viewpoint, the connection between needle and space could be read as a matter of Newtonian gravitation. But Bacon's way of uniting what Smith calls 'the most opposite and distant objects' insists on the relation between real things as well: a simple needle, the empirical fact of space and continents. These are not connected by invisible spirit but by acts of historical mind. Indeed, Bacon had already embodied his sense of the inductive interconnections between inventions with the same example, or rather an example the same and different, in an earlier passage of the *Advancement*: 'for the Invention of the Mariners Needle, which giveth the direction, is of noe less benefit for Navigation, then the invention of the sailes which give the Motion' (Bacon 2000: 90). The compass met the sail and the two invented or discovered the New World.

In the *Novum organum*, Bacon held that the art of printing, gunpowder and the compass (or mariner's needle: 'acûs nautae') had produced the modern world: 'these three have altered the whole face and state of things right across the globe' (Bacon 2004 [1620], I.CXXIX:195). Much has of course been made of Smith's Newtonian method, but one may at least wonder whether this textual environment of nails and needles does not inform Smith's philosophical understanding of his own discoveries. It could explain why he moved beyond the examples of the division of labour contained in the early fragments ('First Fragment', 'Second Fragment') – the porter, the baker, navigation – in order finally to associate the momentous force which *he* recognized as changing the world, with the Baconian model. Following out this hypothesis would imply a different chronology among ED and the early fragments than what is usually accepted (for example, WN I.iii n.1). Far from being a 'very trivial' or 'frivolous' example, the pin would then become an 'instance' in the Baconian (and Aristotelian) sense of the term.[35] Indifferent though it may be, the pin figures a world in movement, and the division of labour becomes Smith's name for what Bacon called 'invention'. Thus, as Bacon put it in closing Book I of *his* connected history, 'the art of invention may improve with inventions' (Bacon 2004 [1620] I.CXXIX: 196; my translation).

The *Encyclopédie* was clearly close to this idea. For if I am right to think that Smith imitated Bacon by assimilating the pin to the compass, he would also have observed d'Alembert's doing something similar and he would have understood the appropriateness of the gesture: 'The discovery of the compass' (*la Boussole*), d'Alembert wrote, 'is no less advantageous to humankind than the explanation of the properties of that needle would be to Physics' (*Discours préliminaire*).[36] D'Alembert's echo of Bacon situated his own reflection at the end of the Baconian series and likewise generalized its range. The mathematician thereby acknowledged that there is no ranking system, no one direction, in the world of invention. It showed that rather than serving only the enterprises of the polite intellect, d'Alembert had recognized that invention occurs at every level of society. Newton in his physics and the nameless artisans who have innovated in their crafts (whom d'Alembert calls 'the benefactors of humankind' – *bienfaiteurs du genre humain* – rather than philosophers) are thus placed on something of the same level. The new form given to invention in the *Encyclopédie's* articles could thus diffuse occasions for further innovation by placing every subject in alphabetical order.

Smith's ideas about grammar and connected history reflect similar concerns. But for him the division of labour has a vaster reach than any specific innovation, and the goal is not simply what d'Alembert refers to as advantages (*avantageuse*). The division of labour informs not only the encyclopaedic ordering of knowledge and techniques, but also the order of 'filiation' (to borrow d'Alembert's word), the genealogical order of mankind. As an instance of Baconian invention improving on invention, the division of labour opens social life to unknown possibilities that cannot be predicted and that can be known only by being tried. Perhaps, though, Smith is stepping back from such radically experimental conditions when he stipulates that the benefits of the division are felt universally 'in a well-governed society' (WN I.i.10), and if there are 'proper' divisions, there can surely be improper ones as well. In any case, for Smith, the division of labour becomes the source of nearly everything: the astonishing well-being of the worker in modern times and the difference between the philosopher and the porter, the development of primitive society and the dizzying progress of contemporary production. But more restrictively than with Baconian invention, the division of labour also informs the definition of European man, in contrast to men of other continents, and the definition of man as such, compared to animals.

Acknowledgement

Parts of this paper were delivered as the McMahon lecture at Wesleyan University in 2006. An earlier version of the lecture appeared in French under the title 'De fil en aiguille: les sources de l'*Encyclopédie* vues par Adam Smith', *Lez Valenciennes*, n°. 36, 2005, pp. 105–21. The author is grateful to Doug Den Uyl and the referee for fruitful criticisms and generous encouragement.

Notes

1 The passage could be translated: 'No matter what the subject, you have never covered all the ground there was to cover until you have reached a principle that cannot be proved, defined, illuminated, darkened or denied, without losing some of the light that was thrown on you, and without taking a step into darkness that would end up getting very deep, if you did not set limits to your argument'. This and other French texts from the *Encyclopédie* and from the 'Discours Préliminaire des éditeurs' come from Diderot and d'Alembert (1999). The translations are my own.

2 The autobiography of a founding member of the Society, Alexander Carlyle, is quoted in Emerson (1973). Other sources of general information about the Society are Rae (1965) and Mossner (1980).

3 Unsurprisingly, the 'Letter to the Edinburgh Review' (1756) about European and especially French learning first appeared in the French translation of *Essays on Philosophical Subjects* published in Paris in 1797; in English, both essays from the *Edinburgh Review* were first collected only in 1967, along with Smith's first publication – a 1748 Preface to a book of poetry – in a volume of his 'early writings' (Smith 1967). On several occasions the essay on Johnson had been reprinted in magazines (Smith 1980: 28–9, 230–1).

4 Mizuta (2000) lists only the seven volumes of the engravings from the *Encyclopédie* as present in Smith's library by the end of his life. Unless otherwise specified, references in the text to Smith's ownership of books are based on Mizuta's catalogue.

5 'Mr Alembert gives an account of the connection of the different arts and sciences, their genealogy and filiation as he calls it' ('Letter' 6), Smith writes, but in such a way that the reader cannot guess that d'Alembert expresses the same reservations about the terminology. The fourth paragraph of the *Discours préliminaire* opens: 'Le premier pas que nous ayons à faire dans cette recherche, est d'examiner, qu'on nous permette ce terme, la généalogie et la filiation de nos connaissances'. Note that the subject is the origins of knowledge.

6   Smith's text is treated with remarkable distance by Dugald Stewart, who summarizes it as follows: 'The observations on the state of learning in Europe are written with ingenuity and elegance; but are chiefly interesting, as they shew the attention which the Author had given to the philosophy and literature of the Continent, at a period when they were not much studied in this island' (Stewart I.25). Stewart published the biography in 1794, when Britain was at war with revolutionary France.

7   Cf. the end of the 'Avertissement des éditeurs', at the head of volume III of the *Encyclopédie*.

8   Of course this is not d'Alembert's conclusion with regard to the history of the sciences: 'l'Angleterre nous doit la naissance de cette philosophie que nous avons reçue d'elle' (*Discours préliminaire*).

9   Diderot agreed and expressed similar reservations in the article 'Encyclopédie', which appeared in the volumes Smith had under review.

10 Smith's impatience with amorous discourse continued in TMS I.ii.2.1.

11 It is in fact the shortest work he reviews, Rousseau's second *Discourse*, that receives the longest and most detailed treatment. Smith's close-up takes the form of a series of passages he translates.

12 Anticipating the creation in 1761 of a 'Society for Promoting the Reading and Speaking of the English Language in Scotland', Smith recommends Johnson's Dictionary for 'all those who are desirous to improve and correct their language', since 'in this country [he means Scotland] there is no standard of correct language in conversation' ('Review' 14). Smith no longer invokes Latin as a learned *lingua franca*, nor does he mention broad Scots (Phillipson 1974: 430).

13 Perth was to found an academy in 1760, but it is perhaps another way of describing Scotland's difficulties to say that for the time being, it did not fit into either case. Its achievement in the eighteenth century was to unite institutions (the university, the genre of historiography) with the genius of individuals.

14 The example of Voltaire at the end of the text destroys the neat opposition and thus goes some way to explaining Smith's lifelong admiration of him.

15 Cf. Hume's remarks in a letter written from Edinburgh to his French translator, Abbé Le Blanc, in October 1754: 'I shou'd esteem myself extremely oblig'd to you, if you inform me of any good Writings, which have lately been produc'd in Paris. We are sometimes late of seeing them in this Part of the World. Our English Literature has not, for some years past, been very fertile.' 'Literature' was of course broadly understood, and perhaps 'our' requires a grain of salt. Hume's letter goes on to cite Bolingbroke, James Harris on grammar, and Lord Lyttleton as the contemporary production (Hume 1932, I: 208). Smith's praise of Scottish mathematics was not long in coming (TMS III.2.20).

16 'Of the Rise and Progress of the Arts and Sciences' (Hume 1987: 110–37).

17 Hume was its Librarian from 1752–1757 (Scott 1965: 333–4, n.2). Subsequently Smith ordered part of a set of the *Encyclopédie* for the university library at Glasgow (Ross 1995: 147).

18 Cf. Hume's fragmentary letter to Allan Ramsay, from April or May 1755 (Hume 1932, I.219f.).

19 Brown (1994) argues that this indifferent or 'second-order' zone of morality is the deliberate environment of WN.

20 Delaire 'décrivait la fabrication de l'épingle dans les ateliers même des ouvriers, sur nos desseins, tandis qu'il faisait imprimer à Paris son analyse de la philosophie sublime & profonde du chancelier Bacon; ouvrage qui joint à la description précédente, prouvera qu'un bon esprit peut quelquefois, avec le même succès, & s'élever aux contemplations les plus hautes de la Philosophie, & descendre aux détails de la mécanique la plus minutieuse'. The passage continues: 'Au reste ceux

qui connaîtront un peu les vues que le philosophe anglais avait en composant ses ouvrages, ne seront pas étonnés de voir son disciple passer sans dédain de la recherche des lois générales de la nature, à l'emploi le moins important de ses productions'. The attribution to Delaire (or Deleyre), an author who wrote on Bacon, is inexact; though for reasons that will become obvious at the end of this paper, the association is tantalizing. In fact, the article on pins was completed later on (Proust 1995: 152).

21　Organization by alphabetical order was criticized by the Abbé de Vauxcelles in these terms: 'C'étoit louer le désordre d'un magasin où tout seroit empilé et dispensé pêle-mêle. On fit un jour cette observation à Diderot, qui eut la franchise d'en avouer la justice' (cited by Venturi 1963: 121, n.7).

22　Mizuta (2000: 48) also supports the association with Chambers.

23　William Robert Scott hypothesized that the pin was a late addition, following Smith's contact with the *Encyclopédie*. It is true that the pin has a textual rival, the nail (Scott 1965: 116–7, 333 n.2), which will return later in my account. In any case, the state of the manuscripts, which has been thoroughly studied since the publication of Scott's study, seems to imply that the pin was his starting-point in writing. This is the position of R.L. Meek and A.S. Skinner (1973) in their important article. And yet, as already mentioned, ED begins: 'Chap[ter] 2'.

24　This is the power claimed by the epigraph to the *Encyclopédie*: '*Tantum series juncturaque pollet . . .*' (so valuable are order and arrangement. . .).

25　To see how Smith finds resources, if not a source, in Chambers, it may be useful to compare the passages in greater detail. Chambers opens his Preface in these terms: 'It is not without some concern, that I put this work in the reader's hands; a work so seemingly disproportionate to any single person's experience, and which might have employed an academy. What adds to my apprehensions, is the scanty measure of time that could be employed in a performance, which a whole man's life scarce appears equal to. The Vocabulary of the Academy *della Crusca* was above forty years in compiling, and the Dictionary of the French academy much longer; and yet the present work will be found more extensive than either of them in its subject and design. . .' (Chambers 1728: ii). Smith's article on Johnson cites the Dictionary's title and then commences: 'The present undertaking is very extensive. A dictionary of the English language, however useful, or rather necessary, has never been hitherto attempted with the least degree of success. [. . .] When we compare this book with other dictionaries, the merit of its author appears very extraordinary. Those which in modern languages have gained the most esteem, are that of the French academy, and that of the academy Della Crusca. Both of these were composed by a numerous society of learned men, and took up a longer time in the composition, that the life of a single person could well have afforded. The dictionary of the English language is the work of a single person, and composed in a period of time very inconsiderable, when compared with the extent of the work' ('Review' 1).

26　Grammar here refers to a kind of logic. In a letter of 1763 Smith returned to the question of a 'Plan for a Rational Grammar. . . not only the best System of Grammar, but the best System of Logic' and he associates it with two French works, the Abbé Gabriel Girard's *Les vrais principes de la langue françoise, ou la parole réduite en méthode conformément aux lois d'usage* (1747) and the grammatical articles 'in the French Encyclopedie' (sic). The latter is, to my knowledge, the only other explicit reference to the *Encyclopédie* in Smith's works (*Corr.* No. 69 to George Baird, 7 Feb. 1763).

27　It is hard to imagine that Smith would not have known the *Dictionnaire* though he did not own it. At the very least, he would already have met with Savary in

Voltaire's 'Catalogue de la plupart des écrivains français qui ont paru dans *Le Siècle de Louis XIV*, pour servir à l'histoire littéraire de ce temps', which summarizes Savary's life and works in several lines (Voltaire 1957: 1208). Smith translates from the catalogue in 'Letter' 6.

28 Chambers's flowing, respectful translation strays from the original only when it crowns London in a passage where Savary touted Paris for having the best shops for the making of pins in the English style ('façon d'Angleterre'), and when it qualifies the number of workers employed in the production as 'incredible' rather than 'grand'. The figure of twenty-five operations is clearly Savary's. Presumably he looked into different shops from those of the *encyclopédistes* a generation later, or else technical innovations had occurred.

29 'L'Encyclopédie de Chambers [. . .] n'eût peut-être jamais été faite, si avant qu'elle parut en Anglois, nous n'avions eu dans notre Langue des Ouvrages où Chambers a puisé sans mesure & sans choix la plus grande partie des choses dont il a composé son Dictionnaire. Qu'en auroient donc pensé nos François sur une traduction pure & simple?' Or as d'Alembert put it in the *Discours préliminaire*, on the subject of the mechanical arts, 'Chambers n'a presque rien ajouté à ce qu'il a traduit de nos auteurs'.

30 'Pourquoi l'ordre encyclopédique est-il si parfait & si régulier dans l'auteur anglois [Chambers]; c'est que se bornant à compiler nos dictionnaires & à analyser un petit nombre d'ouvrages, n'inventant rien, s'en tenant rigoureusement aux choses connues, tout lui étant également intéressant ou indifférent [. . .] Les articles de Chambers sont assez régulièrement distribués; mais ils sont vides. Les nôtres sont pleins, mais irréguliers. Si Chambers eût rempli les siens, je ne doute point que son ordonnance n'en eût souffert' (Diderot, art. 'Encyclopédie').

31 Cf. Chambers: 'By means hereof [through the *Cyclopaedia*] a stock of knowledge becomes attainable on easy terms, sufficient for the purposes of most persons, except those who make learning their most immediate profession; and for those too in most parts of science, except that which makes their immediate province. Such a design may perhaps seem most adapted to the uses of men of business [and 'men of pleasure']' (Chambers 1728: xxv). In the Prospectus, Diderot may attack Chambers, but he simply varies metaphors in order to take aim at the same target: 'nous inférons que cet ouvrage pourrait tenir lieu de bibliothèque dans tous les genres, à un homme du monde; et dans tous les genres, excepté le sien, à un savant de profession'.

32 The title page to the third edition of *The Universal Dictionary of Trade and Commerce* (1766) proclaims that the book presents 'Every Thing essential that is contained in Savary's Dictionary'. This appears to be the edition owned by Smith (*Corr.* No. 102 to Thomas Cadell, 25 Mar. 1767, n.4).

33 A locus for the connection *manqué* would be in this staging of philosophical reflection *after* history: 'Il n'en est pas de même de l'ordre encyclopédique de nos connoissances. Ce dernier consiste à les rassembler dans le plus petit espace possible, & à placer, pour ainsi dire, le Philosophe au-dessus de ce vaste labyrinthe dans un point de vûe fort élevé d'où il puisse appercevoir à la fois les Sciences & les Arts principaux; voir d'un coup d'œil les objets de ses spéculations, & les opérations qu'il peut faire sur ces objets; distinguer les branches générales des connoissances humaines, les points qui les séparent ou qui les unissent; & entrevoir même quelquefois les routes secretes qui les rapprochent' (*Discours préliminaire*). But for its arising after history, this staging would be closer to the philosopher than to what I have called the *philosophe*.

34 In the *Novum Organum* [1620], Bacon described William Gilbert's use of an 'iron nail' (*clavus ferreus*) in his experiments on 'verticity' (Bacon 2004, Book II: 328).

35 'An instance is neither an illustrative example, nor a particular use, but any information rich in inductive power, either by the place it occupies in a table or by some prerogative or methodical virtue' (Malherbe 1996: 84). Smith made a grand statement in the Baconian style later in WN (IV.vii.c.80) but it is far less penetrating.
36 'La découverte de la Boussole n'est pas moins avantageuse au genre humain, que ne le seroit à la Physique l'explication des propriétés de cette aiguille'.

Bibliography

Bacon, F. (2000) [1605–33] *The Advancement of Learning*, Michael Kiernan (ed.) Oxford: Clarendon Press.
—— (2004) [1620] *The Instauratio Magna. Part II: Novum organum and Associated Texts*, Graham Rees with Maria Wakely (eds.) Oxford: Clarendon Press.
Brown, V. (1994) *Adam Smith's Discourse: Canonicity, Commerce and Conscience*, London: Routledge.
Burke, E. (1968) [1790] *Reflections on the Revolution in France and on the Proceedings in Certain Societies in London relative to that Event*, Conor Cruise O'Brien (ed.), Harmondsworth: Penguin.
Chambers, E. (1728) *Cyclopaedia, or an Universal Dictionary of Arts and Sciences*, 5th edn 1742, Dublin.
Clifford, J. (1979) *Dictionary Johnson: Samuel Johnson's Middle Years*, New York: McGraw–Hill.
Diderot, D. and d'Alembert, J. (1999) *L'Encyclopédie de Diderot et d'Alembert*, CD-Rom, Paris: Redon.
Emerson, R.L. (1973) 'The social composition of enlightened Scotland: the Select Society of Edinburgh, 1754–64', *Studies in Voltaire and the Eighteenth Century*, 114: 291–329.
Hume, D. (1932) *The Letters of David Hume*, J.Y.T. Greig (ed.), Oxford: Clarendon Press, 2 vols.
—— (1985) [1777] *Essays, Moral, Political, and Literary*, E.F. Miller (ed.), 2nd edn 1987, Indianapolis: Liberty Press.
Lough, J. (1970) *The* Encyclopédie *in 18th-century England and other Studies*, Newcastle: Oriel Press.
Malherbe, M. (1996) 'Bacon's method of science' in *The Cambridge Companion to Bacon*, M. Peltonen (ed.), Cambridge: Cambridge University Press.
Meek R.L. and Skinner A.S. (1973) 'The development of Adam Smith's ideas on the division of labour', *Economic Journal*, 83: 1094–116.
Mizuta, H. (2000) *Adam Smith's Library: A Catalogue*, Oxford: Clarendon Press.
Mossner, E.C. (1954) *The Life of David Hume*, 2nd edn 1980, Oxford: Oxford University Press.
Phillipson, N.T. (1974) 'Culture and society in the 18th-century province: the case of Edinburgh and the Scottish Enlightenment', in L. Stone (ed.) *The University in Society*, vol. II, Princeton: Princeton University Press: 407–48.
Pocock, J.G.A. (1999) *Barbarism and Religion. II. Narratives of Civil Government*, Cambridge: Cambridge University Press.
Postlethwayt, M. (1766) *The Universal Dictionary of Trade and Commerce*, London.
Proust, J. (1995) [1962] *Diderot et l'Encyclopédie*, Paris: Albin Michel.
Rae, J. (1965) [1895] *Life of Adam Smith*, New York: Augustus Kelley.

Ross, I.S. (1995) *The Life of Adam Smith*, Oxford: Clarendon Press.

Savary des Brulous, J. (1723) *Dictionnaire universel de commerce*, Paris: Estienne, 2 vols.

Scott, W.R. (1965) [1937] *Adam Smith as Student and Professor*, New York: Augustus Kelly.

Smith, A. (1795) *Essays on Philosophical Subjects*, London: printed for T. Cadell and W. Davies, and W. Creech.

—— (1967) *The Early Writings of Adam Smith*, J.R. Lindgren (ed.), New York: Augustus M. Kelley.

—— (1976a) *The Theory of Moral Sentiments*, D.D. Raphael and A.L Macfie (eds), Oxford: Clarendon Press; reprinted, Liberty Press (1982).

—— (1976b) *An Inquiry into the Nature and Causes of the Wealth of Nations*, R.H. Campbell and A.S. Skinner (eds), Oxford: Clarendon Press; reprinted, Liberty Press (1981).

—— (1978) *Lectures on Jurisprudence*, R.L. Meek, D.D. Raphael and P.G. Stein (eds), Oxford: Clarendon Press; reprinted, Liberty Press (1982).

—— (1980) *Essays on Philosophical Subjects*, W.P.D. Wightman (ed.), Oxford: Clarendon Press; reprinted, Liberty Press (1982).

—— (1983) *Lectures on Rhetoric and Belles Lettres*, J.C. Bryce (ed.), Oxford: Clarendon Press; reprinted, Liberty Press (1985).

—— (1987) *Correspondence of Adam Smith*, E.C. Mossner and I.S. Ross (eds), Oxford: Clarendon Press; reprinted, Liberty Press (1987).

Stewart, D. (1980) [1794] 'Account of the Life and Writings of Adam Smith, LL.D.', in Adam Smith, *Essays on Philosophical Subjects*, W.P.D. Wightman (ed.), Oxford: Clarendon Press; reprinted, Liberty Press (1982).

Venturi, F. (1963) [1946] *Le Origini dell'*Enciclopedia, Milan: Einaudi.

Voltaire (1957) *Œuvres historiques*, R. Pomeau (ed.), Paris: Gallimard.

Commemorating 30 years of The Glasgow Edition of the Works and Correspondence of Adam Smith

Editor's introduction

The year 1976 saw the publication of the first two volumes of The Glasgow Edition of the Works and Correspondence of Adam Smith, 1976–87, Oxford at the Clarendon Press: *The Theory of Moral Sentiments*, edited by D.D. Raphael and A.L. Macfie; and *An Inquiry into the Nature and Causes of the Wealth of Nations*, edited by R.H. Campbell and A.S. Skinner, Textual Editor, W.B. Todd. The Glasgow Edition provides the only scholarly variorum edition of Smith's works and correspondence.

It is an honour for *The Adam Smith Review* to mark this moment with (written) interviews with Professor Raphael and Professor Skinner. The interview with D.D. Raphael appeared in *The Adam Smith Review*, volume 3, pp. 1–11. The interview with Andrew Skinner is given below.

Questions

1   The period since 1976 when the *Wealth of Nations* was published in the Glasgow Edition has seen a considerable increase in interest in Adam Smith. Did you have any thoughts at the time that this was likely to happen? Were there signs then of an increasing interest in Smith?
2   To what extent do you think that the Glasgow Edition itself contributed to this increased interest – or was it largely the result of other factors?
3   The editorial Introduction to the *Wealth of Nations* has been influential for Adam Smith scholarship. Were there any particular difficulties you experienced in editing the *Wealth of Nations*? Or controversial issues to be weighed in writing the Introduction?
4   Looking back with the benefit of hindsight and further scholarship on Smith, would you now want to make any changes or revisions to your editorial Introduction.
5   What do you see as the most interesting lines of research on Smith during the last thirty years?
6   Has your own thinking on Adam Smith changed during this period?

Vivienne Brown
Editor
April 2008

The Adam Smith Review, 4: 209–214 © 2008 The International Adam Smith Society, ISSN 1743–5285, ISBN 13: 978–0–415–45438–4.

Interview with Andrew S. Skinner

An Inquiry into the Nature and Causes of the Wealth of Nations: The Glasgow Edition 1976

Vivienne Brown has put a series of questions to two of the surviving editors of Smith's *Works*. David Raphael responded in the last edition of this *Review* (2007). For my part it is not easy to confine attention to the *Wealth of Nations* (WN 1976b) for reasons which will become apparent.

I

My interest in Smith dates back to my time as an undergraduate in Glasgow. In the early 1960s the teaching of the history of economic thought was dominated by two men: Alec Macfie (ALM), the Adam Smith Professor, and Ronald Meek (RLM). Meek had been appointed as a lecturer in 1948. The two men were very different in terms of their interests but both subscribed to the old Aristotelian dictum, namely, that if you wish to understand what presently exists you must first understand the origins from which it springs. While the history of economic thought formed a major part of the curriculum it was in no sense antiquarian. Following graduation I had the advantage of an entire calendar year in Cornell where I had nothing to do other than the study of WN and the secondary literature. But I was sidetracked by the publication of S.R. Sen's *The Economics of Sir James Steuart* (1957) and by RLM's (1958) review of it which was subsequently published as 'The rehabilitation of Sir James Steuart' (Meek 1967).

My first foray in the study of the history of economic thought was a thesis on Steuart, conducted under the supervision of RLM who introduced me, crucially, to the work of the Scottish Historical School and to this aspect of Smith's work. It was only at this point that I came to appreciate the relationship which exists between Books V and III of WN. It is in Book V that we find the clearest account of the first two stages of society (hunting and pasture), while it is in Book III that we meet the third and fourth stages (agriculture and commerce) together with an account of the origins of the exchange economy.

The thesis on Steuart brought with it an invitation from the Scottish Economic Society to produce an edition of the *An Inquiry into the Principles of Political Oeconomy* [1767]. This work, which eventually appeared in 1966, was developed under the supervision of ALM. Like Meek, Macfie was an efficient and a helpful supervisor. Quite apart from his knowledge of Steuart, it was Macfie who introduced me to yet another facet of Smith's work – *The Theory of Moral Sentiments* (TMS). Macfie wrote a number of articles on the TMS and its relationship to WN, starting in 1959. These papers were later collected in *The Individual in Society* (1967).

I was thus equipped with some knowledge of the three main components of Smith's contribution.

II

Steuart's *Principles* (1966) was well received (by the discerning few!) and notably by Terence Hutchison. In the event I entered into a long correspondence with Robert Hutchison of Penguin Books. The upshot of this correspondence (which dates from 1967) was an invitation to produce a Penguin edition of the WN. Rather than contemplate an abridgement, it was decided to reproduce Books I–III in their entirety together with a long introduction. The first volume appeared in 1970, whilst the edition was completed, with a separate introduction, in 1999.

The significance to me of the first volume was that it gave me for the first time the opportunity of exploring in a formal way the relationship which I believed to exist between the parts of Smith's system. This approach was based in part on John Millar's account of Smith's teaching from the Chair of Moral Philosophy but was largely based on the concluding sentences of the first edition of TMS and on the Advertisement to the sixth and last edition of that work (1790). Readers will recall Smith's famous statement:

> In the last paragraph of the first Edition of the present work, I said, that I should in another discourse endeavour to give an account of the general principles of law and government, and of the different revolutions which they had undergone in the different ages and periods of society; not only in what concerns justice, but in what concerns police, revenue, and arms, and whatever else is the object of law. In the *Enquiry concerning the Nature and Causes of the Wealth of Nations*, I have partly executed this promise.
>
> (TMS 1976a, Advertisement 2)

The line of argument which was first explored in the Penguin edition has been repeated in a variety of forms in Skinner (editorial intro. WN 1976b; 1987; 1996). A further version of what is in effect an introduction to Smith's work will appear in the second edition of the New Palgrave in 2008. In short I would not change the basic line of argument as developed in the Glasgow edition of WN although it will be clear that subsequent versions of the argument have different emphases. What I would wish to do is to give greater prominence to Smith's 'History of Astronomy' (1980) and to his *Lectures on Rhetoric and Belles Lettres* (LRBL 1983).

The text, however, presented me with some initial problems. As David Raphael has recorded (2007), E.C. Mossner contacted a colleague, W.B. Todd, who visited Glasgow and explained that modern techniques suggested the value of an 'eclectic text', using the first edition as a copy text and then modifying it in the light of later editions. The editors of TMS declined the offer really on the ground that the sixth edition of TMS was a quite different work from the first. The editors of WN (Professors Checkland and Meek) accepted Todd's offer although it is not clear to me that Todd did in fact produce an 'eclectic' text as originally defined. But Raphael is correct in stating that I, as one of the principal editors of WN, had no say in the selection of the text.

However, I had no difficulty in dealing with this problem. To begin with, Todd followed the practice of the editors of TMS in that his copy text follows the edition on which Smith is last known to have worked – the third edition of 1784. On reflection, Todd concluded that 'the third edition can be regarded as supervening even the first in many of its formal aspects, and thus now serves as printers' copy' (editorial intro. WN 1976b, p. 63). There is no methodological tension between the treatment of the texts of TMS and WN. I was also glad to note that the scholar who uses the Glasgow edition may also consult Cannan's version of the fifth edition of WN (1904). I was anxious throughout to avoid any criticism of Cannan, whom I greatly admired – a point which drew a generous compliment from Lionel Robbins, writing in the *Financial Times* (1976).

III

I returned to Glasgow in 1964, having spent the preceding five years teaching political theory – an invaluable experience as it turned out. The move came about as the result of Meek's appointment to the Tyler Chair of Economics, The University of Leicester. I did not have any academic connection with the project of the Glasgow Edition and in fact worked as the secretary to the Editorial Board for a number of years. The Board consisted of the Chairman, Professor C.J. Fordyce, formerly the Clerk of Senate, and all the appointed editors. One of the early losses was the late George E. Davie, whom it was hoped would be able to edit the 'Astronomy'.

My function was purely administrative although it turned out to be very informative. The Board met frequently as the minutes (which still exist) will attest. But there were changes. First RLM retired as one of the editors of WN. This was due in large measure to the amount of work involved in the preparation of LJ. The second resignation was that of Professor Sydney Checkland who had his own agenda. Professor Checkland resigned in my favour, largely on the basis of the work I had already done on the Penguin.

In the late 1960s I found myself as the sole editor facing a deadline of some six years duration. But in the event I persuaded the Board to adhere to their original decision to appoint an economist and an economic historian. This was Roy Campbell, Professor of Economic History in the University of Stirling. This proved to be a very amicable relationship and featured a very useful division of labour. For my part I was primarily responsible for the system of cross references within the WN and for the references to Smith's other works. However, I could not accept a text prepared by another hand so that in effect the work in Texas (editorial intro. WN 1976b, p. 65) was duplicated in Glasgow by myself. There were differences which, as Todd generously acknowledged, were 'resolved' at Glasgow.

IV

Vivienne Brown has asked if the edition has had an impact on scholarship. A glance at Tony Brewer's article in the last edition of this *Review* (2007) suggests that the edition has at least helped. But there is another reason for the 'market penetration' of the *Works*. In the early 1980s we faced a cash-flow problem which made it unlikely that the edition could be completed in the short run. The last volume to be published by the Press was John Bryce's edition of LRBL. I wrote to Ian (later Sir Ian) McGregor, then CEO of the American Company Amax, and later of Coal Board fame. Sir Ian had a close interest in Smith and in fact I met him quite often during his many visits to Scotland. Sir Ian was aware of the problem and put me in touch with the Director of the Liberty Fund of Indianapolis. The Director, while sympathetic, informed us that they could not give cash, but could commission work. The upshot was an agreement to publish the *Works* in paperback – at a price of roughly £5 per volume. This development transformed the impact of the edition as a whole.

But the Fund went further. In another agreement it became possible to put the whole of the *Works* onto the internet, with free access. The Fund also commissioned the index to Smith's *Works* which was prepared by myself and Knud Haakonssen (2001). This volume, together with the internet makes it possible for the scholar (and student) to create their own indices depending on the area of interest.

The technical changes have been completed as a result of an agreement between the Clarendon Press and the American Company Intelex as a result of which Smith's *Works* are now available in CD-Rom. This CD-Rom includes my own book of essays (1996; a by-product of work on the edition) and Mizuta's *Catalogue* (2000). Glasgow University and scholars generally have good cause to be grateful to our American colleagues.

Bibliography

Brewer, A. (2007) 'Let us now praise famous men: assessments of Adam Smith's economics', *The Adam Smith Review*, 3: 161–86, London and New York: Routledge.

Haakonssen, K. and A.S. Skinner (2000) *Index to the Works of Adam Smith*, Oxford: Clarendon Press.

Macfie, A.L. (1967) *The Individual in Society: Papers on Adam Smith*, London: Allen & Unwin.

Meek, R.L. (1967) 'The rehabilitation of Sir James Steuart', in *Economics and Ideology and Other Essays*, London: Chapman & Hall; first published in *Science and Society*, 1958.

Mizuta, H. (2000) *Adam Smith's Library: A Catalogue*, Oxford: Clarendon Press.

Raphael, D.D. (2007) 'Commemorating 30 years of The Glasgow Edition of the Works and Correspondence of Adam Smith: Interview with D.D. Raphael', *The Adam Smith Review*, 3: 1–11, V. Brown (ed.), London and New York: Routledge.

Sen, S.R (1957) *The Economics of James Steuart*, London: G. Bell.

Skinner, A.S. (1987) 'Adam Smith' in *The New Palgrave: A Dictionary of Economics*, J. Eatwell, M. Milgate and P. Newman (eds), London: Macmillan.

—— (1996) *A System of Social Science: Papers Relating to Adam Smith*, Oxford: Clarendon Press; 1st edn 1979.

Smith, A. (1904) *An Inquiry into the Nature and Causes of the Wealth of Nations*, E. Cannan (ed.), London: Methuen & Co.

—— (1976a) *The Theory of Moral Sentiments*, D.D. Raphael and A.L. Macfie (eds), Oxford: Clarendon Press; reprinted, Indianapolis: Liberty Fund (1984).

—— (1976b) *An Inquiry into the Nature and Causes of the Wealth of Nations*, R.H. Campbell and A.S. Skinner (general eds), W.B. Todd (textual ed.), Oxford: Clarendon Press; reprinted, Indianapolis: Liberty Fund (1981).

—— (1978) *Lectures on Jurisprudence*, R.L. Meek, D.D. Raphael, and P.G. Stein (eds), Oxford: Clarendon Press, reprinted, Indianapolis: Liberty Fund (1982).

—— (1983) *Lectures on Rhetoric and Belles Lettres*, J.C. Bryce (ed.), Oxford: Clarendon Press, reprinted, Indianapolis: Liberty Fund (1985).

—— (1980) 'History of Astronomy', in *Essays on Philosophical Subjects*, W.P.D. Wightman (ed.), Oxford: Clarendon Press; reprinted, Indianapolis: Liberty Press (1982).

—— (1999) *An Inquiry into the Nature and Causes of the Wealth of Nations*, A.S. Skinner (ed.), Harmondsworth: Penguin; 1st edn, Books I – III, 1970.

Steuart, J. (1966) [1767] *An Inquiry into the Principles of Political Oeconomy*, A.S. Skinner (ed.), Edinburgh and London: Oliver & Boyd.

Acknowledgement

I am grateful to Brenda Barnett for her secretarial assistance in preparing this interview for publication, Editor.

Symposium on *The Cambridge Companion to Adam Smith*

(ed.) Knud Haakonssen

Introduction

Interdisciplinarity in Smith studies

Fonna Forman-Barzilai

Until very recently, philosophers tended to ignore Adam Smith. They acknowledged his idea of sympathy in the *Theory of Moral Sentiments*, but generally regarded it as superficial and unsophisticated, and tended to dismiss Smith as a minor figure in the shadow of David Hume. Moreover, he was regularly cast aside as a crass materialist who reduced human motivation to selfishness and corrupted the world with a moral justification for capitalism. In this environment, Smith scholarship was left to the mercy of economists and historians of economics who tended to subordinate Smith's philosophy and ignore the complexity of his thought.

This tendency finds its earliest traces in a debate that began among late nineteenth-century German capitalists and Marxists, on the extent to which Smith's two seminal books might be reconciled. The so-called 'Adam Smith problem' turned on how we might reconcile the *Theory of Moral Sentiments* [1759] and its emphasis on sympathy with the *Wealth of Nations* [1776] and its emphasis on self-interest. Are the books consistent or continuous? And if not, which in Smith's mind was prior? Was Smith primarily an ethical or an economic thinker? Were human beings driven primarily by sympathy or self-interest, virtue or vice? *Homo socius* or *homo oeconomicus*? Scholarship on Smith throughout the nineteenth century and most of the twentieth, was dominated by 'present-minded' people who wanted to say something or another about capitalism. In that environment the 'Adam Smith Problem' was most often resolved in the direction of self-interest, with the *Wealth of Nations* and its purported 'celebration of avarice' rising triumphant as the motivating centre of Smith's thought, and the *Moral Sentiments* set aside as aberrant and odd, puerile, academic.

Now, saying something or another about capitalism is a worthy enterprise, no doubt. But as ideology goes, it tends to produce very bad history. And in Smith's case, it seems to have mattered very little where one stood on the political spectrum. Whether one extolled the virtues of capitalism or condemned its excesses and blindness; whether one advocated a small state or big one; there was general agreement about what Smith said and what he meant by it. Whether he was praised by liberals as a champion of individual freedom or maligned by Marxists as an 'evil genius' responsible for

The Adam Smith Review, 4: 217–253 © 2008 The International Adam Smith Society, ISSN 1743–5285, ISBN 13: 978–0–415–45438–4.

inventing the bourgeois ideology, interpretations generally 'converged' around Smith as the founding father of liberal capitalism, leaving posterity with a ridiculously superficial, deeply flawed and selective interpretation of his thought.

Today we perceive how thoroughly the binary formulation of the nineteenth century 'Adam Smith Problem' distorts what Smith meant by sympathy and self-interest, missing fundamentally the overall 'organic unity' and 'coherence' of his moral philosophy and the place of political economy within it – a theme pursued by Knud Haakonssen in his introductory chapter to the *Cambridge Companion to Adam Smith* (2006, CUP) and indeed in all of his work on Smith. Among a good majority of Smith scholars today in the humanities and social sciences, the unity of Smith's system is no longer in serious contention. The nineteenth-century formulation doesn't reflect anything properly attributable to Smith's thought, but serves as a revealing cultural representation of the urgency of nineteenth-century debates about political economy. Haakonssen and Donald Winch, in their conclusion to the *Cambridge Companion*, speculate that Smith 'could hardly have suspected that the question of systematic coherence and/or incompleteness in his intellectual endeavour would constitute an enduring part of his legacy'.

Economists began to lose their hold on Smith's legacy in the 1970s. An important moment in this story of Smith's late twentieth-century recovery came in 1978 when Donald Winch confronted the 'economist's Smith' head-on in his path-breaking book, *Adam Smith's Politics: An Essay in Historiographic Revision*. Inspired by the new (back then it was new) contextual approach to intellectual history associated with Quentin Skinner and the so-called 'Cambridge School', Winch pursued various problems with interpreting Smith's thought through the anachronistic lens of nineteenth-century liberal capitalism. His particular focus was Adam Smith's politics. He wanted to unmask the 'economist's Smith' in order to resuscitate the political elements of Smith's thought, which economists had marginalized or sublimated through their late modern assertion that politics, for better or for worse, was 'epiphenomenal to the more profound economic forces at work in modern commercial society'. Winch demonstrated that Smith was in fact participating in a very old political discourse about virtue and corruption that his contemporaries would have identified readily with the Augustan humanism of Montesquieu and Hume.

One need not share Winch's historiographical orientation, his proclivity for republican sentiments or his preoccupation with Smithian politics to recognize the value of approaching Smith's thought without ideologically-charged assumptions and with sensitivity to how Smith might have understood his own project. When permitted to speak in his own eighteenth-century voice, the 'economist's Smith' begins to lose touch with himself. Smith's view of human motivation is complex and layered, driven as much by passion and imagination as by reason and interest. In fact, Smith argued that the human mind is often deeply resistant to reason, often blown about by 'fits of spleen'. Self-interest takes its place within a rich complex of human motivation. Smith's political economy itself was not the centre of his thought, but rather took its place in a larger project of moral philosophy. What's more, Smith was ambivalent about commercial culture, and deeply critical of the very economic totality he is regularly accused of inventing and enshrining. Despite what history has made of him, he was never a flat-footed optimist about the effects of commercialism on human life. The poorest eighteenth-century European labourer might indeed be better off than 'an African king', Smith famously wrote, but he lamented that modern commercial life rested on a pervasive self-deception about our needs and our happiness, that it tended to corrupt our moral sentiments by encouraging vanity and conspicuous greed, that it sapped our magnanimity and public-spiritedness, and that the division of labour that sustained it dehumanized its participants, rendering them 'as stupid and ignorant as it is possible for a human creature to become'. Only Marx himself rivals Smith's alarm at the life-pursuit of making pin-heads.

The revisionist spirit Winch exhibited in *Adam Smith's Politics* has reproduced itself in waves of scholarship committed to the project of wrestling Smith's thought from the economistic grip, recovering new meanings that have a more solid claim to historical accuracy, have deeper philosophical significance, and are potentially useful for generations no longer preoccupied with or blinded by Marx and his legacy. And as the *Cambridge Companion to Adam Smith* demonstrates, this wave has not been constrained to intellectual history. Smith revisionism – or perhaps we might call it Smith recovery – is a truly interdisciplinary project within the humanities and social sciences. The last thirty years have witnessed a genuine renaissance of revisionist scholarship among moral philosophers, political and social theorists, anthropologists, psychologists, students of communication, of culture, of gender, of literature, among others. Knud Haakonssen's *Cambridge Companion to Adam Smith* captures elements of this, though by no means all of it.

I would like to thank Cambridge University Press for furnishing copies of the *Companion* to each of our participants; the American Political Science Association for hosting our symposium as an 'Interdisciplinary Theme Panel' at their 2007 meetings in Chicago; the International Adam Smith Society for co-sponsoring and publicizing our symposium; and Vivienne Brown and *The Adam Smith Review* for agreeing to publish our papers.

In what follows, each participant has engaged two or three chapters of the *Companion*. We have tried to maintain substantive coherence, so that the presentations could unfold thematically. Most of the chapters have received treatment here. It should be acknowledged at the outset that Knud Haakonssen, as editor, obviously is not answerable for all of what follows, which is why he hesitated writing a reply to our symposium. And yet, as editor, he surely had much to say about the themes covered and authors selected. *Cambridge Companions* are exciting and useful for they promise up-to-date surveys on all central aspects of a thinker's thought. The diversity of topics covered in the *Companion* attests to the astonishing range of themes and issues that exercised Smith. Equally impressive is the diversity of perspectives and disciplinary orientations of the contributors – philosophers, historians of economics, intellectual historians, political theorists, a legal scholar and even a Nobel Laureate economist. And yet, if I have any hesitation about the project as a whole, it relates primarily to authors who are conspicuously missing from the contributors list, and others present who while perhaps interesting here have played little role in the vibrant secondary debates on Smith's thought in recent years. The appearance of a *Cambridge Companion* is an exciting event for bringing together the very best and most accomplished voices on various aspects of a thinker's thought. Given this expectation, I found the contributors list somewhat unsatisfying.

Language, literature and imagination

Ryan Patrick Hanley

The publication of *The Cambridge Companion to Adam Smith* (2006) is a quite welcome event. Specialists have long appreciated both the range and depth of Smith's thought, and now with his canonization, of sorts, in the Cambridge pantheon, it can be hoped that a broad group of students and scholars will be prompted to explore Smith's philosophy. Certainly the volume's three opening essays raise several crucial questions for future exploration. Yet some of these questions are more crucial than others.

The most challenging of these three contributions is Marcelo Dascal's. Entitled 'Adam Smith's theory of language', its first paragraph concludes with the caveat that 'it would be an exaggeration to say that he had a "theory of language"' (79). The effect of such a caveat is to raise doubts concerning the fruitfulness of the approach mandated by the essay's title. Dascal's essay certainly succeeds in demonstrating the ubiquity, and even the centrality, of 'language-related topics' in Smith's teaching and writing (79). At the same time, one gathers from the essay that Smith has little to offer to contemporary language theorists. The author is himself an eminent student of both this theory and its early modern history, and when he concludes that Smith's 'voice in the intensive dialogue that his century sustained on this topic was a relatively minor one' (103–4), we must defer to his expertise in concluding that Smith's intrinsic interest to theorists of language (and historians thereof) is minimal.

Of course, for the majority of the readership of the *Cambridge Companion* (and presumably of this *Review*), of greater interest than the question of how Smith illuminates the theory of language is how the theory of language might illuminate our understanding of Smith. Dascal's contribution points in several promising directions on this front, but it is also unnecessarily difficult to engage. First, the cost of entry into its argument is a working familiarity with technical vocabulary, including such concepts as 'diachronic antonomasia' and the 'cryptoanalyticity of morphologically represented relations' (88, 104). Second, the essay is written at a distance from Smith scholarship. The 47 entries in its bibliography do not include a single contemporary specialist work on Smith, and only one piece – Stewart's 1793 biographical oration – even takes Smith as its principal focus. Given Dascal's own focus on Smith's 'Considerations concerning the first formation of languages', especially noteworthy absences from this bibliography are the recent study of the relations of 'Considerations' to Smith's moral philosophy developed by James Otteson (2002a; 2002b), as well as Christopher Berry's important early treatment of the text (1974). Third, almost a third of the essay is dedicated to a contextualization of Smith's theory of language in a trajectory from Locke to Condillac. This section focuses largely on how Locke's question of the degree to which language is a mirror to the mind spurred a crucial debate over the implications of the Enlightenment's linguistic turn for materialism, scepticism and ethical relativism. This is an important and interesting question, yet Dascal also makes clear that Smith's thoughts on language were largely developed independently of this trajectory; hence his treatment of Smith's review of Johnson's *Dictionary*, which he regards as a 'mixed lot', in which Smith 'does not seem to follow Locke' in important respects, 'nor is he concerned' with the claims of Leibniz (87–8). In the absence of a more precise justification of Smith's place in this trajectory, one regrets that so much space is dedicated to it – and all the more so as the essay's conclusion explains that it is 'for lack of space' that it cannot address such important topics as the treatments of language to be found in both WN and LJ, or the relationship of Smith's theory of language to his spectator theory (105 n34, 107).

Dascal's essay is thus hardly ideal. At the same time, there is much of use here. His introduction points to two central questions: first, the question of how Smith's theory of language 'might help to reconstruct his general underlying epistemology'; and second, the question of how his theory is best situated in 'the context of a century' in which 'the relationship between language and knowledge often functioned as an indicator of a thinker's stance on other philosophical and social issues' (80). Smith's epistemology and his politics of course remain central issues of debate for specialists today, and Dascal introduces several considerations useful to those navigating such waters. To touch briefly on one of the most important: one of Dascal's most interesting themes concerns the role that Smith's assumption of 'natural kinds' or 'natural prelinguistic candidates for proper names' plays in his thought. Dascal considers these as Smith's responses to Locke and his doctrine of antiessentialism (89). But the provenance of this concept is perhaps of less importance than Dascal's cautionary reminder that the idea of 'nature' is both ambiguous and central in Smith. His analysis particularly reminds us of Smith's keen interest in the aesthetic mimesis of nature, and particularly his belief that 'the better a linguistic form *mirrors* sensory input, the closer it is to nature (at least as it appears to us), and consequently, the earlier it is likely to be created' (93). Here too Smith is hardly original: the idea that human arts and creations are to be evaluated on the grounds of their capacity to imitate nature is the fundamental claim of pre-Romantic aesthetics. But Dascal shows that this concept is particularly central to Smith insofar as it is ubiquitous across his corpus, and indeed suggests 'an encompassing notion of "naturalness" of which the "metaphysical" and semiotic versions discussed in *Languages* are nothing but particular cases' (100). Thus, however conventional certain aspects of Smith's theory seem from an eighteenth-century standpoint, these conventions yet remain central to our understanding of the most unconventional – and indeed the most important and enduring – aspects of his thought. By reminding us of this, Dascal helpfully contributes to an ongoing scholarly debate concerning the status and authority of nature in his thought.[1]

Dascal's essay is preceded in the *Companion* by Mark Salber Phillips's excellent piece, 'Adam Smith, Belletrist'. There are many obvious points of natural contact (and even repetition) between the two. Yet Phillips carves out original ground, both vis-à-vis Dascal and with regard to his main subject, the *Lectures on Rhetoric and Belles Lettres*.[2] Dascal has suggested that 'just as Smith's ethics is a theory of the propriety of action, his rhetoric is a theory of the propriety of *linguistic* action' (101). But Phillips turns this view on its head. On his account, Smith's rhetoric is dedicated not to offering norms for linguistic actors, but to offering guidelines for reception or interpretation. To slightly overstate Phillips's subtly-developed case: Smith's rhetoric is directed more to audiences than speakers, auditors rather than orators. It is a perspective that, while unconventional, brings illuminating and valuable results with regard to the three central themes of the essay: first, Smith's pioneering contributions to the teaching of rhetoric as a university subject; second, the insights LRBL provides into his intellectual development and early career; and third, the intrinsic interest of LRBL with regard to the nature of rhetoric (57).

These results are all the more valuable as Phillips helpfully frames his analysis in the context of one of the most interesting questions in current Smith scholarship: namely the degree of Smith's relative debts or allegiances to the ancients and to the moderns. A host of recent scholars from Griswold and Brown to Vivenza and Montes have reopened this question and Phillips provides a helpful extension of their labours (see Montes 2004; and Vivenza 2001).[3] Rightly lamenting the contemporary academic convention that 'emphasizes the ruptures of modernity, not the continuities of the classical' (61), he aims to demonstrate Smith's profound debts to ancient rhetorical theory (a project that also lies at the heart of McKenna's recent book). At the same time, Phillips's Smith is no slave to the ancients. Phillips is quite sensitive to Smith's historical context (the author is himself a historian), which particularly leads him to note the influence of the seventeenth-century French belles-lettres tradition, a crucial but today decidedly underemphasized source of inspiration for Smith and the Scottish moralists more generally. On his account, Smith and the Scottish rhetoricians, working under French influence, 'refocused attention on the ways in which works in a variety of genres are read or received. Thus, rhetorical analysis shifted its concern from the *production* of persuasive *speech* to the *reception* of written *texts*' (64; italics original to text). Herein is the heart of Phillips's contribution. His

Smith was hardly uninterested in making normative interventions in rhetoric. Yet these interventions took a new turn: instead of providing rules to speakers, Smith's goal was 'to elevate the taste of readers' by improving their critical capacities; providing 'aesthetic training' of 'provincial elites' would both improve taste and contribute to the spread of politeness and sociability (64).

Phillips's shift from speakers to audiences leads to several key insights – as well as, I think, one omission. One of Phillips's observations is that literature is today largely divided into the two categories of 'fiction' and 'nonfiction' – itself the consequence of the Romantic emphasis on the 'primacy of imagination' (63). Smith's own approach predated Romanticism – and hence also the reductionism implied in this division – with the consequence that his contributions to 'nonfiction' are marked by sensitivity to both moral psychology and the role of the imagination in reading and interpreting; thus it is argued by Phillips that Smith 'regards literary structures as capturing habits that reflect wider regularities of moral psychology' (71). This observation shapes several discrete claims which tend to focus on the questions of distance and intimacy between the author and the reader. Phillips's emphasis on the prominence of the idea of 'fittingness' in his rhetoric – understood both as the fit of an author's style to his audience's taste and as the fit of an author's style to his own personal character – is especially helpful, and is nicely brought out in a useful commentary on Smith's comments on Swift in rhetoric lectures seven and eight. Here and elsewhere Phillips shows how his approach to prose-writing deemphasized the 'descriptive austerity demanded by Baconian science' in favour of 'a conception of reading that is attuned to sentimentalist immediacy' (68) – an observation that itself suggests intimate ties between Smith's rhetoric and his doctrine of sympathy.

This theme reaches its climax in what is perhaps the most valuable and original aspect of the piece: its discussions of Smith's pioneering contribution to historiography. Phillips insists that this contribution 'deserves to be far better known' (58). Of particular interest, he claims, is that Smith's conception of historiography casts light directly on the limitations of the conventional ancient-modern divide. In this vein, Phillips explains that Smith's vision of history sought to transcend familiar 'humanist cliches about learning by example' (72). Far from simply providing moral lessons, Smith had 'a theory of history in which narrative effects rather than moral examples would be key' (73). In particular, the focus on the centrality of narrative to historiography led Smith to prefer 'indirect description' that speaks to the imagination over heavy-handed didacticism.

Phillips's piece prompts only a single regret. Its shift in normative focus from speaker to audience pays several dividends, but also comes at the cost of deemphasizing the question in which students of Smith's morals or politics are most interested: namely the question of his understanding of the place of rhetoric in commercial and political life. Smith's invocations of the centrality of speech and persuasion to both human nature and commercial exchange are familiar even to casual readers. Given the prominence of these themes in the context of Smith's larger project, it seems not unreasonable to conjecture that at least one of the aims of LRBL may have been to equip the citizens of emerging commercial society with the facility at speaking and persuading needed to flourish in such a society. Phillips's conclusion indeed calls attention to the role of 'persuasion and intersubjective exchange' in Smith's thought, and quotes the crucial passage in LJA that most clearly attests to Smith's understanding of the ubiquity of oratory in ordinary life (77). Yet given the acuity of Phillips's study, one might have wished that he developed this aspect of his piece at greater length.[4]

Let me now turn to Charles Griswold's masterful 'Imagination: morals, science, and arts', the opening essay of the *Companion* as a whole. In both this essay and in his 1999 book (from which the present essay is in part drawn, according to its first footnote; 22 n1), the author shows himself to be not only one of the past half-century's most careful readers of Smith, but also one of its most sophisticated; his piece points in directions that comprehensively develop a vision of Smith with which all serious interpretations have to contend. Part of its novelty is suggested in a comparison with Phillips's essay. Turning from Phillips to Griswold we discover a certain shift. As noted above, Phillips's Smith is a pre-romantic, who wrote prior to the age of imagination's primacy. But Griswold suggests that in fact the imagination is the central and indeed the unifying doctrine of Smith's diverse speculations on morals, economics and philosophy (or 'science') – speculations that, in Griswold's hands, seem more systematic than they are often thought.

Griswold's essay begins by demonstrating how Smith understood the practical utility of the imagination in a range of different areas. In commercial life, the notorious deceptions of the imagination drive our efforts to better our condition. In moral life, the 'sympathetic imagination' suggests a foundation for social bonds and the development of common moral norms. In science, the imagination helps us remedy lacuna in data culled from empirical observation, enabling us to form psychologically satisfying theories. The element common to all of these operations is that the imagination, in an effort to provide 'the satisfaction inherent in order and completeness', necessarily 'rushes in to fill gaps with an account or story that contextualizes the particulars under evaluation' (23, 26). And this language of 'story' is not casual. Griswold, like Phillips, continually emphasizes the centrality of narrative to human efforts to understand and render intelligible a world that might otherwise seem chaotic; hence imagination 'is narrative, not just representational; it draws things into a coherent story whenever possible, filling in gaps and searching for moral or conceptual equilibrium' (23). Again: 'sympathetic imagination is not solely representational or reproductive. It is primarily narrative, seeking to flow into and fill up another situation, and to draw things together into a coherent story, thus bringing the spectator out of him- or herself and onto the larger stage' (26). The ubiquity of such locutions attests to the degree to which Griswold's Smith regards the practical world and our participation in it as 'theatrical' – to use a locution central to his earlier book – or, perhaps more accurately in the context of the present essay, poetic.[5] As the repeated emphasis on story-telling and narrative-creation suggests, for Griswold's Smith 'the imagination is fundamentally creative' (49), and our use of it to make sense of our world is perhaps best understood as an act of *poiesis*. This aspect of the imagination is especially crucial to Griswold's account of the sources of moral value. Throughout his piece Griswold emphasizes Smith's scepticism, and particularly what he takes to be his conviction that we lack definite knowledge of external sources of moral value, thereby necessitating our imaginative creation of moral value for ourselves. Thus his claim that 'the central role played by the imagination in Smith's philosophy is the obverse of his scepticism about the "Platonic" view that there exists a knowable independent order of moral facts', and hence his view of the imagination as the source of 'the constructed or projected nature of value' – itself evidence of 'the nonnatural nature of moral standards' (40).

For Griswold's Smith, then, the imagination is indispensable to our efforts at both comprehending and navigating the world. But this is only half the story Griswold means to tell. For even as the imagination solves one problem, it introduces new problems in its wake. Griswold especially focuses on two shortcomings. First, imagination frequently doesn't go far enough; repeatedly Griswold shows us that in precisely the spheres where we most need it, the imagination comes up short. Thus in moral life, however useful the imagination is in helping forge sympathetic bonds between individuals, 'our fundamental separateness' yet 'is not obliterated' (27–8). Our condition, that is to say, remains one of alienation or individualism; sympathy is 'in a sense deceptive' and our experience of it 'illusory' (29–30). So too in philosophy. However indispensable the imagination may be to our efforts at theory-building, our philosophical systems remain 'mere inventions of the imagination', constructs of the mind rather than representations of the truth of reality (49). Indeed, so far from revealing the truths of nature, philosophy or science resembles a sophisticated form of navel-gazing; what we call the contemplation of nature is in fact merely an act of 'contemplating ourselves' (49). Finally the aspiration to self-knowledge in the fullest sense is, on this account, vitiated by the same problems as attempts to know nature. Attempts at self-knowledge, we are thus told, are mediated through a sympathetic imagination: 'Consequently, the actor has no exclusive epistemic access to his or her own emotions, none that dispenses with the spectator – with the public, with the community, and with "mankind"' (38).

Taken altogether, the suggestion is that while the imagination remains our best (and only) resource in our struggle to understand, its limitations are palpable in precisely those areas of speculation in which we most need it – including the knowledge of the self, the knowledge of others, and the knowledge of the truth. But this is only one of two problems with the imagination:

for if at times the imagination doesn't go far enough, at other times it goes much too far altogether. Fundamental then to Griswold's Smith is the conviction that for all its benefits, the imagination's reach often exceeds its grasp, with disastrous practical consequences; in his words, 'the imagination's deification of moral norms can also create grave risks' (40). These risks are at once both political and moral. Their political aspect emerges in Griswold's focus on the political destabilization consequent to religious sectarianism and factional zealotry. Much of Smith's liberalism, on Griswold's account, indeed can be understood as means of mediating the negative externalities consequent to our necessary recourse to the imagination, religion foremost among these. The moral aspect of these grave risks emerges in Griswold's treatment of the 'moral and political corruption' consequent to the pursuit of commercial ambition, which, while promoting social opulence, simultaneously seems to encourage, if not require, individual restlessness and misery (23; see also 44).[6]

Griswold has offered an admirably unified and subtle reading of Smith's system. Let me now raise two questions in response. Much of this reading rests on the claim that Smith is a sceptic and that his conception of the imagination 'unquestionably represents an appropriation of Hume' (22) – and that it is, in fact, a faithful 'extension of Hume's views' (53 n22). But this demands further scrutiny. That Smith directly appropriates the language of Hume's account of the imagination is undeniable; as Griswold himself notes (22 n2; 53 n22), these debts have been well known at least since Raphael's and Skinner's important contributions in the mid-1970s (see Skinner 1974; Raphael 1977). What particularly demands further scrutiny is the question of whether Smith's appropriation of Hume is indicative of his approbation of Hume – that is, whether his use of Hume's language can reasonably be construed as good evidence of his agreement with the substantial claims of Hume's doctrine. Good reasons exist to think that in fact Smith's appropriation of this language, so far from indicating his agreement with Hume's view, represents a subversion of them. The very fact that Smith speaks of the utility of the imagination in certain types of speculation that takes place at a remove from conventional empiricism (astronomy and cosmology in particular) seems to mark a crucial difference with Hume, whose *Dialogues* (which Smith famously declined to see to press) were dedicated to demonstrating the illegitimacy of precisely this extension of the imagination. This claim requires a more comprehensive account than I can provide here.[7] But suffice it to say that the equation of Smith's epistemology with Hume's has been explicitly questioned in several important recent contributions, and deserves additional careful scrutiny.[8]

Griswold's emphasis on Hume's scepticism raises a more fundamental question as well, one which concerns his view of the conventionality of moral value. Griswold is keen to demonstrate that his sceptical Smith circumvents familiar pitfalls associated with anti-realism or anti-foundationalism. Yet it's not altogether clear how to distinguish his sceptical Smith (or what he elsewhere calls Smith's 'sophisticated emotivism'; see Griswold 1999: 130), with its emphasis on the self-creation of value, from less salutary efforts in this vein that emerged in the wake of the Enlightenment. Griswold's sharpest formulations seem to point down this road; hence his claim that 'considered from a metaphysical standpoint, value is something we communally determine for ourselves, and is not founded on philosophically mysterious entities lodged outside of this-worldly phenomena of human life' (50). All such sources, it is repeatedly insisted, are unavailable: 'morality must ultimately be understood as arising "from us", not as established by nature or the divine'. As 'nonhuman or suprahuman sources' are simply 'inscrutable to us', we are 'left with the one remaining source, namely ourselves' (51). This strong claim naturally leads one to wonder what defence Griswold's Smith might have against charges of thoroughgoing relativism. Griswold himself anticipates this objection, and his preemptive defence is that norms created through intersubjectivity and reciprocal exchanges of sympathy are not relative because they are things we possess and can set to work upon; on these grounds Smith is not to be confused with the relativism that regards moral value as 'formed out of thin air' (53).

This seems right, but it is difficult to see how such a defence can save Griswold's position from a certain circularity. The turn to the imagination, we've been shown, was originally required because we have no access to other sources of value. Yet at the same time we've also been shown that the imagination, left unto itself, is woefully deficient; imagination clearly generates difficulties that imagination alone cannot solve. Put differently: necessity prompts a turn to the imagination but the necessary consequence of this turn is to require access to a standard beyond imagination if we hope to judge and remedy its palpable deficiencies. The question of course becomes whether we in fact have recourse to such a resource; indeed, everything turns on the question of whether the imagination is our only source of value (and a second-rate one at that), or whether it is only one source among several (and not the highest one at that). If such an 'extra-imaginative' standard is in fact unavailable, then the conditions of life would seem tragic. This seems to be the route taken here: 'Smith's reply to the philosophers would be that it is all we in fact have' (54). Yet if Smith's many invocations of both teleological and providential language in fact represent something more than the reflection of a mere 'aestheticized, speculative outlook', as is here suggested (48), then it may well be that Smith himself recognized this potential tragedy and sought to provide us with the tools to circumvent it.

The trajectory of Smith's own literary career perhaps itself suggests the depth of his recognition of this problem. Griswold has elsewhere emphasized the significance of Smith's failure to complete his promised treatise on natural justice (Griswold 2006). Yet Smith's career of course ends not simply with this failure, but rather with the successful completion of the sixth edition of TMS – a project which might be best regarded as dedicated principally to establishing the necessity of the very sources of value that Griswold deems unavailable (or so I argue elsewhere). In any case, Griswold's contribution remains extraordinarily valuable for its comprehensive consideration of what remains one of the most contested questions among specialists: to use the terms of James Alvey's important recent book, whether Smith is an 'optimist' or a 'pessimist' (Alvey 2003). One hopes that Griswold's essay, in conjunction with the burgeoning recent interest in the status of natural religion in Smith's work, will continue to prompt further work on the question of where on this spectrum Smith is best placed.[9]

Notes

1 In addition to the pieces that focus specifically on natural religion cited below, readers interested in Smith's understanding of nature will particularly want to consult Schabas (2003) and Brubaker (2006).
2 The originality of these results is all the more striking given that LRBL has received important studies from several quarters. Most recently – indeed too recent for Phillips to take account of it – is McKenna (2006). McKenna's book provides a helpful supplement to two major studies of Smith's rhetoric, Brown (1994) and Griswold (1999), each of which, for hermeneutical reasons, does not focus on LRBL specifically.
3 A critical survey of recent literature on Smith's debts to antiquity can be found in Vivenza (2004). Also noteworthy are several articles that deserve a wider audience, including Berns (1994).
4 Other studies have however focused on this; see especially Kalyvas and Katznelson (2001).
5 On Smith's conception of the 'theatricality' of human life in the world, see especially Griswold (1999: 63–70).
6 This position is central to Griswold (1999). Others have since sought to respond explicitly to this claim; see especially Fleischacker (2004: 104–18); and Rasmussen (2006).
7 I have sought however to develop it elsewhere; see Hanley (under review).
8 On this front, see especially Schliesser (2005); as well as the differences between Hume's and Smith's conceptions of moral psychology and political theory noted in Pack and Schliesser (2006).
9 Important recent treatments of Smith's conception of natural religion include Hill (2001); Waterman (2002); Alvey (2004).

Bibliography

Alvey, J. (2003) *Adam Smith, Optimist or Pessimist? A New Problem Concerning the Teleological Basis of Commercial Society*, Burlington, VT: Ashgate.
—— (2004) 'The secret, natural theological foundation of Adam Smith's work', *Journal of Markets and Morality*, 7: 335–61.
Berns, L. (1994) 'Aristotle and Adam Smith on justice: cooperation between ancients and moderns?', *Review of Metaphysics*, 48: 71–90.
Berry, C.J. (1974) 'Adam Smith's Considerations on Language', *Journal of the History of Ideas*, 35: 130–8.
Brown, V. (1994) *Adam Smith's Discourse: Canonicity, Commerce, and Conscience*, London: Routledge.

230   *Ryan Patrick Hanley*

Brubaker, L. (2006) 'Does the "wisdom of nature" need help?', in *New Voices on Adam Smith*, L. Montes and E. Schliesser (eds), London: Routledge.

Fleischacker, S. (2004) *On Adam Smith's* Wealth of Nations: *A Philosophical Companion*, Princeton: Princeton University Press.

Griswold, C.L. (1999) *Adam Smith and the Virtues of Enlightenment*, Cambridge: Cambridge University Press.

—— (2006) 'On the incompleteness of Adam Smith's system', *The Adam Smith Review*, 2: 181–6.

Hanley, R.P. (under review) 'Scepticism and imagination: Smith's response to Hume's *Dialogues*'.

Hill, L. (2001) 'The hidden theology of Adam Smith', *European Journal of the History of Economic Thought*, 8: 1–29.

Kalyvas A. and I. Katznelson (2001) 'The rhetoric of the market: Adam Smith on recognition, speech, and exchange', *Review of Politics*, 63: 549–79.

McKenna, S. (2006) *Adam Smith: The Rhetoric of Propriety*, Albany: SUNY Press.

Montes, L. (2004) *Adam Smith in Context: A Critical Reassessment of Some Central Components of His Thought*, London: Palgrave Macmillan.

Otteson, J. (2002a) 'Adam Smith's first market: the development of language', *History of Philosophy Quarterly*, 19: 65–86.

—— (2002b) *Adam Smith's Marketplace of Life*, Cambridge: Cambridge University Press.

Pack, S.J. and E. Schliesser (2006) 'Smith's Humean criticism of Hume's account of the origin of justice', *Journal of the History of Philosophy*, 44: 47–63.

Raphael, D.D. (1977) ' "The true old Humean philosophy" and its influence on Adam Smith', in *David Hume: Bicentenary Papers*, G.P. Morice (ed.), Edinburgh: Edinburgh University Press.

Rasmussen, D. (2006) 'Does "bettering our condition" really make us better off? Adam Smith on progress and happiness', *American Political Science Review*, 100: 309–18.

Schabas, M. (2003) 'Adam Smith's debts to nature', in *Oeconomies in the Age of Newton*, M. Schabas and N. de Marchi (eds), Durham: Duke University Press.

Schliesser, E. (2005) 'Wonder in the face of scientific revolutions: Adam Smith on Newton's "proof" of Copernicanism', *British Journal for the History of Philosophy*, 13: 697–732.

Skinner, A.S. (1974) 'Adam Smith: science and the role of the imagination', in *Hume and the Enlightenment: Essays Presented to Ernest Campbell Mossner*, W.B. Todd (ed.), Edinburgh: Edinburgh University Press.

Vivenza, G. (2001) *Adam Smith and the Classics: The Classical Heritage in Adam Smith's Thought*, Oxford: Oxford University Press; originally published in Italian as *Adam Smith e la cultura classica*.

—— (2004) 'Reading Adam Smith in the light of the Classics', *The Adam Smith Review*, 1: 107–24.

Waterman, A.M.C. (2002) 'Economics as theology: Adam Smith's *Wealth of Nations*', *Southern Economic Journal*, 68: 907–21.

The philosophical subtlety of Smith

Eric Schliesser

When half a decade ago, Christopher Berry circulated drafts of his chapter for the *Cambridge Companion*, 'Smith and science', it was understood to be no mere survey of recent views; it offered cutting edge, revisionist work on Smith's oft-misunderstood views on science.[1] Since I read it first in 2003, I have cited it approvingly in various published papers. It is sad that Berry has had to wait so long for his paper to appear in print while in its absence other authors could appear more original than they were. I have, thus, long agreed with Berry that claims about Smith's supposed scepticism are overblown and the evidence for them often misconstrued (123).[2]

Berry's piece calls attention to some of Smith's otherwise overlooked philosophical debts to a Lockean anthropology (cf. my treatment of Pocock below), which equates the savage mind to children (128). Berry also notes the importance of Hume's essay, 'Of national characters', in order to understand the eighteenth-century distinction between 'moral' and 'physical' causes in Smith's 'soft-determinist', institution-centric explanations (130). Berry, thus, offered, the first serious treatment of Smith's epistemology and metaphysical framework that could accommodate Nathan Rosenberg's old and increasingly influential piece on Smith's institutionalism (Rosenberg 1960).

I have only one minor disagreement with Berry; he implies that Smith is 'a fully paid-up member' of a progressivist 'Enlightenment family' (135). Smith certainly advocates the 'natural progress of improvement' and hopes that with more economic growth (due to extensive division of labour, technological innovation, mutually beneficial trade, protection of property rights, etc.) poverty would diminish and that with the spread of science there would be a 'great antidote to superstition' (135; quoting WN). But Smith also calls attention to the fact that the division of labour itself can cause 'gross ignorance and stupidity' among workers doing dull, repetitive work. Smith advocates commercial progress on humanitarian, moral and political grounds, but he is not blind to its potential, pernicious effects. In their piece in the *Cambridge Companion*, 'Adam Smith's economics', Rothschild and Sen emphasize that while Smith noted many moral improvements associated with commerce (probity, self-discipline, increased support for rule of law, moral independence, etc.), commerce can also stimulate 'human folly and injustice' (Smith repeatedly describes the injustice of European colonialism) and pernicious attempts by business elites to hijack the political process to their narrow and selfish interests (for example, 341–3). This suggests that Smith disagrees with Hume's well-known claim (in 'Of commerce') that commercial improvement coincides with improvement in humanity. For Smith, progress *can* also involve various kinds of moral losses. This helps us better understand Smith's positive treatment of various natives in India, Africa, and America (see Harkin 2002, 2005; Pitt 2005, esp. ch. 2).

Neil de Marchi's 'Smith on ingenuity, pleasure, and the imitative arts', presupposes considerable knowledge of Smith's writings and deliberately (155) does little to introduce the student or other newcomer to Adam Smith or to Smith's views on aesthetics. Nevertheless, this reviewer is grateful for its inclusion in the *Cambridge Companion* because it is one of the more original reflections on Adam Smith to appear in recent years. While some might object to De Marchi's occasional flirtation with anachronism, his paper repays careful study; it is to be wished it will stimulate others to offer serious readings of Smith's generally unappreciated essay on the Imitative Arts, Smith's treatment of so-called 'unproductive' labour, Smith's views on propriety (144), and Smith's views on pleasure. Moreover, it also raises important questions for future research on Smith's response to Plato's concerns about and the relative merits of commerce and the imitative arts (142).

In his treatment of Smith's account of Imitative Arts and WN, De Marchi discerns a 'standard form of response to the four basic causes of pleasure' (151; the four are: 'imitation; colour; form or figure, where pleasure is linked to variety; and rarity, which may also be combined with variety', 149). Given that the full Aristotelian-sounding title of WN proudly announces Smith's interest in causal explanation, De Marchi's approach has additional prima facie plausibility beyond the rich textual evidence he offers. (Of course, it would require a much larger investigation to appreciate how Smith replaces the traditional four Aristotelian causes with a new list or set of lists.) According to De Marchi, '[b]roadly speaking, Smith's four causes all produce a curve of rising, then declining pleasure, although true rarity (in isolation from variety) does not quite fit this treatment' (151). Moreover, this 'common pattern' in the pleasure we derive from objects occurs regardless of any 'insubstantial or substantial characteristics of goods' (154). It could, thus, be fruitful to read 'Of the external senses' treatment of primary and secondary qualities in light of De Marchi's findings!

I am not convinced by De Marchi's argument that Smith envisaged thinking of pleasure in terms of real curves or using these as a 'as a basis for comparing values added' (151). I see little evidence that Smith is a proto-Utilitarian in thinking that there is a natural standard that allows for such inter-subjective comparison. De Marchi cleverly gets around this objection by emphasizing that Smith operationalizes the *expectation* of this pleasure in terms of 'willingness to pay' (151, 153). But leaving this aside, one can still accept De Marchi's bold conjecture that Smith intended to 'put the performing arts (and by implication, since they were the least obviously productive, the arts in general) on the same footing as the durable, physical products' (153–4). This also fits nicely with Smith's rhetoric of treating the arts and sciences as the 'noblest' labour (155). De Marchi cites WN II.iii.2; his reading would have been strengthened by reference to the well known 'deception' of nature passage, where it is asserted that *some* of the unintended achievements of civilization, that is, the arts and sciences, can 'ennoble' our lives (TMS IV.i.10; 183) (see Schliesser 2006a).

I conclude my treatment of De Marchi's essay with one minor quibble: De Marchi claims that for Smith the sentiment of wonder is pleasing (139), yet the textual evidence that he cites suggests that Smith also thought it quite painful (see also Smith's even clearer treatment of it in terms of 'uncertainty and anxious curiosity' ('Astronomy' II.4)).

I had high hopes for J.G.A Pocock's contribution, 'Adam Smith and history'. Pocock is one of the most famous living historians of ideas and one of the leading authorities of eighteenth-century political thought with a keen interest in Hume's and Gibbon's writings on history. I was eager to read a comprehensive view of Smith's treatment of history – a topic often neglected by scholars but fundamental to appreciating Adam Smith's vision. Pocock draws on his background knowledge to analyze Smith in terms of the distinction and divergence between 'civil' and 'natural history'. While Pocock does not work out the details, some such distinction is clearly in place in, for example, Book III of WN. So, I agree with Pocock that Smith exploits a version of the distinction in order to generate evidence for his theory-building ends.[3]

It would be nice if the 'Adam Smith industry' could move beyond a focus on Smith's much-admired piece on the history of astronomy (even while it neglects the pieces on Ancient Logics, Metaphysics, and Physics). For, one can read Book IV of the *Wealth of Nations* as an attempt to write the first major history of economic ideas (Smith practically invents the category of the 'mercantile system' in order to refute the Mercantilists); one can read Part VII of later editions of TMS as an attempt to establish an authoritative (and potentially equally self-serving) history of moral philosophy. Moreover, the long 'digression' on the price of silver over four centuries at the end of WN I is (among other things) a major piece of economic history. In addition, LJ contains a very rich treatment of important aspects of the history of law. This is just a tip of the proverbial iceberg of Smith's many important historical 'narratives' (287). Most of these do not register beyond a mere passing mention in Pocock's piece.

In his essay, Pocock argues that Smith believed in a 'human nature' with 'fixed propensities of behaviour' (275), that Smith did not to believe in 'contingent' change, and that Smith denied that non-Europeans can also be actors of change rather than be mere 'victims' (285). Rather, Smith constructed 'narratives' based on historical inquiry that served other 'philosophical' purposes in his 'system' (286). Smith's is a Eurocentric understanding of the forces of history that makes 'difficult' the extension of the 'concept of "history"' to 'Non-European cultures' (280). Therefore, Smith is 'not a historian' (270) in the proper contextual (that is, Gibbon's) meaning of the term (271). So says Pocock. Much of this is based on sloppy scholarship.

In an earlier review of this *Cambridge Companion* (Schliesser 2007) I called attention to Emma Rothschild's and Amartya Sen's analysis of Smith's emphasis on the agency of the colonized (see 342–44; see also my comments above on Berry's piece). It is also instructive to compare Rothschild and Sen on Smith's views on religion (353) with Pocock's misleading comments (282–3). But given Pocock's towering reputation, these may be thought minor blemishes and not warrant much critical comment.

So, let me offer a more startling example. Here is Pocock pretending to be quoting Smith: 'At all events, the "progress of society" takes place only "in Europe"' (281; the quote-marks within the quote are supposed to be Smith). In context it is pretty clear that Pocock attributes to Smith a Eurocentric position. (Smith is even said to favourably contrast the European 'Goths' to the Asiatic 'Huns'.) Let us compare this with Smith's text:

> And to this day in the remote and deserted parts of the country, a weaver or a smith, besides the exercise of his trade, cultivates a small farm and in that manner exercises two trades, that of a farmer and that of a weaver. To bring about therefore the separation of trades sooner than the progress of society would naturally effect, and prevent the uncertainty of all those who had taken themselves to one trade, it was found necessary to give them a certainty of a comfortable subsistence. – And for this purpose the legislature determined that they should have the priviledge of exercising their separate trades without the fear of being cut out of their livelyhood by the increase of their rivalls. That this was necessary therefore in the 1st stages of the arts to bring them to their proper perfection, appears very reasonable and is confirmed by this, that it has been the generall practise of all the nations in Europe.
>
> (LJA ii.40–1)

One would never learn from Pocock that Pocock is quoting words several sentences apart, in which there is no implied contrast between Europe and non Europeans!

This should alert us to the fact that many of Pocock's central claims are offered without textual evidence. He relies on his own authority or that from the sources he cites. Sometimes he cites Ferguson or Hume rather than Smith, failing to note crucial differences among these three thinkers. In order to illustrate how distorted Pocock's presentation of Smith is, I analyse Pocock's treatment of the longest quotation of Smith in his article. In commenting on excerpts from LRBL, ii.40–1, Pocock writes, 'Smith – if correctly reported – is at this point the inhabitant of a moral and exemplary universe, where a fact's edificatory value outweighs the tedious question of its actuality; he is not living a Lockean universe of probability, or a Mabillonian universe of source criticism' (275).

This claim is a misreading of the content and context of the quoted passage as well as the whole lecture from which it is drawn. First, in Lecture XVIII (Friday 7 Jan. 1763), Smith is self-consciously teaching the proper 'composition' of works of history. Smith's doctrines concern primarily the 'manner' or 'style' of presentation not content; he is explaining the 'order of narration'. Second it is true that Smith often demands that histories should be 'instructive' (this is strangely unmentioned by Pocock) and this could be taken to be a form of edification. Nevertheless, contrary to Pocock's assertion, the main criterion Smith uses to evaluate the order of narration is not its edificatory value, but the degree to which events are causally connected: '[t]here is no connection with which we are so much interested as this of cause and effect'. Smith is reported to have lectured that without this connection, facts remain 'unintelligible' to us. This suggests, third, that by leaving out 'intelligibility' as an aim for history, Pocock is using a (contextually) misleading dichotomy between edification vs. actuality. One can discern an anachronistic deployment of the distinction between facts and values in Pocock! Either way, Smith's focus on intelligibility suggests Smith is far more concerned with actuality than with edification. Without offering a full defence of Smith's position here, historical narratives that purport to be factual must presuppose the intelligibility of these facts. (Is there a historical art without *Verstehen*?) Even if we leave aside Smith's concern for intelligibility, it is puzzling that Pocock fails to note that on the very same page, Smith claims that the 'business' of the historian 'is [to] narrate facts!' And Smith objects against the introduction of speeches into historical narratives on the grounds, 'That tho they be represented as facts, they are not genuine ones'. Contrary to Pocock's assertion, Smith is emphasizing how important facts and causal realism are to intelligible historical narration. Nowhere in the passage cited, does Smith appeal to moral edification. Even the passage that Pocock quotes is introduced with an emphasis on the 'impartiality' of the historian![4]

Moreover, Pocock's selective quotation omits Smith's claim that 'To avoid a dissertation about the Truth of a Fact a Historian might first Relate the Event according to the most likely opinion and when he had done so give the others by saying that such or such a Circumstance had occasioned such or such a mistake or that such a misrepresentation had been propagated by such a person for such Ends'. This suggests that Smith has not departed from the broadly 'Lockean universe' at all; Pocock simply fails to recognize that Smith's use of 'proof' (throughout the lecture and elsewhere) is indebted to Hume's adaptation of Locke (in which 'proof' is the highest degree of probability – a kind of moral certainty; see the first footnote to EHU 6. See also my comments above on Berry's important analysis of Smith's debts to a Lockean anthropology).[5]

Finally, Pocock also misreads the offending sentence ('Now all proofs of this sort show that the matter is somewhat dubious; so that on the whole it would be more proper to narrate these facts without mentioning the doubt, than to bring in any long proof'). Here Smith might be taken to suggest to the aspiring student-historian that it is better to fail to mention how weak one's evidence is. Let's momentarily grant for the sake of argument this is so. In context, Smith claims that if one has a partial interest in those claims of 'whose truth [one is] altogether satisfied' then one is better off to avoid dwelling on long arguments that have the unintended consequence of revealing the weakness of one's position to the reader. Given that Smith is discussing stylistic concerns, all is he is saying here is that one's means should be appropriate to one's ends. So, this might be taken to partially vindicate Pocock's reading. But the whole lecture makes abundantly clear that Smith is not endorsing such partial histories demanded by political and religious 'sects'. Given that Pocock is eager to link Smith's approach to history to his moral philosophy, it is strange that he misses Smith's emphasis on the absolute importance of the historian's impartiality even in a lecture devoted to style; the quoted sentence is an example of a form of history that is not to be endorsed.

Now, perhaps Pocock might be tempted to claim that the importance (in my reconstruction) of Smith's appeal to intelligibility vindicates his dismissal of Smith as a historian; unlike Hume, Robertson and Gibbon, Smith did not write 'histories in which the strangeness of human behavior is not concealed' (276–7), or so Pocock thinks. (Of course, Pocock may not be conflating strangeness with intelligibility.) Now, it's not exactly clear what Pocock has in mind with 'strangeness of human behaviour'. Yet, in the 'History of Astronomy' and the 'History of Ancient Metaphysics', Smith repeatedly comments on the 'strange' doctrine of some innovative thinker (say, Copernicus, Kepler) or wildly speculative thinker (Malebranche). In *Wealth of Nations*, he writes: 'The dream of Sir Walter Raleigh concerning the golden city and country of Eldorado, may satisfy us, that even wise men are not always exempt from . . . strange delusions'. If in Smith's universe even wise men are not exempt from delusions, it should come as no surprise that Smith thinks that common sense is in many respects quite rare (TMS III.2.4;115). If Pocock means that Smith is (contra, say, Montesquieu on the Persians, or Voltaire on the Chinese) no Orientalist, so much the better for Smith. Anyway, for anybody interested in how to begin to understand Adam Smith's views on history in historical context, they are better off reading Mark Salber Phillips' contribution to the same volume or Dario Perinetti's fine essay in another, competing Cambridge Companion (also edited by Knud Haakonssen) (Perinetti 2006).

Notes

1 Disclaimer: I am the co-editor with Leon Montes of a competing volume (2006) *New Voices on Adam Smith* (Routledge) with a foreword by Knud Haakonssen.
2 My comments on Berry's contribution recycle many of my views of his piece published in an earlier review (Schliesser 2007) and appear with kind permission of the editors of *Notre Dame Philosophical Reviews*.
3 But without using that terminology, I treated it in Schliesser (2005a) where I explain how Smith exploits the gap between natural and civil history for evidential and theory-building purposes.
4 For a treatment that cashes out Smith's concern with the impartiality of causal historical explanation (in Smith's published writings), see Schliesser (2006b).
5 See my treatment of these matters (Schliesser 2005b).

Bibliography

Harkin, M. (2002) 'Natives and nostalgia: the problem of the north American savage in Adam Smith's historiography', *Scottish Studies Review*, 3: 25–8.
—— (2005) 'Adam Smith's missing history: primitives, progress, and problems of genre', *English Literary History*, 72: 429–51.
Perinetti, D. (2006) 'Philosophical reflection on history', in *The Cambridge History of Eighteenth-century Philosophy*, K. Haakonssen (ed.). Cambridge: Cambridge University Press.
Pitt, J. (2005) *A Turn to Empire: The Rise of Imperial Liberalism in Britain and France*, Princeton: Princeton University Press.
Rosenberg, N. (1960) 'Some institutional aspects of the Wealth of Nations', *The Journal of Political Economy*, 68: 557–70.
Schliesser, E. (2005a) 'Some principles of Adam Smith's "Newtonian" methods in the Wealth of Nations', *Research in History of Economic Thought and Methodology*, 23A: 35–77.
—— (2005b) 'Wonder in the face of scientific revolutions: Adam Smith on Newton's "Proof" of Copernicanism', *British Journal for the History of Philosophy*, 13: 697–732.
—— (2006a) 'The self-interest of a benevolent philosopher: Adam Smith's conception of philosophy', in *New Voices on Adam Smith*, L. Montes and E. Schliesser (eds), London: Routledge.
—— (2006b) 'Articulating practices as reasons: Adam Smith on the conditions of possibility of property', *The Adam Smith Review*, 2: 69–97, London and New York: Routledge.
—— (2007) Review of K. Haakonssen, *Cambridge Companion to Adam Smith*, *Notre Dame Philosophical Reviews*, 20 Aug. 2007.

Impartiality, utility and induction in Adam Smith's jurisprudence

S.M. Amadae

[I]t is harder than expected to find an attractive account of propriety and virtue that turns on correspondence between spectator and agent. When Smith's difficulties with normative utilitarianism are added, it is easier to see why *The Theory of Moral Sentiments* grew obscure while normative utilitarianism and its intuitionist critics prospered.

(Shaver, *Cambridge Companion*, 212)

Given my affinity for Smith's theory of justice, it took this observation of Robert Shaver's in his chapter, 'Virtues, utility, and rules', to jar me into facing the question: why is it that Smith's jurisprudence has been mainly disregarded while his *Wealth of Nations* is celebrated as the chief blueprint for political economy and free markets? This question warrants attention given that Smith's system of natural liberty is predicated on the natural virtue of justice. In Alexander Broadie's words, in his chapter, 'Sympathy and the impartial spectator', Smith's 'economic theory was developed therefore within the context of a moral theory that goes wide and deep, a context that carries the message that an economic theory has to be developed within a moral philosophical framework' (165). In reading *The Cambridge Companion to Adam Smith*, I found new compelling arguments to both counter apparent weaknesses in Smith's jurisprudence, and to respond to an increasingly prevalent tendency to solve the infamous 'Adam Smith problem' by replacing sympathy with self-interest as the basis of social norms and legal standards.[1]

The origination of social norms and their source of normativity is a germane topic today. I am particularly interested in Philip Pettit's reworking of Smith's use of sympathy, coupled with approval and disapproval, to present an explanation on normativity that is consistent with rational choice theory (RCT). Quoting the utilitarian economist and Nobel Lareaute John Harsanyi, Pettit reminds us that 'People's behaviour can be largely explained in terms of two dominant interests: economic gain, and social acceptance' (Pettit 2002: 309). Pettit's account of norm formation adopts a posture similar to Smith's sentiment of sympathy. According to Pettit, norms arise from a) positively or negatively evaluating another's conduct; and b) directly sanctioning individuals exhibiting disfavoured behaviour. This individualized process of judging others' conduct, insofar as regular patterns emerge, sustains norms as agents seek to conform their actions to others' expectations in order to gain approval and avoid shame. Pettit's defends his theory of norm creation by suggesting that it is consistent with Smith's theory of justice. He quotes Smith: 'What reward is most proper for promoting the practice of truth, justice and humanity? The confidence, esteem and love of those we live with. Humanity does not desire to be great, but to be beloved' (Pettit 2002: 311).

In the following discussion, I contrast a 'classic Smith' rendering of justice developed from the *Cambridge Companion*'s essays with Pettit's version. I discuss the essays of Broadie, Shaver, and David Lieberman respectively, addressing the themes of impartiality, utility and induction in Smith's jurisprudence.

I: Broadie – What role does impartiality play for Smith and is it attainable?

Broadie tells us up front that Smith's impartial spectator is the hero of the Enlightenment (175). This conclusion is fitting as impartiality itself is the key to the Enlightenment inquiry.[2] Impartiality plays a particular role in anchoring justice because, for Smith, it is necessary to attain third-party distance from an injury that permits an unbiased appraisal of whether an individual was actually injured, and has a legitimate cause for resentment. It is the achievement of an impartial vantage point, initially towards the conduct of others, but eventually towards our own conduct, that gives rise to judgments which, when considered society-wide, serve as the basis of the general laws of justice. The subject matter of justice is unique for Smith because, unlike matters of fashion or taste, or of the positive virtues including benevolence and charity, it is exact and categorical (TMS II.ii.2.2). The consensus that emerges on the principles of justice is not a mere social artifact, but instead represents a process of comprehension that may best be compared to the relationship between Newton's principles of motion and our observations of the actual regular motions of the bodies they describe (176–7). Thus, impartiality serves the crucial role of distancing individuals from their private interests, and of permitting the apprehension of a generalizeable appropriateness of fit between circumstances, the passions they arouse, and an agent's reaction. If normativity is considered to embody the recognition of rules which individuals cannot control but must conform to, Smith suggests that the realization of the standards of justice is similar to imagining the laws of mechanics. In both cases, there is a beauty to appraising the harmonious system, and misconstruing the laws of justice or physics leads not only to internal dissonance, but also to a breakdown of social intercourse or mechanical integrity (TMS II.ii.3.4).[3]

In Broadie's analysis, even though a concordance of the spectator's sympathy with an injured party may generate pleasure, there is an important distinction between the sentiments evoked by sympathetic reflection of another's circumstances, and the feeling of concordance produced if agent and observer share like assessments (174). Firstly, impartial sympathy yields a judgment of appropriateness of action independent from any personal utility or implications. In assessing your circumstances and actions as an external observer, your fate is separate from mine, and your realization of ends is immaterial to me. Therefore as I reflect on your reactions, my judgment is not predicated on whether your fate may promote my ends. Second, as the sympathetic judgment is prior to potential concordance among first or third party's perspectives, though concordance may generate pleasure, this pleasure is the unintended outcome of impartial judgment, and does not itself represent the telos or end of judgment. Here Smith suggests that justice has much in common with mathematics because the judgment of normative appropriateness, or philosophically surmising the 'connecting principles of nature', first meets an independent standard of aptness, and only having done so, gives rise to satisfaction.[4] Justice is exact for Smith, precisely in analogue to the general laws of natural science which must stand the test of countless idiosyncratic observations (TMS III.4.7–8).[5]

Broadie's essay focuses more on the feasibility of attaining impartiality, and less on the metaphysics, or basis of the universal basis of approbation; yet he avers with Shaver that this universal basis is *not* any consideration of personal or public utility (Broadie 163; Shaver, 194–203; I concur, 212–19). According to Broadie, the impartial spectator is neither the general 'we' of society, nor an omniscient God's eye perspective: this spectator is human, but has a critical stance, separate from what may be mass consensus or psychosis, as a function of being able to take on an outside observer's role. Crucially, this impartial spectator is not the normal, typical, or average individual, but one who can ultimately serve as the personal faculty of conscience (181). It is well-known that this privileged seat of judgment must exhibit a degree of self-command, and even in many ways must possess commendable virtue (TMS III.2.33; see also Shaver 208). However, Smith's theory of justice functions adequately on the assumption that most of us can be sufficiently impartial in the third person stance to tap in to what Smith argues is generally acknowledgeable conformity of judgment in the case that an individual has been wronged by another (185).

II: Shaver – does Smith's theory of justice depend on utility?

Shaver, I believe, is sympathetic to Smith's project, but worries that 'Smith gave few meta-ethical arguments to keep the twentieth century attentive' (212). Specifically, as is tacit in the preceding discussion, Smith could not in fact articulate the metaphysical basis that secures the uniformity of impartial judgments; neither did he articulate the general rules of juris-prudence that he long promised. Newton deductively postulated his laws of motion, and they seemed (over time) to hold up to empirical verification, but Smith was not able to do the same, even if he did propose the negative virtue commitment upholding the integrity of personhood, property and contract (Lieberman 214–6).

Accepting Smith's theory of convergence of judgments concerning injustices, but leaving aside the source of this convergence, Shaver focuses his essay on the point that Smith consistently disavows any role for utility in justice. Critics of Smith could find a role for utility in three locations throughout Smith's system: (1) as a normative justification for the legitimacy of justice; (2) as the empirical basis of individual judgments over others' actions; and (3) as the rationale for punishment. I agree with Shaver, who in his turn is consistent with Knud Haakonssen's conclusion in his *Science of a Legislator*, that although Smith suggests that his system of justice does serve the public utility, his argument for justice is wholly disconnected from such justification (Haakonssen 1981: 67–74; Amadae 2003: 211). However, the fact that were Smith's system of justice to contradict public utility, it would be suspect, leaves Shaver to conclude that Smith's system offers nothing that we do not gain by a more straightforward derivation of normative justification from utilitarian concerns (197). I will engage this point further, suggesting that a utilitarian account of justice ultimately fails for Smith because it offers a forward-looking, teleological motive for agents' actions causing justice to arise, rather than a backwards-looking appraisal of events that is independent from either realizing self-gain and or any intention of bringing about just consequences.

I do agree with Shaver that perhaps a more important point to distinguish Smith from utilitarian critics is with respect to individual judgments over others' actions. I believe this is the more crucial part of Shaver's argument because Smith is clear throughout *Theory of Moral Sentiments* that he is discovering the *efficient* causes of justice, and not the *final* causes. The question at hand is whether in judging the appropriateness of others' actions, the third person consults how these actions affect public or personal utility. Using utility-based judgment as the explanation of justice runs counter to Smith's entire enterprise because otherwise, insofar as justice is individually beneficial for people, it would necessarily merit intentional action. Smith's unintended consequences argument for the formation of justice assumes that individuals act without awareness that they are contributing to a system of justice; neither in contributing to justice are individuals moved by the prospect of satisfying personal preferences. Shaver argues that according to Smith, 'We are neither smart enough to make reliable utilitarian calcu-lations nor motivated by appeals to utility' (197). Shaver finds that 'The case against explanatory utilitarianism remains. Here Smith is probably right that we often do not, and did not originally, arrive at our approvals by reflections on utility' (201). However, it remains the case that, just as with not contradicting utility for normative justification of justice, individuals' judgments of others actions by and large 'track utility', even if 'utility is not the original or motivating explanation of punishment (201).

Shaver finds Smith's non-utility based rendering of justice reasonable, apart from that Smith identifies a basic difference between judgments about material things which he agrees are subject to personal preference, and judgments about persons, which exhibit 'a special sentiment of approval felt only toward persons' (203). Shaver suggests that Smith's inability to provide reasoning for a categorical distinction in contemplating 'things' or 'people' again gives explanatory utilitarianism the upper hand, as both may serve individuals' ends. He goes on to express concern over Smith's staunch reliance on the impartial spectator, and maintains, counter to Broadie, that impartiality requires a super-human degree of self-command and virtue (208–11). However, perhaps the decisive point here is not how readily accessible impartiality is, but that it does represent an attainable posture.

III: Lieberman – Induction, or how do general rules arise from isolated judgments?

In introducing Lieberman's essay, 'Adam Smith on justice, rights, and law', I take another line from Shaver: 'Smith's "remedy" [for injustices] is to introduce "general rules". . . . These are formulated by induction on past impartial approvals (rather than by deduction from utility or by direction intuition)' (204). It is the question of Smith's delivery on his premise that the general principles of justice can be induced from numerous idiosyncratic and anecdotal cases of judgment that I now turn my consideration.

Lieberman's essay draws attention to the somewhat odd fit between Smith's inductive promise, which Lieberman emphasizes was not kept, and Smith's own historical method. A strength of Smith's method, we learn, is to contrast reflections on justice with the actual historical processes that lead to specific positive laws. Smith delighted in showing that the original aims behind a law's formation may be sufficiently out of synch with a contemporary practice that the law may fail to serve its original purpose. One example is that of primogeniture, which originally served the role of guaranteeing nobles sufficient strength in resources and arms to protect themselves and their subjects. In the eighteenth century, however, this legal convention no longer served the purpose for which it was designed. Lieberman observes of this example that it exemplifies Smith's historical jurisprudence: 'This was the manner in which his historical research frequently complemented the purposes of normative criticism by making clear the antiquated or anachronistic character of many of those positive laws which most glaringly violated natural justice' (229). Lieberman's point in discussing Smith's historical jurisprudence is that Smith acknowledges that in the formation of positive law 'human purpose and normative reflection, as well as . . . political contingency and the machinations of social elites' play a role (231).

Lieberman argues that Smith's project was to contrast positive law, and the processes by which it arises, with the precise principles of natural jurisprudence.

Lieberman echoes what we are familiar with: Smith firmly believed that his system of natural liberty is all that is required to ensure economic growth and opulence. But we are left with the puzzle of how, given the historical manner by which actual laws are formed in accordance with normative reflection, contingency, and elite interest, Smith's inductive method of generating general laws from particular cases of sympathetic impartial judgment can lead to effective law. There seems to be a gap between isolated individuals' sympathetic judgments, and the powers that actually create laws, most often to preserve the property of the rich from the poor (239).

Lieberman provides an innovative solution to this puzzle by considering Book V of *Wealth of Nations* that treats the 'impartial administration of justice'. Lieberman argues that Smith fills the gap between individual cases of impartial judgment and the process of legal formation with the British example of institutionalizing an 'increasing independence of the "judicial" from the "executive" power' (240). He maintains that for Smith, judicial independence is far more important than parliamentary representation in establishing the basis for a just and prosperous civil society. It is crucial for Smith that justice is impartially administered. This impartiality anchors a 'stable structure of rights', and protects the rights of the least well-off Briton equally to the most wealthy's (241). If I accept, with Broadie and Shaver, the *possibility* of impartial judgment, no matter how remote, then the problem of its achievement may be solved by the institutionalization of the conditions for impartiality. In modern societies described by Smith, an independent judiciary makes up for the fact that the distance between the protagonist and the observer may not be sufficiently great as to foreclose on considerations of private interest entering into judgments of appropriate action. If the judiciary is constituted free from political intrigue and personal gain, then it embodies Smith's impartial spectator.

IV: Pettit's RCT Smith

Next I briefly consider the mechanism by which social norms are formed according to Pettit's rational choice-inspired reading of Smith. I must note that Pettit realizes that he is complementing a legally-based coercive-sanctions account with his discussion of informal norms and sanctions; however, Pettit believes he is true to Smith's analysis of how justice arises. According to Pettit: 1) An agent reacts to a set of circumstances. 2) A third party observes this agent's actions and either approves or disapproves. 3) If the outside observer disapproves of the action, and it is effectively costless to apply some form of sanction, then this person will shame the observed agent. 4) Norms then arise, by Pettit's account, because a) there is some sort of uniformity of pattern of negative responses to particular forms of behaviour; and b) these norms are abided by via informal sanctions because individuals seek each other's approval (Pettit 2002: 316–37).

We proceed to examine Pettit's Smith on the themes of impartiality, utility and induction. For Pettit's Smith, impartiality has no role to play. Pettit clarifies: 'Approval in my sense is nothing less than that broad sort of attitude to which acts of expressing approval testify' (313). Approval is an idiosyncratic feature of an individual's preferences and the perceived usefulness of others' actions to satisfy these private preferences. If a norm arises, this indicates a uniformity of preferences among individuals over third parties' actions. In the case of the canonical 'free-rider' problem, each prefers others to contribute to the joint effort, even as each seeks to ride for free. Pettit is interested in how deviance from a norm, or regular pattern of activity, evokes disapproval and censure, which in turn serves as the mechanism by which the norm is enforced. Pettit uses this process of disapproval to account for how norms arise, how they may be justified and enforced, and why agents conform to norms (317). He supposes that the particularly important social norms are those that solve Prisoner's dilemma, or collective-action type situations, in which, unless a particular norm is followed by most or all, the population in question will waste resources (319–27).

Although Pettit does not invoke 'impartiality' as the basis of the judgment leading to sanction, he does invoke 'utility'. The utility in question is that recognized to be lost when agents perceive others as 'free riders', or 'foul dealers' (322, 333). Therefore, for Pettit the decision to sanction another agent is ultimately based on an individualistic cost-benefit analysis: I watch someone free ride on my efforts by using an invalid bus pass, I disapprove and frown at him intently as he gets on the bus. He feels my furious disapproval, and in the future adds this potential sanction into his calculation of whether to cheat the system or not. It is this agent-relative, utility-based cost-benefit analysis that provides the motive force impelling norm creation and stabilization for Pettit. In a collective action problem, everyone sees the benefits of joint cooperation, even if everyone privately seeks to cheat, if he can get away with it. The standard of joint cooperation, then, is mutually preferred to others' free-riding, and serves as a baseline motivating and justifying the punishment of defectors. Pettit draws on utility three times over in his analysis. Once, as an individual's judgment is based on an assessment of utility of another's compliance with specific norms. Twice, because the utility of the norm in achieving mutually preferred outcomes is manifestly evident to any one either looking for justification or for explanation of the abiding value of specific norms. Three-times, as conformity to the jointly preferred norm is achieved by imposing negative utilities on norm breakers.

Conclusion

Pettit puts forward a theory of norm creation that seems to have Smith's imprimatur because it brings self-love to the fore as a single motive for action. Indeed, Pettit's mechanism resembles Smith's in isolating individuals' judgments of others' actions as the inductive base from which generalized rules of conduct are derived. In light of the *Cambridge Companion*'s contributions, we are able to ascertain two equally misleading departures in Pettit's account. First, Smith's jurisprudence is mischaracterized by Pettit who locates the source of social norms in personal preferences rather than impartiality.[6] Second, this misrepresentation of Smith's jurisprudence suggests the practice of deriving just social laws from considerations of agent-relative utility. We must recall that for Smith, the point is not 'I like what you do because your action suits my ends'. The point rather is, 'I approve of your demonstrated passions given my sympathetic reflection on your situation'. Smith provides us with the vantage point to view free-riding as a categorically unjust action that steals the fruit of others' to promote personal ends, rather than simply as an action preferred for oneself, but dispreferred in the case of others (TMS III.ii.22). Smith's jurisprudence demands that standards apply universally to the self and others, and thus provides a rationale for action independent from sanctions and calculations for self gain. Smith's solution to the problem of social order is unconditionally distinct from Pettit's RCT rendering because the efficient cause of justice is non-consequentialist, backward-looking judgment of appropriateness, and not a forward-looking judgment of potential pay-offs.

Smith's classic liberalism premised on impartial judgment of injury to personhood, property and contract, hang in the balance if we accept Pettit's contemporary reading (TMS II.ii.2.2). For the classic Smith of the *Cambridge Companion*, individual judgments over actions are independent from preferences or consequences, may be impartial, and are informed by sympathy. The standards that result from numerous judgments apply equally to others and to the self, and they may guide action independent from considerations of individual gain or external censure. The impartial spectator embodies the Enlightenment idea of inducing generalized law from disparate phenomena regardless of locality or perspective, and serves as template for the institutionalization of rules of conduct dependent on an independent judiciary. Emphasizing Smith's commitment to a judicial system reflecting judgments unencumbered by considerations of self-gain, Emma Rothschild and Amartya Sen in 'Adam Smith's economics' note that the 'reasonably impartial administration of justice . . . [is] the single most important condition . . . for the progress of opulence' (350). Without an Archimedian reference-point in impartial judgment over agents' actions that may apply seamlessly to oneself or to agents at large, Pettit's rendering of Smith's system of natural liberty prospectively reduces justice to a consensual framework for manipulating others' actions in accordance with the preferences of the majority, or of the disproportionately empowered.

Notes

1 See, for example, Buchanan and Tullock (1962); see also Pettit (2002). For discussion of this tendency see Amadae (2003: 133–55).

2 In Smith's words, 'The well informed and impartial observer will bring to view what the Ignorant or prejudiced would overlook', (Mossner 1960: 228).
3 In 'History of Astronomy', Smith acknowledges that 'unprotected by the laws of society. . .[individuals are] exposed, defenseless. . .[and feel their] weakness upon all occasions' (III.2), therefore knowledge of social law is a necessary condition of security and prosperity. Natural philosophy can only be developed after social law is established, and although it is pursued as a 'good in itself', its appreciation grants the achievement of ends (III.5–8).
4 Broadie, 164; Smith, 'History of Astronomy', II.9. For an in-depth discussion of the epistemological parallels between Smith's philosophies of social and natural science see Schliesser (2005).
5 Smith observes, 'What is agreeable to our moral faculties, is fit, and right, and proper to be done . . . Since these, therefore, were plainly intended to be the governing principles of human nature, the rules which they prescribe are to be regarded as the commands and laws of the Deity. . . All general rules are commonly denominated laws: thus the general rules which bodies observe in the communication of motion, are called the laws of motion. But those general rules which our moral faculties observe in approving or condemning whatever sentiment or action is subjected to their examination, may much more justly be denominated as such' (TMS III.5.5–6).
6 In his discussion of the 'Adam Smith problem', Broadie emphasizes that for Smith, sympathy is not a motive at all (165).

Bibliography

Amadae, S.M. (2003) *Rationalizing Capitalist Democracy*, Chicago: University of Chicago Press.
Buchanan, J.M. and G. Tullock (1962) *The Calculus of Consent*, Ann Arbor: University of Michigan Press.
Haakonssen, K. (1981) *The Science of a Legislator: The Natural Jurisprudence of David Hume and Adam Smith*, Cambridge: Cambridge University Press.
Mossner, E.C. (1960) ' "Of the Principle of Moral Estimation: A Discourse between David Hume, Robert Clerk, and Adam Smith": An Unpublished MS by Adam Ferguson', *Journal of the History of Ideas*, 21: 222–32.
Pettit, P. (2002) '*Virtus normative*: rational choice perspectives', in *Rules, Reasons, and Norms*, P. Pettit, Oxford: Clarendon Press.
Schliesser, E. (2005) 'Wonder in the face of scientific revolutions: Adam Smith on Newton's "proof" of Copernicanism', *British Journal for the History of Philosophy*, 13: 697–732.

Whose impartiality? Which self-interest?

Adam Smith on utility, happiness and cultural relativism

Dennis C. Rasmussen

Robert Shaver's chapter, 'Virtues, utility, and rights', in the *Cambridge Companion to Adam Smith* begins by noting that '*The Theory of Moral Sentiments* was a great success upon publication; now it is obscure' (189). 'Obscure' may be a bit of an overstatement, as the existence of this *Companion* attests, but it is certainly true that Smith's moral philosophy is not nearly as widely studied as those of Hume and Kant, for example. Shaver aims to offer one reason why this might be the case, and he finds an explanation in the fact (or, rather, the claim) that Smith's moral theory is weaker than a utilitarian moral theory in many respects. Shaver concedes that Smith's theory is an attractive one, but he points to a number of what he sees as defects in it that might help to explain its relative obscurity. His arguments on this score are numerous, but there are three contentions that seem to be central to his case: that Smith's explanatory moral theory has no real normative weight, that he relies on utility in making (some) normative claims even while insisting that doing so is illegitimate, and that his moral theory is susceptible to a kind of cultural relativism. I will briefly touch on the first two of these criticisms before discussing the third at somewhat greater length.

One of the most appealing elements of Smith's moral theory, Shaver concedes, is that it seems to constitute an improvement over utilitarianism as a description or explanation of our moral psychology: our moral feelings – approval and disapproval, gratitude and resentment – are generally motivated not by utilitarian calculations but by feelings or sentiments. People typically demand that murderers are punished, for example, because they feel outrage or resentment and not because they calculate that doing so may make society better off in the long run by deterring other potential murderers. Yet, Shaver notes (195–6), Smith also frequently makes normative claims in TMS; in addition to describing the way people *do* in fact make moral judgments, Smith seems to suggest that people *ought* to act in such a way that an impartial spectator would approve of them. And Shaver suggests that this is where he runs into trouble.

First, Shaver asks (196–8), how does Smith justify his normative conclusion – that we ought to follow the dictates of the impartial spectator

– based on his premises? Where does the normative weight come from? He implies that Smith does not have a good answer. This is far too large and complicated an issue to resolve here, but we can note that Smith could equally ask, why are we morally obligated to maximize utility – or to obey the categorical imperative, for that matter? Shaver seems to be seeking a level of normative purchase that is rarely found outside of theological arguments. Moreover, the divide between an explanatory moral theory and a normative one is perhaps not as stark as Shaver implies: it does not seem entirely tautological to claim that following the dictates of the impartial spectator is moral because that is what we *mean* when we say that someone is a moral person. Charles Griswold rightly notes in his chapter, 'Imagination: morals, science, and arts', in the *Cambridge Companion*, that even if our moral norms do not 'correspond to some completely mind-independent reality', such norms 'are nonetheless "real" in the sense that they organize the world; that we rely on them in making decisions, from the most inconsequential to the gravest; and that we both appeal to them and develop them in praising and blaming our fellows, which praise and blame, in turn, guide much of human life' (54).

Shaver's second key criticism (198–9) is that there are instances in TMS in which Smith appeals to utility in making normative claims, despite his opposition to normative utilitarianism. For example, Smith argues that a sentinel who falls asleep at his watch ought to be executed, in accordance with common laws of war, even though to an observer this punishment seems to far exceed the crime, because this kind of carelessness can endanger an entire army (TMS II.ii.3.11). He also implies that it is proper to feel more gratitude toward someone who tries to help you and succeeds than toward someone who tries equally hard but fails, because rewarding realized rather than latent virtue ensures that people will try harder to do good; rewarding luck is desirable because it promotes happiness or utility (TMS II.iii.3.2–3). Shaver contends that these kinds of apparently utilitarian statements fit uneasily within Smith's spectatorial moral theory.

It is entirely possible, however, to account for these moral judgments through impartial spectatorship, without recourse to the idea of utility. While we as partial spectators may sympathize with the sentinel who accidentally falls asleep, an impartial spectator would presumably also sympathize with the great multitude of people whose lives were thereby put into danger and thus resent the sentinel's ostensibly minor infraction more. Similarly, an impartial spectator might approve of realized virtue more than latent virtue because he sympathizes with the person (or people) being benefitted. This is not to say that these judgments do not contribute to utility; in fact, Smith explicitly concedes that morality sometimes *seems* to arise from utility and often *does* serve a utilitarian purpose (the sentinel example is found in a chapter of TMS entitled 'Of the utility of this constitution of Nature'). Indeed, he seems to believe that moral action generally benefits both the individual who so acts and the society of which he or she is a part; James Otteson has (to my mind persuasively) argued that the 'meta-argument' of Smith's moral theory 'takes the form of a hypothetical imperative: if you wish to obtain a tranquil and happy psychological state, then you should abide by the system of morality that has arisen naturally and unintentionally in the way described in TMS' (Otteson 2002: 236; cf. TMS III.5.7). Smith's claim is not that moral actions are not conducive to utility or happiness, but rather that the utility or happiness that results from an action is not what makes that action moral; normative utilitarianism conflates the 'efficient' and 'final' causes of our moral sentiments (TMS II.ii.3.5).

The third major worry about Smith's moral theory that Shaver mentions (193–4, 200) is that it entails a kind of historicism or cultural relativism that he himself sometimes seems to want to resist. Given that Smith's theory is based on sentiments and that people's sentiments vary widely from time to time and place to place, there does not seem to be any room in his theory to appeal beyond the particular morality of one's own culture. Insofar as morality consists of what 'we think' or 'we approve', there does not seem to be any way of judging one culture's moral standards to be superior to another's, or of criticizing a practice that an entire society has adopted. Even an impartial spectator seems to have no standards by which to judge other than those of his own society; he simply judges by those standards impartially. Yet Smith often criticizes practices that he sees as appalling, such as slavery and infanticide, even though he is well aware that in some societies (such as the city-states of ancient Greece) these practices have been accepted by virtually everyone (TMS V.2.15). Shaver suggests that Smith has no valid grounds on which to launch such a criticism: even if we were to grant that the viewpoint of the impartial spectator defines morality and provides some kind of normative weight, there is still no room within such a viewpoint to criticize the morality of a culture as a whole.

This last charge seems to me the most compelling and illuminating of the three. There does appear to be a degree of cultural relativism inherent in Smith's moral theory, and moreover Shaver appears to be right to suggest that this problem (if indeed it is a problem) arises in precisely the area where Smith's theory improves on utilitarianism, its more plausible description or explanation of real-world moral phenomena. The more realistic one's explanatory moral theory, the less normative bite that theory will tend to have on a societal level: any theory that accurately captures people's moral judgments is forced to account for the fact that different people and different societies vary immensely in the judgments they make. Nor is this whiff of cultural relativism in Smith's thought entirely a disadvantage, as Samuel Fleischacker (2005) has stressed in a recent essay on this subject: most people *do* tend to share many or most of the moral standards of their society on a basic, 'gut' level, and to say that most almost everyone is simply and obviously *wrong* in their moral judgments seems implausible as well as demeaning.

On the other hand, Shaver does not give due weight to the possibilities within Smith's moral theory for resisting this kind of cultural relativism. Stephen Darwall (1999; 2004) has argued, for instance, that Smith's notion of the impartial spectator is inherently connected to a belief in the basic dignity of all other human beings, and thus that it stands as a kind of precursor to Kant's categorical imperative. Adopting the viewpoint of the impartial spectator leads people to see that everyone is of equal worth, and that there is no good reason to prefer themselves or their kind over others. And Charles Griswold (1999: 198–202, 349–54, 363–4) has noted that the notion of the impartial spectator does allow people to separate themselves to some degree from their culture's moral standards, particularly because such a spectator would fully sympathize with each actor in a given situation – including, for example, a slave or an unwanted infant. Thus, the impartial spectator might view practices such as slavery or infanticide as unacceptable even in the case where an entire society had accepted them; he would simply conclude that these societies were being partial.

Yet Shaver could rightly insist that neither of these responses are wholly satisfactory. After all, accepting that the viewpoint of the impartial spectator *can* rule out slavery and infanticide even in ancient Greece seems to require retreating somewhat from the notion that the impartial spectator is built out of actual spectators – out of what 'we think' or 'we approve' – and that people properly learn what is right and wrong through their upbringing and their interaction with others. But this idea seems central to Smith's moral theory, and it is also one of its more attractive features, as Shaver notes – it is precisely what makes Smith's explanatory theory so powerful. Either way one tries to solve the problem, it seems, the solution will come with a price: the theory can be given more normative bite at the cost of reducing its explanatory power, or it can retain its explanatory power at the cost of accepting a degree of cultural relativism. Of course, the price of giving the theory more normative bite – that of reducing its explanatory power – is one that utilitarianism has paid from the outset.

I turn now to Pratap Mehta's chapter, 'Self-interest and other interests', in the *Cambridge Companion*, which examines the role of self-interest in Smith's thought. Contrary to the hoary old reading according to which Smith is an apostle of selfishness who builds his economic palace on the granite of self-interest (Stigler 1971: 265), Mehta shows that self-interest in fact plays a nuanced and complicated role in his writings, and that it is just one of a whole range of human motivations that he recognizes. In particular, Mehta argues that the idea of self-interest is suffused with moral connotations even in WN, that even TMS makes plenty of room for a proper pursuit of self-love, and that for Smith it is the imagination, rather than self-interest, that is the more fundamental spring of human action.

The claim that self-interest has moral undertones in WN is most certainly correct, even if it will not come as a surprise to many contemporary Smith scholars. So far from attempting to emancipate economics from the restraints of morality (as is contended by Cropsey 2001 and Minowitz 1993), Smith shows in WN how self-interest can *serve* morality. For instance, the famous passage on the butcher, the brewer, and the baker (WN I.ii.2), which has so often been read as endorsing self-interest at the expense of morality or benevolence, in fact demonstrates that self-interest can serve a moral purpose: if we can rely on the self-interest of the butcher, brewer, and baker for our dinner then we do not *have* to rely on their benevolence, like beggars or slaves. Smith saw this kind of dependence as a sure path to servility and moral corruption and argued that the interdependence of the market can help to ameliorate these problems (LJA vi.6; LJB 204–5). Further, Mehta notes (250), appealing to the self-interest of the butcher, brewer, and baker forces us to focus on *their* interests rather than our own; even if this does not make us benevolent toward them, it does at least make us other-regarding.

Mehta also rightly argues (250–2) that Smith was concerned to show that we are the best judges of our own interests, and that other people (particularly legislators) should not presume to know what is good for us better than we ourselves do. In other words, rather than trying to replace a public-spirited motive with a self-interested one, Smith was concerned to determine who the relevant determinants of a person's interests are and to ensure that an equality of interests prevails. Still further, Mehta shows (252–3) that Smith (like many other thinkers of his time; cf. Hirschman 1997) saw reasonable self-interest as a benign alternative to a host of far more dangerous passions – especially pride, which causes people to do things like maintain colonies, go to war, and enslave people, all in opposition to their real interests. There are, then, numerous ways in which self-interest serves moral purposes in WN.

Mehta's claim that TMS makes plenty of room for a proper pursuit of self-love will be, if anything, even less controversial among Smith scholars. The reader of TMS can hardly fail to note Smith's claim that prudence, the virtue that directs people in their care for themselves, is fully approved of by the impartial spectator, even if does not provoke ardent love or admiration, and that it is connected to a number of other virtues such as frugality, industry, reliability, and so on (TMS VI.1).

In the last part of the chapter, Mehta is particularly concerned with the question of why people act in opposition to their (apparent) self-interest when they labour more than is necessary to satisfy their needs. This is a good example of an extremely common instance in which viewing people in wholly utilitarian terms simply fails to explain the facts; why do we continually strive to 'better our condition' even when we have everything we need, and when labouring is a painful burden? Smith's answer, of course, is that this striving is largely the result of the imagination, which leads us to put ourselves in the shoes of the wealthy and to contemplate how happy we would be if we had their wealth, and if people looked up to us in the way we tend to look up to the rich (TMS I.iii.2.1). We continually strive to 'better our condition' not out of any material need but out of vanity and a trick of the imagination. This, it seems, is why Mehta sees imagination as a more fundamental spring of human action in Smith's thought than self-interest: imagination is what leads people to pursue their self-interest, or rather to continue striving to 'better their condition' even when doing so is *contrary* to their (apparent) self-interest. The imagination *overrides* pure self-interest in a way that drives the economy in an important sense (WN II.iii.31).

Yet Mehta fails to adequately answer the question of why Smith applauds the seeming disconnect between our perceived self-interest and our true self-interest. He rightly notes that according to Smith happiness consists of a kind of psychological ease or a state of 'tranquillity and enjoyment' (TMS III.3.30); he also rightly notes that Smith thinks continually striving to 'better our condition' requires relentless toil and anxiety and thus undermines our tranquillity (TMS IV.1.8). Mehta remarks that there is something 'deeply odd' and even 'disquieting' about Smith's discussion of happiness, above all his claim that 'the accumulation of the means to happiness, although distinct from happiness and possibly inversely related to it, leads to the general benefit of society' (266–8). According to Mehta, 'This is the language of consolation. Most human endeavor is not aimed at procuring real satisfaction or a secure happiness, but, in transcending ourselves through our imaginations, we embark on the toil that keeps industry in motion and makes opulence a possibility' (269). Such language, however, does not seem particularly consoling. How, after all, could constant toil and the accumulation of the *means* to happiness lead to 'the general benefit society' even if it is *inversely related* to true happiness? What good is 'opulence' if attaining it makes everyone miserable?

This issue is one that I have addressed elsewhere (Rasmussen 2006), so I will not go into detail about it here except to note that Smith *is* ultimately concerned with people's happiness, and not just their opulence or their *means* to happiness. For instance, he writes that 'the happiness of mankind . . . seems to have been the original purpose intended by the Author of nature, when he brought them into existence' (TMS III.5.7), and claims that 'all constitutions of government . . . are valued only in proportion as they tend to promote the happiness of those who live under them. This is their sole use and end' (TMS IV.1.11). Smith hoped and believed that both the spontaneously organized moral system outlined in TMS and the spontaneously organized economic system outlined in WN would promote this happiness. Yet this concern for people's happiness did not make him a utilitarian, at least in the conventional sense of the term; Smith would not have advocated a moral or economic system that pursued only 'the greatest good for the greatest number', because he was concerned not with aggregate totals but with ensuring that *every individual* has a certain basic level of resources, independence, and chances for contentment, as Emma Rothschild and Amartya Sen demonstrate in their excellent chapter in the *Cambridge Companion*, 'Adam Smith's economics'. While Shaver and Mehta raise a number of thought-provoking questions about Smith's thought, in the end his thought is rather more convincing and less disquieting than they depict it.

Bibliography

Cropsey, J. (2001) *Polity and Economy: with further thoughts on the principles of Adam Smith*, South Bend: St. Augustine's Press.

Darwall, S. (1999) 'Sympathetic liberalism: recent work on Adam Smith', *Philosophy and Public Affairs*, 28: 139–64.

—— (2004) 'Equal dignity in Adam Smith', *The Adam Smith Review*, 1: 129–34.

Fleischacker, S. (2005) 'Smith und der Kulturrelativismus', in *Adam Smith als Moralphilosoph*, C. Fricke and H. Schütt (eds), Berlin: Walter de Gruyter.

Griswold, C.L. (1999) *Adam Smith and the Virtues of Enlightenment*, Cambridge: Cambridge University Press.

Hirschman, A. (1997) *The Passions and the Interests: Political Arguments for Capitalism Before its Triumph*, Princeton: Princeton University Press.

Minowitz, P. (1993) *Profits, Priests, and Princes: Adam Smith's Emancipation of Economics from Politics and Religion*, Stanford: Stanford University Press.

Otteson, J.R. (2002) *Adam Smith's Marketplace of Life*, Cambridge: Cambridge University Press.

Rasmussen, D. (2006) 'Does "bettering our condition" really make us better off?: Adam Smith on progress and happiness', *American Political Science Review*, 100: 309–18.

Stigler, G. (1971) 'Smith's travels on the ship of state', *History of Political Economy*, 3: 265–77.

Book reviews

Christel Fricke and Hans-Peter Schütt (eds.), *Adam Smith als Moralphilosoph*

Walter de Gruyter, 2005, 374 pp.

ISBN Hardback: 3110180375

Reviewed by Keith Tribe

This collection of essays arises from a conference held in Heidelberg during June 2003 and organised by the Institute of Philosophy at Karlsruhe University. All of the contributions have been substantially revised, and in fact more than half of them then translated into German. This is itself a matter requiring some discussion, although it is also worth noting here that Christel Fricke, who now teaches (in English) at the University of Oslo, managed to secure from this institution a publication subsidy for the book when German sources proved unforthcoming: so that the Norwegians have subsidised the publication in German of commentary on a writer in English.

While this does testify to the strong international interest in Adam Smith, and especially the relatively recent revival of interest in Adam Smith as a Scottish philosopher, there are several problems arising from the appearance of this work in German, some of which the editors readily acknowledge. Most obviously, it is a pity that such a substantial collection will be inaccessible to the great majority of its potential interested readership. The editors discuss at some length their decision to translate nine out of fifteen contributions from English into German, rather than six into English, but seem to neglect entirely consideration of their potential readers – a point of some irony given the manifest object of their book. Their own, quite understandable, reservations regarding quite what it means to discuss and write in a foreign language in an international context increasingly dominated by the English language are allowed to trump the simple point: that contributing to international discussion in languages other than English runs the risk of making little contribution at all. One does not here have to rehearse the argument about English as a foreign language, and what kind of basic English 'world' English might be; it should be enough to recognize that while most native users of English might be fluent, this does not necessarily mean that they all speak or understand the language *for the purposes here* any better than the editors (for example). It took a Frenchman (Pierre Force) to point out that George Stigler did not understand what Smith meant by 'self interest'. My own experience with the difficulty of learning German while

The Adam Smith Review, 4: 257–318 © 2008 The International Adam Smith Society, ISSN 1743–5285, ISBN 13: 978–0–415–45438–4.

working as a *Gastarbeiter* was considerably helped once I realised that most of the Germans I came across did not speak the language perfectly either.[1]

A second point sheds light on the gap that exists between the approach that modern philosophers take with respect to Adam Smith and that of historians and political theorists. The editors briefly discuss the existing German translations of *Wealth of Nations* and *Theory of Moral Sentiments* at the end of their introduction, under the somewhat dismissive heading 'Technisches'. It is correctly noted that there is a good modern translation of the former available; but unfortunately they refer in their bibliography to the wrong book (p. 375). The 'good modern translation' is by Monica Streissler, published in 1999; the one they list is Horst Claus Recktenwald's *Wohlstand der Nationen*, published in 1976. Quite apart from the general shortcomings of Recktenwald's translation, he used the wrong edition of *Wealth of Nations*, presumably thinking, like Cannan, that the reference edition should be the last one published in Smith's lifetime.[2] Monica Streissler made her translation from the Glasgow edition, which is based upon the third edition of 1784. It is true that Recktenwald's edition is still available as a cheap paperback, but whether that is a good thing is quite another matter.

Most of this brief editorial comment on translation is devoted to the appropriate way in which 'moral sentiments' should be rendered into German, although as previously noted they neglect a third possible variant offered by the Kosegarten translation of 1791 (listed in the bibliography on p. 376). More importantly, they are faintly dismissive of Eckstein's 1926 translation of *Theory of Moral Sentiments*, implying that there is not for this work a 'new, complete' translation to hand as there is for *Wealth of Nations*.[3] As already suggested, this might be a positive advantage, and not a matter to be regretted. Some important points are passed over here: that Walther Eckstein's German translation of *Theory of Moral Sentiments* was the first modern, scholarly edition of *Moral Sentiments* in any language; that, while the great achievements of Edwin Cannan are not in any way diminished, Eckstein set entirely new and lasting standards for Smith scholarship in general; and that the editors of the Glasgow edition relied heavily on Eckstein's work.

And so the editors insist on directing their discussion of Adam Smith to a German-speaking audience while at the same time being apparently indifferent to the relative merits of the translations of Adam Smith available to this German-speaking audience. Some of this at least is owed to the perspective that they adopt as philosophers, an approach with which I am (quite plainly) unsympathetic. Why is this?

The most simple response is that, having spent about thirty years arguing off and on for a conceptual-historical approach to eighteenth- and nineteenth-century economic discourse and against the grid readings of economists, I now encounter philosophers embarked upon a similar enterprise. My working assumption is that Smith is important because of what he wrote, and so we need to try and understand what he wrote, and why. There is also a sense in which Smith is important because of what other people have written about him; but this is an entirely different matter, although one that can also involve a historicising perspective.[4] To begin work on the former we have to consciously identify the latter, and set it to one side. By doing this we might hope to gain a clearer understanding of the problems that Smith was seeking to resolve, rather than short-circuiting this through the constant translation of the words of Adam Smith into the terms and preoccupations of subsequent discourse. For my preoccupation with 'translation issues' above is not just an expression of personal interest (although as a professional translator it is this as well), but rather with the wider issue of how we today can best understand work written over two centuries ago. It of course seems deceptively simple: we native English-speakers can pick up a copy of *Theory of Moral Sentiments* and read it – as Knud Haakonssen rightly notes, Smith's 'English is so close to modern usage that I have not modernized his spelling or punctuation, but some readers may occasionally find some forms archaic' (2002: p. xxix). But is it really that easy? For all Recktenwald's faults, there is possibly something in the liberty he takes with the title of Smith's second book – 'The Welfare of Nations' – although he is probably thinking of the kind of *Wohlstand* that German readers in the 1970s associated with Adam Smith, and not Smith's idea of welfare.[5] For while 'the annual produce of land and labour' fits into the schema of measurable year on year growth of the kind first formulated in the mid-twentieth century, 'wealth' and 'welfare' always meant more than that in the eighteenth century.

My argument is that if we are to learn anything new from Adam Smith we have to pay close attention to what he wrote;[6] the more we use Smith as a sounding-board for current disciplinary preoccupations, the more we just get back what we put there in the first place. Philosophers are of course free to use the writings of Smith in any way they see fit; but we should not assume that anything resulting from such readings tells us anything very much about Smith. This is an academic discipline talking to itself, not addressing the problem of how we can learn from seeking to understand what Adam Smith wrote.

There is of course a difference of perspective, but one of which we should be aware. The contributors to this volume produce serious and well-argued essays that turn on various problems related to what appears to them to be Smith's moral philosophy, but where Smith is for the most part brought into line with modern argument, not *vice versa*. The first essay by James Otteson for example sets out from the idea that the moral 'standards' shared among the members of a society constitute themselves in a manner analogous to a market process (p. 16). These 'standards' therefore emerge as 'institutional facts' in the sense used by John Searle, he suggests (p. 20). But notice that the mechanism upon which all this rides is a market process in which Otteson assumes that Smith thinks markets are the same sort of thing as Otteson does. Now it is a fact too little observed that modern economists know little about markets, in the sense that they tend to assume that 'everyone knows' what a proper market looks like and think the matter not worth much reflection. The entire sub-prime crisis of the autumn of 2007 was built upon this reflex. But not even Léon Walras thought markets to be a straightforward matter – his account of market process rests on an appreciation of *different sorts of market*, from trading floor in a commodity market to street stall to small shops. They were all very different, and this seems to me a rather better point of departure in understanding how social action translates into economic process. If we look at the work of Chartres on eighteenth-century agricultural markets in England (1990), or Persson on European grain markets (1999) and Miller on eighteenth-century French grain markets (1999), we can immediately see that things are more complicated in a way that is going to affect the manner in which Adam Smith thought about them, and in a way that we might not immediately grasp. I am not proposing that we might in some way reduce Smith to a historical context of our construction; rather that by understanding the problems surrounding markets in Smith's time we are helped to detach ourselves from the imposition on Smith of our own conceptions. And so when Smith directly talks of markets, or alludes to market-like processes, something we tend to think we understand,we have to be especially upon our guard.

The editors suggest in their introduction that the motivation for the compilation of these essays arises from a disjunction in the contemporary assessment of Smith's standing as a moral philosopher. Historians of economics do now acknowledge that Smith has to be approached as much as a moral philosopher as an 'economist'; but until very recently moral philosophy paid scant regard to his work. Insofar as he is assigned a place in the history of philosophy it is between the moral psychological plausibility of Hume and the normative universalism of Kant (p. 2). However, as usually happens with conference proceedings, this editorial understanding is not systematically developed in the course of the volume. The editors distinguish three broad groups among their fifteen papers: James Otteson, Christel Fricke, Carola von Villiez and Georg Lohmann treat the *Theory of Moral Sentiments* as a project seeking to establish normative foundations; the following eight contributors – Samuel Fleischacker, Carles Griswold, Aaron Garrett, Stephen Darwell, Vivienne Brown, Kate Abramson, Robert Solomon and Allan Gibbard – deal with Smith 'from the point of view of issues that play an important role in current moral-philosophical discussion' (p. 3); while the final three contributions consider Smith's moral philosophy in its historical context.

The majority of these papers then not only present Smith as a moral philosopher, he is rediscovered as a moral philosopher who 'talks our language'. Only three contributors distance themselves from this stance, and approach Smith with that degree of uncertainty which permits Smith to begin to speak for himself. As Kate Abramson so rightly states in the closing lines of her paper, 'We can take an interest in Smith as a figure in the history of philosophy, or as a source that might sustain contemporary discussion in moral philosophy; but we will learn most if we simply let Smith be Smith' (p. 250). The following paper, Robert Solomon's 'Sympathy for Adam Smith' opens by acknowledging that Smith's concept of 'sympathy' is neither unambiguous nor used in the same sense at it is today, and proceeds to analyse the term starting from the reasonable point that '. . . what 'sympathy' means [for Smith] is certainly rather unclear' (p. 254). Likewise Georg Mohr's paper on 'Moral sense' seeks to reconstruct Smith's own usage through extended discussion of Shaftesbury and Hutcheson. Only in these three papers does the reader get a sense of how understanding Smith's moral philosophy is a problem that cannot be resolved simply by applying elements of the moral philosophy of today.

Notes

1 But I must say that it was like a poke in the eye with a sharp stick (a swiftly-administered *Dorn im Auge* perhaps) when I read in James Otteson's essay that Smith was of the view that 'allgemeine moralische Standards' (p. 16) are constituted in a manner analogous to a market process – a view which I will discuss below, but where I here take exception to the casual use of anglicisms that are entirely redundant, for the German word *Maßstab*, lit. 'measuring stick/rod/staff', should be used here by a translator. And now that I look at the word that precedes it, whatever happened in this book to *sittlich*, as in Kosegarten's translation of 1791: *Theorie der sittlichen Gefühle*? In their discussion of the proper translation of the title of *Theory of Moral Sentiments* into German (pp. 12–13) this is entirely neglected by the editors.
2 See the comments on this by William Todd in 'The Text and Apparatus' (Smith 1976: p. *64*).
3 Knud Haakonssen for example freely acknowledges Eckstein's 'pioneering effort' in his own edition of *Theory of Moral Sentiments* (2002: p. xxix).
4 These two distinct endeavours are essayed in my attempt to establish what Smith actually wrote about foreign trade in *Wealth of Nations* (2006) as regards the first; and my essay on the 'Adam Smith Problem' (2008) as regards the second approach.
5 There is more than an echo here of Ludwig Erhard's *Wohlstand für alle* (1957), a work which epitomises the flight forward of the *Bundesrepublik* into the 1950s and away from the 1940s.
6 Which is about all there is to go on; the situation is similar with William Shakespeare, and the arguments that rage about Shakespeare's intentions and how we might construe them as an important resource for intellectual history.

Bibliography

Chartres, J. (1990) 'The marketing of agricultural produce, 1640–1750', in *Agricultural Markets and Trade 1500–1750*, J. Chartres (ed.), Cambridge: Cambridge University Press.
Erhard, L. (1957) *Wohlstand für alle*, Düsseldorf: Econ-Verlag.
Miller, J.A. (1999) *Mastering the Market: The State and the Grain Trade in Northern France, 1700–1860*, Cambridge: Cambridge University Press.
Persson, K.G. (1999) *Grain Markets in Europe, 1500–1900: Integration and Deregulation*, Cambridge: Cambridge University Press.

Smith, A. (1976) *An Inquiry into the Nature and Causes of the Wealth of Nations*, R.H. Campbell, A.S. Skinner, W.B. Todd (eds), Oxford: Clarendon Press.

—— (2002) *Theory of Moral Sentiments*, K. Haakonssen (ed.), Cambridge: Cambridge University Press.

Tribe, K. (2006) 'Reading trade in the *Wealth of Nations*', *History of European Ideas*, 32: 57–89.

—— (2008) '"Das Adam Smith Problem" and the origins of modern Smith scholarship', *History of European Ideas*, 34 (forthcoming).

EDITORS' RESPONSE

Christel Fricke and Hans-Peter Schütt's response to review by Keith Tribe

We would like to thank our reviewer, Dr. Keith Tribe, for taking the trouble and writing this review. And trouble it seems to have been as he expresses a general lack of sympathy with the way philosophers read texts in the history of philosophy.

We take all the points our reviewer mentions about the English language as the new *koine* and confess that – in our choice of German as the only language – the volume we edited may not find quite as many readers as it would have done had we edited it in English. However, there are some philosophers left in Germany who take the liberty of using German as their philosophical language and who want to keep their linguistic tool updated. The volume is addressing them in the first place. The gaps we have left in our introduction and bibliography can easily be filled by anyone consulting the study of the publication history of Adam Smith's writings which Keith Tribe himself has coordinated (Tribe 2002).

Keith Tribe attributes our failures mainly to the fact that we are philosophers, whereas he is a sociologist, historian and professional translator. Philosophers we are indeed, as are most of the contributors. Philosophy is one of the rare academic disciplines in which scholars try to find answers to certain questions (such as: 'What are the moral norms?' and 'What is the source of their authority?') by relying – at least to some extent – on the history of their subject. Our interest in the history of philosophy typically goes beyond purely historical research. We do not hesitate to consider the history of philosophy as a 'gold mine of philosophical ideas', of ideas to be not only discovered but also exploited for further use by studying the philosophical texts 'seriously and systematically' (Darwall 1995: ix). This approach to the history of philosophy raises a number of hermeneutical difficulties which have been discussed extensively by (mostly German) philosophers. We cannot help reading and understanding historical texts with our own minds as they have been formed during our lifetime; Adam Smith's work is no exception. There is no escape from the 'hermeneutic circle', whether for philosophers, historians, or anyone else. Why should we at all care about learning from Adam Smith as a moral philosopher (and even Keith Tribe does not consider such an interest as illegitimate) if we were not philosophers ourselves and moral philosophers in particular? Smith himself read the history of moral philosophy (and Aristotle and the Stoics in particular) in order to learn from them. All the scholars who contributed to our volume follow him in this respect, and we would like to thank them for their contributions. Our reviewer provides very little information about the various topics and arguments of these contributions, but this would probably have taken too much trouble.

Bibliography

Darwall, S. (1995) *The British Moralists and the Internal 'Ought'*, Cambridge: Cambridge University Press.

Tribe, K. (ed.) (2002) *A Critical Bibliography of Adam Smith*, H. Mizuta (adv. Ed.), London: Pickering & Chatto.

Istvan Hont, *Jealousy of Trade: International Competition and the Nation-State in Historical Perspective*

Harvard University Press, 2005, 560 pp.
ISBN Hardback: 0674010388

Reviewed by Laurence W. Dickey

During the last twenty years, Istvan Hont has published extensively on the role of political economy in the thought of European and British thinkers in the seventeenth and eighteenth centuries. Written between 1983 and 1994, the seven essays collected in this volume constitute a major contribution to our understanding of why and how so many early modern European thinkers made the interplay between political and economic thinking the main focus of their work. Taken together, the essays show how these thinkers responded to the increasing global competition for markets among the world's emerging commercial states and trading empires. Just as instructively, the essays show how these market states developed a commercial ideology that explained why peace and plenty rather than destructive commercial wars would be the result of free trading among the commercial nations of the world.

As the book-jacket of *Jealousy of Trade* (henceforth JT) indicates, Hont is regarded as a leading member of an 'influential' school of historiographical thinking – the so-called 'Cambridge School'. Since the 1970s, this school has focused its research efforts on connecting the emergence of political economy as a focus on intellectual life to changes precipitated by the expansion of trade in the Atlantic World during the seventeenth and eighteenth centuries. As a result of its work, the Cambridge School has fundamentally changed our overall understanding of political thinking in early modern European history. More specifically, it has shifted discussion of the intellectual history of the Enlightenment – in America as well as Europe – from showing it to be an 'Age of Reason' to explaining how it pointed the way from an Age of Conquest to an Age of Commerce. In this framework, it is not so much the Scientific revolution or the anti-Christian secular outlook of the French *philosophes* that explains the intellectual history of the Enlightenment as the way a new and emerging commercial ideology came to dominate the thinking of the age, including conception of what it meant to live in a civilized society rather than a martial one. It is well-known, moreover, that the Cambridge School identified the thinkers of the Scottish Enlightenment as main contributors to the themes that connected commerce to political economy on the one hand and to the civilizing process on the other.

Hont's association with the Cambridge School became evident to scholars in 1983 when he and Michael Ignatieff edited a magnificent volume of essays on the rise of political economy in the Scottish Enlightenment. As it turns out, the essays in *Wealth and Virtue* (henceforth WV) were written mainly by scholars who subsequently have been grouped together as the Cambridge School. The key theme in WV had to do with what has long been known as the 'paradox of progress' problem. At the heart of this problem is the thesis that holds that as trade expands and commercial societies become wealthier and more civilized, those same societies begin to suffer from a range of domestic dislocations that threaten social, political and religious upheaval. In explaining how Scottish thinkers addressed problems such as these, WV shows how many of the nineteenth century's criticisms of capitalism had their origins in the Enlightenment itself. Depending, then, on which strand in the paradox is emphasized, we get either a commerce-leisure-cosmopolitanism argument about the Enlightenment or one that raised all kinds of questions about the overall coherence of the Enlightenment project itself. The great merit of WV is showing how the two strands of the paradox argument existed simultaneously rather than successively in Enlightenment thinking.

Hont contributed two essays to WV; both are included in JT. Of the two, 'The rich country–poor country debate in the Scottish enlightenment' (henceforth RCPC) is Hont's signature piece – a truly brilliant essay that is filled with remarkable erudition, exacting scholarship and notes that command the reader's attention. Reading RCPC years ago profoundly changed the way I thought about the Enlightenment. Shortly thereafter, I read (in manuscript) Hont's equally compelling essay 'Free trade and the economic limits to national politics: neo-Machiavellian political economy revisited' (henceforth FT) to the same effect. From that point on, I realized that understanding the trade policy of commercial states in Europe – even between different entities within the same trading empire – was very much on the mind of key Enlightenment figures from the 1690s until late in the eighteenth century.

The RCPC and FT essays contain the core argument of JT. They account for about one-third of the page count of the seven essays collected in this volume. For the most part, the other essays revolve around themes either addressed or alluded to in the two core essays. But because the connections between all the essays are not obvious to readers of the separate essays, Hont uses the Introduction he recently wrote for JT to explain the relationships between all the essays. To that end, he divides the Introduction into two parts. In what he (37) calls Section II (37–156), he discusses specific points of intersection among the essays and explains why the essays are thematically grouped the way they are. In Section I (5–37), his claim is that although the seven essays in JT are 'closely connected by their subject matter', the 'jealousy of trade' theme serves to 'make the connections' even 'more explicit' (5). The thirty-two pages that he devotes to this theme is what I wish to focus on in this review.

Section I of the Introduction, Hont tells us, is 'a preamble to the entire volume', for it provides 'a genealogy of the theme "jealousy of trade"' (5). The aim of the genealogy is 'to clarify the role of reason of state in the shaping of political economy' (37) – that is to say, the aim is to clarify how matters of national security and the preservation of markets insinuated their way into policy decisions regarding trade. Although he should have but does not elaborate, Hont means something quite specific by 'genealogy' (5), for he has borrowed the idea of genealogy from a Cambridge colleague, Raymond Geuss, and uses it as a conceptual device to bring the essays in JT into what Max Weber would call meaningful relationship with each other (Geuss 1999). Knowing that – what a genealogical approach to history entails – tells us much about the structural ribbing of JT.

According to Geuss (4, 11, 13–14), a genealogy offers an account of an 'historically contingent conjunction' of a number of 'separate' and 'diverse' factors, when interpreted as a developmental sequence, form themselves into a 'synthesis of meaning' – into what Weber in his methodological writings called a complex historical meaning. The challenge of genealogical history, Geuss says, is twofold: to explain the processes and circumstances that bring the 'separate strands of meaning' into relationship with each other; and to write about the connectedness of these separate strands while 'disentangling' each from the others in order to grant it historical autonomy. As Geuss notes, writing history this way involves showing how the separate strands of meaning constitute 'successive layers' in a larger meaning complex that is formed over time. On those terms, the 'jealousy of trade' theme that Hont proposes to approach genealogically is actually a composite historiographical concept, the layers of which refer to particular moments of an unfolding historical process. Among philosophers of historical methodology, Wilhelm Dilthey would say that jealousy of trade is an historiographical concept which simultaneously encompasses the moments of which it is the result and expresses the connectedness that provides the developmental sequence with its overall conceptual unity.

There are, then, organizational and narrative difficulties that arise once one decides to explore the jealousy of trade theme genealogically. First, a balance must be struck between the general and the particular in the narrative. On one level, in an essay collection of this sort, that balance need not be an issue, for each of the seven essays was originally written to stand on its own. On another level, though, balance needs to be established between the essays as particulars and as constituting a more general whole. After all, as Hont notes, the essays do not connect themselves. Hence the task of the long Introduction Hont wrote for this volume.

For a scholar like Hont, whose learning is as broad as his command of his subject is deep, the challenge of the Introduction is to know when to let go of particulars for the sake of developing clearer lines of more general interpretation. Here, I think, the problem is that Hont uses the Introduction to JT not only to talk about 'the historical genealogy of jealousy of trade' as the organizational nexus of the entire volume (Section I: 5–37) but also to add particulars about the individual essays that follow (Section II: 37–156). As the page count of the sections reveals, there is a lack of proportionality between the two, with the result that the particular overwhelms the general at precisely the point where the general has to be the priority. Notwithstanding this organizational issue, Section I of the Introduction provides an argument that is designed to give coherence to all the particulars that follow. What is that argument?

If we begin with the notion that jealousy of trade is a composite historiographical concept whose layers form themselves into a larger synthesis of diachronic meaning, then Hont's task in Section I is to identify the separate layers/moments/processes that are encompassed by the concept. Taking a cue from David Hume, who addressed the issue of jealousy of trade in writings of the 1750s, Hont begins his genealogy in the seventeenth century, for it was then that a 'conflation' of three different processes occurred (8). First, the quest for 'national glory' by means of warfare became increasingly expensive (16), creating a persistent demand on the part of the King/State/ Nation for revenue to fund military projects aimed an enhancing 'national security' or imperial expansion. Second, although national self-defence had been an abiding concern of European thinkers since the renaissance, it was not until the seventeenth century that statesmen began to see profit from trade as a funding source for national security and/or military adventurism. Given this orientation, it was but a short step to seeing the protection of trade routes, colonies and lucrative commercial markets as well as institutionalization of monopolistic trade practices as matters of state – that is, of political and military necessity. Third, and finally, the success of Holland in its long war with Spain in the late sixteenth and early seventeenth centuries taught European statesmen two things: that economic 'plenty' was rapidly becoming the basis of political power in the modern world; and that state promotion of commercial expansion was the best way to ensure the political and military integrity of a nation (23). Two commonplace sayings of the seventeenth century, both of which figure prominently in the jealousy of trade argument, speak powerfully to the changing understanding of statecraft in early modern European history: money is 'the nerve of war' (16); and the longest purse rather than the longest sword is the winning formula for warfare in the modern world.

While describing this initial moment of synthetic meaning in the genealogy of jealousy of trade – a moment, he says, is epitomized in Colbert's management of France's transformation from a territorial monarchy geared to conquest to a trading empire interested in commerce (22 ff.) – Hont offers his own reflections on how this seventeenth-century moment shaped long-term tendencies in the political thinking of early modern Europe. His view is that once the interests of government and trade could be seen dovetailing in public debates about national security, economics had to become a matter of 'reason of state' (11 ff.). And so it became, with the result that the related but 'premodern' (because 'pre-economic') notions of 'reason of state' (Machiavelli) and 'jealousy of trade' (Hobbes) were transformed so as to take heed of the new roles trade and international economic competition played in the growing rivalries between commercial states in the modern world (9). Hont signals this fundamental change in political thinking by calling economically informed reason of state 'truly modern' – that is, to use his own revealing language, 'post-Machiavellian' and 'post-Hobbesian' (9, 11 ff.). As he knowingly put it, neither Machiavelli nor Hobbes had given priority to protecting or expanding trade in their discussions of national self-interest. Accordingly, Hont follows Hume in presenting modern reason of state as a 'post-Machiavellian development' (p. 9).

Although Hont uses the phrase 'post-Machiavellian reason of state' (13) as another way of entering into jealousy of trade, he also seems to sow confusion when he occasionally calls jealousy of trade 'economic neo-Machiavellianism' (9). In fact, at one point he says, 'Jealousy of trade was an extrapolation of Machiavellianism to the modern trading economy' (9). His explanation of how he can use terminology this way draws our attention to the second layer (that is, synthetic moment) in the jealousy of trade concept.

In Hont's work (24 ff.), economic neo-Machiavellianism expresses a widely held eighteenth-century perception that, despite the shift of political thinking from conquest to commerce, premodern Machiavellian currents still informed the policies of many trading states when it came to matters of political economy. In this context, Hont dwells on the anti-Machiavellian outlook of thinkers who associated the cut-throat politics of international economic competition with Machiavelli's notion of a 'politics of [national] increase' (16, 18, 21) – that is, with the imperialistic and mercantilistic economic policies of some of the larger trading empires. On that score, anti-mercantilist writers of the eighteenth century regarded neo-Machiavellian political economy as a 'shadow' clouding the vision of statesmen of modern commercial societies (29, 35), a shadow that allowed what Benjamin Constant would later call the spirit of conquest to persist into an Age of Commerce (Constant 1988). As an alternative to this 'corrupt' reason of state, anti-Machiavellian writers recommended free trade and liberal political economy as the key to 'good' reason of state (16).

As Hont perceptively shows, the persistence of Machiavellianism in eighteenth-century thinking about reason of state was a policy consequence of a failure to understand how free trade worked in the modern commercial world. Here the argument was that jealousy of trade corrupted the judgment of governmental officials, prompting them aggressively to pursue bellicose mercantilist rather than pacific liberal trade policies with regard to economic rivals. What these officials failed to see was that when applied to international commerce, free trade, in Hont's words, 'would not remain a zero-sum game' but rather would redound to the interest of all (37).

As we learn from Hont in JT as well as from others before him (e.g. Gilbert 1961) and Albert Hirschman (1977), this is the promise of *doux-commerce* – the thesis found in the writings of Montesquieu and Hume as well as John Adams that under the auspices of free trade policy commerce would unite in peace, plenty and cosmopolitan fellowship, not divide in war, the trading nations of the world (Dickey 2004). Throughout JT, Hont explains what lies behind the promise of *doux-commerce*. Three of his arguments are of special interest because they form the second layer of the genealogy of trade argument.

First, he devotes much attention to the 'retrospective histories' (6) written by anti-Machiavellian writers who wish to advance the agenda of liberal political economy by showing how commerce not only created more wealth for trading nations but, in the process, produced more civilized and enlightened citizens as well. Second, he dwells on how Montesquieu and Hume realized that the operation of the so-called 'self-balancing [economic] mechanism of international free trade' (36) – an eighteenth-century discovery Jacob Viner has told us (Viner 1937; Dickey 1993: 226 ff.) – ensured that sooner or later economic laws of production costs (e.g., wages, prices and quantity of money) would militate against the permanent concentration of wealth in richer countries relative to poorer ones. In accordance with this awareness, Montesquieu and Hume as well as Benjamin Franklin labelled as uninformed reason of state policies that reacted in heavy-handed economic, political and military ways to economic rivals. Better, they said, to adjust to the built-in competitive advantage that poorer nations had in certain economic areas than to try to vitiate those advantages through misguided reason of state policies. Third, even though the self-balancing mechanism suggested that it would be futile for a rich nation to try to preserve market shares by way of unnatural means, the reality of lost markets, unemployment and decline in national wealth weighed heavily on statesmen, inclining them to formulate policies that flew in the face of the economic logic of what Viner called the 'automatic mechanism'. It is fair to say, therefore, that the anti-Machiavellian writers and *doux-commerce* theorists regarded this 'rich country–poor country' moment as the true test of modern reason of state, for it required the statesmen of the former to adhere in practice to the cosmopolitan outlook that the *doux-commerce* thesis promised would inform civilized reason of state policy – which is to say, the expectation was that statesmen would sacrifice the short-term national interest of their countries for the sake of the long-term economic well-being of the trading community as a whole. Hont underlines this point by citing Hume to the effect that this would happen were the statesmen of rich countries to 'adopt . . . enlarged and benevolent sentiments' toward their poorer trading partners (36).

In this, political economy's doctrine of free trade needs a healthy dose of anti-jealousy moralism to achieve the 'commercial mutuality' (37) and cosmopolitan fellowship promised by *doux-commerce* theorists. As Hume suggested in the 1750s, this is the moment of decision of modern reason of state – the moment when the emerging civilized ideals of 'humanity and cosmopolitan fellowship would triumph over national self-interest without denigrating the economic system that powered the civilizing process itself (Hume 1987: 253–80). Indeed, in the final analysis it is the assimilation of humanitarian and cosmopolitan values to free trade that enabled truly modern (that is, liberal) reason of state to arise and inform the commercial policies of market states – which means that liberal political economy is an ethical/ moral as well as an economic system of value (Haskell 1985). Or, to put it another way, modern reason of state may be said to supplant Machiavellian reason of state because benevolence has become the moral means to the economic end of reciprocity among the market states of the world.

This brings us to a final consideration about the rich country–poor country moment in eighteenth-century political economy. Conventionally considered, the free trade doctrine of liberal political economy is viewed as having the potential to knit the trading nations of the world together into a community of cosmopolitan fellowship. One of Hont's great insights involves turning this view upside down (especially chapter 7, 147–56). For once the dynamic of the rich country–poor country argument is factored into the liberal outlook it becomes clear (as Hume and Josiah Tucker both appreciated) that, while in the short run the good will shown by a rich country to a poor country will allow the latter of become more prosperous, in the long run that same good will redounds to the economic interest of the rich country. There seems to be, therefore, an economic pay-off for rich countries to promote cosmopolitanism in the political economy of the eighteenth century. And insofar as the long-term end justifies the short-term means, it would appear that cosmopolitanism is the means by which rich countries sustain the so-called imperialism of free trade.

Although the means and ends aspects of liberal political economy are difficult to separate, the fact is that in the context of the rich country–poor country debate a commercial and civilized society's only recourse for long-term economic viability involves adopting a short-term moral attitude towards its less advantaged rivals. As Tucker, Hume and Smith all recognized, the decision to proceed this way grew out of calculations about long-term national interests and not from any endorsement of utopian hopes for cosmopolitan fellowship. The problem was that means and ends tension in liberal political economy soon became obvious to nineteenth-century critics of capitalism/industrial society. For example, in 1843 the young Friedrich Engels, himself writing about 'trade jealousy', mocked 'modern liberal economics' for its ideological 'sophistry and hypocrisy', its 'sham philanthropy' and its 'sham humanity'. Accordingly, he saw 'all the [liberals'] beautiful phrases about . . . world citizenship' as an ideological 'cover' to 'conceal the immoral nature of trade' (Marx and Engels 1983: 278–83). Indeed, for Engels playing up the 'humanity' of free trade involved 'misusing morality for immoral [economic] purposes'. Thus, when Engels asked, 'when have you [liberal economists] been moral without being interested', we have no trouble grounding the remark in the rich country–poor country debates of the eighteenth century.

In the most general terms, then, Hont's conception of jealousy of trade draws attention to two clusters of meaningful and related action in the history of political economy: the 'military revolution' of the seventeenth century; and the rich country–poor country problem of the eighteenth century. Moreover, and without labouring the point, he says that the 'international market rivalry' of the eighteenth century produced insights into the politics of the modern world that 'continue to be relevant for the twenty-first century' (4). With his eyes firmly fixed on the challenges of today (5), Hont goes on to say (especially 111–56) that today's debate about 'globalization . . . lacks conceptual novelty' (155). One only has to read about the European Union in a recent article in the *New York Times* (3 Mar. 2006) by Floyd Norris to appreciate this point: to wit: 'Despite all the talk in Europe about one market, nationals will still count for more than the central operation. And governments [France in this case] will use their power when and as they wish'. Hont's book grounds this way of looking at things in the history of early modern Europe and warns us about the many ideological paradoxes of being modern.

Bibliography

Constant, B. (1988) *Political Writings*, B. Fontana (ed. and trans.), Cambridge: Cambridge University Press.

Dickey, L. (ed.) (1993) A. Smith, *An Inquiry into the Nature and Causes of the Wealth of Nations*, Indianapolis, IN: Hackett.

—— (2004) '*Doux-commerce* and humanitarian values: free trade, sociability and universal benevolence in eighteenth-century thinking', in *Grotius and the Stoa*, H.W. Blom and L.C. Winkel (eds), Aasen: Van Gorcum, pp. 271–318.

Geuss, R. (1999) *Morality, culture, and history*, Cambridge: Cambridge University Press.

Gilbert, F. (1961) *To the Farewell Address: Ideas of Early American Foreign Policy*, Princeton: Princeton University Press.

Haskell, T.L. (1985) 'Capitalism and the origins of the humanitarian sensibility', *American Historical Review*, 90: 339–61.

Hirschman, A.O. (1977) *The Passions and the Interests: Political Arguments for Capitalism before its Triumph*, Princeton: Princeton University Press.

Hont, I. and Ignatieff, M. (eds) (1985) *Wealth and Virtue: The Shaping of Political Economy in the Scottish Enlightenment*, Cambridge: Cambridge University Press.

Hume, D. (1987) *Essays Moral, Political, and Literary*, Eugene Miller (ed.), Indianapolis: Liberty Fund.

Marx, K. and Engels, F. (1983) *Letters on Capital*, A. Drummond (trans.), London and Detroit: New Park Publications.

Viner, J. (1937) *Studies in the Theory of International Trade*, New York: Harper and Brothers.

Iain McLean, *Adam Smith Radical and Egalitarian: An Interpretation for the 21st Century*

(With a foreword by Gordon Brown)
Edinburgh University Press, 2006, 272 pp.

ISBN Hardback: 1403977917

Reviewed by Leonidas Montes

It is not often that one has the opportunity of reading a good academic book with a foreword by the British Prime Minister. We all know that Gordon Brown is not George W. Bush. The Prime Minister certainly can write a reasonably good two-page foreword on Adam Smith. He has his academic credentials. Moreover, he is also a Scot. Although Gordon Brown was born in Glasgow, he attended Kirkcaldy High School. His father was minister of Kirkcaldy parish church. So like Smith, Gordon Brown is a native of Kirkcaldy.

According to the author, this book emerges as a response to Gordon Brown's challenge, which is to answer the following four questions:

1   Is Smith, the author of the invisible hand, also the Smith of the helping hand?
2   Would the Adam Smith who has been the inspiration behind the right-of-centre Adam Smith Institute be more likely to feel at home with the left-of-centre John Smith Institute?
3   Or, is Smith of *The Theory of Moral Sentiments* the Jekyll to the *Wealth of Nations* Hyde?
4   Is it possible two centuries and more on from his famous work the *Wealth of Nations* to find a way of reconciling his apparently contrasting views: that social behaviour is influenced by sympathy and that economic behaviour is motivated by self-interest?

You don't need to reach the end of the book to know these answers. The title of the book already suggests in advance an affirmative answer to questions 1, 2 and 4. For those familiar with Smith, question 3 is also rather common. In my view, the crucial issue of this book is whether the author actually needed these questions by Gordon Brown to write this book. More challenging is whether the book could have been better without Gordon Brown's challenge. My guess, with an academic bias, is yes. McLean is at his best when he explains the Scottish Smith of the eighteenth century, not Brown's Smith of the twenty-first.

In his Preface McLean sets out that the purpose of his book, besides tackling Brown's challenge, 'is to explain the Scottish Smith of the eighteenth century to the citizens of the twenty-first'. As the title of the book suggests, McLean's Adam Smith is radical and egalitarian. And his radical egalitarianism is rooted in Scotland. Throughout his book, the author is concerned with the Scottish context. And he knows it well, achieving an interesting and accessible narrative.

The first chapter is entitled 'The Life of an Absent-minded Professor'. In this lively introductory chapter McLean goes through some well-known aspects of Smith's life with a special concern for the context in which he lived. For example McLean explains the situation surrounding the Snell Exhibition. He argues that Smith didn't accept this scholarship to become an Episcopelian priest, neither did he use it in bad faith (5–8). In endnote 5 he gives an interesting opinion about the legend of Smith reading Hume while at Oxford. In endnote 7 there is a delightful story about David Hume, regarding his house at the famous development in Edinburgh, New Town. McLean also explains Hume's reading of Lucian while he was dying, and how Smith reacted to his death. Although he mentions that the prudent public Smith did not publish Hume's *Dialogues concerning Natural Religion*, he does not mention that Hume left him money to do so. Was it a last joke from Hume, whose last wish could have been to trouble his too prudent friend?

In 'A Weak State and a Weak Church' McLean goes over Scotland before and after the 1707 Act of Union arguing that a weak state and church contributed to the shaping of the Scottish Enlightenment. He explores Smith's relationship with Robert Burns, a theme that fascinates the author throughout the book. Chapter 3, 'A Non-religious Grounding of Morals: Smith and the Scottish Enlightenment' deals with the context surrounding the Aikenhead case, who was hanged in 1697 for blasphemy. McLean recalls that Smith was well aware not only of the Aikenhead case, but also of the execution of Jean Calas in 1762. Briefly he goes over Mandeville and Rousseau, and tackles Smith's invisible hand not as Rothschild's killing hand, but as Hayek's hand of unintended consequences. For Maclean the invisible hand represents 'Smith's profound insight [is] that order can arise spontaneously' (p. 53). Then he briefly tackles sympathy and the impartial spectator, suggesting that 'Smith's philosophy . . . is profoundly egalitarian' (p. 55). McLean explains the change of the famous and long Atonement passage, for that peculiarly short sentence of Tartarus and Elysium (TMS II.ii.3.12), with its notorious Humean flavour. He ends up with some interesting remarks on the famous chess board passage (TMS VI.ii.2.16).

Chapter 4, 'Merriment and Diversion: Smith on Public Finance and Public Choice', goes over Smith's political economy, explaining Smith's take on physiocracy and mercantilism. Smith is not Steuart, as we all know. Then McLean explains Smith's four stages theory, suggesting that 'Smith can indeed be called a man of the Left, but not for the labour theory of value' (69). I believe this is generally shared by almost everybody, regardless of political preferences. McLean briefly mentions the militia and Standing Army issue, and how Smith might have changed his mind on this point. Although Smith was a founding member of the Poker Club, and its purpose was literally 'to stir up the militia cause', in WN he defends a professional army. I personally think this is a fascinating subject, and one would have wished, as in many other passages of McLean's book, that the author could have delved a bit more into this issue. Then McLean proceeds to explain why Smith's position on taxes and education can be deemed as left-wing. But he finishes up with Smith's concern with incentives. The latter would prompt us to see Smith as a public choice minded person, especially when he thinks about politicians.

In a special chapter devoted to 'The Invisible Hand and the Helping Hand', McLean begins by too readily dismissing the Adam Smith Problem. Then he comes back to the invisible hand. As has been already suggested, although he is proposing a reading from the left, he is not Emma Rothschild when it comes to the invisible hand. Intellectual honesty leads him to James Otteson's *Marketplace of Life*. The invisible hand would follow the principle of Hayek's spontaneous order. According to McLean, Emma Rothschild 'perhaps underplays the underlying *concept*' (87). However, the invisible hand 'may require the helping hand of government' (89). Then McLean shows his concern of a 'capture of Adam Smith by the American right' blaming a 'staunchly conservative-libertarian think tank'. He is referring to 'Liberty Fund of Indianapolis – to which all scholars are in debt' (91).

The next chapter is entitled 'The French and American Smiths'. After underlining the Quebec Act of 1774, McLean briefly goes over Madison, Jefferson and Hamilton, in order to confirm 'that Madison was wholly Adamite, Jefferson was more naively Jamesian and Hamilton was almost entirely Jamesian' (109). On France he challenges some commonly held views on Smith and the French Revolution, giving an interesting contrast on how the French Enlightenment, through Condorcet's letters, understood sympathy, or actually could not understand it (117–18). This interpretation might suggest that McLean's reading of Smith's sympathy might also be more Hayekian than a lefty could wish!

The last chapter, 'Adam Smith Today', attempts to show that Smith would favour the French trilogy of 'liberty, equality and fraternity'. McLean claims that Smith could be Schumpeterian, but also a precursor of general economic equilibrium theory. I would agree with the former, but not the latter. Smith's relationship with models, and particularly with general economic equilibrium theory, is more complex (see Montes 2003). As we all know, Smith was certainly an egalitarian. So, as part of Gordon Brown's challenge, the author suggests that we should know that 'TMS sets out a system of egalitarian and post-Christian ethics which attract moralistic and frugal politicians of the Left to this day' (130). On this, I believe Smith was much more sceptical about politicians.

Then McLean moves to a general account of a Marxian Smith and a conservative Smith, to end up with his favoured 'Social-Democratic Smith', that is a Brownian Smith. McLean is honest enough: 'It would be going too far to claim that Gordon Brown's Adam Smith is "the only" Adam Smith . . . the modern Right can legitimately lay claim' (147). To wrap up he gives six arguments that are common with 'Adam Smith's Gordon Brown (and equivalently with Gordon Brown's Adam Smith)' (147–8). Although some of us would not share McLean's notion of equivalence, we would agree with the last sentence of his book: '[Smith] is one of the chief architects of the modern world'.

All in all, this book is very good reading, but throughout the different chapters one has the sense that the author could have gone deeper into some issues that he raises. There is much awareness of Smith's context, but in my view Gordon Brown's influence hampers McLean's concern with our Adam Smith of the Scottish Enlightenment. It is certainly encouraging to have Gordon Brown writing a Preface. Actually he had introduced the 2002 Edinburgh Lecture on Adam Smith (held at Edinburgh University as part of the 'Enlightenment Lecture Series 2001–2'). It is beneficial that a book like this one could have a broader audience. The Foreword can help out on that. But after reading the book, which is a good book, one has the feeling that Gordon Brown represents a deus ex machina for a good representation. If it opens up with Brown's challenge, and ends up answering this challenge, McLean's contribution is not there. It is in the middle, when he shows us in a very accessible manner his own view of Adam Smith and the Scottish Enlightenment.

Ian McLean suggests that 'a good rule of thumb to follow in opening a book on Smith is to ask "Does the author show awareness that Smith was a Scot, and that eighteenth-century Scotland was very different from eighteenth-century England?"' (153). The author is loyal to this rule of thumb. Although most aspects are well-known to a Smith scholar, one could argue that the book, paraphrasing Hume's letter to Smith after the publication of *Wealth of Nations*, 'has Depth and Solidity and Acuteness, and is so much illustrated by curious Facts' (*Corr.* p. 186). But let me add that when the author warns us that he might 'have missed important contributions', he is right.

The author reminds us that Gordon Brown's MP constituency includes Kirkcaldy. But McLean's radical and egalitarian Adam Smith of the Scottish Enlightenment is much better when it is not part of Brown's political constituency. Then it is a great reading. And overall it is a book to recommend for general readers and Smith scholars.

AUTHOR'S RESPONSE

Iain McLean's response to review by Leonidas Montes

I thank Leonidas Montes for his supportive and perceptive review. I have little to disagree with, but I focus on his more critical points.

> *(T)he crucial issue of this book is whether the author actually needed these questions by Gordon Brown to write this book.*

As Montes points out, Gordon Brown's four questions, and my answers, are no surprise to the community of Smith scholars, or more generally of (Scottish) Enlightenment scholars. Therefore, in an obvious sense I did not *need* the questions. And Smith scholars may find it frustrating that I spend a lot of my rather short book dealing with questions which to them (us) are pretty trite. But bear in mind that my primary audience is the interested general reader.

On the other hand, as Montes delicately puts it, Gordon Brown is not George W. Bush. Furthermore, his Edinburgh lecture, and his foreword to my book, are not speechmakers' confections. When the finance minister (now prime minister) of a large industrial democracy asks intellectual questions on the interpretation of Adam Smith, I think that scholars have not only an opportunity, but indeed a duty, to try to answer them. Adam Smith talked to policymakers and they talked to him. That has rather gone out of fashion, which I think is a shame. As Brown explains in his Foreword, I have also been an academic adviser to anybody in government who was prepared to listen, on contemporary issues of UK public policy. I admire Smith's role as a policy adviser, which is why I give it more prominence than most authors of short books on Smith. In this spirit of revisiting an Enlightenment that is interested in policy as well as in pure theory, I was particularly pleased that Edinburgh University Press – the Strahans and Cadells of our day – agreed to publish my book.

> *McLean's radical and egalitarian Adam Smith of the Scottish Enlightenment is much better when it is not part of Brown's political constituency.*

If Montes merely means that the parts of my book that deal with Smith in his contemporary context are better than the parts which deal with the present day, then I thank him for the praise and accept the criticism. If, however, he means that I overemphasize the Scottish and even more closely the Fife context, then I disagree. As I say in my Preface, Adam Smith, Gordon Brown, and I are all Fifers. Not only do Scottish mentalities (then and now) differ from English, but even east coast Scots differ from west coast Scots.

Smith saw how the Union of 1707 had damaged Kirkcaldy and boosted Glasgow, because it switched Scotland's trade from the east coast to the west. When Hume writes to Smith in 1769 that he has a 'View of Kirkaldy from my Windows' and jokily invites his friend to meet half-way, regretting that 'There is no Habitation on the Island of Inch-keith', I think it is (in its way) important for modern readers to know that:

- you can still see that view from Hume's stair window (I checked it as part of my field research); and that
- there is still no habitation on Inchkeith, which lies half-way between Edinburgh and Kirkcaldy in the firth of Forth.

(T)hroughout the different chapters one has the sense that the author could have gone deeper into some issues that he raises.

I would have loved to do so, but I had a word limit and an intended audience to think about. In retrospect, I should have gone deeper into the rich variety of modern interpretations of TMS. I agree that I should also have said more about militias and standing armies (and, perhaps, the Second Amendment). But I don't apologize for being as curt as I am about the Adam Smith Problem. I just can't understand how or why anyone takes it seriously. Likewise, I acknowledge that I am brusque about attempts to rehabilitate Sir James Steuart. I appeal to the Salieri-and-Mozart test that I mention in a footnote. Read Steuart and Smith side by side and decide which of them is an economist.

Smith's concern with incentives . . . would prompt us to see Smith as a public choice minded person, especially when he thinks about politicians.

Absolutely it would, and should. I try to bring out parallels between Smith and some modern public-choicers, notably Mancur Olson. Olson was a Smithian in lots of ways including his personality (a Norwegian farm boy from Nebraska advising governments in Washington – does it remind you of somebody 200 years earlier?). The risk here is to assume that if somebody is in the public choice tradition, he necessarily shares the normative political views of a William Niskanen or a George Stigler. Smith's comments about merriment and diversion, which I borrow for a chapter title, show that he knows politicians are driven by self-interest, and that they promote special interests including their own. But this did not lead him to believe that all of them were selfish, all of the time, or that it was futile for him to advise those who were prepared to listen. In return, *they* respected *him*.

While I am at it, let me say that I did not intend to 'blame' the Liberty Fund for their munificent support of Smith scholarship. Nothing blame-worthy there; and I am glad for the opportunity to make my view clear. My complaints against groups who have tried to capture Adam Smith for a conservative agenda are not directed at the Liberty Fund, and I am sorry that that paragraph was carelessly worded.

McLean's reading of Smith's sympathy might also be more Hayekian than a lefty could wish!

Montes sees Smith as much more closely related to Hayekians (including, presumably, Austrian economists) than to general equilibrium theorists. I don't disagree, but I have two responses:

1   for what it is worth, (some) general equilibrium theorists talk of Smith as if he is one of them;
2   Consider, for instance, this from WN V.ii.e.10 (with my emphasis). I think it has a general equilibrium flavour, and it is not the only such passage:

> Both ground-rents and the ordinary rent of land are a species of revenue which the owner, in many cases, enjoys without any care or attention of his own. Though a part of this revenue should be taken from him in order to defray the expences of the state, *no discouragement will thereby be given to any sort of industry.* The annual produce of the land and labour of the society, the real wealth and revenue of the great body of the people, might be the same after such a tax as before.

In conclusion, I repeat my thanks both to Montes and to Prime Minister Brown for setting me off down this road.

Leonidas Montes and Eric Schliesser (eds), *New Voices on Adam Smith*

Routledge Studies in the History of Economics
(With a foreword by Knud Haakonssen) Routledge, 2006, 364 pp.

ISBN Hardback: 0–415–35696–2

Reviewed by Caroline Gerschlager

Introduction

The present collection of papers on Adam Smith edited by Leonidas Montes and Eric Schliesser comprises the contribution of fourteen scholars who defended doctoral theses on Adam Smith in the US and Europe between 2000–2004.[1] The main purpose of the collection is the 'broadening of the study of Smith' (8), because as the philosopher Knud Haakonssen asserts in his foreword, 'our understanding . . . has been severely hampered by narrow economic boundaries' (xviii). Against this background most of the contributions voluntarily adopt a philosophical perspective;[2] rather than a 'reconsideration of his views in economics' (8). In other words, the dominant philosophy of the present collection on Adam Smith is to provide '*more* than economics'.

The chapters are heterogeneous. They give priority to Adam Smith the philosopher, and his fame as a founding father of economics does not much interest them, a fact that potential economic readers may find puzzling. In this review I suggest considering the philosophical foundations of Adam Smith that the present collection proffers from an economic point of view.

Adam Smith lived and wrote in times of change and his work is above all indicative of this change: it anticipates much of the new – Smith the visionary and contriver of a new economic system, for example – but still contains many remainders of the old. The present collection shows how Adam Smith was anchored in both of these worlds and I have therefore chosen it as a leitmotif for the following discussion.

I

The first section (three chapters) deals with Adam Smith's sources and influences.

Ryan Hanley reminds us of Smith's admiration for Aristotle and his ethics, which he reconstructed in his *Theory of Moral Sentiments*. Hanley particularly focuses on Smith's views of virtue as a means of constraining, or better still, educating ordinary self-love, or selfishness. Hanley's intention is to draw attention to Smith's role as an antecedent and advocate of virtue ethics in moral philosophy. He concludes with the political role that Smith provided for the 'wise and virtuous man' [who seeks the] 'material betterment of the lowest of ranks' and is needed in the new society 'as reformer and legislator of a great state' (20).

Edith Kuiper adopts a feminist reading and makes us aware of how much Adam Smith's new system of thought was still influenced by the old gender prejudice. Her reading glaringly reveals Smith's blindness with regard to the issue of women, which – probably to the surprise of many economists – was already on the agenda in Adam Smith's days. In her analysis Kuiper illuminates the quality and the intensity of the issue in the eighteenth century by drawing on popular women's pamphlets of the time.

Robert Mitchell illuminates Smith's insistence on human psychology and finally also on human foolishness in relation to his concept of a system making innovative use of the power of abstraction. Mitchell points out that Smith's systematization of society in *The Theory of Moral Sentiments* paved the way for understanding and controlling the mechanisms of social change and progress in the conservative and radical political theories of the Romantic age after him.

Hanley meticulously reconstructs Smith's discussions of the virtuous character and his debts to Aristotle. From an economic point of view, however, the importance he attributes to the individual character in Smith overlooks the fact that *The Theory of Moral Sentiments* also conveys important insights into the specific 'weakness' of virtue (Schneewind 1990: 63), one of which is that the appeal to virtue does not suffice to countervail the excesses of self-love in society. Smith was adamant that society depends on moral rules and bounds (TMS III.5.2:163) and his modernity consists in his analysis of the way these rules were generated and why they were pursued.

Kuiper's reading is commendable and it should be noted that it is also the only article in the collection that is critical of Adam Smith.

Mitchell aptly highlights the complexity of Smith as a (Scottish) systematizer, on which alternative political ideologies have been able to build after him, and his contribution is also the first in the collection to suggest that Smith is difficult to classify as an author.

II

The second section (five chapters) focuses on moral philosophy and – from a different perspective – confirms Mitchell's estimation that Smith is indeed difficult to classify. Economists regard questions about the foundations and the appropriateness of morality as being fuzzy and are not always interested in asking them for that reason. This section could nevertheless be interesting for economists as it shows the extent to which Smith, the founding father of political economy, was still concerned with moral bounds.

So what moral standards did Smith actually recommend? A double standard, says Carola von Villiez. Fonna Forman-Barzilai also maintains that Smith provides *various levels* of abstraction in relation to moral standards, and Patrick Frierson deals with their social construction and potential development.

Notwithstanding the heterogeneity of the contributions to this section, they all have in common their rejection of the idea that Smith provided a 'one recipe' approach to ethics. As a consequence, they also reject the dominant view in philosophy that Smith's standards can be conceived in utilitarian terms solely. Thus, Chad Flanders points out that Smith's utilitarian justification of the 'irregularity of sentiments' and their distorting role on human judgment is not 'the whole story' (203).

The authors show from different perspectives how difficult it is to assign Smith to one single approach. However, there are two observations to be made from the economic perspective.

Adam Smith was important as a thinker who separated economics from moral philosophy. Whether this is justified or not has been a recurrent theme in the history of economic thought, to wit the infamous 'Das Adam Smith Problem'. But it is clear that the actual separation also mirrors the new role of both the economic and the moral domain in society. It is therefore remarkable that this separation and its consequences for moral philosophy are not brought up at all in philosophical discussion.

It is also striking that the present focus on ethical standards leaves out the significance that Adam Smith attributed to institutions. From an economic perspective, ethical human conduct (and education) is improbable in society without appropriate institutions to support it. The authors do not really appreciate this aspect, with the exception of Lauren Brubaker, who makes an explicit link between Smith's ethical and economic systems.

III

The third section (three chapters) deals with Adam Smith's economics.

In her reconstruction of Adam Smith's economic arguments against Bernard Mandeville's fable of the bees and by drawing on his *Lectures of Jurisprudence* Jimena Hurtado-Prieto reveals that Smith disagreed on many important accounts with Mandeville, in whom he saw an advocate of the old mercantilist economy who wanted to conserve the old hierarchy in which the poor had no prospects for becoming rich.

With the development of the economy the use of paper money also increased, and Maria Pia Paganelli is interested in the status that Smith attributes to this innovation. She claims that according to Smith the over-issue by banks of paper money could best be held in check by market forces.

Leonidas Montes studies the influence of Isaac Newton's new insights on Adam Smith's thoughts on the economy. He takes on the standard economic claim that Smith's system is to be seen as already containing the germs of general equilibrium theory. According to him Newton's insights into the order of the universe and their proper application to the social world sought by Smith, particularly his emulation of 'Newton's third law of action and reaction' (257), would not bring about equilibrium but rather disequilibrium.

Hurtado-Prieto's focus on the differences between Smith's new economic conception and that of Mandeville is original and illuminating. It should nevertheless be pointed out that they both shared the insight that human intention is not always and not necessarily the cause of what is produced by human (inter-)action.

Paganelli's contribution on the role of paper money in Adam Smith is an attempt to reconstruct Adam Smith as an early member of today's free banking school. According to this school, market competition (among issuing banks) is the most efficient means for controlling the supply of money in the economy. Her claim is not convincing, as it is precisely in relation to money issuance by banks that Smith detected what we today would call market failure (cf. also Young 2005: 109).

I agree with Montes on the conceptual difference between Smith's dynamic conception of the economy and twentieth-century general equilibrium theory in general. I would also have agreed with him if he had simply claimed that there is more to Adam Smith's economics than general equilibrium theory. However, I disagree when he denies that Newton's influence on Smith totally rules out such a conception too. It is significant that Smith thought of his 'system of natural liberty' in terms of a 'Utopia' (WN IV.iii.43: 471), a state of perfection that might well be associated with the end-state vision of competition in general equilibrium. The idea of a Utopia, in which competition is finally at rest, is similar to Newton's idea of a vacuum, where the bodies neither accelerate nor slow down and in which obstacles have been removed.

IV

Modern economies are dynamic and modern economic theory needs to understand the determinants of their innovation and change. The fourth section (three chapters) on Adam Smith and knowledge deals mainly with these issues and first touches on a most topical *economic* issue of our days. For Craig Smith, the key to understanding Smith's theoretical approach to social and economic change is to understand the role played by human knowledge. What drives man to seek knowledge and understanding in the first place? Craig Smith holds that for Smith 'we have an emotional need for understanding in order that our minds are able to function smoothly' (295).

Estrella Trincado analyses Smith's anti-utilitarian foundations of human identity. She contends that for Smith the experience of present time and not some fiction in the past or the future forms the basis of all human behaviour in the market. Accordingly, the ultimate motivation to create wealth in Smith does not lie in making money but in 'the enjoying of feelings such as curiosity and creation' (321).

These insights into knowledge (and human identity) that are at odds with standard economic approaches are partly presented in the form of rational reconstructions from a twentieth-century (Hayekian) perspective, which at the same time also denies any possibility of control in relation with social and economic change at all. While it is well known that Scottish intellectuals at the end of the eighteenth century – and above all Adam Smith – proposed a new understanding of social and economic change that could not be seen as the result of conscious action (Wood 1982), this important abstraction, on which both authors build their different reconstructions, does not necessarily imply that all responsibility for and attempts to control social and economic change are also to be rejected outright, as the Hayekian suggests.

In the final chapter of the collection on Smith's philosophy, Eric Schliesser is also more sensitive on this issue and highlights the existence of a political dimension in the *Wealth of Nations*. He claims that 'forms of exchange take place in a political context' implying that for Smith '[i]ndividual freedom is bound up with our membership in political society' (347). For Smith, Schliesser says, philosophical knowledge is important for the creation of the correct institutional framework for the system of natural liberty. This knowledge is a specific because it transcends the partiality of private interests. With this view Schliesser's analysis also nicely rounds off the collection, as a similar concern for impartiality required in the political realm has also been suggested by Hanley in the first chapter.

Conclusion

The philosophical perspective of the present collection offers an understanding of Adam Smith's values and beliefs that are at the foundation of his thought in general and his economic thought in particular. The heterogeneity of the contributions reveals an ambivalent picture of his philosophical foundations. Smith was still committed to the old while at the same time also anticipating the new. Accordingly, he was concerned with Aristotle and his ethics, while building on Newton, whose laws on motion rendered Aristotle's account of the universe obsolete. Francis Bacon, another emblematic figure of the new, referred to the problem in cognitive terms: [The human mind is not like a blackboard.] On a blackboard we first cross out the old in order to write down the new, in the human mind we can only cross out the old after having inscribed the new (The Refutation of Philosophies"/from Redargutio Philosophiarum/"1608 quoted by Krohn 1987: 38 [translated from the German by the author]). Smith had not yet crossed out the old and this is why his work will remain for us moderns both complex and difficult to grasp and a rich source of 'wonder' and 'surprise' ('Astronomy' 1:33). The present collection of *New Voices* with its philosophical focus is a perfect case in point.

But a never-ending interest in Adam Smith also exists for those who have been focusing on the economist in him. What philosophers have concluded for their domains, namely that Adam Smith is an author who is difficult to classify, has been revealed repeatedly by historians of economic thought. One example of this is the discussion of 'Das Adam Smith Problem', which deals with the relation between his economic and his non-economic work and is experiencing a vigorous revival today. Historians of economic thought have also revealed the different understandings of Adam Smith that have accompanied the development of economic thought until today. The provision of multiple reference frames that allow different schools of thought to repeatedly identify with an author is clearly an attribute of any classic author.[3]

Let me conclude with a critical observation on the presentation of this collection. The heterogeneity of the perspectives and ideologies would have been more readily accessible if it had had a helping hand by the editors. The introduction, in which the editors offer a historical account of the Smith industry, could have benefited from a focused rationale on the broadening of Smith scholarship. Although interesting, it does not prepare the reader for the 'less familiar' (8) portrayal of Adam Smith.

However, the collection meets its goal and offers a diversification of Smith scholarship and it is certainly of great interest to philosophers that Smith, who is mainly known as the founding father of economics, has an important and rich philosophical side as well. The book will also be attractive to an audience with an economic focus in so far as it accepts to cross disciplinary boundaries and explore other than economic sides in Smith.

Granted also the editors' rejection of any attempt at reconsideration of Smith's economic ideas, the foundations of Smith's thought would in general also be of interest to economists if the editorial couple (which constitutes an alliance between a trained economist and a trained philosopher) had explicitly pointed out the potential links between his philosophy and his economics.

Notes

1 Five theses at University of Chicago, one at George Mason University, one at University of Washington and one at University of Notre Dame in the USA, the universities of Bremen, Madrid, Glasgow, Cambridge, Amsterdam and Paris X Nanterre in Europe.

2 Although of fourteen authors, five did their PhD in economics, for the most part they also adopt a philosophical perspective in their contributions; nine authors did their PhD in humanities (philosophy and literary studies) and political and social theory.

3 As Medema (2006) has shown the 'Old Chicago Smith' is in many respects not compatible with the 'New Chicago Smith'. And both of which are incompatible on many accounts with another recent reception of 'Adam Smith, [the] behavioural economist' (Ashraf *et al.* 2005).

Bibliography

Ashraf, N., Camerer, C.F., and Loewenstein, G. (2005) 'Adam Smith, behavioural economist', *Journal of Economic Perspectives*, 19:131–45.

Krohn, W. (1987) *Francis Bacon*, Munich: Beck.

Medema, S.G. (2006): 'Adam Smith and the Chicago School', Available <http://ssrn.com/abstract=902220> (accessed 1 May 2007).

Schneewind, J.B., (1990) 'The misfortunes of virtue', *Ethics*, 101: 42–63.

Smith, A. (1976) *An Inquiry into the Nature and Causes of the Wealth of Nations*, R.H. Campbell and A.S. Skinner (eds), Oxford: Clarendon Press; Glasgow Edition.

—— (1976) *The Theory of Moral Sentiments*, D.D. Raphael and A.L. Macfie (eds), Oxford: Clarendon Press; Glasgow Edition.

—— (1980) 'History of Astronomy', in *Essays on Philosophical Subjects*, W.P.D. Wightman, J.C. Bryce and I.S. Ross, (eds), Oxford: Clarendon Press; Glasgow Edition.

Wood, G.S. (1982) 'Conspiracy and the paranoid style: causality and deceit in the eighteenth century', *The William and Mary Quarterly*, 39: 401–41.

Young, J.T. (2005) 'Unintended order and intervention: Adam Smith's theory of the role of the state', *History of Political Economy*, 37 (Annual Supplement): 91–119.

EDITORS' RESPONSE

Eric Schliesser and Leonidas Montes's response to review by Caroline Gerschlager

On behalf of our contributors, we thank Caroline Gerschlager for her thorough and thoughtful review. It is rare that a review attempts to do justice to all the articles in an edited volume. We also very much enjoyed her Baconian twist in responding to the papers in *New Voices on Adam Smith*. First we offer a few responses to Gerschlager's criticisms. Then we correct some oversights so as to leave readers of ASR not with a misleading impression about the aim of *New Voices* and several of the papers in it. Even as a summary it falls short of accuracy.

We were a bit surprised when we read that Gerschlager merely chose to consider 'the philosophical foundations of Adam Smith that the present collection proffers from an economic point of view'. Given the range of Smith's thought, we find an exclusive focus on this perspective a bit limiting. It is also seriously misleading because even *Wealth of Nations* is not only a book in economics. As most readers of ASR would recognize, WN includes lengthy treatments of economic history (digression on silver), history of various social institutions (including education, warfare, taxation, etc; parts of Book V), history of political economy (Book IV), institutional reform (Book V), among other things. This is why we cannot agree with her odd claim that Smith separated 'economics from moral philosophy'. Her explanation for this division looks rather obscure, and at times it seems that she would have wanted more attention to the famous 'Das Adam Smith

Problem'. The whole point of *New Voices*, however, is to explore the exciting work being done on other dimensions of Smith's thought. Gerschlager's claim is more puzzling because it flatly contradicts the explicit moral to be drawn of Jimena Hurtado-Prieto's analysis of Smith's criticism of Mandeville (240), in a chapter that was highly praised by Gerschlager. It also contradicts Schliesser's contribution to *New Voices*. In her review, Gerschlager does not note that Schliesser frames his treatment of Smith's conception of philosophy in terms of Smith's debate with Rousseau over the value of commerce, an argument pursued through TMS and WN. (See Sen and Rothschild's contribution to the *Cambridge Companion to Adam Smith*, 2006, for an excellent recent treatment of reading *Wealth of Nations* as part of Smith's contribution to moral philosophy, or Fleischacker's *On Adam Smith's* Wealth of Nations, 2004.)

Gerschlager misses a 'helping hand of the editors'; we must admit we have more of a preference for the invisible type. Our introduction seems to bother Gerschlager because it simply gives a 'historical account of the Smith industry'. We duly emphasized the 'partial' and 'opinionated' element of that enterprise, but we still believe that at least it provides a good starting point to any scholar interested in the state of the art of Smith studies. More important, we were surprised to read about our 'rejection of any attempt at reconsideration of Smith's economic ideas'. Yet, while we would have accepted the charge of brevity, Gerschlager appears to have ignored our calling attention to work by Vernon Smith, James Buchanan and Amartya Sen (among others).

We are also puzzled by Gerschlager's insistence on comparing Smith's remarks on 'Utopia' with Newton's treatment of the vacuum. There is a very important dis-analogy: besides drawing on Boyle's experiments, which established a limited vacuum in the laboratory, Newton thought he had firmly established the existence of celestial vacuum on a grand scale. In WN, Smith uses the language of Utopia to make clear that there is as of yet nowhere a system of liberty. Moreover, in context, Smith's remarks might suggest that he did not expect a system of natural liberty to be reached. It is not so much an expected end-state, but part of a process.

Gerschlager is correct to emphasize the heterogeneous nature of the contributions; this we see as an advantage of this collection. However, we did call attention to some surprising themes running through many of the papers: four papers (Hanley, Flanders, Trincado, Frierson) undermine the once fashionable reading of Smith as a utilitarian; two papers (Hanley, Brubaker) attack the still strong consensus that view Smith as a modern Stoic; six papers (Mitchell, Montes, Trincado, Smith, Forman-Barzilai, Schliesser) attack the claim that Smith is some kind of sceptic; two papers read Smith as offering a kind of virtue ethics (Hanley, Frierson) (5).

Gerschlager is not much interested in the papers on moral theory in section II of *New Voices*. But her brief comments are seriously misleading. This is especially to be regretted because some readers of ASR could be interested in details of Smith's moral philosophy. We should simply remember that Smith's moral philosophy lectures, following Hutcheson, included Political Economy, Ethics, Jurisprudence and Natural Theology. In fact Gerschlager fails to note that Carola von Villiez's paper is a careful comparison of Smith and Rawls. She does not mention either that Fonna Forman-Barzilai evaluates Smith's treatment of pluralism and cultural relativity. Forman-Barzilai is quite critical of Smith, thus, putting to rest Gerschlager's claim that only Kuipers's contribution would be critical of Smith. Gerschlager also fails to mention that Frierson's paper is a Smithian contribution to environmental ethics, and Flanders' represents an original contribution to the problem of moral luck. Incidentally, Gerschlager could have read all of this in the editors' introduction.

Finally, we think it very strange to attribute to Craig Smith and Estrella Trincado the claim 'that all responsibility for and attempts to control social and economic change are also to be rejected outright'. It is true that in a lone footnote (309), Craig Smith's paper brings Adam Smith's thought into conversation with Hayek, but if we have to interpret Craig Smith's reading of Adam Smith from a contemporary economic point of view, we think it is more appropriate to read Smith as a precursor of human capital theory and the application of it to economic growth. Trincado evaluates Smith with ideas from Husserl, Ricour, Borges and while concerned with illuminating Smith's economics she does so by invoking 'postmodern' conceptions of time.

In sum, we believe readers of ASR interested in *New Voices* will find new trends in Adam Smith scholarship that might foster future research. We simply expect that this thorough review may be a starting point for anyone who, according to Gerschlager, 'accepts to cross disciplinary boundaries and explore other than economic sides in Smith[2] (p. 277). And this includes all those interested in the history of economics.

Tiziano Raffaelli, *Ricchezza delle Nazioni: Introduzione alla lettura*

Carrocci editore, 2001, 215 pp.

ISBN Hardback: 88–430–1746–2

Reviewed by Maria Pia Paganelli

The title of Tiziano Raffaelli's book translates as '*The Wealth of Nations*: introduction to its reading'. The book is relatively short and divided into three sections. The first, on 'The birth of a new knowledge', is subdivided into a) Ethics, law, and economics: the system of Adam Smith; b) Beyond *the Adam Smith Problem*; c) The social implication of moral theory; d) Justice; e) Toward the analysis of the commercial society. The second part, on 'Market and accumulation', is subdivided into a) The plan of work; b) Division of labour as a model of the dynamic process of discovery and skill creation; c) Exchange, market and origin of money; d) The three original sources of income; e) Prices and economic progress: theory and facts; f) Social classes and the evolution of commercial society; g) Accumulation. The last section is on 'History, political economy, and the role of government' and it includes a) The unnatural progress of modern Europe and the end of the feudal system; b) Two systems of political economy: criticism of mercantilism and praise of physiocracy; and c) The general principles of government. A chronology of the life and works of Smith closes the book.

The book has no introduction or preface by the author. We are not told who the intended audience of the book is. Given its title and structure it seems the book is meant as a textbook, or at least as a book to be read by students as an Adam Smith primer and/or as a complement to the *Wealth of Nations* (WN).

Raffaelli takes us onto the familiar road of WN by sliding in and out of Smith's time. For many of Smith's ideas, Raffaelli expounds on their origins, their standing in Smith's time, and how we understand them today. For example, Raffaelli parallels the narration of Smith's position on the origin and use of money with Hume's and Hobbes', spells out its Aristotelian origins, and restates the problem in terms of the game theoretical language of coordination problems. Despite a technical imprecision (where a change in quantity demanded is described as a change in demand) Raffaelli is successful in the difficult task of combining modelling with contextual analysis. Modelling Smith decreases with the progression of the book, though, leaving the reader to question whether Raffaelli's 'translations' of Smith's ideas into modern economic language is simply a gimmick to capture the attention of today's economic students who are used to the modern language, or rather a technical description truly required for clarity's sake.

Raffaelli's road through WN may be familiar to someone well acquainted with Smith. Raffaelli's road, though, at times becomes circuitous, like a mountain road, with sharp and sudden turns which open unexpected and beautiful views. And like on a mountain road, breaches in the horizon are short, quick, and leave the rider with a craving for more, wondering how the full view could be. For example, Raffaelli takes the reader along the path of Smithian value and price, describing the standard distinction between nominal and real measurements. He claims, in my translation, that for Smith 'labour is a necessary sacrifice for production and the fundamental cause of the value of the good. . . . But a problem arises: not all quantities of labour are the same. Yet we need to make comparisons. To do that, we need to take into account not only time, but also hardship, and skills "for which it is not easy to find a precise measure" (ivi [WN] p.83). Here the central theme of *The Theory of Moral Sentiments* (TMS) peeps out – finding an objective criterion for the relationship among individuals – since the price of an individual's labour is the esteem given by other individuals' (52). We are given a spectacular glimpse into what Raffaelli may mean by considering Smith's work as an uncompleted trilogy – TMS and WN are two of the three tassels, the third of which would have been something close to Smith's *Lectures on Jurisprudence*. But then Raffaelli moves on, leaving the reader with the unfulfilled desire for more. Similarly, in the third section of the book, Raffaelli elucidates Smith's position about the British colonies by contextualizing the debate. Raffaelli explains how Smith, even if aware of the practical impossibility of his idea, made a radical political proposal: the full parity of representation of the colonies in the British parliament, which would include, if needed, moving the parliament to America, given the heavier fiscal load with which America could be burdened. Raffaelli then states, again in my translation, that 'it is interesting that the second utopia in WN, after the one about free trade, is about building a great state, modeled on ancient Rome. The cosmopolitan ideal of free trade and the cosmopolitan institution of the empire are interlinked, as when Smith states that "the liberal system of free exports and free imports" would make the diverse states of a continent similar to "the provinces of a great empire" (WN p. 456)' (158). This is a spark on the fuel of the reader's curiosity. But it is also the end paragraph and the end of a section of the book. Raffaelli moves on to a different topic.

I fear that the book may be too rich for its dimension and scope. Reflections like the two mentioned above are relatively frequent. Most of the time, they consist of one lonely sentence. On the one hand they make the book a treasure hunt for the scholar familiar with Smith. Yet, at the end of the hunt, we are left with only little tastes, rather than a full meal, and a feeling of hunger. On the other hand, I wonder how much of this wealth of ideas will be picked up by a novice student who is reading Smith for the first time (or Raffaelli's book instead of Smith).

Unfortunately, because the book is only available in Italian, readership will be limited. Many readers could appreciate the bibliography though. It is usefully divided into sections that separate Smith's works and their direct references texts from what Smith used as sources, and literature contemporary to Smith as well as secondary literature on Smith contemporary to us now. This last section is rich with names of Italian scholars and works in Italian. A non-Italian reader would therefore learn how productive Italian scholarship has been, even if the language barrier may not allow any further exploration. Yet, what one may wish would be a longer bibliography of works in English. Evensky, Samuels, and Young are among the many economists whose works were published before 2000. Fleischacker and Griswold are among many philosophers not mentioned. There are over thirty books on Smith published in English in the 1990s alone and a booming number of relevant articles, the very large majority of which are apparently unnoticed by Raffaelli, or at least they are unmentioned by him. By Raffaelli's references alone one might wonder if, outside of Italy, scholars have lost interest in Adam Smith – luckily that is not the case.

I think Raffaelli's book could be a useful book for the (limited) audience of Italian readership. I wish it was longer and many more themes were developed more fully.

AUTHOR'S RESPONSE

Tiziano Raffaeli's response to review by Maria Pia Paganelli

I greatly sympathize with Maria Pia Paganelli's sense of being at loss in reviewing a book whose aim and role are not well specified. This gives me the opportunity to reconsider what I tried to accomplish when writing *Introduzione alla lettura* to the *Wealth of Nations*. The book is the concise, revised version of lectures in the History of Economic Thought delivered to philosophy students in the academic years 1995–6 and 1996–7. The lecture notes were first circulated in 1998 by the internal publishing service of the University of Pisa, under the more ambitious title of *Adam Smith interprete della società commerciale* (no translation needed). When I decided to make them into a book for a wider audience, especially for students of other Universities, Carocci offered to publish it in a series devoted to introductions to the classics of philosophy. The series already included Aristotle's *Metaphysica*, Kant's three Critiques, Vico's *Scienza Nuova*, Descartes's *Meditationes* and has since been enriched with works by Nietzsche, Wittgenstein, Spinoza, Schopenhauer, Hegel and Heidegger. At a time when economics and philosophy were establishing closer relations than ever before, and since I myself was interested in promoting this process, I could not resist the temptation to bring back to its birthplace the masterpiece that is generally considered to have severed the links between economics and moral philosophy. I seized this opportunity, accepting word limits which, among other things, compelled me to substitute many quotations with page references to Smith's own works. This may be troublesome for the general reader, but should create no problem for students who are supposed to read the *Introduzione* with the *Wealth of Nations* (and Smith's other works) wide-open on their desk. The aim and collocation also affected the bibliography, which is limited to articles and books referred to in the text, where preference is given to works in Italian, with no concern for the completeness that would be required in a book of a different kind. In no way was this meant to give the impression that 'outside of Italy, scholars have lost interest in Adam Smith'. Since its publication, the book has been put to task as a teaching tool, used always as a guide, never as a substitute, to reading the *Wealth of Nations*, and has proved its worth for the audience of Italian students, for whom it was originally conceived. In the unusual task of lecturing on the history of economics to philosophy students, Smith's book turns out to be very effective as a means for illustrating the basic principles and pervasiveness of economic reasoning (I love to think that my introduction helped with the task). For this purpose, now and then Smith's way of reasoning is translated into the rudiments of modern economic analysis, without resorting to excessive technicalities. The main idea is to show how economic incentives work at the margin of an enormous variety of human motivations, according to the model set up in the chapter on wage and profit differentials. The lottery, widespread throughout the *Wealth of Nations* to represent the essence of human decision under uncertainty, extensively applied also to political contexts, is what best epitomizes Smith's uses of economic explanations (it also tells a lot about his attitude towards human life). This, rather than capturing the attention of today's economics students, is the educational aim of the limited use of economic models. They are not 'required for clarity's sake' – though they may sometimes be helpful – but they are a means to familiarize the student with economic concepts and their history, as also are references to Ricardo, Marx, Mill and Marshall, which would be out of place in another context. Having tried many other ways of teaching philosophy students what it means to think 'en economique', I have come to the conclusion that no book can perform the task better than Smith's masterpiece. From the opposite perspective, when I taught economics students in Cagliari, I found that Smith's book is unique to show the philosophical foundations of economic reasoning. My introduction should help bridge the gap between the two disciplines, without losing sight of any part of the *Wealth of Nations*, which is perused through all the meanders and digressions on prices, commerce, money, taxation and their history, always calling attention to the enlightening passages, pearls of irony and lively intuitions that are scattered in the crevices of the text, and trying to make sense of what look like gratuitous divagations. Students are asked to skip no part of a book that is proverbially considered to be prolix and has invited many an abridgment. This is the background, aim and outcome of the publication of *Introduzione alla lettura* to Smith's *Wealth of Nations*.

Another consequence of length limits was that the first chapter, devoted to Smith's general system of thought and especially to *The Theory of Moral Sentiments*, had to be summarized. Furthermore, I know that many remarks, which the reviewer kindly points out as interesting, act as sheer bookmarks to be developed in the class-room (expert readers can make a note of a topic and develop it by themselves, in case they find it of some interest). Notwithstanding these limitations, hopefully the book conveys an interpretation that is neither too cryptic nor too trivial. Basically, it supports the traditional view that places the *Wealth of Nations* at the centre of Smith's system, against modern attempts to 'relocate' the gist of his thought (this too may explain some oddities in the bibliography). Its relative novelty, if any, is that it reaches this conclusion not by ignoring his other works, *The Theory of Moral Sentiments* in particular, but by fully integrating them into the picture. To take an example, it maintains that the main function of sympathy does not so much consist in curbing self-interest – though it does it in so far as its outward manifestations must be kept within the limits with which the detached, impartial spectator can sympathize – but in establishing a working ('*plain and palpable*', in Smith's effective terminology) criterion of social hierarchy by means of its – morally defective – predilection for wealthy people. Sympathy for wealth is the natural mechanism capable of placating the anxiety caused by the social mobility originating from the collapse of feudal ranks and orders. To work effectively, the new criterion requires compliance with the simple and non-exigent rules of justice, in their turn dependent on sympathy and resentment, in a paradigmatic case of 'the economy of nature' and of good coming out of evil. Prudence and self-control are also considered to strengthen rather than weaken people's desire for wealth – the historical specification of the 'desire to better one's condition' – the satisfaction of which is achieved by parsimony, the key 'minor' virtue on which the whole edifice of the *Wealth of Nations* rests (93, 113). The outcome of this complex mixture of feelings and institutions is the market, which for Smith represents a suitable answer to the problem of finding inter-subjectively accepted criteria to establish working hierarchies in a society that no longer relies on birth, age and other old-fashioned criteria of social ranking. Thus, commercial society is conceived as a system that does not depend on high moral standards. Similarly, it also economizes on cognitive faculties thanks to the localized, semi-detached niches of activity produced by the division of labour, a theme often resumed by modern and contemporary economics. This 'economy of nature', in both the moral and the intellectual sphere, provides a clearer and wider understanding of the 'invisible hand' than do purely economic applications, as in the passage that directly introduces the famous metaphor in the fourth book of *The Wealth of Nations.* It is the ability to function on the presupposition of human qualities that are easily attainable which commends commercial society as a working system, while at the same time its anthropological model rather unfavourably compares with that of previous social systems (as attested by Smith's appreciation of the generosity, magnanimity and disinterested behaviour that characterize ancient and medieval society).

Introduzione alla lettura also pays great attention to the last three books of the *Wealth of Nations* and in general to Smith's politics, after Forbes and Winch, often referring to Machiavelli, Hobbes, Locke, Montesquieu, Hume and Rousseau. The third book is vindicated as a milestone of the philosophy of history, against Schumpeter's dismissive judgment. Particular emphasis is placed on Smith's worries about the key problem of finding out who is to perform the political function, which requires those human qualities that commercial society tends to displace. Hence his scepticism and a sophisticated attempt to resurrect aristocratic values and, after due retraining, the aristocracy itself, along lines that would exert their influence on Hegel, Mill and Tocqueville. Not by chance *Introduzione alla lettura* ends with a discussion of the relationship between Smith's concern for politics in the *Wealth of Nations* and the remarks, inspired by the French Revolution, that were added to the sixth edition of *The Theory of Moral Sentiments*.

Not only are all economists 'Adam's sons', independently of their school affiliation, but Smith's ideas are also seminal for an understanding of the wider field of human and social affairs. *Introduzione alla lettura* tries to focus on the architectural conceptions for which the *Wealth of Nations* – 'the other book', as once Smith referred to it – deserves to be considered one of the great classics of the history of ideas, not out of place in the library of philosophy students, perhaps in a more prominent position than the book Smith directly devoted to moral philosophy.

D.D. Raphael, *The Impartial Spectator: Adam Smith's Moral Philosophy*

Clarendon Press, 2007, 150 pp.

ISBN Hardback: 019921333X

Reviewed by Charles Larmore

'Imagination is decaying sense', wrote Thomas Hobbes in the *Leviathan* (I.2). When we imagine, we picture to ourselves what we once perceived, calling up past images and combining them as we please. Imagination cannot expand our knowledge. It is only fancy, playing with the remains of sense experience by which alone we make contact with reality. Not surprisingly, this conception seemed irresistible to many early empiricist thinkers. Hume was the first to break its hold, arguing that the basic structural features of experience – the continuity of objects over time, the causal connections between events – do not derive from the senses but instead from the imagination, operating through the association of ideas. Yet he never managed to avoid the sceptical suggestion that they are therefore *merely* the work of the imagination, without any correlate in the world. It was Hume's younger friend, Adam Smith, who unambiguously raised the imagination to the rank of an organ of knowledge. If empiricism is the view that all our knowledge of the world comes from experience, then experience according to Smith must be understood as more than simply registering the givens of sense. Only if we imagine how what we perceive might look or act under various circumstances does it become intelligible.

Smith's 'History of Astronomy' (written before 1758, though published only posthumously) applied this view to the natural sciences. So long as we can imaginatively extend what we perceive without running up against contrary experience, we feel secure in our knowledge. Yet even when we come upon phenomena which 'appear solitary and incoherent with all that go before them, which therefore disturb the easy movement of the imagination', science turns to the imagination, postulating principles and mechanisms that will 'introduce order into this chaos of jarring and discordant appearances, allay this tumult of the imagination, and restore it . . . to that tone of tranquillity and composure, which is both most agreeable in itself, and most suitable to its nature' (II.12). Social life, of course, was the main area in which Smith pursued this thesis. In society, one mind runs up against another and must turn to the imagination to harmonize their differences.

We try to see the world from other people's point of view and envision how they will regard what we do. In this way we arrive at the idea of an 'impartial spectator' as a common standard of right and wrong. That the imagination lies at the heart of our moral thinking is the grand theme of Smith's *Theory of Moral Sentiments*.

D.D. Raphael's new book, short but incisive, is a most welcome contribution to our understanding of Smith's ethics. Raphael is a notable philosopher in his own right as well as a specialist on both Smith and eighteenth-century British moral thought as a whole. He explains clearly and engagingly why Smith was not simply the great economist who also happened to write on ethics. *The Theory of Moral Sentiments* is a remarkable work, whose insights have yet to be fully appreciated. Raphael declares – too diffidently, I think – that it is 'not one of the great classical texts in its field', though 'it has a prominent place among texts of the second rank' (1). This verdict is true only if the first rank is limited to the two masterpieces which have defined the very meaning of moral philosophy and shaped Western culture itself in manifold ways, Aristotle's *Nicomachean Ethics* and Kant's *Groundwork of the Metaphysics of Morals*. Smith's *Theory* is not a landmark of this magnitude. But it does lay out a position that no moral philosopher can afford to ignore. I say this even if I find it far less promising than Raphael himself.

As he rightly claims, the concept of the 'impartial spectator' was Smith's great theoretical achievement. Its significance, however, depends on more basic notions and we must look first at what Raphael says about them. Most fundamentally, Smith followed his two Scottish predecessors, Hutcheson and Hume, in believing that 'moral judgment begins with the reaction of spectators to the actions and motives of other people' (16). Raphael underscores this assumption several times (14, 27, 31), indicating that other philosophers have begun their theory of moral judgment from the standpoint of the agent who must determine what to do. The suggestion is that so controversial a premise may have momentous consequences – as indeed it does, though Raphael never explores what gains and drawbacks may be involved. In fact, yet a third perspective might be adopted, not that of a spectator or an agent, but that of a conversational partner discussing with others what is best to do, and one might further wonder why any of these stances should be considered prior to the others, as though the source of moral thinking had to be one single capacity. I will return to this question at the end. Now the topic is Smith's own approach.

Its starting point, examined in the first chapter of the *Theory*, is our ability to take up another's point of view. Smith had little to say about the sorts of circumstances which impel us to do so. His concern was with the way that putting ourselves in other people's place is essential to our evaluating what they feel or do. If we believe that we would react similarly in their situation, then we approve of their conduct. If not, then we disapprove. According to Smith, this exercise of the imagination gives rise to approval through the operation of sympathy. Unfortunately, he was not consistent in his idea of how sympathy works.

Sometimes he talked as though sympathizing meant undergoing the same emotions as the person we contemplate, and at other times as though it were a different kind of emotion that only we as bystanders can feel. When we see other people unhappy, do we feel their sorrow, no doubt less intensely, or do we feel a sorrow at their sorrow – a reflective kind of sorrow which they themselves need not feel, unless they choose to look at their misfortune from the outside? The second account is surely the better one. For when I sympathize with another, I generally do not lose sight of the fact that the two of us are different persons and that the distressing events befell the other, not me. Sympathy is not a contagion. After all, the emotion Smith wanted to describe is the one we feel when putting ourselves imaginatively in a situation we fully know is not our own.

The second account implies, however, that the feeling of sympathy cannot serve to explain approval. If the sorrow we feel in seeing others unhappy is a sorrow at their sorrow, then it presupposes our approval of their reaction to their situation. As Raphael correctly remarks, 'Smith took it for granted that Hume had demonstrated beyond challenge that moral distinctions arise from feeling' (7). Whence his title, *The Theory of the Moral Sentiments*. But in fact the way that Smith based approval on the imagination makes approval instead a function of reason. When we put ourselves in other people's shoes, we imagine what we would then feel and do, and if this agrees with their reaction, then we approve of it and only thus feel sorrow at their sorrow or joy at their joy. Our approval is therefore rooted in what we think there would be reason to feel or do in their situation. This explains why, as Smith maintained, we may sympathize even with the dead (TMS I.i.1.13) – not because we feel what they do (they feel nothing), but because imagining ourselves in their condition we think we would have reason, if *per impossibile* we could then feel, to regret immeasurably what had happened.

Moral approval is just one species of approval in general. We might, for instance, endorse another's awe before a beautiful landscape without expressing thereby a moral judgment. I think that Raphael overlooks this distinction in the criticisms he makes of the *Theory*'s analysis of moral evaluation. Smith distinguished between the 'propriety' and the 'merit' of actions. An action is appropriate to the extent that the passions animating it are suitable to their object, a matter we judge by imagining what we would feel and do if confronted with a similar situation (TMS I.i.3.6). An action is meritorious to the extent that it has beneficial instead of hurtful consequences for those whom it affects (TMS I.i.3.7; II.i.introduction.2). Here too judgment requires imagination, since to determine an action's merit we must put ourselves in the place of those affected and imagine how we would then feel.

Now Raphael holds that for Smith judgments of propriety and judgments of merit are 'different kinds of moral judgment' (22) and that the former by themselves amount to judgments of 'right and wrong' (25, 31). And thus he complains, quite justifiably if Smith took such a view, that judging moral right and wrong requires attention to consequences. The interpretation is flawed, however. 'I may be mistaken', Raphael amiably notes, 'in identifying Smith's propriety and impropriety with right and wrong' (25). He undoubtedly is. For Smith, moral judgment considers both merit and propriety, and it is this dual focus that constitutes its special nature. Such is the thesis he advanced right at the beginning of the *Theory*, just after defining the difference between propriety and merit, and by way of indicating that if he spent so much time emphasizing the importance of the former, it was not in order to suggest that it is the only factor involved in moral judgment, but instead to correct his contemporaries' one-sided emphasis on the latter:

> Philosophers have, of late years, considered chiefly the tendency of affections, and have given little attention to the relation which they stand in to the cause which excites them. In common life, however, when we judge of any person's conduct, and of the sentiments which directed it, we constantly consider them under both these aspects.
>
> (TMS I.i.3.8)

Raphael is right to think that the object of this criticism was Hume (22, 25). But he misses the fact that the correction Smith proposed was that moral judgment, in contrast to other forms of evaluation, entails evaluating an action in both respects at once. This is why near the end of the *Theory*, in surveying the different philosophical approaches to the nature of virtue, he concluded that theories which reduce it to propriety fall short:

> There is no virtue without propriety, and wherever there is propriety, some degree of approbation is due. . . . [Yet] though propriety is an essential ingredient in every virtuous action, it is not always the sole ingredient. Beneficent actions have in them another quality by which they appear not only to deserve approbation but recompense.
>
> (TMS VII.ii.1.50)

In Smith's theory, then, our judgments of moral right and wrong look at both motives and consequences. They do so, however, from a specific point of view, once we learn to distinguish morality from social convention and personal preference. This standpoint is that of the impartial spectator. When we place ourselves in another person's position and ask ourselves whether we would feel and act the same way, we arrive at a moral verdict about that person only if we regard our imagined reactions as those of which an impartial spectator would approve. Raphael lays most stress on the specific role such a standard plays in our judgments about our own conduct (4, 31). In his view, Smith's story of how we develop this 'demigod within the breast' and thus acquire what is called conscience makes up his 'enduring contribution' to moral philosophy (127).

In general, Smith observed, reflecting upon what we have done or might do requires looking at our motives 'as at a certain distance from us', and therefore we cannot evaluate them except by taking up the viewpoint of some spectator we regard as authoritative, and asking ourselves whether they would meet with approval (TMS III.i.2). When young, we lean upon the opinions, real and imagined, of family and associates (even fictional characters) to judge the worth of our conduct. Such is the form that conscience first takes. Raphael points out a tendency in the first edition (1759) of the *Theory* to leave the matter there, effectively reducing conscience to social convention. It was, he shows, the criticisms of Sir Gilbert Elliot that spurred Smith to push his developmental story further in subsequent editions so as to explain why individual conscience can transcend existing attitudes (36–8). We come to realize that those whom we deem wise and good would differ in their verdicts on our conduct. Having to iron out their differences, we cease to identify with any one of them when we reflect and develop the abstract standard of a truly 'impartial spectator'. This was Smith's mature position. Its strength, Raphael avers, is explaining how conscience has its origin in social forces that nonetheless propel it to become a tribunal above society.

Yet this account makes it all the plainer that Smith did not really found morality upon sentiment, much as he wanted to do so. I already pointed out how on his view our moral judgments take their cue, not from how we feel when imagining ourselves in other people's position, but from how we think we would feel if our circumstances were thus. It now appears that, if we are indeed thinking morally, we must determine how we would feel by reference to how we should feel according to an impartial spectator. The ultimate basis of our moral judgments must therefore be the reasons we suppose such a supreme authority would have for approving a certain reaction on our part and thus a certain feeling or action on the part of the person whose conduct we are judging. In the end, it must be reason, not sentiment, which is the basis of morality.

But there is more. How exactly, according to Smith, are we to suppose that the impartial spectator, gazing upon us and others, would determine whether to approve of various feelings and actions? On this score, he said precious little. He came perilously close to explaining correct moral judgment as whatever judgment the impartial spectator would express. Yet such judgments would have to embody rather complex assessments, balancing for instance the different factors of propriety and merit in the actions under appraisal. By what principles are we to imagine the impartial spectator to operate? Smith never explained.

This lacuna is not accidental. It occurs because the impartial spectator is imagined as simply a spectator, not as an agent as well, who grasps the reasons for acting one way rather than another in the given situation and issues on this basis evaluations of others. A moral theory cannot succeed if, like Smith's, it analyzes moral judgment by reference just to a spectator's standpoint. Moreover, even the agent's standpoint may prove inadequate, if it turns out that the reasons agents have to act in a certain way must, if morally acceptable, be ones they can suppose that those affected by the action could see grounds to endorse. The standpoint of people having to justify to one another the way they act seems also essential. The limitations of Smith's theory, which I do not believe Raphael perceives, lie in its view of what morality is all about. Is the fundamental moral relation one between a person who acts and another who looks on and appraises? Certainly not, even if judging others has a role to play. The fundamental relation is between a person who acts and another whose possibilities of action are thereby affected. Morality is a matter of how we ought to treat one another.

AUTHOR'S RESPONSE

D.D. Raphael's response to review by Charles Larmore

I am grateful to Professor Larmore for the commendatory remarks in one part of his review. In the main, however, he is critical; and rightly so, for the primary function of philosophers is to exercise critical thought and questioning. It is therefore incumbent upon me to be critical in my turn. So here goes.

The two chief features of Larmore's review are, first, an emphasis on the role of imagination in *The Theory of Moral Sentiments*, and second, a claim that Adam Smith, in this book, founded morality upon reason rather than sentiment, despite his desire to do the opposite.

I agree with Larmore on the first point. It would have been helpful to readers if he had explicitly said that I highlight, as he does, the role of imagination in Adam Smith's moral theory. The second chapter of my book is entitled 'Sympathy and Imagination', and in it I say right away that, of the two, imagination plays the larger part, although Smith himself seems to think that sympathy has the chief role.

I began by suggesting that the title of the first chapter in both of Adam Smith's books indicates the primary cause of the subject-matter. The first chapter of the *Moral Sentiments* is entitled 'Of Sympathy', and the first chapter of the *Wealth of Nations* is entitled 'Of the Division of Labour'. I suggested that these titles indicate Smith's view that the moral sentiments are founded on sympathy, and that the increase of national wealth is founded on the division of labour. I then added that, in the case of the *Moral Sentiments*, the foundational element should include imagination as well as sympathy, and that imagination is more significant than sympathy.

The second feature of Larmore's view, rationalism in Smith, seems to me less sound. He says that basing approval on the imagination makes approval a function of reason. 'Our approval is therefore rooted in what we think there would be reason to feel or do' in the situation that we are appraising (p. 296).

This, Larmore says, explains why, according to Smith, we can sympathize with the dead: such sympathy is not a sharing of feeling (since the dead feel nothing) but a matter of thinking 'we would have reason, if *per impossibile* we could then feel, to regret immeasurably what had happened' (p. 296). So Larmore believes that Smith has in mind a rational process, thinking 'we would have reason . . . to regret'. But Smith himself explains his view of sympathy with the dead in terms of 'the fancy' or 'imagination', with no allusion whatsoever to reason.

> The idea of that dreary and endless melancholy, which the fancy naturally ascribes to their condition, arises altogether from . . . our lodging . . . our own living souls in their inanimated bodies, and thence conceiving what would be our emotions in this case. It is from this very illusion of the imagination, that the foresight of our own dissolution is so terrible to us.
>
> (TMS I.i.1.13)

Larmore concludes his review with a criticism of the limitations of Smith's theory. The theory, he says, assumes that 'what morality is all about', 'the fundamental moral relation', is 'one between a person who acts and another who looks on and appraises.' This is not altogether fair. Smith's book is indeed chiefly about moral judgment, but not simply about the moral judgment made by 'another' (p. 299). Nor is it entirely about the judgments that are passed upon action. Some parts are about the character of moral action itself. They are largely about the virtues, prudence, justice and beneficence, but also about the place of utility in morally approved action. However, I would agree with Larmore that 'morality is a matter of how we ought to treat one another' (p. 299), and I would concede that this is not central in Smith's treatment of the subject.

Larmore is mistaken in saying that I do not perceive the limitations of Smith's theory. My book was an examination of the positive content of Smith's theory, not a statement of what I myself take to be the essentials of morality. Larmore is evidently familiar with something of my earlier books, and he must know that my idea of 'what morality is all about' is near enough to his own.

On my first acquaintance with the British moralists of the seventeenth and eighteenth centuries I was not much impressed with the contribution of Adam Smith, or indeed with that of Hume. Richard Price was the thinker that appealed to me. My mentors were the Oxford deontologists, H.A. Prichard, Sir David Ross, and E.F. Carritt, and the book that most attracted me to philosophy was G.E. Moore's *Principia Ethica*, not so much for its doctrine as for its clarity and simplicity of expression. When I came to read some of the British moralists I was delighted to find that Moore's famous argument about the 'naturalistic fallacy' was presented, plain as a pikestaff, near the beginning of Richard Price's *Review of the Principal Questions and*

Difficulties in Morals. I guess that Larmore would think that Price and the Oxford deontologists knew 'what morality is all about'. Later, however, I came to see that Hume was a great philosopher on ethics as well as epistemology. Much later still, long after editing Smith's *Moral Sentiments*, I found myself concluding that this book was far more illuminating than Hume's work on ethics.

So much for what Larmore has written. It remains to say something of what he has not written. I am surprised that he says nothing about the main difference between the sixth edition of the *Moral Sentiments* and the preceding editions, namely the inclusion of an extensive new Part on the character of virtue. This is the chief feature of the book that Larmore is reviewing. Does he think that it is of little importance? Adam Smith is best known for the *Wealth of Nations*, and some of the economists who have discussed it have written about the difference between the hard-headed realism of that work and the supposedly idealistic character of Smith's earlier book on ethics. Attention to the sixth edition of the *Moral Sentiments*, written long after the *Wealth of Nations*, would show them that their view of the mind of Adam Smith needs revision.

Since the reviews editor has asked me to comment at some length on Larmore's critique, I take the opportunity to mention a point that puzzles me a little, namely Larmore's own opinion of the *Moral Sentiments*. He says that it is 'a remarkable work, whose insights have yet to be fully appreciated' (p. 295), and that I am too diffident in excluding it from the great classical texts in the field of moral philosophy. He thinks that this view of mine is true only if the great texts are limited to Aristotle's *Nicomachean Ethics* and Kant's *Groundwork of the Metaphysic of Morals*. That appears to imply that Larmore would rate the worth of Adam Smith's book more highly than I do. Yet he then qualifies his praise of the book with 'I say this even if I find it far less promising than Raphael himself' (p. 295), which seems to imply that he rates it less highly than I do.

I am, incidentally, surprised that Larmore confines his top team to Aristotle's *Nicomachean Ethics* and Kant's *Groundwork*. I would have said that the list should include Plato's *Republic*, Spinoza's *Ethics* and Kant's *Critique of Practical Reason*. Of course one regards Aristotle's book as far better grounded than Plato's, but the *Republic* is surely one of the few really great works in the history of moral philosophy. That goes for Spinoza's *Ethics* too. Few of us would adopt it as our guide for life, yet it is an overwhelmingly challenging book that should never be ignored in philosophical thought about human conduct. Again, while Kant's *Groundwork* is more readable than the second *Critique*, we must surely accept that the latter is more definitive of Kant's thought on the philosophy of practice, including moral practice.

It is perhaps worth noting in this connection that Adam Smith's own survey of the history of moral philosophy, in the final Part of the *Moral Sentiments*, begins with Plato's *Republic* before going on to Aristotle's *Nicomachean Ethics*. He does not mention Spinoza, of whom, I imagine, he knew nothing.

He was well versed in ancient philosophy and was especially influenced by Stoic thought. With Kant the influence was the other way around. There is some evidence that Kant took an interest in Adam Smith, notably on aesthetics but also on ethics. This is a topic on which we are particularly indebted to the researches of Samuel Fleischacker (1991). Adam Smith was remarkably well-informed about contemporary books in French, and fairly well interested in Italian works, but apparently not at all in German writings. If I am not mistaken, the only German books in his library were translations of his own two books (Bonar 1894; Mizuta 2000).

I conclude with a niggle at a trifling point which Larmore treats as important. He purports to quote me as holding 'that for Smith judgments of propriety and judgments of merit are "different kinds of judgment" (22)' (p. 296), while in fact, he says, Smith holds that 'moral judgment . . . entails evaluating an action in both respects at once' (p. 297). Oddly enough, Larmore supports this criticism with a quotation in which Smith says: 'though propriety is an essential ingredient in every virtuous action, it is not always the sole ingredient. Beneficent actions have in them another quality by which they appear not only to deserve approbation but recompense' (TMS VII.ii.1.50). If propriety is *not always* the sole ingredient of virtuous action, it sometimes *is* the sole ingredient, and so a judgment of propriety is not necessarily also a judgment of merit.

On page 22 of my book I did not in fact use the words 'different kinds of judgment'; I wrote of 'different forms of moral judgment'. But no matter; the meaning is roughly the same. However, all I meant is that, since the concept of propriety differs from the concept of merit, the judgment that an action is appropriate differs from the judgment that the action is meritorious. Would Larmore want to deny that? I did indeed express some hesitation about identifying Smith's propriety and impropriety with right and wrong, but that does not affect the perfectly obvious point that propriety differs from merit, so that a judgment (statement, proposition) that an action is appropriate differs from a judgment that the action has merit. In modern English we would rarely speak of propriety and impropriety as normal moral qualities of human action, though we would speak of merit and demerit in much the same way as Adam Smith. It seemed to me that the modern equivalent of Smith's propriety and impropriety was right and wrong, but it is not always quite clear that one could make the substitution and therefore I said that I might be mistaken in this understanding of Smith's terms.

Bibliography

Fleischacker, S. (1991) 'Philosophy in moral practice: Kant and Adam Smith', *Kant-Studien*, 82: 249–69; cited in I.S. Ross, *The Life of Adam Smith*, Oxford: Clarendon Press, 1995, pp. 193–4.

Bonar, J. (1894) *A Catalogue of the Library of Adam Smith*.

Mizuta, H. (2000) *Adam Smith's Library: A Catalogue*, Oxford: Clarendon Press, 2000.

Craig Smith, *Adam Smith's Political Philosophy: The Invisible Hand and Spontaneous Order*

Routledge, 2006, 209 pp.

ISBN Hardback: 0415360943

Reviewed by James R. Otteson

Although a growing amount of scholarship in recent years has focused on Adam Smith's political philosophy, there has been little sustained investigation into 'spontaneous order' explanations in general and their connection to, or dependence on, Adam Smith's work in particular. Craig Smith's book is a welcome attempt to address this lack.

Craig Smith has several goals in this book (I shall use both his first and last names to distinguish him from Adam Smith; I apologize in advance for the redundancy). One goal is to investigate the general nature of spontaneous-order (SO) explanations of social phenomena, with a special emphasis on Adam Smith's use of them. A second is to isolate the part of such explanations that invisible-hand (IH) arguments play, again with a special emphasis on Adam Smith's contribution. A third is to argue that Adam Smith's use of such arguments – and their use by others in the Scottish Enlightenment period – led them to adopt 'classical liberal' political positions, what Craig Smith proposes to call 'British Whig Evolutionary Liberalism' (3).

I cannot address all of this book's many good individual discussions. Its main topic, however, desperately needed attention: there are so many interpretations of Adam Smith's use of 'invisible hand', and so many uses of SO explanations, that searching out their roots cannot but help us assess their usefulness today – especially as other disciplines, including evolutionary psychology, linguistics and game theory, have 'discovered' or come to use such explanations on their own.

Thus one of the first important things Craig Smith does is distinguish between SO arguments and IH arguments. He sees the latter as a subset of the former:

> Unintended consequences arguments are one way of approaching social and historical processes, of this there is a subset concerned with the analysis of the formation of complex social orders which we have termed spontaneous order thought. Within spontaneous order analysis

social change is viewed as an evolutionary process describing the gradual and cumulative nature of change in a neutral manner. Thus the results of this evolution may be vied as either benign or malign orders. Benign orders are explained by invisible hand arguments.

(14)

This is a good start: these terms often get confused, and it is well to begin by stipulating a plausible taxonomy. But his formulation of IH arguments seems too strong. He writes that they refer 'to some mechanism which ensures the benign outcome of unintended consequence style arguments' (14). But why should one think that IH arguments guarantee – or 'ensure' – benign results? Why not 'increase the chances of' or 'tend overall toward'? This is not mere pedantry. One of the chief attractions of Adam Smith as a philosopher is the fact that he generally eschews universal, exceptionless claims. His use in the *Wealth of Nations* of IH arguments suggests the rather more qualified conception: individual actions tend toward the benefit of others without the latter's benefit being intended by the former. Even if Adam Smith believes that overall the IH mechanism conduces to everyone's benefit, his extensive discussions of the deviations political and social orders can take – clergy, politicians, and businessmen can all waylay or impede progress and growth – suggest that Adam Smith's conception of the IH mechanism held it to be a tendency but not a guarantee.

Craig Smith proceeds to show the use of SO and IH arguments by Adam Smith and other eighteenth-century Scots in several fields, including history, morality, jurisprudence, and political economy. His careful and deliberate discussion shows not only how pervasive such arguments were in their work but also just how powerful such explanations could be. One particularly fecund use is in explaining the human social phenomenon of morality.

In chapters 3 and 7, Craig Smith shows how SO and IH arguments, especially as wielded by Adam Smith, can explain a great deal – indeed, a surprisingly large proportion – of human morality. In these chapters, Craig Smith presents a sketch, based on Scottish notions of unintended social behaviours and practices and a Hayekian elaboration of the view, of how we could come to have the particular roster of general rules of behaviour we have. It is a plausible story: mutual adjustment to one another, with successful attempts at cooperation and behaviour getting reinforced by their success and unsuccessful attempts receiving no reinforcement and therefore withering and eventually dying. Human morality, on this account, is based on some constants in human nature – like self-interest, a desire for, as Adam Smith puts it, mutual sympathy of sentiments, and a natural affection humans feel for their own kind or for those they know – and develops gradually, by fits and starts, experiments, and trials and errors, into habits of behaviour that can themselves develop into rules of morality.

Explanations of human morality along these naturalistic, evolutionary lines have become commonplace today, as researches into evolutionary psychology have proceeded apace. Craig Smith's discussion shows that the Scots – in particular Hume, Adam Smith and Ferguson – understood more elements of such explanations of morality than they have been given credit for.

But the story of human morality must be more complex than Craig Smith represents. He writes, for example, that 'for a practice to become habituated and socialized by repetition, it must fulfil some use in order for that repetition to occur' (41); moreover, 'the practice must have some recurring utility that prompts its repetition' (42); and again, 'Though habits are unintentionally acquired regularities of behaviour they are not eternal, nor are they immutable. Habits survive . . . because they succeed. They allow an efficient reaction to the environment' (121). Perhaps that is true in the abstract or for the most part, but surely not in every particular case. Human beings are not always rational: they often do things that do not conduce to their own benefit, and they even, it seems, do things when they know full well they ought not (this is what was known in the ancient Greek world as *akrasia*). Habits sometimes seem to have a kind of inertia that resists changes of environment or utility (why do we still shake hands when we meet people, for example?); people feel pride, envy or jealousy, all of which might negatively influence our habitual behaviour; people might have an intellectual investment in a way of thinking or in a moral, religious or political worldview that they are loath to give up even when evidence suggests they are mistaken or not conducive to utility; and so on. Moreover, even if it is true, as Craig Smith suggests, that human action is purposive – that is, serving some end or other – it does not follow that all human action conduces to utility. Many of our ends, alas, are either neutral with respect to utility or even positively destructive of it, and if history has shown anything it would seem to have demonstrated that destructive ends can endure for quite a long time.

Craig Smith's story also gives no explanation for distinctively *moral* judgments. We can give a 'naturalistic' account of where humans in fact get the codes of behaviour that they follow, and we can give an 'evolutionary' account of how such codes change over time. But what would distinguish the judgments we make as a result of such social-evolutionary selection from other kinds of judgments? Why, on this account, would the judgment 'one ought not to hurt others' be qualitatively distinct from a judgment like 'one should not swim for an hour after eating', 'one should not clip one's toenails in public', or 'one should wear black to a funeral'? We have here various species of prudential judgments – maxims that, if followed, might allow us to get along better with others or promote our health – but it is not clear that there is anything particularly 'moral' about them, at least not as 'moral' is standardly conceived.

Perhaps Craig Smith is correct that 'Moral rules provide a species of stability of expectations by expressing the "done thing" that is expected of group members' (134) and moreover that 'Moral practice has no other function than the facilitation of mutual adjustment within the group: it is part of the invisible hand that facilitates social benign spontaneous orders' (135).

Many of the recent researches into the potential evolutionary bases of human morality and our 'moral sense' would seem to corroborate this conception of morality. But one must be careful. Even if Craig Smith's genealogy of human morality along Scottish SO and IH lines is correct, it does not follow that morality is nothing other than these prudential, strategic and historically contingent rules. There is a strong sense among most people that there is substantially more to morality properly understood – indeed, that morality often requires us to 'do the right thing' even in the face of what prudence would counsel. Now perhaps people who believe such things are misguided; still, more would have to be shown than a just-so story about where human moral judgments might have come from. Craig Smith writes, 'Moral rules do not have their origin in a rational calculation . . . It is the deep esteem of others that acts as the inducement to follow moral rules' (134). Another important tradition in moral thought, however – epitomized perhaps by Kant – holds a very different view, and, even if this other tradition is utterly mistaken, simply saying so does not prove it.

I say this as someone who is largely sympathetic to SO and IH explanations of human morality and of other human social orders. I think they represent perhaps the most intriguing and promising line of inquiry today into morality in particular and human social orders in general. However promising they are in outline, however, they are frustratingly difficult to work out in detail, precisely because the details are so complex. One element that contributes significantly to the complexity of human social orders, an element Craig Smith does not address in this discussion, is that humans do sometimes act intentionally. Craig Smith writes 'Social change and the progress of knowledge are not only often unnoticed as they gradually occur, but are often unintended' (63). True: this is perhaps the crux of SO and IH explanations. But sometimes they *are* intended. Can SO and IH explanations accommodate cases in which individuals or groups do deliberately work out moral, social or political systems or codes? It would seem that no account of human social orders would be complete until it encompasses, or can plausibly encompass, the entire range of human behaviour – including intentional and unintentional action, rational and irrational action, utilitarian and disutilitarian ends, and so on.

My suspicion is that SO and IH explanations might be able to accommodate this impressive range of human action and human motivation, and Craig Smith's discussion of their applications to several areas of human activity strengthens my suspicion. Perhaps his discussion should be considered, then, an important early step in elaborating such explanations, indeed clearing a path for future work. For that, his book is most welcome. I hope it inaugurates a series of sustained investigations into what might be not only the Scottish Enlightenment's greatest philosophical insight but also one of the most powerful and promising explanatory mechanisms of human social orders we have. Craig Smith's book is not only welcome but has been too long in coming: let us hope others see its promise and follow his lead.

AUTHOR'S RESPONSE

Craig Smith's response to review by James Otteson

I'd like to thank James Otteson for his thoughtful and rigorous review of my book, and also for handling the stylistic difficulty of reviewing a book on Smith by someone called Smith with aplomb.

He correctly identifies my project as one of ground clearing. Much has been written about the invisible hand and, as Gavin Kennedy's blog demonstrates, a great deal of it might charitably be referred to as confused at best. My project in this book was to provide a taxonomy that would introduce some clarity to the discussion of ideas of spontaneous order and unintended consequences, while at the same time demonstrating the significance of the contribution of Smith and his fellow eighteenth-century Scots to the appreciation of these difficult concepts.

Otteson observes that my taxonomy is perhaps a little too strong in its attribution of certainty of benign results as a qualifier for the use of the term invisible hand. Instead he prefers to view tendencies to produce benign results as sufficient for the application of the term. This is a reasonable complaint. My use of certainty referred to the use of invisible hand explanations as retrospective explanatory devices. I fully accept that the more conditional generalizations that Smith tends to make, especially when he is advancing policy advice, are given in terms deliberately open to exceptions. In this respect my consideration of Smith as part of a putative tradition of explanatory social theorists presents a strong interpretation of the term invisible hand (stronger indeed that that deployed by Smith himself). This, I feel, is warranted by my desire to use the term as part of a prescriptive taxonomy: a project that lends itself to robust definitions for clarity of conceptual reconstruction.

Many of Professor Otteson's comments relate to my handling of what is, in my view, the particularly fraught relationship between explanatory social theory and moral philosophy. This is made especially difficult as spontaneous order thinkers tend to blend what we now regard as distinct intellectual endeavours. He rightly notes that my parsing of Smith for the purposes of this book stresses the social theory, and while I obviously acknowledge that Smith is a moral philosopher of great stature, I felt (and still feel) that his consideration of spontaneous order is conducted as part of his discussion of what we would now regard as sociological theory rather than normative moral philosophy. Smith's interest, shared by almost all of those in the tradition of thought that I identify at the start of the book, is in explaining how we experience morality and how common moral beliefs are generated.

It is for this reason that I have played up the place of utility and sociability in the generation of moral norms. It is quite correct to observe that some purposive decisions are irrational, and that we often act in ways that generate disutility. However, it is another thing to say that long term shared group norms (the spontaneous orders outlined in the taxonomy) that generate disutility will persist in perpetuity. Habit and custom are indeed 'sticky' but not permanently bonding. This is precisely why thinkers like Smith are attracted to evolutionary accounts of social change while recognizing the limits of utility based explanations (see Smith's criticism of Hume's account of justice in Book IV of TMS). My observation that practices serve a purpose, or function, if you wish, was intended to demonstrate that part of the spontaneous order project of conjectural history is concerned with constructing retrospective accounts of the generation and alteration of social level patterns of behaviour. It was later in the development of sociology that the issues of agent understanding and meaning came to be of central concern, but this in itself need not preclude the application of the spontaneous order approach. My point is that actors understand themselves to have achieved something by an action and that this is the function that marks repetition. Like handshaking we can see the purpose of a practice alter through time, and we can note that people continue to engage in the practice through habit and without awareness of the original function or indeed the 'latent' function. But as Hume famously observed of justice, the explanation of its origins in terms of utility may be distinct from the reason that we attach moral approbation to just actions. Thus our personal experience of moral judgment may bear little relation to prudential reasoning, but the unintended nature of the generation and evolution of moral norms should lead us to expect this.

I agree with Professor Otteson that it is a weakness of the spontaneous order tradition that its explanatory accounts of the generation of morality sit uneasily next to the normative arguments that are usually to be found in the same works. It is clear that this understanding of morality needs to do more to answer the points made against it by other (notably Kantian) understandings of moral judgment. It is one of my main contentions that Smith and others draw a link between their explanatory theory and their endorsement of broadly classical liberal policy prescriptions. These are taken as lessons from the science of man. What is unclear is whether the tradition of spontaneous order as a whole can develop a more nuanced moral philosophy that will move the individual experience of moral decisions beyond the observation that they are largely guided by habit, custom and socialization while taking account of our intuitions that morality is a distinct form of human experience.

Professor Otteson also raises the issue of the place of intentional action in a theory of unintended consequences. In one sense this is built into the theory – purposive actions produce unintended consequences – of more significance however is the idea that we intend an action, design an institution and it operates exactly as we had intended. This, I think, is handled by my model of the theory: it doesn't happen, because social institutions do not exist in a vacuum. Evolutionary social change and the limited foresight possessed by the human designers mean that even the most prescriptive of institutional designs adapt and change in reaction to unforeseen and uncontrollable consequences – as Smith's 'man of system' discovers (TMS VI.ii.2.18). Indeed if they did not, they wouldn't really be that interesting – the only explanation needed would be the testimony of the designer and the assessment of the observer as to how successfully the institution attained its stated goals.

I must thank Professor Otteson for his review and for the very useful comments on my taxonomy. And I join him wholeheartedly in his call for more investigation into these important themes from Smith. If my book has played some small part in provoking discussion and encouraging this enterprise then it will have served one of its most important intended purposes.

Jan Toporowski, *Theories of Financial Disturbance: An Examination of Critical Theories of Finance from Adam Smith to the Present Day*

Edward Elgar, 2005, 195 pp.

ISBN Hardback: 1843764776

Reviewed by David M. Levy

Jan Toporowski's *Theories of Financial Disturbances* poses enormous difficulties for the reader. Some of this difficulty is simply the nature of the project which might be viewed in part as a translation from the mathematics in which the modern economic discussion of financial instability is found. This is a short book expounding economic thinking by literally dozens of subtle economists' thoughts on financial instability in texts ranging from François Quesnay in the middle of the eighteenth century through Robert Schiller of today. Adam Smith and the classical economists get two chapters. Thorstein Veblen, Rosa Luxemburg, Ralph Hawtrey, Irving Fisher and Hyman Minksy get a chapter each. Maynard Keynes gets two chapters. The work of Marek Breit, Michal Kalecki and Josef Steindl is considered together 'in the shadow of Keynes'. The exposition is often in terms of other economists, Knut Wicksell, F.A. Hayek, Robert Lucas, whose work is assumed to be known.

There is a reason that Keynes gets two chapters. Indeed, we start with Keynes to get a sense of the layout of the argument. Then turn to Adam Smith and Toporowski's interpretation of Smith. Then we will give some ideas of what the reader can expect elsewhere.

Keynes' distinctions

Keynes visualized economic activity taking place over time. The critical distinction which Keynes made in the *General Theory* was between savings and investment. Savings is a motive, a desire to consume in the future. Investment is an act, the creation of an asset which will produce income in the future. Purchasing a security might not be an investment from a social point of view; it might simply be a change in the ownership of an existing asset. This is one of the important reasons that Keynes' theory is an aggregate theory – it needs to distinguish clearly between the creation and the transfer of assets.

There are simple formula which embody this understanding. Society's income (Y) can be consumed today (C) or saved (S). Thus, Y = C + S. This is an expression of motivation. The activities which are allowed are expenditure on current consumption (C again) or investment (I). With investments come assets and finance enters the story. Thus, Y = C + I. Now comes the trick. S is a motive, the desire to postpone consumption. What activities allow this motive to be affected? Of course, I is one activity. But there is another; one can postpone consumption by adding to one's money holdings, which we denote by ΔM. Thus, S = I + ΔM.

For Keynes it is absolutely critical that there is no automatic mechanism by which the money holdings of society can be changed by the expenditure of real resources. This passage is appropriately quoted by Toporowski (89): 'Because money cannot be easily produced (it 'has both in the long and in the short period, a zero, or at any rate a very small elasticity of production') . . .'. If $\Delta M = 0$ then for equilibrium S=I. And in the Keynesian specification of the consumption function, there is only one level of Y which equates S to I so there is only one equilibrium level of Y. That may or may not be a full employment level of Y. Thus, Keynes denied what the classics had asserted. For them all levels of Y are consistent with full employment. That would require, in the Keynesian formulation, that all amounts of ΔM are possible. Given the Keynesian world in which money was a policy variable, this would be a very tricky argument to make.

For Adam Smith and those who followed, money was produced inside the market economy. Britain was viewed as a small economy inside a large world in which gold was used widely. Smith had supposed that the market for money cleared quickly:

> If there were in England, for example, an effectual demand for an additional quantity of gold, a packet-boat could bring from Lisbon, or from wherever else it was to be had, fifty tuns of gold, which could be coined into more than five millions of guineas.
>
> (WN IV.i.12)

If we start with Walras's Law – the excess demand for money equals the aggregate excess supply of goods – then Smith's adjustment principle suffices to obtain Say's Law – the aggregate excess supply of goods is zero because any ΔM is feasible (Peart and Levy 2003). Nassau Senior, who doesn't enter into Toporowski's account, worked an example of how equilibrium in the classical system is affected when a sudden contraction of the money supply resulted from a bank panic (Senior 1828: 27).

Toporowski does not consider what the automatic adjustment of a gold standard does for the classics' argument. On this issue, as J.E. Cairnes' pointed out, W.S. Jevons' work is fully classical (Cairnes 1863). Toporowski's reference to Jevons' *Theory of Political Economy* (82) is not germane to Jevons' discussion of adjustment to disequlibrating events. This is found in his *Money and the Mechanism of Exchange*:

> A further objection to a paper money inconvertible into coin, is that it cannot be varied in quantity by the natural action of trade. No one can export it or import it like coin, and no one but the government or banks authorized by the government can issue or cancel it. Hence, if trade becomes brisk, nothing but a decree of the government can supply the requisite increase of circulating medium . . . Now, even the best-informed government department cannot be trusted to judge widely and impartially when more money is wanted. Currency must be supplied, like all other commodities, according to the free action of the laws of supply and demand.
>
> (Jevons 1875: 236–7)

Toporowski on Smith

Toporowski starts his chapter on Smith with two passages separated by ellipses (p. 15) which in the *Wealth of Nations* occur ten pages apart. The first passage is Smith's familiar statement of people's 'absurd presumption in their own good fortune' so that people systematically overestimated their good fortune in gambles (WN I.x.b.26); the second is Smith's statement that projectors takes large gambles (WN I.x.b.43). This is supposed to show that Smith worried about the financial instability from projectors taking unwarranted gambles. This is an important passage so let me *emphasize* what Toporowski deletes:

> The establishment of any new manufacture, of any new branch of commerce, or of any new practice in agriculture, is always a speculation, from which the projector promises himself extraordinary profits. These profits sometimes are very great, and sometimes, more frequently, perhaps, they are quite otherwise; *but in general they bear no regular proportion to those of other old trades in the neighbourhood. If the project succeeds, they are commonly at first very high. When the trade or practice becomes thoroughly established and well known, the competition reduces them to the level of other trades.*
>
> (WN I.x.b.43; emphasis added)

This, Toporowski argues, lead Smith to defend usury laws, much to the horror of his later admirers.

Toporowski seems rather more interested in recruiting Smith for the financial instability cause than to considering how Smith gets his conclusion. The 'absurd presumption' passage quoted occurs in Smith's explanation of how the net advantages of employment are equalized by competition. Smith also explains that people pay to take risks in part because of the approbation which greats successful gambles. Adding approbation to a standard gambling model has surprising results (Levy 1999). If one wish to take Smith's argument seriously on a technical level, it seems useful to suppose that the desire for approbation enters consideration as a motive independent of material income (Levy and Peart 2004). The second paragraph has Smith's important claim that new investments have a different distribution of returns than old investments. Perhaps usury laws might be viewed as a way to trim out the extremes? Paganelli (2003) who develops this point must have appeared in print too recently for Toporowski to benefit from her research.

Insights

Let us turn from aspects of arguments which Toporowski does not see to those he will help us see. Perhaps his sharpest insight is for economic arguments which depend upon heterogeneity of agents. He notes that Irving Fisher's emphasis in 1907 is on the '*inequality* of foresight' (76). This same appeal to heterogeneity of foresight is found in Fisher's eugenic arguments from that period (Peart and Levy 2005: 114–15). There are fascinating references to Stendl and Kalecki's appeals to 'inelasticity of rentier's savings' (115, 150). Famously, Keynes' consumption function specified that the percentage saved increased as income rose. Why might that be? The Fisherian account of differential foresight would suggest a time preference interpretation of Keynes' consumption function in which richer people are where they are in the income distribution because of their superior foresight. They save more as a share of income than poorer people. Toporowski gives hints of places to look but not solutions.

Toporowski also sees the effect of differential rewards upon economic models themselves. Economists hired by the central bank have personal interests at stake from their modelling activities. Money matters to economists because it matters to our friends and those who hire our friends:

> The labour market is extraordinarily efficient in providing economists who will do what they are paid to do, just as the tradition of deference in the profession and our increasing dependence on finance will always ensure a sympathetic reception to their endeavours. Thus the activities of the central bank acquire a quasi-mystical power and authority that, in the view of most economists, make money and the rate of interest the key to human welfare . . .
>
> (136)

If this is true, and I cherish a letter from Milton Friedman which expresses an opinion about the impact of the Federal Reserve's employment of monetary economists which differs only in detail, then how do we propose to judge such motivated modelling efforts? Drastic remedies might be required (Levy and Peart 2008).

Conclusion

What a reader might get out of Toporowski's book will depend greatly upon what gets brought to the book. You won't be told what the rational expectations hypothesis is. You won't be told what the Friedman–Phelps criticism of the purported 'trade-off' between unemployment and inflation is (132). Indeed, if you know, Toporowski's account becomes a rather amusing puzzle of just why he expressed it in the way the way he does.

The ideal reader of this book is one who knows a good deal about twentieth-century work on the economics of financial instability. The book may help to explain why workers in financial instability see Adam Smith as one of their own. If you can pay the price of admission then you may well see things which you hadn't seen before. I did.

Bibliography

Cairnes, J.E. (2003) [1863] 'Have the discoveries of gold in Australia and California lowered the value of gold?', in *W.S. Jevons: Critical Responses*, S.J. Peart (ed.), I: 29–32.

Jevons, W.S. (1875) *Money and the Mechanism of Exchange*, London: H.S. King.

Keynes, J.M. (1936) *The General Theory of Employment, Interest and Money*, London: Macmillan.

Levy, D.M. (1999) 'Adam Smith's katallactic model of gambling: approbation from the spectator', *Journal of the History of Economic Thought*, 21: 81–91.

Levy, D.M. and S.J. Peart (2004) 'Sympathy and approbation in Hume and Smith: A solution to the other rational species problem', *Economics and Philosophy*, 20: 331–49.

—— and —— (2008) 'Inducing greater transparency', *Eastern Economic Journal*, 34: 103–14, forthcoming.

Paganelli, M. (2003) '*In medio stat virtus:* an alternative view of usury in Adam Smith's thinking', *History of Political Economy*, 35: 21–48.

Peart, S.J. and D.M. Levy (2003) 'Post-Ricardian British economics, 1830–1870', in *Blackwell Companion to the History of Economic Thought*, W. Samuels, J. Biddle and J. Davis (eds), Malden, MA: Blackwell.

—— and —— (2005) *The 'Vanity of the Philosopher': From Equality to Hierarchy in Post-Classical Economics*. Ann Arbor: University of Michigan Press.

Senior, N.W. (1998) [1828] *Three Lectures on the Transmission of Precious Metals.* Vol 2. *Collected Works of Nassau William Senior,* D. Rutherford (ed.), Bristol.

AUTHOR'S RESPONSE

Jan Toporowski's response to review by David M. Levy

In his last book, *Travels with Herodotus* (*Podróże z Herodotem*) Ryszard Kapuściński quotes a passage that T.S. Eliot included in his 1944 essay on

Virgil, but which could just as easily have been written about economics today:

> In our age, when men seem more than ever prone to confuse wisdom with knowledge, and knowledge with information, and to try to solve problems of life in terms of engineering, there is coming into existence a new kind of provincialism which perhaps deserves a new name. It is a provincialism not of space but of time; one for which history is merely the chronicle of human devices which have served their turn and been scrapped, one for which the world is the property solely of the living, a property in which the dead hold no shares. The menace of this kind of provincialism is that we can all, all the peoples on our globe, be provincials together; and those who are not content to be provincials, can only become hermits.
>
> (Kapuściński 2007: 271)

I quote this because it summarises the fundamental principles behind my own approach to the history of economic thought. These principles were not made clear when I wrote at the beginning of *Theories of Financial Disturbance* that 'The origins of this book lie in a somewhat belated "literature review" for my book *The End of Finance*' (Toporowski 2005: 8). The historian is concerned with the events of the past, and the historian of economic thought is rightly concerned with the economic ideas that have animated intellectuals and policy-makers in the past. Both aim to present some kind of 'authentic' or true account of the past. However, as an economist my purpose is the rather different one of showing how the ideas of past economists can illuminate our present reality and policy dilemmas. Hence my admission that 'I have not done full justice to the totality of the ideas of many of the writers discussed here. This is most notable in the cases of Adam Smith . . .' (5). I then refer to this injustice as 'my wilful distortion of the works of these great writers. . .' (5). As I make clear in the Introduction to the book under review, my purpose is to add further criticism to those macro-economic and finance theories widespread today that suppose that there exists in the real world a state of perfect financial intermediation, so that 'Financial institutions exist solely to facilitate the rational choices of economic agents, and residual error terms record the irrational choices of economic agents'.

In his perceptive review, David Levy has correctly identified the weaknesses in my treatment of Adam Smith, and my own ignorance of such authors as Nassau Senior and J.E. Cairnes. A more careful historical approach would have revealed more to me, and I discuss this further below. At this stage, I want to go back to the starting point in my book, a starting point that was not the Book of Genesis that commences a historical narrative, but a taxonomy of theories of money and finance that encompasses the ideas found later in the book. This taxonomy distinguished three types of finance theory: The first of these is general equilibrium theory, in which no causative or even dynamic process can be identified, because by definition a static equilibrium holds between all variables. Change can be imposed on the system by varying one of the factors in the general equilibrium. But it can be any factor, and no systematic source of disequilibrium or change can be identified. The most recent versions of this kind of approach, in dynamic stochastic general equilibrium models, postulate various arbitrary 'shocks', and then trace the trajectory of adjustment in the model to a new equilibrium. But, unlike the business cycle theories of the first half of the twentieth century, these models do not identify any particular kind of 'shock' as prevalent in an economy. New Keynesian models are arguably of this kind, even though they suggest that particular kinds of rigidities may give rise to less than fully efficient use of resources. Once this inefficient general equilibrium has been established, these models give no indication of how change takes place in the system.

The second type of finance theory is what I called in the book 'reflective' finance. In Classical and New Classical writing, in which firms and consumers are supposed to calculate in terms of 'real' rather than monetary values, then financial parameters come to be determined by relations obtaining in the sphere of production, distribution and consumption. This is very apparent in, say, the Marxian theory of interest in which the rate of interest is largely significant as a factor in the averaging out of rates of profit across firms and activities in the economy, or in the neo-classical theory where it is brought into equilibrium with the marginal productivity of capital. Schumpeter and even Wicksell held this 'reflective' view.

The third type of finance theory is what I called 'critical' finance, not because its exponents were critical of finance, although by and large most of them were, but because they regarded finance as playing an independent role in disturbing the activity of production and distribution. This is most obvious in, for example, credit cycle theory. However, the only credit cycle theory that penetrates into today's economics textbooks, the financial accelerator theory associated with Bernanke and Gertler, is itself a pale revenant of Austrian credit cycle theory which really only allowed temporary, policy-driven, deviations from a Ricardian equality between saving and investment that is supposed to determine the rate of interest. Hence, while I would accept that my book deals with financial instability, the foundation for my examination, and the typology of finance presented above, is the macroeconomic significance of finance. It is because of their lack of systematic macroeconomic vision that I explicitly omitted from my consideration Hobson, Polanyi, Douglas and Gesell (7).

David Levy commences his review with a consideration of Keynes, and Keynes, and his Post-Keynesian followers, would no doubt enter a strong claim to his pre-eminence in overthrowing monetary and financial orthodoxies. I began my book with a discussion of the Physiocrats and Adam Smith because it seemed to me that here was the first systematic economic discussion of how finance could operate perversely in the economy. I should perhaps have devoted more attention to the French discussion of interest.

It is now obvious to me that the difference between Quesnay and Turgot on the question of the rate of interest lies precisely in Quesnay's adherence to a pure monetary/financial theory of interest, whereas Turgot regarded interest as bringing saving into equality with investment (18–20). Quesnay accepted that the rate of interest would affect investment. But he saw no reason why investment should influence a rate of interest determined in money and financial markets. The usury laws were for Quesnay (and later for Say) a way of preventing the rate of interest from rising to squeeze out legitimate commerce and production.

On this question, Smith clearly sided with Quesnay. This, I believe, was the foundation of Smith's later disregard for Bentham's *Defence of Usury*. Smith's familiarity with the Quesnay–Turgot debate on interest illuminates Smith's position on usury in a way that has not hitherto been appreciated in the English language discussion of Smith's views on interest. Without that familiarity, Smith's later disregard for Bentham's *Defence of Usury* appears anomalous, and was perceived as such by liberal political economists from John Stuart Mill to George Stigler. Drawing attention to the French background to Smith's view of interest is the modest, but I hope significant, contribution that my book makes to Smith studies.

Other criticisms of David Levy I have to accept because they highlight what I now regard as a general flaw in my book, caused by the haste with which I had to complete it, under professional circumstances that would not allow me to write a more fully considered study. In particular I regret that I did not make clear how fundamentally the Companies Acts of the 1860s, and similar company legislation passed at around the same time in other capitalist countries, changed the institutions of capitalism. These reforms extended the credit system to expand capital markets. As the supply of bank credit became more elastic, the capital market based system gave rise to the over-capitalization of companies. This is the institutional foundation for the critical finance theories, from Kalecki to Minsky, that I examine in Part III of my book, 'In the shadow of Keynes'. Unfortunately I have only really been able to develop this insight since the publication of my book, as a result of a more extensive reading of Minsky, and a recent re-reading of Karl Niebyl's *Studies in the Classical Theories of Money*. This last book highlights how money and credit changed with the development of capitalist production. I would have liked to have been able to show how this process affected finance in the twentieth century.

As David Levy points out, I could have given a fuller account of Adam Smith's views on the financing of speculative enterprise. Smith's well-known observation of the propensity of entrepreneurs to exaggerate their financial prospects, due to vanity, should have stood as a warning against the Companies Acts and the subsequent financial inflation. Such legislation and the consequent inflation of capital markets has been perennially justified on the grounds of supplying far-sighted public benefactors with the finance that they need for their speculative undertakings. What transpired, however, was not a general decline of capitalism into fraud and financial instability, although such incidents are never far from inflated financial markets. Instead business corporations developed new mechanisms for coping with such possibilities by raising capital in excess of their productive needs. Excess capital is then turned over in the capital markets in the kind of balance sheet operations that Minsky was to analyze.

The other omissions to which David Levy refers, those of Nassau Senior, Cairnes and Jevons, I find less critical. These authors, wedded to the classical quantity theory of money, located their theories of money and finance firmly in the process of exchange. They were thus unable to give any account of macroeconomic financial disturbance beyond price changes and the kind of mercantile speculations that so exercised nineteenth-century authors.

It is rare for an author to have the opportunity to have his after-thoughts so focused by an insightful and scholarly reviewer, and then to have the opportunity to publish those after-thoughts. For both I am very grateful.

Bibliography

Kapuściński, R. (2007) *Travels with Herodotus*, London: Penguin Books.

Notes for contributors

Submissions to *The Adam Smith Review* are invited from any theoretical, disciplinary or interdisciplinary approach (max. 10,000 words, in English). Contributors are asked to make their arguments accessible to a wide multidisciplinary readership without sacrificing high standards of argument and scholarship. Please include an abstract not exceeding 100 words.

Please send all submissions, suggestions and offers to edit symposia to the Editor: Professor Vivienne Brown, Faculty of Social Sciences, The Open University, Walton Hall, Milton Keynes, MK7 6AA; v.w.brown@ open.ac.uk. Email submissions are welcomed. Alternatively please send three hard copies in double-spaced type.

Please prepare your manuscript for anonymous refereeing and provide a separate title page with your name. Interdisciplinary submissions will be sent to referees with different disciplinary expertise. Submitted articles will be double-blind refereed and commissioned articles will be single-blind refereed. All contributions must be in English; it is the author's responsibility to ensure the quality of the English text. Where quotations in languages other than English are provided, authors are asked to provide a translation into English.

Final versions of accepted papers will need to conform to the ASR Guidelines for Authors (Harvard reference system), but submitted papers are welcomed in any format.

Submission to *The Adam Smith Review* will be taken to imply that the work is original and unpublished, and is not under consideration for publication elsewhere. By submitting a manuscript, authors agree that the exclusive rights to reproduce and distribute the article have been given to the Publishers, including reprints, photographic reproductions, microfilm, or any other reproductions of a similar nature, and translations. Contributors will receive a complimentary copy of the volume in which their contribution is published.

Books for review

Books relating to Adam Smith or of more general relevance for Adam Smith scholarship will be considered for review in *The Adam Smith Review*. It is editorial policy to invite authors to respond to reviews of their work. Offers to review works published in languages other than English are welcomed.

Please send books for review to the Book Reviews Editor: Professor Fonna Forman-Barzilai, Department of Political Science, University of California, San Diego, La Jolla, CA 92093–0521, USA; ffb@ucsd.edu.

Announcements

Conference: 'The Philosophy of Adam Smith', 6–8 January 2009, Balliol College, Oxford

The Adam Smith Review and the International Adam Smith Society are organizing a conference commemorate the 250th anniversary of the publication of the first edition of Adam Smith's *Theory of Moral Sentiments* (1759).

Plenary talks

Stephen Darwall (Professor of Philosophy, University of Michigan), 'Smith on Honour and Respect'

Charles Griswold (Professor of Philosophy, Boston University), 'Tales of the Self: Adam Smith's Reply to Rousseau'

Knud Haakonssen (Professor of Intellectual History, University of Sussex), 'Smith and Epicureanism'

David D. Raphael (Professor Emeritus of Philosophy, Imperial College), 'The Virtue of TMS 1759'

Emma Rothschild (Fellow, King's College Cambridge; Visiting Professor of History, Harvard), 'TMS and the Inner Life'

Geoffrey Sayre-McCord (Professor of Philosophy, University of North Carolina), 'Is the Impartial Spectator's Vision 20/20?'

In addition 40 papers have been selected for presentation from an outstanding response to the call for papers.

The plenary talks and a selection of the submitted conference papers will be published in a special issue of *The Adam Smith Review*, vol. 5, 'The Philosophy of Adam Smith', V. Brown and S. Fleischacker (eds), to be published autumn 2009.

Conference website: www.adamsmithreview.org/conference.

Other conferences

An international Adam Smith conference celebrating the 250th anniversary of *The Theory of Moral Sentiments* will be held in Oslo, Norway, 27–29 August 2009. It will be jointly hosted by three Oslo based research institutions: the Centre for the Study of Mind in Nature (CSMN/Christel Fricke and Raino Malnes); the Centre for the Study of Equality, Social Organization, and Performance (ESOP/Kalle Moene); and the Seminar on Theory of Science (Ragnvald Kalleberg). The organizers will invite philosophers, economists, political scientists and sociologists to comment on Adam Smith's moral theory from their respective points of view. Further information will be posted under the following address: www.csmn.uio.no/.

SMITH in GLASGOW. The University of Glasgow, where Smith was both student and professor, will host a Conference under the auspices of the University and the Faculty of Law, Business and Social Sciences' Adam Smith Research Foundation (www.glasgow.ac.uk/asrf). The Conference will be held between 31 March–2 April 2009. Recognising the breadth of Smith's interests and range of his work at Glasgow, the Conference will be organised along four themes: (i) Smith, Scotland and the Enlightenment; (ii) Smith and Culture, Literature and the Arts; (iii) Smith and Moral Philosophy; and (iv) Smith and the Social Sciences. Each theme will have a plenary lecture (Nick Phillipson, Jim Chandler, Tom Campbell and Amartya Sen respectively) and a series of up to four workshops/seminars. The organiser is Chris Berry from whom more information may be sought (c.berry@lbss.gla.ac.uk).